Advances in Computer-Supported Learning

Francisco Milton Mendes Neto
Federal Service of Data Processing, Brazil

Francisco Vilar Brasileiro
Federal University of Campina Grande, Brazil

INFOSCI Information Science Publishing
Hershey • London • Melbourne • Singapore

Acquisitions Editor: Michelle Potter
Development Editor: Kristin Roth
Senior Managing Editor: Jennifer Neidig
Managing Editor: Sara Reed
Copy Editor: Kim Barger
Typesetter: Jessie Weik
Cover Design: Lisa Tosheff
Printed at: Yurchak Printing Inc.

Published in the United States of America by
Information Science Publishing (an imprint of Idea Group Inc.)
701 E. Chocolate Avenue
Hershey PA 17033
Tel: 717-533-8845
Fax: 717-533-8661
E-mail: cust@idea-group.com
Web site: http://www.idea-group.com

and in the United Kingdom by
Information Science Publishing (an imprint of Idea Group Inc.)
3 Henrietta Street
Covent Garden
London WC2E 8LU
Tel: 44 20 7240 0856
Fax: 44 20 7379 0609
Web site: http://www.eurospanonline.com

Library of Congress Cataloging-in-Publication Data

Advances in computer-supported learning / Francisco Milton Mendes Neto and Francisco Brasileiro, editors.
p. cm.
Summary: "This book clarifies the new technologies, applications, and research in computer-supported learning. It helps students, teachers, and researchers gain a larger understanding of this field and the trends that are driving computer-supported learning forward"--Provided by publisher.
Includes bibliographical references and index.
ISBN 1-59904-355-6 (hardcover : alk. paper) -- ISBN 1-59904-356-4 (softcover : alk. paper) -- ISBN 1-59904-357-2 (ebook : alk. paper)
1. Computer-assisted instruction. 2. Educational technology. 3. Internet in education. I. Neto, Francisco Milton Mendes, 1973- II. Brasileiro, Francisco, 1965-
LB1028.5.A25 2006
371.33'4--dc22
2006015056

British Cataloguing in Publication Data
A Cataloguing in Publication record for this book is available from the British Library.

Advances in Computer-Supported Learning

Table of Contents

Preface

Nowadays, computers are considered one of the most important instruments for supporting the learning process. This is mainly due to the fact that they allow the use of resources with various interaction modes, the friendly interface of many of their applications (most notably the so called Web-supported applications), the variety of multimedia resources supported by them, and their crescent acceptance and utilization worldwide. Moreover, thanks to the expansion of computer networks, such as the Internet, they are an important ally to eliminate geographical barriers. These barriers are characteristics of the face-to-face learning process and impede the transference of knowledge in a massive way. In summary, computers interconnected by worldwide networks provide the required support for alternative solutions in the educational area.

Computer-supported learning (CSL) was created mainly for anyone that, due to financial, social, or geographical reasons or due to physical incapacity, could not attend a formal school. Its main goal was to facilitate the access to education to people that did not have conditions of obtaining instruction by the conventional methods. However, CSL has evolved to a much broader role in the learning process.

The use of CSL to provide education allows more flexibility in the acquisition and in the knowledge transfer than the face-to-face learning. In the current knowledge economy, the knowledge required by people is daily updated. CSL allows adapting the training materials to the current needs of the students more easily than in the face-to-face learning approach. In the latter, training materials are quickly outdated, because they are usually prepared with great antecedence. CSL also offers the necessary structure for supporting, controlling, and addressing the knowledge to a target public. CSL can be used to promote coordination and cooperation among the students themselves, as well as among the students and the instructors. Due to all that, CSL is a research area that has great practical and theoretical importance, and has rapidly grown as an area of educational practice, in both academic and business training.

Challenges Faced by CSL

It is an enormous mistake to think that the implementation of this learning modality is easier than face-to-face learning and requires less work. Its implementation is indeed a complex task, involving many factors and variables. As examples of these factors, we can cite: the great diversity of both the target public and the training goals; the variety of learning environments available today; the distinct levels of familiarity of students and instructors with the employed technology, and so forth. CSL designers need to understand this complexity and carefully plan what to do, before designing their CSL solutions.

The successful implementation of CSL trainings requires a broad comprehension of the learning requirements that should be satisfied by the training, of the audience profile and, mainly, of the technology used. This technology involves both the technology supporting the learning environment as well as the technology being used by instructors and students for interacting among themselves and with the environment. Although technology is important for supporting the CSL environment, the use of a particular technology without a well developed educational plan is frequently not effective.

Contribution of This Book

This book has an overall objective to present new technologies, applications, and research in the CSL area. It intends to help the readers to obtain a larger understanding of both the potential of this learning modality and the trends that are being followed to make CSL as much or more effective than face-to-face learning.

As said before, the implementation of CSL is not a trivial task. The accumulated experience and know-how of the researchers in this area, who have invested time and effort in studying CSL problems, are, therefore, important success factors. This book shares this know-how with the readers. Our intent is to show the current trends, practices, and challenges faced by CSL designers. These include from theoretical assumptions and empirical researches to practical implementations and case studies.

CSL is a genuinely interdisciplinary area that strives for creating a better comprehension of the requirements of the learning process that is mediated by a diverse set of computer technologies. Therefore, this book is addressed to a wide audience, including scholars, academics, educators, researchers and professors working in (higher) education and corporate education, students, and CSL beginners and experts with interest in the CSL research area. Given its depth and breadth of coverage, this book is also of interest to researchers in the fields of education and psychology, working in various disciplines, such as education, cognition, social, and educational psychology, didacticism, and, mainly, computer science applied to education. Besides, the book is helpful for industrial trainers and business professionals entrusted with the implementation of distance learning and CSL applications.

The major scholarly value of this book is to provide a general overview of research on CSL and its applications, as well as a notion of the recent progress in this area. This overview can support future academic research with the background provided by the experts that contributed to this book. Also, it indicates to the readers what they should do (best practices) and should not do (bad practices).

In relation to the contribution to information science, technology, and management literature, one important improvement, which is provided by this book, is the discussion on new methodologies, technologies, and approaches that are being used in CSL and their advantages and challenges. The topics covered, which include the current best practices in CSL, can also stimulate the implementation and the use of CSL in higher education and industrial trainings. In addition, this book serves to highlight some of the most important gaps in the development of CSL tools, patterns of interaction, online courses, and so forth.

Organization of This Book

The book is organized into 15 chapters that are divided into three sections with five chapters each. The first section, "New Approaches for Teaching and Learning Online," presents works on innovative approaches and methodologies for undertaking CSL. It covers subjects that span from CSL design models and desirable design elements for CSL systems, to peer review and learning management systems, including a thorough description of a major initiative of integrating CSL in a traditional distance course. In the following we give a brief description of each of the chapters that comprise this section.

Chapter I, by Inan and Lowther, does a comprehensive review of CSL design models with emphasis on the key dimensions and elements of effective teaching and learning within an online environment, such as learning activities, learning environments, and assessment of student learning. The chapter highlights the trend of creating online environments that are able to support student-centered constructivist learning.

In Chapter II, Coffey proposes a set of desirable design elements for a system targeted to support distance learning. The advocated elements range from the potential benefits of having an explicit realization of a viable pedagogical theory as the underlying basis for the software, to the value of presenting a customizable interface, and the need for allowing the share and reuse of instructional resources. These principles are further developed in the context of a prototype system that is also presented.

Chapter III, by Kern et al., discusses the important issue of peer review in education. Although the subject is discussed from a computer science education point of view, the conclusions can be easily extrapolated to other areas. By reporting on the current practice of peer review in computer science education, the authors discuss the attained results, the tools available, as well as the different approaches in use. They end up by discussing the relevant issues of a methodological approach for a continued and regular large-scale adoption of peer review.

In Chapter IV, Watson et al. discuss Learning Management Systems (LMS) as an essential technology to fulfill the educational requirements of the information age. They advocate the use of LMSs as one way to effectively support the customized learning-oriented paradigm that we face nowadays. They also discuss the directions for further growth and development of LMSs.

Chapter V, by Aydin et al., concludes Section I with a thorough description of how the Anadolu University of Turkey has integrated CSL to its traditional distance courses. Building a CSL infrastructure for approximately 1 million students is a challenging endeavor. The experience reported by the authors will certainly be useful to whoever is involved with a similar task.

The second section of the book is titled "Main Issues and Trends in CSL." It presents some of the newest issues and future trends in the CSL area. It covers new areas such as the Semantic Web and technologies for sharing and reusing instructional material. It also discusses the implementation of CSL in the corporations. A brief description of each of the chapters of this section is presented next.

In recent years we have experienced a phenomenal increase in the number of e-learning initiatives put together by both the industrial and the academic sectors. Unfortunately, many of these initiatives have fallen short of their objectives. In Chapter VI, Ertl et al. postulate three theses aiming at overcoming the disillusionment and the problems that were encountered during the initial euphoric phase of e-learning. Together, these theses provide a framework that can be used to support the implementation of successful e-learning initiatives. The authors provide examples that further substantiate the applicability of their theses in the implementation of sustainable e-learning initiatives.

The next two chapters address applications of the semantic Web on CSL. In Chapter VII, Adán-Coello et al. discuss relevant applications of semantic Web technologies in the field of education. They argue that the possibility of describing resources via the use of metadata that are suitable for being autonomously processed by computers allows the creation of self-organizing networks that can be the core of intelligent educational systems able to reuse information and integrate learners, authors, teachers, and educational institutions. Chapter VIII, by Branco Neto, discusses the problems that arise from the gap between the visions of two communities involved with Web-based learning initiatives, namely those that study the learning process and those that design and implement CSL technologies. After presenting some of the technologies proposed by both communities, the author proposes a way to put them together with the support of semantic Web technologies.

In Chapter IX Nascimento discusses the important issue of reusing and sharing information. This chapter introduces the SCORM standards for creating skills to support the conception and development of e-learning devices. The author shows that the use of SCORM in association with new technologies and techniques such as Metadata Harvesting, XML, RSS, and Feedreaders allows the understanding of the dissemination of Open Archives initiatives and Learning Objects Repositories in a variety of contexts. This, in turn, provides a better comprehension of how to design and develop CSL contents such that they can be more efficiently stored, distributed, shared, and reused.

Concluding the second section of the book, Chapter X, by Lee et al., deals with the issue of CSL in the corporations. They define CSL in a corporate setting as the delivery of lessons to employees via the Internet or the corporation's intranet. The chapter discusses the many challenges in providing CSL in such a setting and the possible solutions.

The final section, "Coordination, Collaboration, and Communication Technologies for CSL," presents a series of chapters illustrating the new ways of coordination, collaboration, and communication that can be implemented for improving CSL. This section starts with a discussion on the role of collaboration in online learning environments. Chapter XI, by Bonk et al., reviews the nature of online collaboration from several dimensions, including the task, social, and technological ones. They emphasize the importance of awareness support into each of these dimensions and suggest key knowledge elements in each type of awareness. The chapter is concluded with examples of awareness support for online collaboration.

Then, in Chapter XII, Lucena et al. introduce an approach to develop and analyze collaborative systems based on the 3C (communication, coordination, and cooperation) collaboration model. A case study based on the AulaNet learningware tool and on the material of an information technology course is used to support the discussion.

Chapter XIII, by Khine, describes the use of a tool that enables users to participate in discussions by attaching notes to video footage in a collaborative way. The use of this type of tool is relatively recent in the educational domain. The author also describes the results of the study and the way that this tool can be used in order to improve the interaction among learners in other training settings in CSL environments.

In Chapter XIV, Furtado et al. describe EGA (educational geosimulation architecture), which is an architecture for the development of pedagogical tools for training in urban activities. The construction of this architecture was based on MABS (multi-agent based simulation), GIS (geographic information systems), and ITS (intelligent tutoring systems). The authors advocate the advantages of this architecture to fulfill the lack of efficient tools adequate to the use in trainings of urban activities with high risk and/or high cost.

Finally, Chapter XV, by Qiu, focuses on the design tradeoffs related to the project, deployment, and authoring of interactive learning environments. Qiu describes a combination of design choices in a software tool used for authoring and delivering learn-by-doing environments.

Acknowledgments

The editors would like to thank all of the authors that have submitted their chapter proposals for this book. We would also like to thank our peers that have acted as reviewers, giving invaluable help in the selection process. We are grateful for the support provided by the staff at Idea Group Inc. in preparation of this book. In particular, we are indebted to Ms. Kristin Roth, Development Editor, for helping us keep on track with our schedule. Finally, we would like to thank our families (Luana, João Pedro, and Maria Eduarda; Patrícia and Gabriel) for their patience when our work has kept us from them.

Section I

New Approaches for Teaching and Learning Online

Chapter I

A Comparative Analysis of Computer-Supported Learning Models and Guidelines

Fethi Ahmet Inan, The University of Memphis, USA

Deborah L. Lowther, The University of Memphis, USA

Abstract

This chapter presents a comprehensive analytical review of computer-supported learning (CSL) design models and guidelines according to the level of emphasis regarding key elements and dimensions of effective teaching and learning within an online environment. The key elements encompass learning activities, learning environment, and/or assessment of student learning. Ultimately our purpose was to identify components that experts considered as critical to achieving effective CSL environments in order to use this information as a framework to design, develop, and implement CSL. The results indicate that the trend in CSL design and development models and guidelines is to create online environments that support constructivist learning that is student-centered, presents resources in varied formats, supports discussions and/or collaborative and/or problem-based learning as well as independent student research and use of resources.

Introduction

When computer-supported learning (CSL) is coupled with the limitless connectivity of the Internet, educational opportunities expand beyond barriers of traditional learning environments. Learning via interactive, virtual Web-based communities and environments now extends into today's K-12 classrooms, universities, and the workforce. CSL allows education to occur independent of the place and time (Moore & Kearsley, 1996) and provides learners opportunities to search, discover, and utilize information according to their own individual needs (Dabbagh & Bannan-Ritland, 2005; Khan, 1997). Basically, the Internet is a flexible, interactive, and resource rich system that supports student-centered learning (Hill & Hannafin, 2001).

The use of CSL environments is gaining more popularity each day; the number of Web-supported or Web-based courses in training, colleges, and K-12 levels are increasing significantly in the United States (Allen & Seman, 2004; Picciano, 2001; Setzer & Lewis, 2005). For example, approximately 54,000 Web-based courses were offered by 1,680 different institutions in 2002 (Simonson, Smaldino, Albright, & Zvacek, 2003). Over 1.9 million students enrolled in online courses in the fall of 2003, and predictions indicate the number will increase to over 2.6 million in 2004 (Allen & Seman, 2004).

Regardless of capabilities of the delivery medium, typical CSL applications and practices continue to be teacher-directed and delivery-centered (Carr-Chellman & Duchastel, 2001; Naidu, 2003). Merely delivering course content through use of the Web is a common phenomenon in that many course sites are primarily text driven repositories for syllabi, course notes, and electronic presentations (Palloff & Pratt, 1999). Although online publishing of course syllabi and PowerPoint lecture notes can be of value, developing an effective online course involves much more than just transforming existing course materials to a Web format (Burch, 2001; Discenza, Howard, & Schenk, 2002). Yet, this widely used instructional medium is often developed and implemented upon the basis of "what works" in traditional settings, institution-specific guidelines, or recommendations found in a research article or textbook. "Traditional" approaches often include no or limited use of the attributes and functions of the Web that enable the creation of student-centered learning environments. Considerations for developing student-centered environments include selecting the most appropriate method for presenting content, engaging students in learning activities, and supporting the needs of individual learners (Hirumi, 2002b; Naidu, 2003).

Most would agree that in order for CSL to be effective, research-based models and guidelines should serve as the structural foundation for systematically planning, designing, developing, and implementing the CSL environment. However, the task of selecting a model becomes daunting in that numerous options are presented in current literature. This chapter used a variety of methods to address these concerns. An initial approach involved operationally defining elements, dimensions, and attributes of CSL models. From these definitions, an analysis schema was developed to assess the frequency with which these components are addressed in "effective" CSL models. It is important to note that the purpose of this chapter is not to report on the "quality" of CSL models and guidelines, but rather to present the results of a comprehensive analytical review of published models and guidelines.

Description of Analysis Schema

The analysis schema for the CSL models and guidelines was created by an extensive review of research on effective teaching and learning in CSL environments (Driscoll, 1999; Hannafin, Hill, & Land, 1997; Hill & Hannafin, 2001; Hirumi, 2002b; Jonassen, Peck, & Wilson, 1999; Land & Hannafin, 2000; Schunk, 2004). The procedure used to create analysis schema includes the following steps: examination of literature, identification of key elements related to teaching and learning in a Web-based learning environment, and grouping these identified elements into main categories. First, to identify key elements, the researchers examined a selection of articles and books related to effective teaching and learning in CSL. Following the examination, a list of key elements was created. For instance, names like "project-based learning," "performance based assessment," "scaffolding," "accessibility," and "testing" were used. Second, the elements that fit together meaningfully were grouped into major elements such as "learning activities," "assessment format," and "assessment source." These major elements enabled the researcher to identify the main dimensions. Lastly, main dimensions were formed, namely, "learning" and "assessment." After an analysis schema was developed, the researchers began testing this schema to ensure comprehensiveness of the items. The schema was slightly modified during this pre-analysis process. After the schema was finalized (see Table 1), all articles were reviewed based on the final version of analysis schema.

Understandably, *learning* and *assessment* emerged as the two major elements impacting CSL design and development. As seen in Table 1, Learning is comprised of a variety of instructor-planned *activities,* which occur within an *environment* that consists of different components. When designing CSL, instructors have the option of including student activities that can range from traditional to student-centered methods. Traditional activities would include the use of didactic approaches (e.g., online lecture notes or videos) to disseminate

Table 1. Elements, dimensions, and attributes of computer-supported learning environments

Elements	Dimensions	Attributes
Learning		
Activities	Discussions	▪ Generally, planned conversation between students, students-teacher. ▪ Can be moderated ▪ Academic focused, Not social or informal discussion ▪ Can be synchronous or asynchronous ▪ Examples: Group brainstorming sessions, guided debate
	Collaborations	▪ Students work together to understand content, solve problems and/or create product. ▪ Typically planned and facilitated ▪ Examples: Peer reviews, group projects
	Interactive Communication	▪ Student initiated communication between themselves by means of web-based communication tools. ▪ Topics are student-selected and may be non-course related ▪ Enable interpersonal relationships/interactions
	Problem-based	▪ Student-centered activities to solve authentic, ill-structured problem(s) ▪ No specific path to solve the problem ▪ Students assume roles of researchers ▪ Generally involve student collaboration to produce a group product
	Project-based	▪ Students construct an artifact or develop a product ▪ Teacher designates specific path of learning outcomes ▪ Learner controls pace of project completion ▪ May involve student collaboration and production of a group product ▪ Examples: Goal based scenarios, Web Quests
	Didactic	▪ Instructor-controlled dissemination of content ▪ Typically lecture format in the form of audio, video, or text
	Independent / Resource-based	▪ Students follow self-learning activities that may include a wide range of resources, learning activities and assignments: ▪ Independent work to gather fact or answer question ▪ Students are responsible for completing individual assignments ▪ Examples: Writing an individual research paper, reading chapters and answering end-of-chapter questions.
Environment	Scaffolding	▪ Support strategy or mechanism to assist student learning ▪ Procedural, conceptual, metacognitive, and strategic ▪ Not feedback
	Feedback	▪ Providing information to student action or product ▪ Upon request from students or nature of task ▪ Goes beyond the "correct" and "incorrect" ▪ Mostly, use accepted criteria
	Learner Control	▪ Amount of control learners have over their own learning process ▪ Can include navigation, pacing, content, practice, and feedback choices
	Teacher as Facilitator	▪ Supportive, not directive role ▪ Active monitoring of individual or group learning ▪ Academic focus
	Usability	▪ Navigation and orientation ▪ Ease of use ▪ Consistency of design

Table 1. continued

	Learner Support	▪ Student access to instructor or facilitator for: - Course-related (e.g., assignments) - Learning (e.g., understanding concepts) - Technical (e.g., uploading assignment)
	Course Content- Text Only	▪ Organization/structure of the materials ▪ Script for audio/video materials ▪ Content downloadable
	Course Content - Multimedia	▪ Different content presentation with different media format (e.g. audio, video)
	Flexibility	▪ Accommodating individual preferences considering access to resources and scheduling ▪ Address learners with disabilities
Assessment		
Format	Knowledge	▪ Recognition or recall of conceptual knowledge ▪ Objective based assessments ▪ Test, quizzes, survey
	Performance	▪ Demonstration of knowledge ▪ Commonly involve use of rubric, checklist or rating scale ▪ Products from project / problem based learning ▪ Examples: Portfolio, role playing, presentation
Source	Instructor	▪ Instructor assesses student knowledge and performance
	System	▪ System produces reports regarding student participation, number of posts
	Student (self)	▪ Students use guided reflection ▪ Feedback by self-scoring by system
	Peer	▪ Reflection from peers for student learning progress or product
Profile		
Origin	Constructivism	▪ Learners are the center of the design activity and have major learning responsibility ▪ Use of communication tools to promote interaction and social activities. ▪ Encourage problem-based and cooperative learning, self-evaluation, and student reflection ▪ Assessment practices involve real life problems in authentic settings (Driscoll, 1999; Jonassen et al., 1999; Mishra, 2002).
	Cognitivism	▪ Instruction is designed to promote individual information processing and decrease cognitive overload. ▪ Uses strategies to promote encoding and increase retrieval of information efficiently ▪ Considers learners prior knowledge, competencies, and metacognitive abilities (Schunk, 2004)
	Behaviorism	▪ Instruction is designed to promote individual pacing in which learners proceed step-by-step with immediate reinforcement ▪ Content is divided into small frames or chunks ▪ Assessment involves measuring behavioral objectives (Mishra, 2002)
Audience	Higher Education	▪ Intended and tested for college or higher level education
	Training	▪ Intended for online training development
	Generic	▪ Applicable for multiple adult audiences

course content and the use of independent learning. On the other hand, student-centered choices might include collaborative, project-based learning that embeds student discussions and interactive communications. Once the activities are chosen as a basis of achieving the course objectives, an effective learning environment can be designed.

Multiple options are available to create learning environments that support traditional and/or student-centered activities. These include the provision of scaffolding resources to address remediation needs, instructional feedback to increase learning, and the teacher acting as a facilitator of the "virtual" classroom. Additional dimensions of the learning environment include flexibility to meet individual needs, usability of the course management software, the level of student support, and types of resources (text, multimedia, and supplemental) available to students. The intent of all CSL courses is student achievement of course goals. Therefore, the next critical element of designing online environments is assessment.

Two elements of *assessment* are addressed: format and source. The *format* of the assessment does not differ from that which would be used in a non-CSL course in that it addresses knowledge or performance-based measures. The difference occurs in the *source* of the assessment. Within a CSL environment, students can be assessed by the instructor, peers, or self-evaluations using text or audio comments added to documents, completion of online rubrics, graded assignments returned to students, or scheduled video conferences. The CSL system can also provide assessment data in the form of participation (e.g., e-mail, discussion boards, online chats) records. As with the other design considerations, selection of the appropriate assessment format and source should be determined by overall course goals.

Identified CSL Models and Guidelines

In order to identify target models and guidelines, an extensive literature search was conducted. The review was initiated through the use of electronic libraries (e.g., ERIC, EBSCOhost, PsychINFO) and search portals (e.g., google.com). This was followed by a review of non-digital refereed journals and books. Moreover, references of the articles located through the above searches were scanned. First, over 75 articles related to the teaching and learning process of CSL were gathered. After initial examination, some articles were eliminated based on whether they provided a guideline or model for design and development of CSL. This review process resulted in the identification of over 28 models and guidelines that addressed at least one of the criteria categories identified in the analysis schema: learning activities, learning environment, and/or assessment of student learning. A brief description of each model or set of guidelines is presented in Table 2.

Table 2. Descriptions of CSL models and/or guidelines included in analysis

Model #	Authors	CSL Model and/or Guideline Description
1	Alonso, Lâopez, Manrique, and Viänes (2005)	Describes an instructional model for e-learning that utilizes a blended learning approach. Authors base the model on information processing theory and social constructivist theory in that the self-paced design addresses cognitive load, attention, and metacognition with supporting collaborative activities.
2	Berge (2002)	Provides a framework for implementing constructivist philosophy to create dynamic learning environments which incorporate student-centered learning activities, social interactions, instructor facilitation, and student self-evaluation and reflections.
3	Burch (2001)	Provides a framework for designing communication in web-based courses. Communication is examined from the user interface (web site design) viewpoint in an effort to allow the learners and web site to interchange messages using two-way communication.
4	Carr-Chellman and Duchastel (2001)	Discusses a set of essential components for designing and developing online courses. Components include student support, content, student assessment, social interaction and collaboration, communication, and theoretical origin.
5	Cooper (2002)	Based on the practices of online business computer application courses, the author provides a framework of instructional strategies and management techniques for online courses. Starting from planning the online course, the author primarily portrays application of strategies and techniques for the initial classroom meeting; creating and managing interactions, providing various course materials, and student testing.
6	Egbert and Thomas (2001)	Applies a traditional instructional design model to develop graduate level online courses. In addition to design guidelines, the authors incorporate student-centered strategies such as problem-based learning and discussions.
7	Fisher (2001)	Presents an analysis of web-based instructional practices. The intent of the resulting guidelines is to direct educators when developing online course materials.
8	Gillespie (1998)	Presents a comparison of a traditional vs. a non-traditional process employed to develop web-based learning. The new model focuses on helping students to develop higher-order thinking and problem solving skills.
9	Graham, Cagiltay, Lim, Craner, and Duffy (2001)	Uses the seven principles developed for evaluating teaching in traditional, face-to-face courses as a general framework to evaluate online courses. Authors use this framework to provide guidelines for design and development of online courses.
10	Hall, Watkins, and Eller (2003)	A model of designing web-based learning environments, which consists of seven components: directionality, usability, consistency, interactivity, multimodality, adaptability, and accountability.
11	Hirumi and Bermudez (1996)	Focuses on analysis, design, development, and evaluation of interactive web-based instruction. The authors examine development of graduate level instructional units by employing strategies to promote interactivity, active learning, and development of learning communities.
12	Hirumi (2002a)	Introduces a three-level categorization of web-based interaction. The author extends traditional interaction types (student-student, student-teacher, student-content) with student self-interaction and student-instruction interaction. Within this environment the interactions are connected to grounded instructional strategies within a organized framework.
13	Ingram and Hathorn (2003)	Presents a model based on the instructional design model of Dick, Carey, and Carey (2001). It assists novice designers to focus on the instructional components of online learning such as content presentation, instructional strategies, and interaction.

Table 2. continued

14	Janicki, Schell, and Weinroth (2002)	Describes the development of a model that guides the creation of web-based instruction by blending behavioral, cognitive, and constructivist learning theories. The model focuses on development of stimulating and interesting content, student engagement, multiple forms of presentation, detailed assessment and feedback.
15	Johnson and Aragon (2002)	Discusses a conceptual framework to guide development of online courses through the synthesis of multiple theoretical perspectives. The authors provide seven pedagogical factors that the designer should consider (1) individual differences, (2) motivation, (3) cognitive overload, (4) authentic context, (5) social interaction, (6) student engagement and practice, and (7) student reflection.
16	Khan (2000)	Describes a comprehensive framework to guide development of online learning materials, courses, and programs. The framework consists of eight components to embrace pedagogical, technological and administrative issues.
17	Koszalka and Bianco (2001)	Describes practical implications of instructional design process for online learning. The authors examine three design elements; information, instruction, and learning with regard to their contribution to the teaching and learning process.
18	Lefoe, Gunn, and Hedberg (2002)	Examines pedagogical, technological, student support, and administrative challenges and problems of online learning. Based on categorization of these challenges, the authors provide recommendations for implementation - taking student perspectives into account.
19	MacDonald, Stodel, Farres, Breithaupt, and Gabriel (2001)	Introduces the Demand-Driven Learning Model (DDLM), which is a framework for designing web-based learning environments. The model consists of five components: superior structure, content, delivery, and service, and learner outcomes.
20	Mason (2001)	Introduces a model to categorize online programs according to their formation. Furthermore, author provides pedagogical perspective for teaching in an online environment.
21	Moallem (2001)	Introduces a combined model for designing and developing web-based courses by employing constructivist and objectivist learning theories. Also presented are evaluation findings from implementation of the model.
22	Naidu (2003)	Examines the capabilities and limitations of e-learning. The author provides a contemporary perspective on pedagogical approaches to improve efficiency of online learning.
23	Oliver (1999)	Describes a framework for the critical design elements of online learning. These elements include the course content, learner support, and learning activities. The author demonstrates how different web tools address these design issues.
24	Schnitz and Azbell (2004)	The model and guidelines address full capabilities of available technologies. Authors provide a model that leverages the advantages offered by available web-based technologies to overcome challenges of online learning.
25	Schrum and Benson (2002)	A book chapter that examines challenges of online learning from the perspectives of learners, online educators and program administration. Authors categorize and provide solution approaches to overcome these challenges.
26	Shearer (2003)	Presents an inclusive list of critical variables and factors to consider when designing online instruction such as learner control, interaction, and access. Distance education is examined from print to two-way video conferencing technologies to display how these technologies address and align with designing online environments.
27	Trentin (2001)	Approaches the design of online courses by examining the course plan and the communication architecture. Key elements addressed in the course plan include learning needs, prerequisites, educational strategies, evaluation criteria, course activities and resources, the schedule and mode of operation. The communication architecture addresses communication requirements, network services, and logical communication structure.
28	Zheng and Smaldino (2003)	Presents essential components of designing instruction for online learning environments. Based on pertinent instructional design models, the authors identify critical elements of online learning (learner analysis, content organization, instructional strategies, and evaluation) and provide suggestions to improve the quality of online instruction.

Table 3. Schema analysis of CSL models and guidelines by elements and dimensions of CSL environments

ELEMENTS	DIMENSIONS	MODEL #									
		1	2	3	4	5	6	7	8	9	10
Learning											
Activities	Discussions		x		X	X	X	x		X	
	Collaborations	X	X		X				x	X	
	Interactive Communication		X			X		x			
	Problem-based	x	X		x			x	x	x	x
	Project-based	x	X				X			X	
	Didactic	x									
	Independent / Resource-based	X	X		X	x	x		x		X
Environment	Scaffolding				X	X	x				
	Feedback		X	x	X	X			X	X	
	Learner Control	x	X		x				X	X	
	Teacher as facilitator		x	x		x			X	X	
	Usability			X		x	X	X			X
	Student support	X						x			
	Content- Text Only	X		X	X	x	x	X	x		x
	Content - Multimedia			x	x	x	x	x	x		X
	Flexibility					x				x	X
Assessment											
Format	Knowledge					X			x	X	x
	Performance		X		X	x	X		x	X	x
Source	Instructor		X		x	x	X			X	
	System					x					
	Student (self)		X			x	x				
	Peer				x					X	
Profile											
Origin	Constructivism	X	X	x	X	x	x	x	x	X	X
	Cognitivism	X		X		x	x	X	x		x
	Behaviorism	X				x	x	x	x		
Audience	Higher Ed.	X	X	X		X	X		X	X	
	Training										
	Generic				X			X			X
ELEMENTS	DIMENSIONS	MODEL #									
		11	12	13	14	15	16	17	18	19	20
Learning											
Activities	Discussions	x	x	X		X	X	X	X	X	X
	Collaborations	x	x			X		x	X	X	X
	Interactive Communication					X		x	X	X	
	Problem-based		x	X	X	x				X	
	Project-based		x			X		x		X	
	Didactic		x	x							x
	Independent / Resource-based	X		X	x	x	X	X		X	X
Environment	Scaffolding							X		x	
	Feedback	X	X		X	X		x	x	X	
	Learner Control		X		X	x			X	X	
	Teacher as facilitator		X		x	x	x	X		X	x
	Usability		x		X	x	X			X	
	Student support	x					X	x	X	X	
	Content- Text Only	X		X	x						
	Content - Multimedia	X	X	X	X	X			X	X	X
	Flexibility				x		X		x	x	

Analysis of CSL Models and Guidelines

Each of the 28 identified CSL models or set of CSL guidelines was assessed on the degree to which the elements, dimensions, and attributes listed in the analysis schema were addressed or supported, for example, fully supported ("X") or

Table 3. continued

Assessment											
Format	Knowledge	X		X	X	x	x			X	X
	Performance				x	X		X		X	x
Source	Instructor	X		X	x	X	x	X		X	
	System									x	x
	Student (self)			X	x					X	
	Peer	x				X		X		X	X
Profile											
Origin	Constructivism		X	x	X	X	X	X	X	X	
	Cognitivism	X	x	x	X	X	X				
	Behaviorism		x	x	X	X	X				
Audience	Higher Ed.	X				X		X	X	X	
	Training									X	
	Generic		X	X	X		X				

ELEMENTS	DIMENSIONS	MODEL #							
		21	22	23	24	25	26	27	28
Learning									
Activities	Discussions	X		X		x	x	X	x
	Collaborations	X	X	X				X	
	Interactive Communication			X		x		X	x
	Problem-based	X	X	X				X	
	Project-based	X	X		X				
	Didactic	X							
	Independent / Resource-based	X	X	X					x
Environment	Scaffolding	X	X	X					x
	Feedback	X	X	X					X
	Learner Control	X	X	X	X	X	X		x
	Teacher as facilitator	X	X	X	X				X
	Usability						x	X	
	Student support			X		X		X	X
	Content- Text Only				X	x	X	X	x
	Content - Multimedia		X	X	X	x	X	X	x
	Flexibility		X	X			X	X	
Assessment									
Format	Knowledge	X			x	x		X	X
	Performance	X	X		X	x		X	X
Source	Instructor	X			X	x		X	x
	System							X	
	Student (self)	X						x	
	Peer		X					x	
Profile									
Origin	Constructivism	X	X	X	X	x	X		X
	Cognitivism	X	X			x	x		x
	Behaviorism	X						x	x
Audience	Higher Ed.	X		X		X		X	
	Training							X	
	Generic		X		X		X		X

Table 4. Frequency of CSL dimension occurrence by degree of emphasis

ELEMENTS		DIMENSIONS	EMPHASIS	
			Full	Partial
LEARNING	Activities	Discussions	13	8
		Independent / Resource-based	12	7
		Collaborations	11	4
		Problem-based	8	8
		Project-based	7	3
		Interactive Communication	7	4
		Didactic	1	4
	Environment	Feedback	13	4
		Content – Multimedia	13	8
		Learner Control	11	6
		Teacher as facilitator	10	7
		Content- Text Only	9	7
		Usability	8	4
		Student support	8	3
		Flexibility	6	5
		Scaffolding	5	4
ASSESSMENT	Format	Performance	12	6
		Knowledge	9	7
	Source	Instructor	11	6
		Peer	6	3
		Student (self)	3	5
		System	1	3
PROFILE	Origin	Constructivism	18	7
		Cognitivism	8	10
		Behaviorism	5	8
	Audience	Higher Education	16	0
		Generic	11	0
		Training	2	0

partially supported ("x"). The analysis results can be seen in Table 3. These results were then summarized into frequencies with which each component was fully or partially supported or emphasized in the published models and guidelines (see Table 4).

Further analysis revealed a positive trend in CSL environments that is supportive of constructivist learning (n = 18). This philosophy is reflected in the types of learning activities that were most commonly mentioned, for example, engaging students in discussions (n = 13), independent work involving locating and researching a variety of resources (n = 12), collaborative learning (n = 11), as well as problem-based activities (n = 8) (see Figure 1). A similar pattern was seen with regard to learning environments. Almost half of the CSL models and guidelines suggested that the online learning environment should provide feedback (n = 13); offer content in a multiple formats (audio, video, virtual interactions) (n = 13); allow students to control a variety of learning variables

Figure 1. Learning activities by frequency of strong emphasis in CSL models and guidelines

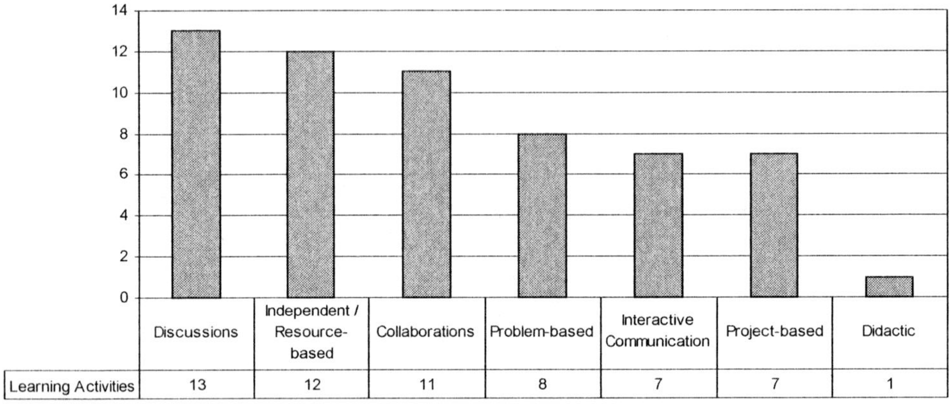

Figure 2. Learning environment by frequency of strong emphasis in CSL modules and guidelines

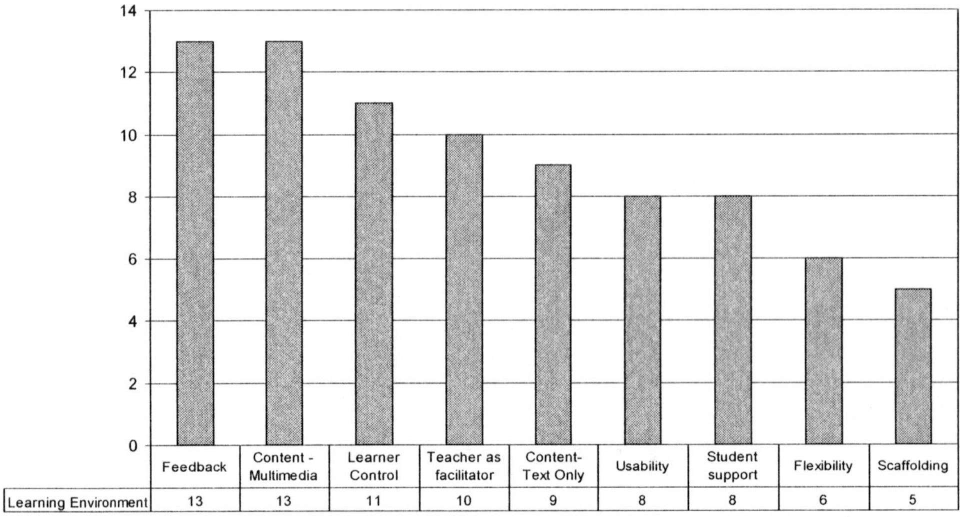

(e.g., pace, types of resources) ($n = 11$); and have teachers serve as facilitators of learning ($n = 10$) (see Figure 2). With regard to the suggested assessment format, there were no considerable differences between knowledge and performance-based measures; however, there was a slight preference for instructors and peers as the assessment source.

Discussion

As seen, the trend in CSL design and development models and guidelines is to create online environments that support constructivist learning that is student-centered, presents resources in a variety formats, and supports discussions and/or collaborative and/or problem-based learning as well as independent student research and use of resources. The guidelines also suggest that teachers should serve as facilitators and students should be able to receive feedback and have control over various aspects of their learning. Additional recommendations included using both instructors and peers to conduct assessments of student knowledge and performance. Since these proposed environments are different from traditional instructional settings, CSL teachers are faced with new design and development considerations for learning activities and environments.

Learning Activities

Social learning has long been an important topic of interest among educators due to its well-established benefits. Students can construct and develop knowledge, attitudes, and values through interaction with others (Woolfolk, 1995). Similarly, learning can occur vicariously when students learn by observing others (Schunk, 2004). As seen in the results, there is a prominence of group-based approaches that emphasize social learning (Brush, 1998; Jonassen, Howland, Moore, & Rose, 2003). In addition, group-based learning often leads to the creation of a learning community that continuously produces and shares information and artifacts while engaging in collaborative learning and reflective practices (Dabbagh & Bannan-Ritland, 2005; Palloff & Pratt, 2003). Guidelines for creating effective learning communities involve the inclusion of:

- Active interaction involving both course content and personal communication
- Collaborative learning evidenced by comments directed primarily student to student rather than student to instructor
- Socially constructed meaning evidenced by agreement or questioning, with the intent to achieve agreement on issues of meaning
- Sharing of resources among students
- Expressions of support and encouragement exchanged between students, as well as willingness to critically evaluate the work of others (Palloff & Pratt, 1999, p. 32)

Learning Environment

Design and development of tools and learning environments that support the creation and support of learning communities and/or collaborative learning is an emerging issue for two primary reasons. First, for cooperation to take place, students must have a shared workspace (Jonassen et al., 2003). The well-established research of the Computer-Supported Intentional Learning Environment, now known as the Knowledge Forum, has addressed these issues. Their approach has involved examining online knowledge building, organization and sharing systems that support student learning through the generation and sharing of learning artifacts to receive feedback, and update their knowledge (Dabbagh & Bannan-Ritland, 2005).

The second issue is a growing concern that the individual differences of learners may not be met when CSL courses increase the focus on group-based activities. Differences among the learner's skill, aptitude, and preferences can influence learning progress in online environments (Chen, Czerwinski, & Macredie, 2000; Jonassen & Grabowski, 1993). For example, studies that match instructional strategies or content presentation with student learning preferences show that students perform better in matching situations in which instructional treatment is designed to meet individual characteristics (Bajraktarevic, Hall, & Fullick, 2003; Ford & Chen, 2000, 2001; Graff, 2003)

Although CSL has many features that support meeting individual student learning goals and preferences, in reality, online courses rarely tailor content or the environment to address individual differences. As this study revealed, individual differences were most frequently accommodated by providing instructional material in a variety of formats. Students are expected to benefit from being able to select and utilize the materials that best match their own individual preferences. In other words, the system, although not personalized, is designed to compensate for individual differences by providing multiple options.

Most Web-based learning environments usually provide optimal content presentation, instructional strategies, assessment methods, and interface. The designers/developers expect learners to acclimate and benefit from the provided learning environment (Chen et al., 2000). However, these learning environments are usually limited in that they do not provide immediate teacher support and feedback. Indeed, if the user is inexperienced or not comfortable with the learning environment, many instructional advantages can be lost (Oliver & Herrington, 1995).

Several adaptive methods (i.e., adaptive interface, content, and navigation) have been used to address these concerns (Brusilovsky, 2001). Unfortunately these methods only address adaptations of the Web-based context, rather than instructional aspects (Carro, 2002). Adaptive methods should go beyond this limitation to take in support, feedback, interaction, assessment, collaboration, and social context, which are included in adaptive Web-based learning environments (A-WBLE) (Inan & Grant, 2004). A-WBLE does this by incorporating different instructional strategies, resources, and learning settings that account for individual differences in the online environment (Inan & Grant, 2004).

Conclusion

We examined CSL design models and guidelines according to the level of support or emphasis regarding identified elements and dimensions of effective teaching and learning within an online environment. The key elements encompass learning activities, learning environment, and/or assessment of student learning. The purpose of this analysis was not to report on the "quality" of CSL models and guidelines, but rather to present the results of a comprehensive analytical review of published models and guidelines. In the effort to provide the most comprehensive model review possible, and in accordance with the parameters of the developed analysis schema, some articles that have significant merit in the field were excluded, not based on the quality of the model that was presented, but due to the absence of the particular characteristics that were being studied. Ultimately, our purpose was to identify components that experts considered as critical to achieving effective CSL environments to enable developers and practitioners to use this information as a framework when designing, developing, and implementing CSL. The key findings are summarized:

- There is a prominence of group-based approaches that emphasize social learning that engages students in collaborative work, which often is problem-based and involves the joint creation of products with considering peer feedback as the assessment source.
- Self-learning activities are more prevalent than those that use a didactic, instructor-controlled dissemination of content.
- There was a positive trend in CSL environments that is supportive of constructivist learning, which is reflected in the types of suggested learning activities, for example, engaging students in discussions, collaborative learning, and problem-based activities.
- The most common method of addressing the individual differences and needs of learners was to provide instructional material in a variety of formats, for example, video, PowerPoint lecture notes.

- There were no considerable differences between the emphasis on knowledge or performance-based assessments; however, the most common source of assessment was the instructor and/or peers.
- Explicit student support and scaffolding did not receive substantial attention, which is surprising considering the lack of face-to-face interactions found in traditional settings.
- Most models were designed and tested for college or higher education.
- In spite of prevalent constructivist perspective applications, behaviorist and cognitivist strategies were not diminished from researchers' attention.

Overall, the proposed direction of CSL courses is promising as the prominent models and guidelines suggest a break from traditional approaches of using online environments as a means of distributing text-based information to be learned in an independent, self-paced manner. The new approaches utilize the inherent features of today's Web-enhanced environments to create learning communities that may result in even higher levels of learning than traditional settings.

References

Allen, I. E., & Seman, J. (2004). *Entering the mainstream: The quality and extend of online education in the United States, 2003 and 2004.* Nedham, MA: The Sloan Consortium.

Alonso, F., Lâopez, G., Manrique, D., & Viänes, J. M. (2005). An instructional model for Web-based e-learning education with a blended learning process approach. *British Journal of Educational Technology, 36*(2), 217-235.

Bajraktarevic, N., Hall, W., & Fullick, P. (2003). *Incorporating learning styles in hypermedia environment: Empirical evaluation.* Paper presented at the Adaptive Hypermedia and Adaptive Web-Based Systems Workshop, Budapest, Hungary.

Berge, Z. L. (2002). Active, interactive, and reflective e-Learning. *Quarterly Review of Distance Education, 3*(2), 181-190.

Brush, T. A. (1998). Embedding cooperative learning into the design of integrated learning systems: Rationale and guidelines. *Educational Technology Research and Development, 46*(3), 5-18.

Brusilovsky, P. (2001). Adaptive hypermedia. *User Modeling and User-Adapted Interaction, 11*(1/2), 87-110.

Burch, R. O. (2001). Effective Web design and core communication Issues: The missing components in Web-based distance education. *Journal of Educational Multimedia and Hypermedia, 10*(4), 357-367.

Carr-Chellman, A., & Duchastel, P. (2001). The ideal online course. *Library Trends, 50*(1), 145-158.

Carro, R. (2002, July). *Adaptive hypermedia in education: New considerations and trends.* Paper presented at the World Multiconference on Systemics—Cybernetics and Informatics, Orlando, FL.

Chen, C., Czerwinski, M., & Macredie, R. (2000). Individual differences in virtual environments: Introduction and overview. *Journal of the American Society for Information Science, 51*(6), 499-507.

Cooper, L. (2002). Online courses: Strategies for success. In R. Discenza, C. Howard, & K. Schenk (Eds.), *The design and management of effective distance learning programs* (pp. 125-140). Hershey, PA: Idea Group Publishing.

Dabbagh, N., & Bannan-Ritland, B. (2005). *Online learning: Concept, strategies, and applications.* Upper Saddle River, NJ: Pearson Education.

Discenza, R., Howard, C., & Schenk, K. (2002). *The design and management of effective distance learning programs.* Hershey, PA: Idea Group Publishing.

Driscoll, M. (1999). *Psychology of learning for instruction.* Boston: Allyn & Bacon.

Egbert, J., & Thomas, M. (2001). The new frontier: A case study in applying instructional design for distance teacher education. *Journal of Technology and Teacher Education, 9*(3), 391-405.

Fisher, M. (2001). Design guidelines for optimum teaching and learning on the Web. *Journal of Educational Technology Systems, 29*(2), 107-118.

Ford, N., & Chen, S. Y. (2000). Individual differences, hypermedia navigation, and learning: An empirical study. *Journal of Educational Multimedia and Hypermedia, 9*(4), 281-311.

Ford, N., & Chen, S. Y. (2001). Matching/mismatching revisited: An empirical study of learning and teaching styles. *British Journal of Educational Technology, 32*(1), 5-22.

Gillespie, F. (1998). Instructional design for the new technologies. *New Directions for Teaching and Learning, 1998*(76), 39-52.

Graff, M. (2003). Learning from Web-based instructional systems and cognitive style. *British Journal of Educational Technology, 34*(4), 407-418.

Graham, C., Cagiltay, K., Lim, B.-R., Craner, J., & Duffy, T. M. (2001). *Seven principles of effective teaching: A practical lens for evaluating online courses*. Retrieved June 18, 2004, from http://ts.mivu.org/default.asp?show=article&id=839

Hall, R. H., Watkins, S. E., & Eller, V. M. (2003). A model of Web-based design for learning. In M. G. Moore & W. G. Anderson (Eds.), *Handbook of distance education* (pp. 367-375). Mahwah, NJ: L. Erlbaum Associates.

Hannafin, M. J., Hill, J. R., & Land, S. M. (1997). Student-centered learning and interactive multimedia: Status, issues, and implications. *Contemporary Education, 68*(2), 94-97.

Hill, J. R., & Hannafin, M. J. (2001). Teaching and learning in digital environments: The resurgence of resource-based learning. *Educational Technology, Research & Development, 49*(3), 37-52.

Hirumi, A. (2002a). A framework for analyzing, designing, and sequencing planned e-learning interactions. *Quarterly Review of Distance Education, 3*(2), 141-160.

Hirumi, A. (2002b). Student-centered, technology-rich learning environments (SCenTRLE): Operationalizing constructivist approaches to teaching and learning. *Journal of Technology and Teacher Education, 10*(4), 497-537.

Hirumi, A., & Bermudez, A. (1996). Interactivity, distance education, and instructional systems design converge on the information superhighway. *Journal of Research on Computing in Education, 29*(1), 1-16.

Inan, F. A., & Grant, M. M. (2004). Applications of adaptive technologies in online learning. *Proceeding of the World Conference on E-Learning in Corporations, Government, Healthcare, & Higher Education, 2004* (Vol. 1, pp. 2701-2706).

Ingram, A. L., & Hathorn, L. G. (2003). Design your Web site for instructional effectiveness and completeness: First steps. *TechTrends, 47*(2), 50-56.

Janicki, T. N., Schell, G. P., & Weinroth, J. (2002). Development of a model for computer supported learning systems. *International Journal of Educational Technology, 3*(1), 1-16.

Johnson, S., & Aragon, S. (2003). An instructional strategy framework for online learning environments. *New Directions for Adult and Continuing Education, 2003*(100), 31-43.

Jonassen, D. H., & Grabowski, B. L. (1993). *Handbook of individual differences, learning & instruction*. Hillsdale, NJ: Lawrence Erlbaum Associates.

Jonassen, D. H., Howland, J., Moore, J., & Rose, M. M. (2003). *Learning to solve problems with technology: A constructivist perspective* (2nd ed.). Upper Saddle River, NJ: Merrill Prentice Hall.

Jonassen, D. H., Peck, K. L., & Wilson, B. G. (1999). *Learning with technology: A constructivist perspective.* Upper Saddle River, NJ: Prentice Hall.

Khan, B. H. (1997). *Web-based instruction.* Englewood Cliffs, NJ: Educational Technology Publications.

Koszalka, T. A., & Bianco, M. B. (2001). Reflecting on the instructional design of distance education for learners: Learning from the instructors. *Quarterly Review of Distance Education, 2*(1), 59-70.

Land, S. M., & Hannafin, M. J. (2000). Student-centered learning environments. In D. H. Jonassen & S. M. Land (Eds.), *Theoretical foundations of learning environments* (pp. 1-24). Mahwah, NJ: Lawrence Erlbaum Associates.

Lefoe, G., Gunn, C., & Hedberg, J. (2002). Recommendations for teaching in a distributed learning environment: The students' perspective. *Australian Journal of Educational Technology, 18*(1), 40-56.

MacDonald, C. J., Stodel, E. J., Farres, L. G., Breithaupt, K., & Gabriel, M. A. (2001). The demand-driven learning model: A framework for Web-based learning. *The Internet and Higher Education, 1*(4), 9-30.

Mason, R. (2001). Models of online courses. *ALN Magazine, 2*(2). Retrieved May 27, 2005, from http://www.aln.org/publications/magazine/v2n2/mason.asp

Mishra, S. (2002). A Design framework for online learning environments. *British Journal of Educational Technology, 33*(4), 493-496.

Moallem, M. (2001). Applying constructivist and objectivist learning theories in the design of a Web-based course: Implications for practice. *Educational Technology & Society, 4*(3), 113-125.

Moore, M. G., & Kearsley, G. (1996). *Distance education: A systems view.* Belmont, CA: Wadsworth Publishing Company.

Naidu, S. (2003). Designing instruction for e-learning environment. In M. G. Moore & W. G. Anderson (Eds.), *Handbook of distance education* (pp. 349-365). Mahwah, NJ: Lawrence Erlbaum Associates.

Oliver, R. (1999). Exploring strategies for online teaching and learning. *Distance Education, 2*(20), 240-254.

Oliver, R., & Herrington, J. (1995). Developing effective hypermedia instructional materials. *Australian Journal of Educational Technology, 11*(2), 8-22.

Palloff, R. M., & Pratt, K. (1999). *Building learning communities in cyberspace: Effective strategies for the online classroom.* San Francisco: Jossey-Bass.

Palloff, R. M., & Pratt, K. (2003). *The virtual student: A profile and guide to working with online learners.* San Francisco: John Wiley & Sons.

Picciano, A. G. (2001). *Distance learning: Making connections across virtual space and time.* Upper Saddle River, NJ: Prentice-Hall.

Schnitz, J. E., & Azbell, J. W. (2004). Instructional design factors and requirements for online courses and modules. In C. Cavanaugh (Ed.), *Development and management of virtual schools: Issues and trend* (pp. 158-177). Hershey, PA: Idea Group Publishing.

Schrum, L., & Benson, A. (2002). Establishing successful online distance learning environment: Distinguishing factors that contribute to online courses and programs. In R. Discenza, C. Howard, & K. Schenk (Eds.), *The design and management of effective distance learning programs* (pp. 190-204). Hershey, PA: Idea Group Publishing.

Schunk, D. H. (2004). *Learning theories: An educational perspective.* Upper Saddle River, NJ: Pearson Education.

Setzer, J. C., & Lewis, L. (2005). *Distance education courses for public elementary and secondary school students: 2002-03* (No. NCES 2005-010). Washington, DC: National Center for Education Statistics.

Shearer, R. (2003). Instructional design in distance education: An overview. In M. G. Moore & W. G. Anderson (Eds.), *Handbook of distance education* (pp. 275-286). Mahwah, NJ: Lawrence Erlbaum Associates.

Simonson, M., Smaldino, S., Albright, M., & Zvacek, S. (2003). *Teaching and learning at a distance: Foundations of distance education.* Upper Saddle River, NJ: Pearson Education.

Trentin, G. (2001). Designing online education courses. *Computers in the Schools, 17*(3/4), 47-66.

Woolfolk, A. E. (1995). *Educational psychology.* Needham Heights, MA: Allyn & Bacon.

Zheng, L., & Smaldino, S. (2003). Key instructional design elements for distance education. *Quarterly Review of Distance Education, 4*(2), 153-166.

Chapter II

Integrating Visual Representations of Knowledge with Learning Management Systems: Design Principles for Advanced Computer-Based Learning Support

John W. Coffey, The University of West Florida, USA

Abstract

After a review of literature pertaining to representative constituent parts of contemporary learning management systems (LMS) and features of other systems that support visual representations of information and knowledge in support of learning, a summarization of desirable design elements for a system that is meant to support distance learning is developed and elaborated. These elements include the potential benefits of having an explicit realization of a viable pedagogical theory as the underlying basis for the software, the possible benefits of integrating a variety of capabilities in as simple and usable a fashion as possible, the value of presenting a customizable interface, and the desirability of providing for sharing and reuse of instructional resources. The chapter concludes with a description of a prototype system that embodies many of the principles laid out in the paper.

Introduction

Interest in distance learning as a means of providing anytime-anywhere education is rapidly increasing today (Honawar, 2005). Most distance learning course delivery is based upon a variety of software capabilities that span a wide range from basic Web sites with e-mail through sophisticated Learning Management Systems (LMS) that transparently provide seamless presentation of a variety of electronic media and many other services. Modern systems that support distance learning include a variety of market-leading LMS products such as WebCT (2005), Desire2Learn (2005), and Sakai (2005). Other systems such as Tuft's VUE (2005) and the Florida Institute for Human and Machine Cognition's CmapTools (Cañas, Hill, Carff, Suri, Lott, Eskridge, Arroyo, & Carvajal, 2004) provide significant networked pedagogical support through visual representations of information and knowledge, without attempting to be full-featured learning management systems.

These systems embody a variety of approaches and technical support features for distance learning facilitation. Most have features such as support for e-mail, threaded discussions, instant messaging, student and faculty access to course instructional materials, grade posting capabilities, sophisticated search, and the like. However, some important differences do exist. The basic goal of this article is to point the way to a synthesis of ideas from LMS capabilities, systems presenting visual representations of information and knowledge, and other ideas, to a new type of system to support distance learning.

This chapter starts with an overview of software that provides support for distance learning, followed by some representative LMSs and other pedagogically-motivated software that supports visual representations of knowledge. Based upon this review, a framework for computer-supported learning technologies that arise from a pedagogical grounding and that provide advanced capabilities for effective distance learning course delivery is developed. The framework is based upon a number of principles that point the way to possible design features for well-integrated, next-generation software systems that support distance learning. Following this discussion, a prototype software system that illustrates a realization of many of the principles will be described. The next section of this chapter contains background information pertaining to software support for distance learning.

Overview of Software for Distance Learning

This review contains descriptions of basic issues pertaining to computer-mediated delivery of distance learning courses, and a range of features and concerns pertaining to modern online learning support software. This review is in service of laying the groundwork from which basic principles pertaining to the design of distance learning systems can be culled. A later section in this chapter enumerates and describes these basic principles.

In an extensive survey of European use of LMS technology, Paulsen and Keegan (2002) conclude that the typical tool suite includes course development tools that are often standard Web page development software, student and tutor tools, and administrative systems. Development tools may or may not be part of an LMS. Student support tools might include chat and e-mail, videoconference tools, and so forth. These tools may be part of a tool suite, or separate applications. Paulsen and Keegan conclude that teacher tools to track student progress are limited and that at that time, not a single LMS provided an integrated comprehensive examination capability. This fact reveals a trend in LMS evolution toward inclusion of assessment capabilities. Collis and Strijker (2002) make the distinction between an LMS as a system that provides capabilities to track learner progress, and a learning content management system (LCMS) that provides capability and support for the development and tracking of content. These capabilities might be made to work together via an application program interface (API) if they do not exist in the same application suite. Integration into the same application potentially provides improved simplicity of use.

Kirk (2002) divides the aggregate distance learning support infrastructure into three segments: content providers, the technology sector that delivers hardware and software for authoring, collaboration, and management of learning resources, and support services. Kirk claims that e-learning can be faster, better, and cheaper than face-to-face classes for just-in-time learning in corporate settings if systems are tailored to students' learning styles, and appropriate consideration of instructional methodologies is made. An implication of Kirk's work is that effective systems should have a grounding in some sort of pedagogy.

Kirk's article also addresses the issue of content reuse, which he deems critical to the efficiency he claims is possible with e-learning. The issue of reuse of instructional materials raises several concerns, including issues such as formats for metadata used to identify suitable resources, the possibility of student preferences for one type of resource over another, and sequencing of resources. Bohl, Schellhase, and Winard (2002) describe problems with the major reusability initiatives and emerging metadata standards by the AICC (2005) and the

Advanced Distance Learning Initiative (ADL, 2005). For example, they cite the very basic fact that it is possible to meet minimal requirements for reuse and standards compliance, while not providing the instructor with any evaluation data.

The interface for distance learning software is an important issue. Most of the widely used commercial systems have a standard Web-page portal look and feel. A significant potential alternative is software that presents visual representations to organize learning resources. A number of visual representations of knowledge have been created to externalize and make explicit knowledge regarding what a person knows about a domain. These representations and accompanying tools include concept maps (Novak & Gowin, 1984), semantic networks (Fisher, 1990), and mind maps (Buzan & Buzan, 1996). These representations and their accompanying tools help users to externalize and organize what they know about a knowledge domain. As examples, *SemNet* (Fisher, 2000) permits creation of Fisher's semantic networks *Mind Manager* (Mindjet, 2005) facilitates creation of mind maps, Tuft's VUE program (VUE, 2005) and the Institute for Human and Machine Cognition's (IHMC) CmapTools (Cañas et al., 2004) provide capabilities to create concept maps. Concept maps are directed graphs in the mathematical sense of the word, that have concepts on the nodes and linking phrases on directed arcs between the concepts.

In summary, management and delivery of distance learning courses may be based upon technology spanning the range from simple Web pages to richly featured, dedicated software. LMS can be used to augment face-to-face courses, in hybrid approaches (part face-to-face and part distance), and in distance learning contexts. Obviously, they have achieved wide use in support of distance learning course delivery. Adherence to standards for learning resources and metadata affords the best chance, but not an ultimate answer, to the problem of resource reusability, since the standards themselves have their deficiencies. Alternatives to standard Web-based, textual representations of course content exist, and may play a salutary role in the learning process. Such visual representations of knowledge hold significant potential to present a better organizational basis for courses. The following section elaborates features of LMS and other pedagogical systems based upon visual representations of knowledge.

Sample Systems to Support Distance Learning

A large number of both LMS and other pedagogically motivated systems have been created and are in use. Although it is beyond the scope of this paper to attempt a comprehensive review of all these systems, this section enumerates typical features found in widely-used LMS, and features found in pedagogical systems based upon visual representations of knowledge. LMSs in the market are mature and reflect the state of the practice today. Design ideas from tools based upon visual representations might be integrated with these market leading systems to produce a new generation of tools to support distance learning. Some representative systems from these categories are discussed next.

Learning Management Systems

A number of competing LMSs are in use in the United States today. These include WebCT, Desire2Learn, and Sakai. These systems have attained substantial market share with modest differentiation among their basic capabilities. A survey of capabilities reveals elements of support for import of student information via interface to other enterprise systems, support for collaboration, for the management of learning resources, and for assessment. The next sections survey features of several representative systems.

Desire2Learn

Desire2Learn™ (2005) provides a fairly standard suite of capabilities. The front page affords access to all relevant courses for instructors or students, news postings, a calendaring system, e-mail, help, and a personal file storage area. Each course has provisions for course content, typically organized on a week-by-week basis, links to other content such as that on the Web, threaded discussions, chat rooms, a dropbox for deliverable submissions, a provision for delivery of quizzes, and an area to post and view grades. Students and faculty can see a list of students in a class, their e-mails, and those who are currently logged into the system. The software enables the course creator to build a course out of content that has been created externally, for instance in a presentation manager or word processor, and then imported into the LMS.

WebCT

WebCT (2005) provides a range of tools that the tool designers group into three categories: organizational tools, communication tools, and student learning activities. The organizational tools include calendaring, a search tool, and a syllabus for the course. The communication tools provide announcements to the class, instant messaging, discussion threads, e-mail, and the ability to determine who is online. The student learning activities toolset provides assessment capabilities to create quizzes, self-tests, and surveys. The assignment capability supports individual or group assignments that are submitted online.

As in other software suites, discussion threads can be graded as part of a participation component of the course. Grades are maintained in a spreadsheet-like format. WebCT provides capabilities to form and manage groups, to set up private threaded discussions for them, and to manage group grades. Event tracking of student interactions with WebCT include: the number of mail messages read, accesses to the calendar, the number of course resources the student has accessed, the number of assessments and assignments started and completed, and total time spent on them.

The Sakai System

Prior work that evolved into the Sakai Project (Sakai, 2005) originated at the University of Michigan and Indiana University, and has led to the creation of a product that is called a "collaboration and learning environment" (CLE). This environment is being developed to assist instructors, students and other users in creating course and project Web sites. It is an ongoing development in an approach to software creation that the leaders of the project call "community software development."

In Sakai, each user can create or can have access to one or more workspaces. Workspaces can correspond to courses or projects. A student's workspaces show up as a series of tabs (one for each workspace) across the top of the main window. Within each course or project, a student can select a menu that provides access to tools. Tools and capabilities in the current release afford access to schedules, and an announcements board, access to discussion groups, assignments, a dropbox, a chat room, an e-mail archive, news groups, and Web content for the course or project.

In support of collaboration, students can see other students who are on the system at any given time and can use the communication capabilities to collaborate. No explicit collaboration medium is specified; rather the tool provides collaboration infrastructure in terms of the communication tools and sharable resources associated with courses and projects. The various capabilities associated with workspaces are chosen by the course creator and/or the student.

The widely-used systems identified here have somewhat overlapping feature sets. While each has some unique features, the main differentiator among them is the nature of the user interface. While these systems provide implicit support for active learning and capabilities to support collaborative work, they do not have explicit pedagogical conceptual frameworks upon which they are based. They all are like standard information systems with the addition of features needed to support instruction, such as grade books, search, and communications capabilities.

Table 1 contains a high-level summary of the capabilities of the LMS that have been surveyed in this section. As can be seen in Table 1, capabilities might be grouped into features that support management of learning resources, features

Table 1. Summary of typical capabilities of LMS

Management of learning resources • Syllabus • Course content area • Links to other resources • Personal file management • Assignment submission capability • Guided tours of resources
Communication/Collaboration Support • Email • Discussion threads • Chats • Announcements board • Pager • Group project board • Who is on the system
Assistance with the LMS • Glossary of terms pertaining to LMS • Help with features of the software
Assessment • User statistics tracking • Quizzes - create, deliver, grade, generate statistics • Grade graphing and release to students
Participant Listing and Access • Instructor • Staff • Students • Groups • Import of Class lists

that support communication and collaboration among students and instructors, help features for the software itself, assessment and grading capabilities, and logistical support for functions such as the import of grade rolls from other enterprise systems.

Criteria for the Evaluation of LMS

Hall (2003), writing from a business perspective, enumerated criteria for the evaluation of LMS. These criteria included standard information systems concerns including high availability, scalability, usability, interoperability, stability, and security. The availability concern is described in terms of having to make the system available to many categories of potential users of the system, including students, teachers, and content creators. Related to the availability concern is the need for a stable, robust system, since online learning should be available anytime, anywhere. The scalability issue arises because of the rapid growth in demand for such services, and the anticipation of increasing loads in the future. Hall states that usability criteria include easy-to-use interfaces and the ability to create learner-centered, self-paced instructional schemes. Hall states that interoperability is fostered by compliance with industry standards such as those coming from AICC (AICC, 2005), SCORM (ADL, 2005), and IMS (IMS, 2005). Finally, security is an obvious concern for learning management systems both in academic and business settings.

Pedagogical Systems Supporting Visual Representations of Knowledge

It is highly desirable that computer systems that support distance learning have grounding in a theory of learning. Modern pedagogical theory takes a constructive view of learning that emphasizes the integration of new knowledge into existing knowledge through the individual constructions of learners. As an example, Ausubel's assimilation theory (Ausubel, 2000; Ausubel, Novak, & Hanesian, 1978) is an empirically-grounded, constructive learning theory that holds that learning is the process of progressive differentiation of details and integrative reconciliation of new knowledge with existing knowledge. Ausubel presents evidence for the benefits of subsumptive learning facilitated by advance organizers. Advance organizers are factors in learning that present a global view of the important ideas to be learned and some indication of how they are related. concept maps (Novak & Gowin, 1984), a pedagogical tool of Assimilation Theory, are visual representations of knowledge that have been used as advance organizers.

This section contains a description of two systems that support visual representations of knowledge in the form of concept maps, Tuft's VUE system, and the Florida Institute for Human and Machine Cognition's CmapTools. A great many systems of this type exist, but the ones cited have been selected because they are representative of the types of features and capabilities found in such systems. Generally speaking, these systems have clearly defined groundings in pedagogical theory, less emphasis on information management, and more disparate feature sets.

Tuft's VUE

Tuft's visual understanding environment, VUE (VUE, 2005), is a system that affords capabilities to organize course resources around a visual representation of knowledge based upon concept maps. The goal of the tool is to make the integration of electronic content into courses simpler and their organization more obvious, for both instructors and students. VUE's authors state that users have numerous tools to help locate digital information, but they have relatively few tools that can be used to organize and understand all the resources they find. The purpose of VUE is to fill that gap.

The idea behind VUE is that faculty and students use concept mapping to make explicit the important ideas in a course and the relationships among them, and then use the concept maps as organizers. Accordingly, VUE provides a visual representation of knowledge in the form of a concept map that serves as an organizer for other instructional content. VUE also provides search and filtering capabilities to help students identify relevant resources and to attach resources to concepts in maps.

A separate goal of the environment is to foster sharing of concept maps and associated learning resources. The authors of the system describe the concept maps that are augmented with other resources as content maps. VUE also has a "pathways" feature, an implementation of the idea of guided tours as described in hypermedia literature.

VUE is described as an information management application that provides an interactive, concept mapping interface to digital resources accessed via the Web, ftp servers, or local file systems. VUE is compliant with metadata standards including OKI (OKI, 2005). VUE lacks some of the basic course management features of the systems described earlier, but it has different strengths, including a visual representation of the knowledge in the course.

CmapTools

CmapTools (Cañas et al., 2004) are described as a "knowledge modeling toolkit." They were originally created as a knowledge elicitation environment, and have evolved into a rich featured set of tools to support face-to-face and online learning. CmapTools combine elements of content management and capabilities for course and learning resource structuring with evaluation and search capabilities based upon the creation of concept maps by students.

CmapTools feature a modeless concept map editing tool, which means the user does not need to switch between modes when drawing concepts or links between items. The editor provides the ability to populate concepts in concept maps with accompanying resources by drag-and-drop capabilities. Multiple resources can be associated with a concept, where they can be grouped as text, graphics, digital audio or video, links to Web sites, and so forth. A variety of icons may appear at the nodes in the concept maps to indicate groups of resources. The user can click on an icon to get a pull-down menu indicating the resources of a particular type that are associated with the concept. CmapTools has many features that support collaboration, including threaded discussions that can be associated with a node, and both asynchronous and synchronous collaboration on the construction of concept maps and knowledge models—aggregates of linked Concept maps and accompanying electronic resources.

CmapTools have many other pedagogically-grounded capabilities including a recording capability that allows the instructor to record the steps followed by the student in creating a concept map. The system also has a concept recommender that attempts to determine the topic of a concept map from the most general concepts, and then performs a context-sensitive search for concepts to suggest to the creator of the map. The development effort for CmapTools has included extensive internationalization efforts, and the Tools have been used in more than 150 countries.

This section has reviewed feature sets of representative LMS and pedagogical systems that support creation and presentation of visual representations of knowledge. The next section seeks to draw from the previous discussion to develop a set of design principles for a system to provide advanced support for distance learning.

Design Principles for Advanced Distance Learning Support Systems

This section outlines elements of a computer-based learning environment that can provide effective support for distance education. Some of these elements are drawn from the literature reviewed in the previous sections; other ideas included here are meant to fill gaps in the current state of the practice. It is recognized that this set of elements is continually evolving, and that new capabilities that are emerging will continue to change the distance learning software landscape over time. The current set of principles start with the possibility of designing such systems in a way that reflects a contemporary theory of learning. Additionally, such systems should provide an integrated, human-centered interface that supports collaboration, assessment and reuse of instructional resources. The learning environment organizer (LEO) to be described in a later section of this article embodies many of these principles.

Grounded in a Pedagogical Framework

Most modern LMS do not have explicit pedagogical underpinnings (Szabo & Flesher, 2002). They are essentially tools that afford capabilities to make postings of schedules, syllabi, instructional materials, homework, and other assignment submissions in electronic format and accessible at a distance, combined with network-based communication capability.

Krawchuk (1996) described categories of the advance organizer, a pedagogical concept from Ausubel's assimilation theory, which includes those based upon text, text and graphics, or purely graphical presentations. The concept map is a pedagogical tool in the latter category that has been described as an advance organizer. The linking phrases elaborate the relationships among the concepts. The VUE and CmapTools systems described previously provide support in the form of graphical advance organizers based upon concept maps. The LMS described earlier have standard Web-based interfaces. concept map-based representations embody Ausubel's notion of a graphical advance organizer, and might be used as the interface for development and deployment of a courser.

Rationale for this feature: LMS have an implicit pedagogical stance that is dictated by features and intended modes of use, for instance, most support active learning experiences and collaborations. Grounding system design in an explicit realization of pedagogical principles holds promise to improve on such systems. Additionally, with regard to the potential use of visual representations to organize a course, the homily "a picture is worth a thousand words" is salient.

Integrated System

Modern computer-supported learning systems might potentially integrate additional functionality in more usable ways. This section describes forms of integration that might be incorporated.

Integrated Support for Assessment

Systems to support distance learning might have an integrated capability to perform a variety of types of student assessments. An integrated evaluation system could be used to assess student interests and other educational attributes such as learning styles, as well to provide support for academic attainment, evaluation, and testing. Ideally, an integrated student model could be culled from the assessment capability, and made accessible to both the student and the instructor, in an easy-to-understand format.

Integrated assessment capability raises a number of issues that must be addressed, but it also holds great promise. Issues with computerized assessment include varying facility with computers among users as well as reliability and security concerns. Since distance learning courses are typically computer-based and offered over the Internet, it might be assumed that the majority of students enrolling in such courses have enough facility with computers not to be at a significant disadvantage compared to others. Reliability concerns pertain to problems such as dropped connections during examinations, and are clearly important. Security issues are equally important in light of privacy laws that require controlled access to student information and the need to protect resources such as examinations that are used in determining grades.

Additionally, the problem of determining who is actually taking the examination is an issue in distance learning courses. Several alternative approaches can be employed to address this problem. The first approach is local proctoring of examinations in testing centers. The second, and generally more feasible, is that courses have examinations that do not require closed-book, individual completion and are the equivalent of take-home examinations. Given that these issues are addressed, evaluation capabilities become powerful contributors to distance learning courses.

Rationale for this feature: This capability could help instructors who are conducting distance learning classes learn more about their students, perform better assessment, and help students understand more about their own approaches to learning.

Support for Collaboration

Collaboration at a distance poses special problems that are not present in face-to-face classes.

If learning is to take place at a distance, collaboration may be asynchronous through threaded discussions and e-mail, or synchronous, through instant messaging capabilities and real-time audio-video, real-time collaborative editing of documents at a distance, and so forth. Additionally, support for collaboration should be in the form of highly targeted (versus general) threaded discussions and instant messaging facilities pertaining to specific topics rather than to the entire course.

Support for collaboration can also encompass the collaborative development of items to be evaluated for grades. A system that allows free exchange of information regarding the interests of students fosters the formulation of collaborative teams. The ability to assess student interests might be provided by an integrated evaluation system as described previously.

Most current systems provide support for threaded discussions in a form that places many separate discussion threads in a single forum. An organizing factor that produces discussion threads at the individual topic level would advance the state of practice of this capability. Synchronous collaboration tools such as instant messaging would also benefit from being associated with a context, for instance with an individual topic, in order to limit the number of different discussions going on at once. The lack of a specific context for a chat detracts from the utility of these capabilities to foster learning.

Rationale for this capability: It is widely held that collaboration in the learning process is beneficial. While some elements of learning (e.g., computer programming) must inevitably have an individual component, much is to be gained through collaboration. Well thought out, network-based systems can address difficulties in collaboration imposed by distance learning.

Seamless Integration of Students' and Instructors' Learning Resources

Most of the systems described earlier provide repositories for students' documents. A system should help students find educational resources easily and support electronic filing of new resources that individuals might want to retain. The organizational capability should allow the student to arrange materials seamlessly with the instructor's course materials. The most basic idea behind this principle is that an advance organizer of some type might serve as the organizing factor for the course presentation and materials. The instructor's materials can be accessed via the organizer. The student's resources could be stored and accessed within the advance organizer as well, organized by topic and co-located with the instructor's resources.

Rational for this capability: The advantages of such an approach for both the instructor and student include:

- A single repository for materials provides convenience in accessing and comparing student's and instructor's materials
- Efficiencies in studying
- Detailed content and other resources are couched in a global context of the course as represented by the advance organizer

Integrated Support for Development and Deployment

A system that integrates development with deployment allows the instructor who is developing the course to see what the student will see in the deployed course. Rather than building distance-learning content with standard, separate authoring tools, an integrated development-delivery environment is both desirable and necessary in order to attain the types of integrations described in this section.

Rationale for this capability: The advent of WYSIWYG interfaces for stand-alone computers revolutionized human-computer interface. The same principle applies to systems for assembling and managing all the artifacts of the learning process.

Human-Centered and Customizable

The idea of human-centered computing is intuitively simple to grasp but difficult to realize. Besides the obvious need for an intuitive interface, two basic principles of human-centered computing might be identified with regard to human-centeredness in computer-supported learning: easy access to the right information and learning resources and tailorable information bandwidth.

Affording Easy Access

Easy access is more than the ability to locate a particular piece of media. It should include the ability to customize an information space in such a way that frequently accessed resources, even in large numbers, are still easy to find. A variety of types of information and resources should be easily accessed, including instructional content, intuitive representations of student progress, artifacts of collaborations, assignments, tests and test results, and other evaluation items. Two different approaches are possible to support this capability:

1. anstructional items and student items are grouped and indexed; and
2. a display can be dynamically constituted with items that have been accessed frequently near the top and those that are less-frequently accessed near the bottom.

Information regarding the number of times a student has visited a page, or the less reliable statistic of how long a student has spent on a page, can be used to determine the importance of a document to a student. The former provides an indication of importance of a document and might potentially be used in the selection of favorite documents that should be made easily accessible. The latter is not a highly reliable statistic since the amount of time a page is open does not necessarily reflect the amount of time the student spent actively working with it.

Tailorable Information Bandwidth

Tailorable information bandwidth is corollary to easy access. It has at least two orthogonal dimensions. The first dimension is the ability to display either more or less information in the information space. The second dimension is to be able to navigate from global, conceptual views of a knowledge domain down to a focus on detail, and back out to the global view again. Work in the area of information visualization might suggest ways to pursue these goals. This is an emerging area of research in which some work has been done (Tergan & Keller, 2005).

Rationale for these capabilities: The basic goal is to create computer systems that are able to extend human capabilities in ways that conform to the needs and modes of interaction that are intuitive to the user, rather than requiring the user to adapt to the interaction modes and capabilities of the system. This is the most significant shortcoming of current LMS. The course developer, instructor, and the student must all learn the typically complex interactions with the system.

Support for Reuse of Resources and Reconfiguration of Courses

Creation of electronic instructional resources entails a significant investment of time and effort. Reuse is possible for course organizations, instructional content, and evaluation items such as tests. Given rapidly evolving bodies of knowledge in most disciplines and the need to deliver courses that are appropriate for disparate constituencies, the ability to modify resources associated with a course and course curricula itself are important capabilities that should be fostered by computer-supported learning systems.

Reuse of electronic resources, as envisioned in the IMS (IMS, 2005) and ADL/SCORM (ADL, 2005) initiatives, is highly appealing. Tagging educational resources with standard meta-data tags provides a means of fostering reuse. The Dublin Core Meta-data Initiative (DCMI, 2005) is an open forum that seeks to develop base standards for annotating documents. The base descriptors are a good starting place for document annotations, and the many initiatives to develop standardized domain-specific descriptors holds promise to foster greater reuse in the future.

Rationale for this feature: The obvious rationale pertains to potential efficiencies gained through reuse. A potential tradeoff pertains to the generic nature of reusable instructional materials that might be less effective than other, specifically tailored materials that support clearly targeted learning outcomes in specific contexts.

An Example System

A prototype software system named LEO, a learning environment organizer (Coffey & Cañas, 2003), embodies many of the principles enumerated in the previous section. LEO is part of CmapTools (Cañas et al., 2004), a knowledge modeling toolkit that has been under development for several years at the IHMC. LEO is grounded in Ausubel's assimilation theory (Ausubel, 2000; Ausubel, Novak, & Hanesian, 1978), and the software has features suggested by several aspects of assimilation theory. LEO is a highly integrated system that provides capabilities to individualize instruction and learning, to track student progress, and to assess academic progress and other traits of the learner. LEO also provides support for the reuse of educational materials and course organizations. Figure 1 contains a graphic depicting various elements of the interface provided by LEO.

Figure 1. The interface to LEO, a learning environment organizer

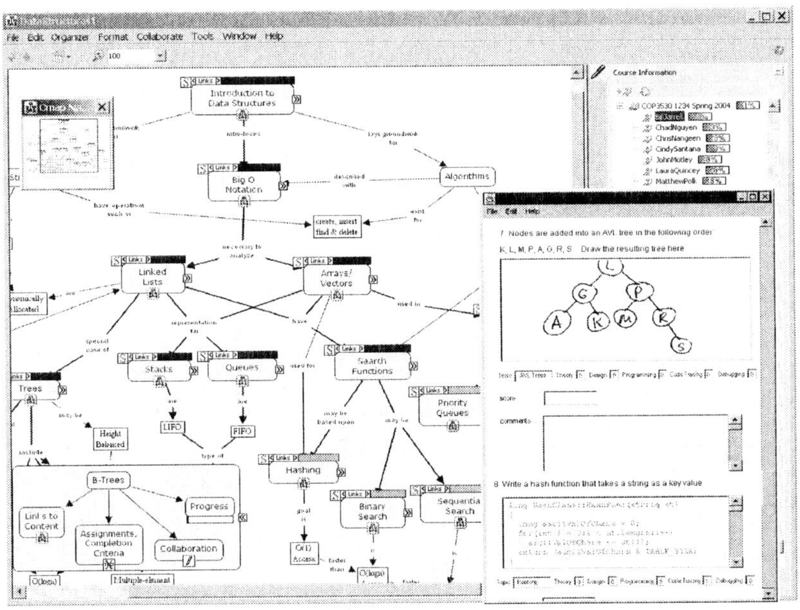

General Features of LEO

As can be seen in Figure 1, the interface to the course is based upon a concept map-like representation with two types of nodes—ones with adornments that correspond to the topics in the course, and others without adornment—that elaborate the relationships among the topics. The representation is an advance organizer showing the major concepts and their relationships in the course, with the most important concepts selected as the course topics. All adornments can be either shown or hidden. When they are shown, they provide the interface for the course, including access to all functionality. When they are hidden, the representation is essentially a concept map of the course, depicting the global organization of the most important concepts, created by an expert on the topic.

As can be seen in Figure 1, individual topics in the course have rectangular bars on the top that are color-coded to indicate student progress. The codings include: completed topics (coded black), topics for which the student is ready by virtue of having completed the prerequisite topics (coded light gray), the current topic on which the student is working (coded gray), and topics for which the student is not ready (coded with an 'X').

Students can customize their environments by highlighting parts of the organizer and de-emphasizing other parts. Students can show or hide the categories of topics or the explanatory nodes in the organizer. They can also open topic nodes such as the one in the bottom-left of Figure 1 to reveal details such as the links to content, completion criteria such as assignments and tests, collaboration tools, and a progress indicator. Students can also hide these details of the topics and reveal only the general view of links, completion criteria, collaboration, and progress. The student can navigate from the organizer into what is termed a knowledge model, also structured by concept maps, which elaborates details pertaining to the topics in the course.

Figure 1 also contains a graphic of the features in the display that the instructor sees. The portion in the top right of the larger window shows student information on a class that has been selected. It is possible from that display to access an individual record pertaining to an individual student or collaborating group and to view student progress as the updated color codings on the topic nodes.

Evaluation Capabilities

LEO provides a range of evaluation capabilities for students. Students can take electronic tests and other evaluation instruments directly from the learning environment (Coffey & Webb, 2002). The window in the bottom right of Figure 1 is an electronic test illustrating interaction modes by which the student can respond to a question, including point-and-click, fill-in-the-blank, and by writing or drawing by hand. This capability supports assessment of academic attainment, student interests, student learning styles, or any other type of evaluation the instructor wishes to administer. Such non-academic evaluations are potentially extremely helpful when trying to know students better in a distance setting. Results of tests are stored in student models that include progress through the course.

Integrated Features of LEO

The software is a highly integrated system that provides for creation and use of an organizer for the course, a much more information-rich representation of the topics than that contained in a traditional syllabus, an integrated interface to tests and other assessments the instructor might wish to administer, and support for collaboration at a fine-grained level. The support for collaboration is fine-grained in the sense that discussion threads and instant messaging are attached to individual topics and therefore focused at the topic level rather than at the course level. In Figure 1, the opened node on "B-Trees" reveals the icon that affords access to the collaboration tools and the other resources.

A course organizer affords easy access to all the salient information pertaining to a topic in the course at the topic level—the links to content, assignments, collaboration tools, and progress. Additionally, the student can tailor the information bandwidth by showing or hiding parts of the organizer, showing or hiding the details of a topic, and viewing a small context window (shown in the top left in Figure 1) with the large window serving as a focus region.

LEO and Reuse of Learning Resources

LEO provides for reuse of course materials and organizers by providing easy editing and linking capabilities. The drawing capability when editing a course is modeless. Links can indicate prerequisite relationships between topics (indicated in Figure 1 by heavy lines) or explanatory links (indicated by the lighter lines). Resources are characterized by a variety of descriptors. CmapTools, in which LEO resides, provides powerful search capabilities to find relevant resources. Resources can be added into an organizer by drag-and-drop capabilities to create hypermedia links. Further discussion of the capabilities that LEO inherits from CmapTools may be found in Cañas et al. (2004).

LEO provides capabilities to create meta-data records for resources associated with the course. Metadata records are structured according to Dublin Core (DCMI, 2005) standards and the format described in the ADL/IMS specification, as presented in the sharable content object reference model (ADL, 2005).

Organizers contain links to course content that are read when a request to generate metadata records is issued. The metadata records contain a variety of information that can be automatically derived from system information. The names of the course, topics, and individual media are all stored in the organizer and can be automatically taken from there. Resource types are also stored in the resources themselves. The course instructor's name is the default value for creator, but all attributes may be edited. When resources are imported into CMapTools, attributes, including a description of the file itself, may be provided. If this information is recorded when the resource is imported into CmapTools, it will be automatically captured for the metadata record. The metadata generator gets the creation date of the file from the system. The software provides editable default values for copyright status and placeholders for keywords that might be associated with the media, topic, or course. These values may also be edited.

Trends in Tools to Support Distance Learning

Numerous software capabilities have been developed to support distance learning. The advent of the Internet brought about tools such as e-mail, threaded discussions, and instant messaging. These capabilities are now routine components of LMS and other online systems that are used for teaching and learning. Current LMS look like standard information systems with additional capabilities such as grade books and collaboration capabilities to support distance learning. Although still relatively primitive, assessment capabilities have been added to LMS in the last few years. Additionally, LMS are typically integrated with other enterprise systems such as student record-keeping systems.

While providing implicit support for active learning and explicit capabilities to support collaborative tasks, these systems generally lack any other commitment to a theory of teaching and learning. It is likely that, in the future, the pedagogical underpinnings of such systems will become more explicit and evident.

Successful LMS now have a plethora of features, and, as with other commercial software, the proliferation of features is a basic trend. The evolution in LMS generally is toward more powerful, well-integrated feature sets. It is anticipated that new features will continue to proliferate, and assessment capabilities will continue to evolve. It remains to be seen if advances in the organization and presentation of learning resources and the interface to new capabilities will reign in the increasing complexity of use that feature proliferation entails.

The systems described here that are based upon visual representations of knowledge such as concept maps, have relatively more clearly identifiable pedagogical underpinnings. Often these systems lack some of the basic information system capabilities that might be incorporated into an application that provides comprehensive support for distance learning. It is likely that these systems will continue to incorporate more features of LMS, or at least, to interface more seamlessly with LMS. Visual organizers hold potential to ameliorate the problem of the additional complexity due to feature proliferation.

A system such as LEO points to a potential synthesis of ideas from traditional LMS and those systems that afford a visual representation of knowledge. The explicit pedagogical underpinnings of this approach and the more intuitive means of organizing learning resources have appeal.

Conclusion

The goal of this article is to survey features of LMS and pedagogical software based upon visual representations of information and knowledge to distill principles of advanced systems that support distance learning. It contains a review of the current state of the practice in learning management systems regarding the features they have that might support distance learning. Several exemplars of commercially deployed LMS are described. The LMS are characterized by relatively minor differentiation of basic features. They differ mostly in terms of particulars pertaining to how their functionality is achieved and how they look and feel. The LMS have interfaces that are typical of the current state of the practice for Web page/portal design.

Additionally, several pedagogical systems that utilize visual representations of knowledge are identified and described. The interface to CmapTools is through concept maps themselves, which are augmented with accompanying electronic resources that are represented as icons on the nodes. The VUE software is also based upon concept maps with links to individual documents. VUE has adopted compliance with external data and metadata standards such as OKI. The systems that are based upon visual representations of knowledge do not compete directly with the LMS described here.

On the basis of this survey, several principles for the design of software that will provide high-quality support for distance learning have been identified. These principles include the desirable attribute of basing the design of a system to support online learning on an explicit pedagogical theory, having a highly integrated, customizable system with a simple, intuitive interface, and the development of a scheme that provides easy access to individual documents even if many are present. The idea of customizable software in general and the idea of customizable information bandwidth in particular, are expressed in this work. An integrated assessment capability with more flexibility than those found in contemporary systems is possible and described here.

LEO, a learning environment organizer, embodies many of the principles elaborated in the discussion. LEO presents both the course developer and the student with a visual representation of the knowledge in the course in the form of a concept map. The nodes of the concept map are augmented with facilities of several types including links to instructional content, a means of linking assignments, tests, and other educational activities associated with a topic, and communication tools that are represented at the topic rather than at the course level.

LEO is based upon the idea of a graphical advance organizer, supporting this central idea from Ausubel's assimilation theory. LEO also provides the basic information system functionality of LMS. As such, it bridges the gap between commercial LMS and systems that provide visual representations of knowledge as the interface. The assessment capabilities of LEO, while still a prototype, point the way to next-generation, assessment systems that are tightly integrated into a learning management system.

Acknowledgments

The author would like to acknowledge the significant contributions of his dissertation advisor, Dr. Alberto Cañas, in the formulation of ideas contained in this work. The author would also like to thank Chad Carff, Michael Webb, John Wernicke, and Michael Wooten for the many insights they gleaned and provided in the process of developing LEO. This work was partially funded by the Office of the Chief of Naval Education and Training, USA.

References

ADL. (2005). Advanced distributed learning. Retrieved April 4, 2006, from http://www.adlnet.org/

AICC. (2005). *Welcome to the AICC Web site.* Retrieved April 4, 2006, from http://aicc.org/

Ausubel, D. P. (2000). *The acquisition and retention of knowledge, a cognitive view.* Dordrecht, The Netherlands: Kluwer Academic Publishers.

Ausubel, D. P., Novak, J. D., & Hanesian, H. (1978). *Educational psychology: A cognitive view* (2nd ed.). New York: Holt, Rinehart and Winston.

Bohl, O., Schellhase, J., & Winard, U. (2002, October 19-23). A critical discussion of standards for Web-based learning. In M. Driscoll & T. C. Reeves (Eds.), *Proceedings of E-Learn World Conference on E-Learning in Corporate, Government, Healthcare, and Higher Education* (pp. 850-855). Montreal, Canada. Association for the Advancement of Computers in Education.

Cañas, A. J., Hill, G., Carff, R., Suri, N., Lott, J., Eskridge, T., et al. (2004, September 14-17). CmapTools: A knowledge modeling and sharing environment. In A. J. Cãnas, J. D. Novak, & F. M. González (Eds.), *Proceed-*

ings of CMC 2004, The 1st International Conference on Concept Mapping (pp.125-133). Pamplona, Spain.

Coffey, J. W. & Cañas, A. J. (2003). LEO: A learning environment organizer to support computer mediated instruction. *Journal of Educational Technology Systems, 31*(3), 275-290.

Coffey, J. W., & Webb, M. (2002). AMEE: Annotated multifaceted electronic evaluation. In M. Driscoll & T. C. Reeves (Eds.), *Proceedings of E-Learn World Conference on E-Learning in Corporate, Government, Healthcare, and Higher Education* (pp. 207-213). Montreal, Canada. Association for the Advancement of Computers in Education.

Collis, B., & Strijker, J. (2002, June 24-29). New pedagogies and reusable learning objects: Toward a different role for an LMS. In *Proceedings of Ed-Media 2002 World Conference of Educational Multimedia and Hypermedia and Telecommunications* (pp.334-339). Denver, CO. Association for the Advancement of Computers in Education.

Desire2Learn. (2005). *Desire2Learn: Innovative learning technology.* Retrieved April 4, 2006, from http://www.desire2learn.com/welcome.html

Dublin Core Meta-Data Initiative. (2005). *Dublin core metadata initiative: Making it easier to find information.* Retrieved April 4, 2006, from http://dublincore.org

Fisher, K. M. (1990). Semantic networking: The new kid on the block. *Journal of Research in Science Teaching, 27*(10), 1001-1018.

Fisher, K. M. (2000). SemNet software as an assessment tool. In J.J. Mintzes, J.H. Wandersee, & J.D. Novak (Eds.), *Assessing science understanding* (pp. 197-221). San Diego, CA: Academic Press.

Hall, J. (2003). Assessing learning management systems. *Chief Learning Officer*. Retrieved April 4, 2006, from http://www.clomedia.com/content/templates/clo_feature.asp?articleid=91&zoneid=29

Honawar, V. (2005). Education department tracks growth in distance learning. *Education Week, 24*(26), 6.

IMS. (2005). IMS Global Learning Consortium, Inc. Retrieved April 4, 2006, from http://www.imsglobal.org/

Kirk, J. J. (2002). *E-learning: An executive summary.* Available in Educational Resources Information Center (ERIC ED461762). Retrieved April 28, 2006, from http://www.eric.ed.gov/ERICDocs/data/ericdocs2/content_storage_01/0000000b/80/0d/bf/40.pdf

Krawchuk, C. A. (1996). *Pictorial graphic organizers, navigation, and hypermedia: Converging constructivist and cognitive views.* Unpublished doctoral dissertation, West Virginia University.

Mindjet. (2005). *Mindjet, visual thinking*. Retrieved April 4, 2006, from http://www.mindjet.com/us/index.php

Novak, J. D., & Gowin, D. B. (1984). *Learning how to learn*. Cambridge, UK: Cambridge University Press.

OKI. (2005). Open knowledge initiative. Retrieved April 4, 2006, from http://web.mit.edu/oki/

Paulsen, M. F., & Keegan, D. (2002). European experiences with learning management systems. In *Web-education systems in Europe* (pp. 4-25). ZIFF Papiere. Available in Educational Resources Information Center (ERIC ED477513). Retrieved April 28, 2006, from http://www.eric.ed.gov/ERICDocs/data/ericdocs2/content_storage_01/0000000b/80/22/2c/ce.pdf

Sakai. (2005). Retrieved April 4, 2006, from http://www.sakaiproject.org/cms/

Szabo, M., & Flesher, K. (2002, October 19-23). CMI theory and practice: Historical roots of learning management systems. In M. Driscoll & T. C. Reeves (Eds.), *Proceedings of E-Learn World Conference on E-Learning in Corporate, Government, Healthcare, and Higher Education* (pp. 929-936). Montreal, Canada. Association for the Advancement of Computers in Education.

Tergan, S.-O., & Keller, T. (Eds.). (2005). *Knowledge and information visualization: Searching for synergies* (LNCS 3426). Heidelberg: Springer-Verlag.

VUE. (2005). *VUE online: Visual understanding environment*. Retrieved April 4, 2006, from http://vue.tccs.tufts.edu/

WebCT. (2005). *WebCt: Learning without limits*. Retrieved April 4, 2006, from http://www.webct.com/

Chapter III

Peer Review in Computer Science: Toward a Regular, Large Scale Educational Approach

Vinícius Medina Kern, Instituto Stela, Brazil

Roberto Carlos dos Santos Pacheco,
Federal University of Santa Catarina, Brazil

Luciana Martins Saraiva, Instituto Vias, Brazil

Joyce Munarski Pernigotti, Porto Alegre City Hall, Brazil

Abstract

Several experiences with peer review in computer science education have been reported in the literature. What is needed to turn it into a continued, regular educational approach? We try to answer that question beginning by presenting the skills required by computer science international curricula, as well as the skills exercised in peer review, an approach that can match those requirements. The practice of peer review in computer science education is reported, revealing very positive results, but with little sign of institutionalization and long-term application. The learning outcomes, the software available, the types of student work reviewed, and the different approaches are detailed. The issues of a methodological approach for continued, regular, large scale application are discussed.

Introduction

Computing is pervasive in society, and it continues to grow in influence. The discourse on this influence goes from admonishing advice, as in "Tools get under our skin" (Talbott, 1995, p. 30), to technological overenthusiasm. No matter what the stance is, computers are originally built, programmed, and run by people.

Computer science international curricula and codes of ethics and professional responsibility demand from computer scientists the mastering of non-technical skills for which they are not prepared by the university. Given that this request has been in writing for more than a decade, it is possible that future accreditation processes demand from computer science courses a clear strategy for the development of those non-technical skills.

Peer review, the quality control system of science, has been applied to computer science education with the aim of exercising students' non-technical skills such as autonomy, collaboration, cooperation, and critical thinking. A reviewer has to read an unpublished paper with an open mind, with no presumption about its quality. This is closer to what an instructor does when grading a paper than what a professional does when reading published material (Smith, 1990). It is also cause of anxiety and occasional enthusiasm or resistance.

Initiatives of student peer review reported in the literature are generally successful. However, they seem to fade out, since several authors quit publishing on the subject and there is no notice of their efforts becoming larger, institutional initiatives. While there is a considerable body of knowledge on technical aspects of peer assessment and evaluation (Falchikov & Goldfinch, 2000; Topping, 1998), there is still little light on how to guarantee the benefits of peer review and on how to make it accessible to a larger number of instructors and students.

There is need to create and make advanced educational approaches that promote non-technical skills of computing professionals. As Haddad and Draxler express:

> *Countries and institutions seem to be willing to invest huge amounts of money in ICT projects with little knowledge of their potential benefits, but are unwilling to invest a small fraction of these amounts in research and development to protect their large investments and improve their effectiveness.* (Haddad & Draxler, 2002, p. 200)

This article discusses the advance of peer review as a pedagogical approach in computer science education. The next sections present the rationale for using it, review the practice, and consider the directions to make it a regular, continuous, and even large scale institutional or multi-institutional program.

The Case for Peer Review in Computer Science Education

Current computer science international curricula (Mulder & van Weert, 2000; Shackelford, Cross II, Davies,Impagliazzo, Kamali, LeBlanc, et al., 2005; The Joint Task Force on Computing Curricula [IEEE-ACM], 2001) reflect the growing need for non-technical skills of computing professionals. Contributes to this growing need the fact that computing is "the defining technology of our age" (IEEE-ACM, p. 9), making "the era of the solo asocial programmer ... come to an end" (Mulder & van Weert, 2000, p. 32).

Skills and capabilities of communication, teamwork, self management, and professional development are required (IEEE-ACM, 2001, p. 9). The International Federation for Information Processing (IFIP) Curriculum Framework (Mulder & van Weert, 2000, p. 32) has 3 of its 12 core curriculum themes dealing with non-technical issues: social and ethical implications, personal and interpersonal skills, and broader perspectives and context.

It is stressed that "learning experiences must build such skills (not just convey that they are important) and teach skills that are transferable to new situations" (Shackelford et al., 2005, p. 36). There is no consensus or general recommendation, however, on how to build those skills. Peer review has been used in education with that purpose, making students go through all steps of scientific production. In the process, they exercise personal, interpersonal, cognitive, and meta-cognitive skills. They also come into close contact with ethics and professional responsibility.

As authors, students select a topic, review the literature, design and execute an experiment, interpret the results, write, and submit a paper for review. As referees, they have the chance to assess the work of their peers and report their review in an objective and impersonal way. As authors of refereed papers, they get feedback on what their colleagues understood from their work and on what changes should be made. They can think about the feedback received, re-elaborate their work, and see it published.

There is a good guide on the task of the referee in computer science (Smith, 1990) to help students understand the process of knowledge building with peer review, with shared responsibility for the quality of published work. Feedback plays a central role. Students need to know how to give and receive it. It is a duty after all, as expressed in the Association for Computing Machinery (ACM) code of ethics and professional responsibility:

> *Accept and provide appropriate professional review. Quality professional work, especially in the computing profession, depends on professional reviewing and critiquing. Whenever appropriate, individual members should seek and utilize peer review as well as provide critical review of the work of others.* (Association for Computing Machinery [ACM], 1992, section 2.4)

The effectiveness of peer review for science, as its quality control system, has been intensely questioned. Bacchetti (2002) argues that, besides failing to identify flaws, it also finds flaws that do not exist, therefore blocking the dissemination of good research. Stehbens (1999) deplores the suffocation of highly innovative research because of conflict of interest and reviewers' failures. The author states that peer review is "ineffective in detecting fraud, plagiarism, poor quality and gross error" (Stehbens, 1999, p. 35), and that plagiarists and fraudsters may find their way into reviewing committees.

All these vulnerabilities seem less harmful for education than for science. The concrete, final results are critical for science, but much less important for education. The educational gain of peer review lies in the process—the exercise of autonomy, critical thinking, cooperation, collaboration, expression, and reflection.

Peer review in education is an attempt to overcome the pitfalls of repetition-based learning, which is insufficient for the development of skills required for computer scientists. To develop those skills, students should keep a stance similar to that of a researcher who acts as referee (Kern, Saraiva, & Pacheco, 2003). This includes the commitment to principles and objectives, and high standards of ethics and professional responsibility.

Lehtinen, Hakkarainen, Lipponen, Rahikainen, and Muukkonen (1999, pp. 14-15) report "a growing body of evidence that cognitive diversity and distribution of expertise promote knowledge advancement and cognitive growth." Scientific production with peer review allows for the exercise of a diversity of skills—personal, interpersonal, and cognitive skills at various levels—from comprehension to analysis, synthesis, and evaluation. Several educational applications of peer review in computer science, with their learning results, are discussed next.

Figure 1. Peer review in computer science education (1st part, 1989-2001)

Reference	Object of peer review	Process choices	Outcomes
Hartman (1989), Illinois State U., US	Data Structures micro-themes – "so short… it can be typed on a single five-by-eight inch note card."	Does not describe process, only recommends peer evaluation.	Not systematically measured, but learning results are reported positive.
Hafen (1994), Penn State U., US	Senior-level Database papers.	Topic selection, draft, peer critiques in groups of 4, final paper. Peer evaluation workshop. Best papers published.	Ten papers (among 24) chosen. Positive, helpful peer criticism, "surprisingly smooth for a first effort."
Cunningham (1994), U.Waikato, New Zealand	Papers on game-playing computing experiments by 3rd-year Artificial Intelligence students.	Short assignments posted to a conferencing system. Students had 3 days to review at least one paper. Blind review in specific form.	Alleviated instructor overload usually associated with writing exercises. Author senses fear of embarrassment as motivator of student engagement.
Davies and Berrow (1998), U. Glamorgan, UK	Reports and papers of 16 part-time non-computing graduates ("from humanities to engineering") in a Computer Studies course.	Double-blind (leaking: word processor "Properties"). Students chose what to review. Tutor marking and grading. Focused on higher-order learning skills.	Inconclusive on the effectiveness in promoting higher-level learning skills. Individuals with high adaptability and more open to Risk and Challenge made more positive responses. No correlation between positive attitudes and effectiveness.
Gehringer (2001), North Carolina State U., US	Research papers, Web pages, programs, assignment proposals, literature review in 8 courses (cited: 1st- and 2nd-semester Programming, Oper. Syst., Comp. Ethics, OO Systems, and grad. reading courses).	Peer review and grading of submissions and reviews. Double-blind. The PG Web system: author-reviewer interaction; authors can re-submit; Web publishing of final result.	Students in 3 classes were asked whether peer review was helpful to the learning process, averaging 3.57 to 4.24 on a 1-5 scale (5 being "very useful").
Liu et al. (2001), Natl. Chiao Tung U., Taiwan	Papers on Operating Systems by 143 3rd-year undergraduate students, during 18 weeks.	Blind, 3 rounds, 6 randomly assigned reviews. WPR Web-based system with forum for peer interaction.	"… students … performed better … displayed higher level thinking skills, i.e., critical thinking, planning, monitoring, and regulation."

Figure 2. Peer review in computer science education (2nd part, 2002-2005)

Reference	Object of peer review	Process choices	Outcomes
Saraiva (2002), Univali, Brazil	Papers by students of 3rd-year course on Databases and environment-related courses (Oceanography, Environmental Engineering, and Law). Law students refused to participate.	Double blind, one review. Efficacy studied with content analysis by psychologist researcher.	3 categories of students' discourse found: Collective Work, Feedback, and Resistance. Resistance considered evidence that approach requires a learning paradigm shift. Approach considered efficacious.
Kern, Saraiva, and Pacheco (2003), UFSC and Univali, Brazil	Papers on Databases by 6th-semester undergrad. and on modeling and requirements engineering by graduate students of Production Engineering.	Double blind, one review, full editorial cycle with publication. Multidisciplinary team (Computing, Psychology).	Good affiliation from graduates. Varied results from undergraduates – from affiliation to strong refusal to participate.
Moreira and Silva (2003), USP-São Carlos, Brazil	Software projects, papers, lab experiments and lit. review by groups of grad. and undergrad. students of various courses (one Java distance education course).	Open review on WebCOM system, followed by face-to-face debate. Multidisciplinary team (Computing, Psychology)	Students reported uneasiness or embarrassment (22%). Mostly positive, however, about learning to give and accept criticism. "Less demanding on staff."
Sitthiworachart and Joy (2003), U. Warwick, UK	Large programming modules of a Unix shell programming course for undergraduates.	Peer assessment Web-based software runs automatic tests on submitted programs. Marking by 3 peers. Marking on feedback.	Preliminary evaluation. Peer assessment system "has successfully helped students to develop their understanding of computer programming."
Nunes (2005), Univali, Brazil	Senior-level projects in a Systems' Analysis & Design course in 16 weeks.	Face-to-face critique of individual proposal, group proposal, design, and implementation – by reviewers, based on critiqued documentation.	Heated debates, peer pressure from reviewers because they become implementers. Referees' work compared to auditing. High instructor overload.

Initiatives in Computer Science Education

Peer review has gained attention in conferences dedicated to computer science education (Cassel & Reis, 2003) and there are educational initiatives reported in the literature. Figures 1 and 2 summarize these initiatives in historical order, informing the outcomes and exposing the variety of objects (papers, projects, etc.) and process choices (about blinding, number of review cycles, etc.). The initiatives are described next, detailing the quality of outcomes, the supporting software, and discussing their small-scale application and lack of regularity.

As a general appraisal of the experiences cited in Figures 1 and 2, the learning effects range from inconclusive to very positive. There are many areas of computer science in which peer review can be used, as suggested by the work of Gehringer (2001) in eight different courses, although that does not mean that peer review is advisable for any course.

It is noticeable that there are independent initiatives from all around the world. Courses range from first-semester to the senior level and graduate school. Student assignments include the usual object of peer review, papers (in full or partial editorial cycle), to software projects of varied extension, but also lab reports, Web pages, and so forth. Review cycles are one or more, blind or open, with written or face-to-face critique, and several variations of grading—by the instructor, self-evaluation, peer-evaluation, or a combination of those.

Help from other disciplines is frequent. For instance, two independent Brazilian initiatives (Kern, Saraiva, & Pacheco, 2003; Moreira & Silva, 2003) started in 1997 have psychologists working together with computer science instructors. Other initiatives also include psychologists in the staff or in the research team.

The typical focus of the reports has evolved. While the first papers tend to dedicate more space to descriptions of the assignments, the process, and the supporting software, the latter tend to give more emphasis to the outcomes in terms of cognition, meta-cognition, and student affiliation.

Quality of Outcomes: Research Results

About one third of the reports on the application of peer review in computer science education are anecdotal. This is consistent with a review by Topping (1998) on peer assessment in higher education, using as keywords peer assessment, peer marking, peer correction, peer rating, peer feedback, peer review, and peer appraisal. Those studies on Topping's survey that included data gathering and treatment concluded that peer assessment is adequately reliable and valid in a wide variety of applications.

Among the research results in our review in Figures 1 and 2, Saraiva (2002) conducted an evaluation of peer review's efficacy as a pedagogical approach using content analysis. She is the third author of this paper, and the instructor was the first author.

Students of two different offerings of the same sixth-semester course on database design were asked to write a paper in group and blind-review, individually, two papers from their peers. Twelve students in one course offering served as referees for 10 students in the other offering, and vice-versa. Reviews followed usual referee report formats. The instructor graded the original submission, the feedback, and feedback internalization demonstrated in the final version of the paper.

Efficacy was investigated by means of a collective semi-structured interview with the students of each course offering, with the following questions (Saraiva, 2002):

- What is peer review?
- What was easy in this peer review experience?
- What was hard in this peer review experience?
- Which suggestions do you make for a future application of peer review?
- Does this method promote learning?
- Do you recommend using it in other courses?

The answers were group consensus. The statements were categorized using content analysis in Collective Work, Feedback, and Resistance. Collective Work and Feedback condensed positive responses from the students, while Resistance expressed their discomfort and difficulties regarding the experience.

Collective Work aspects included the comprehension of science's method to evaluate research results, the acknowledgment of the dependence on referees' commitment, and the existence of conflicts of interest. Feedback aspects included the understanding that criticism should be well explained and that various referee reports are needed, in an effort to eliminate bias. Resistance is related to students' complaints about the method: They do not know how to write a paper; it is too time-consuming; it is hard to write; it is confusing to read so many papers (although each referee was assigned two reviews).

This peer review of student papers on databases was a pilot for a wider experiment (Saraiva, 2002) with undergraduate students of environment-related courses in oceanography (12 students, ninth-semester), environmental engineering (40 students, first-semester), and law (20 students, ninth-semester). The instructors were contacted, and the proposal was explained before they presented the assignment to their students.

It is interesting to know that in one of the courses (law), Resistance aspects were strong enough to make students simply refuse taking part in peer review. Nonetheless, the method was considered efficacious, despite of and *because* of Resistance—evidence that peer review requires a learning paradigm shift, moving the instructor from the center of the learning process, asking from the students: autonomy, responsibility, and reflection.

Liu, Lin, Chiu, and Yuan (2001) used peer review in an operating systems course, with 143 third-year undergraduates, during 18 weeks. Students had to choose among eight course topics, review the literature, and write a paper summarizing the main ideas and suggesting future development. The review was blind, in three rounds, with six randomly assigned reviews, using the WPR Web-based system with forum for referee-author interaction.

Students responded (64.71%) that they benefited from using peer review and that it is effective as learning strategy (Liu et al., 2001). A qualitative analysis of meta-cognition revealed that critical thinking and monitoring were used more frequently than planning and regulation, but 77% of reviewers demonstrated these four kinds of higher level thinking (Liu et al., 2001).

Students' performance on assignment, quality of review, and final examination were compared. Multiple correlations among the three were significant. However, the authors identified four categories of learners, according to assignment and review performance (Liu et al., 2001): strategic adapter (both scores high), effective reviewer (high score for the quality of reviews, but not capable of using the feedback received to achieve a high assignment score), self-centered learner (high assignment score, but not capable of giving good feedback), and failure (both scores low).

Davies and Berrow (1998) evaluated the effectiveness of computer supported peer review in the promotion of higher level learning skills of 16 part-time graduates of varied backgrounds in a computer studies masters course. The authors contend that many higher education computer-based learning projects in the United Kingdom are concerned with lower-level learning skills such as imparting knowledge and developing comprehension, but few projects focus on higher-level skills such as application and analysis, and fewer still address the object of their study: synthesis and evaluation (Davies & Berrow, 1998).

Their study involved a combination of psychometric measures, qualitative interview, and final module grades. The psychometric measures, taken at the beginning of the module, were anticipatory anxiety and locus of control (Rotter,

1966)—a measure of people's beliefs on what are the main causes of events in life—their own actions (internal locus of control) or things outside their control (external locus of control).

They found no significant relationship between final module grades and anticipatory anxiety. Students with an internal locus of control performed significantly better than externals. The semi-structured, qualitative interview on the positive and negative aspects of the experience was assessed with content analysis, revealing students' feeling of positive interdependence and individual accountability, however lacking appropriate collaborative skills, group processing, and one-to-one promotive interaction (Davies & Berrow, 1998), important for cooperative learning.

A post hoc measure of Adaptation-Innovation revealed that individuals with high Adaptability and more open to Risk and Challenge responded more positively regarding the usefulness and preferences for the learning environment (Davies & Berrow, 1998). However, the study was not conclusive regarding the development of analysis and evaluation skills.

Quality of Outcomes: Informal Accounts

The informal, anedoctal reports from the instructors who led the peer review experiences in computer science education give an overall positive appraisal of the learning effects. There is nothing like "I'd rather not do it again"; however, the quality of the appraisals has convergences and divergences. Among the concordant points, it can be mentioned:

- **Meta-cognition:** Students usually recognize that they can benefit from studying the work of colleagues and reflecting about their own work. This seems to be a strong contribution of peer review: to make students exercise high-level cognitive skills.
- **Amount of feedback:** Peer review can provide much more feedback than an instructor and staff could provide.
- **Strong need for guidance:** Instructors stress the need for guidance to help students acquire the necessary knowledge and experience to evaluate other peoples' work. Some students may not be able to make good reviews, even with all the help necessary.
- **Problems with dropouts and delays:** Since peer review is a cooperative effort, when a student drops out of the class someone is going to get less reviews. This is especially harmful when some student ends up with no peer review. Delays are also harmful to the process.

The reports diverged, however, with regard to the stances of students, the choice for blind or open review, and instructor workload.

- **Student affiliation vs. resistance:** Students demonstrate goodwill and enthusiasm regarding their participation in peer review according to some authors, for instance, Hafen (1994) and Gehringer (2001). Some students even recommend that the method be extended to other courses. Other authors report student feelings of uneasiness or embarrassment (Moreira & Silva, 2003), or even strong resistance to do the work (Kern, Saraiva, & Pacheco, 2003). Whether the fact that both experiences were conducted in Brazil is only a coincidence or there are cultural issues involved is a subject of further research. Interestingly, Saraiva (2002) sees the resistance-affiliation polarization as an evidence of peer review's strength, since the method requires from students attached to repetition-based learning that they shift their learning paradigm and accept responsibility, take an active role, and be critic.
- **Blind vs. open review:** Most experiences use double-blind review, an approach that can avoid some conflicts of interest and be less emotionally challenging for students. Open critique, on the other hand, may be a better exercise to prepare for professional activity, since it can be interactive and demand argumentation. It is possible, however, that students "let personal involvement interfere" (Moreira & Silva, 2003, p. 54). There are no research results giving a full comparison of the two approaches regarding their merits and shortcomings.
- **Instructor overload:** There is no consensus on the instructor overload effect—some say it alleviates workload (Cunningham, 1994; Moreira & Silva, 2003), and some say it increases workload (Kern et al., 2003; Nunes, 2005). Naturally, this depends on how the assignments are organized, which in turn depends upon students' preparedness to take charge, without assistance, of tasks such as "make a summary," "find authoritative sources in the literature," and so forth. In our experience, working with ill-prepared students takes extra effort to make peer review work. Also, graduate students tend to fulfill their tasks with minimal help; undergraduate students may require intense monitoring and guidance.

Problems, Failures, and Successes in Our Experience

This section gives an in-depth informal account of our experience with peer review (Kern et al., 2003), especially in undergraduate computer science. There were mistakes, failures, and successes that are worth mentioning. The motivation came from the participation of the first author, as student, in a peer review of papers on CAD-CAM by graduate students, guided by Dr. Jan Helge Bøhn, at Virginia Tech.

Given the excellence of the learning experience, the application of peer review in a course on databases was started by the first author in his return to teaching at Univali, in Brazil, in 1997. It was performed with double-blind, one-cycle individual peer review of papers written in groups, with two reviews per referee and about five reviews per paper.

The first result was the acknowledgment of the reach of students' unpreparedness for academic studies, in several cases including the simple ability to form phrases. While it is common that educators all over the world diagnose a decay in education quality, the dimension of the crisis in Brazil may be interpreted through the results of the PISA 2000 exam (Organization for Economic Co-operation and Development [OECD], 2001): taking the average scores of 15-year-old students from several countries, the Brazilian average is more than 3.7 standard deviations below the average of average scores from the OECD countries. This happened in reading, the exam in which Brazilians performed best. The relative performance was even worse in math and science.

The peer review method continued to be used in undergraduate school. The first experience in graduate school was conducted in 1999, in production engineering, with good results. In the same year, however, a specific class of undergraduates resisted to the point of failing to turn in the assignments. The instructor sought help in educational psychology to investigate opportunities for improvement. A psychology student, under supervision, assisted the professor during the 2001 school year, then another student during the 2003 school year.

The gap between the instructor's and students' expectations became clear. While the instructor wanted to give the students a high-level learning experience, most of them were unprepared and attached to their repetition-based learning strategy. A competent literature review, for instance, was above the capacity of most students.

Some changes in the method were then adopted. The grades for the peer review project, responsible in the first experience for only 20% of the total grade, were altered to over 50%. The assignment was broken in smaller tasks, all graded. The review process received stronger guidance, and the grading of reviews received higher weights.

The following experiences produced better papers and, especially, better reviews. The reviews began to significantly impact the overall quality of the papers, revealing students' understanding and commitment to the objectives of peer review. The criticism captured the opportunities for improvement, but also misconduct—in the second semester of 2002, among 58 referee reports from 29 students, two pointed different cases of copy of material from the internet, giving the URL address of the sources.

Undergraduate peer review has, since then, generated a number of research and graduation (capstone) projects. Among the eight computer scientists graduated at Univali by the end of 2003, two developed their final projects from research started in databases, in the sixth semester.

Figure 3. Software used in peer review

Reference	Peer review software	Staff and other support	Software functions
Hartman (1989)	No details.	No details.	No details.
Hafen (1994)	No specific software.	University grant for publication, student volunteers.	Not mentioned; apparently only hard copies were used.
Cunningham (1994)	No specific software; local conferencing system.	Not mentioned (apparently run by the instructor alone).	Only upload-download in a discussion group at the local conferencing system.
Davies and Berrow (1998)	No specific software; posting to local network.	Not mentioned.	Only upload-download; personal use of text editors (some MS Word users failed to remove identifying headers, disclosing authorship).
Gehringer (2001)	PG, Peer Grader system.	Teaching assistants apparently available.	Login, Web submission, pseudo-random reviewer allocation, double-blind communication via shared Web page, peer grading, review of peer grading.
Liu et al. (2001)	WPR, Web-based Peer-Review system.	Assistants available.	New course, Web submission, versioning, random allocation of 6 reviewers, double-blind peer review.
Saraiva (2002)	No software.	Not available.	None.
Kern, Saraiva, and Pacheco (2003)	No specific software; e-mail traffic.	Not available.	E-mail centered in the instructor.
Moreira and Silva (2003)	WebCOM, Web Course Manager.	Assistants apparently available.	New assignment and deadlines, referee allocation, student or group signup, work and review submission, access to other groups' works, grading by the instructor.
Sitthiworachart and Joy (2003)	Web-based peer assessment.	Not mentioned.	Submission, automatic tests on programs, blind peer marking – yes/partial/no answers, comments, marking on marking, marking calculations.
Nunes (2005)	No specific software; discussions through e-mail.	Not available.	E-mail.

Software and Help Used

The initiatives outlined in Figures 1 and 2 vary with regard to software and help available, summarized in Figure 3. Author-referee interaction, marking and grading, versioning, setting multiple deadlines, feedback on feedback, and automatic tests add to a preliminary list of functional requirements given by Kern et al. (2003): Web site configuration of assignment, publication of call-for-papers and review form, student signup, submissions, referee allocation, acknowledgment of reception, and author notification.

Although software can alleviate much of the administrative work, Figure 3 shows that peer review can be handled without software support. There is a number of freely available conference software that cover most functional requirements of educational peer review, as described by Snodgrass (1999), although none of the reports cited use them.

Regularity and Scale of Application

The outcomes of peer review initiatives in computer science education are generally positive, led by one instructor or small group, but with no sign of continued development and large scale application. Although the authors cited in Figures 1 and 2 have more papers on the subject than those cited here, it is worth mentioning that no author was found to publish on the subject for more than a four-year interval.

Why isn't peer review applied in a larger scale (e.g., as an institutional or multi-institutional program) and regularly, if the outcomes are positive as they seem to be in terms of cognitive and meta-cognitive skills, including social, writing, analytical, ethics, and critical thinking aspects? Are there other approaches that can better fulfill the same learning objectives? Are there *any* approaches that can fulfill those learning objectives?

Our study in Figures 1 and 2 shows that peer review can be conducted by a single instructor with minimal or no help. Peer review addresses the development of non-technical skills prescribed by the IFIP curriculum (Mulder & Van Weert, 2000). It makes future computer scientists give and receive feedback, a professional responsibility (ACM, 1992) that is also part of software processes such as extreme programming (Beck, 1999) and feature-driven development (Coad, LeFebrve, & De Luca, 1999).

If the benefits of peer review in education are not replaceable by other approaches, then it seems advisable that it be part of an educational policy, not an individual initiative. But what are the requirements for peer review as a regular, large scale educational method? The next section explores this issue.

Making Peer Review a Regular, Large Scale Educational Method

The literature depicts only one large scale educational application of peer review; however, it does not involve computer science students. It is a multi-university effort conducted in 2001 in the United States, described by Trautmann, Carlsen, Yalvac, Cakir, and Kohl (2003). They involved 411 science and science education students from 11 colleges and universities in a double-blind online peer review of simple toxicology experiment reports, with the objective of enhancing student understanding of the nature of science. Faculty was recruited through a mailing list from the National Association for Research in Science Teaching.

The results suggest that multi-university peer review potentiates student learning beyond the possibilities of individual classrooms. Students used positive statements to describe the experience. Mismatches in student ability frustrated some expectations, since not every review was insightful, although there was no offensive language. The authors report that peer review has been continued on a smaller scale after the multi-university experiment (Trautmann et al., 2003).

No account or plan to make peer review an institutional, regular educational method was found in the literature. Implementing peer review may not be as straightforward as the reported experiences suggest. In fact, the positive learning outcomes might not be there if it were not because of highly motivated instructors mentoring and leading the process. The status of peer review in education, therefore, is:

- source of varied, important learning results (for which there are no other encompassing approaches in computer science);
- destabilizer of students' role, causing resistance or affiliation;
- endeavor of a few self-motivated instructors; and
- temporary, isolated projects that tend to fade or disappear.

Whereas the first two points are important characteristics of peer review in education, the two last points should be changed if we expect to extend peer review to become a regular practice. They are interrelated—when the mentor quits lecturing the course, or changes jobs, or retires, or gets tired from attempting to be the "guide on the side" instead of "the sage on the stage" with the risks associated to a process of change, then the project ends, or it dims because of the lack of leadership.

Despite that, the advance of educational peer review in computer science, from individual to institutional initiative, may be mounting. Reports in the literature indicate (Figures 1 and 2) that the practice becomes more widespread. At the same time, peer review as a professional duty (ACM, 1992), accreditation procedures, and the demand for non-technical skills from international curricula (IEEE-ACM, 2001; Mulder & Van Weert, 2000; Shackelford et al., 2005) may have computer science department heads, chairs, and curriculum coordinators having to answer to questions such as this, mentioning three of the 12 IFIP core curriculum themes (Mulder & Van Weert, 2000):

How do you approach social and ethical implications, personal and interpersonal skills, and broader perspectives and context in computer science?

If "using student peer review" is to be the answer, it is important to recognize that the availability of computers and software alone will not render the expected results. There is need to take into account the subjective processes involved in learning—the different cognitive styles and the modifications that take effect in the students' and instructor's perceptions. Peer review is effective as an educational method only if the students shift their stance from traditional learning. They have to *use* the instructor as a guide instead of only following his instructions—and this is a challenging demand.

Many of the same drawbacks of computer-mediated peer review are observed in distance learning (Van der Geest & Remmers, 1994). Pernigotti (2004) studied the situations that tension the educational practices in distance learning, with similar demands from students and instructor as those from peer review. Three critical factors affect and tension the educational practices in such a setting (Pernigotti, 2004):

- the denaturalization of autonomy as characteristic of adult learning;
- the stance of students, instructors and other staff as learners and teachers; and
- the necessary student affiliation.

Autonomy is an important premise of adult learning. Nevertheless, this premise is at times contradicted in adult learning processes by resistance to change. Saraiva (2002) observes that the demand for autonomy may cause resistance and anxiety at the individual and at the collective levels, but it is important to recognize that people in this situation are defending something they consider important and under threat because of the change process.

Overcoming resistance, the fear of change, is part of the learning process. It is one of the tensions in the process of student affiliation, which is not always autonomous. This suggests that an intense monitoring of the learning process by the managers of educational peer review may be needed, at least in the first experiences of students *and* instructors.

The stances taken by students and instructors in peer review generate tension. Both need to be learners and teachers, stances that do not correspond to the *functions* of students and instructors, but to *perspectives* adopted in the learning experience. Their positions change constantly, like nomad tents that have to be set up at each movement.

The instructor investigates students' needs and potentials for learning. As observed by Topping (1998), in the context of peer assessment, the instructor can scrutinize and clarify assessment objectives and criteria. The instructor acts as learner, ceasing to be on stage, in the center of the learning process. The students, in the same way, are co-authors of the learning process, acting as teachers.

Student affiliation to peer review requires the adaptation of the process to the individual, not the opposite. The learning environment, usually conceived and managed from the instructor's viewpoint, needs the student's desire to take part, to be in the game. This poses a challenge to build learning communities that seize the desire of part of the group to belong to that community.

Affiliation manifests itself in students' commitment, affecting the quality of feedback, a central issue for the method. Feedback itself affects affiliation and the learning outcomes. Topping (1998) and Gueldenzoph and May (2002) recommend that feedback be formative, during the process, and not only summative, correctional, at the end of the process.

Autonomy, students' and instructor's roles, and affiliation are the tension points that interfere in the achievement of the objectives of educational peer review. The fulfillment of requirements of educational peer review as a regular method, for continued application, depends on reorganizing and redirecting students' and instructors' actions, much more than on an undue emphasis on the enabling computational technology.

Conclusion

This article discussed the advance of educational peer review in computer science from the current individual initiatives to a regular, continuous, institutional program. The reasons why peer review should be used in computer science education were given. The literature was reviewed to summarize the variety of objects, courses, levels, and process choices with which peer review has been applied to computing education. The learning outcomes were commented, and the issues that affect its advance to a regular method were raised.

Although the leading edge of software technology may create new technologies for use in educational peer review, the critical factor for its advance lies in the tension points that affect educational practices. These tension points can be summarized as: demand for student autonomy, roles of students and instructors, and student affiliation to the process.

There are software environments used by existing peer review initiatives in computer science. Freely available conference management software can fulfill most functional requirements. New software, however, should provide for the assessment of process' results. For instance, there is need to better monitor students' learning in the process of peer review. The tracking of a student's record as author and reviewer in the continued application of peer review is important. Riggs and Wilensky (2001) propose an algorithm for automated rating of reviewers that could be used to monitor students' record, as it is related to the formation of professional responsibility.

From the variety of details in existing educational approaches to peer review and from the diverse situations that tension its educational practice, it can be inferred that there is not one peer review, but many. The common issue is how to deal with those tensions to create a learning environment in which students want to take part and respond to the demand for autonomy, responsibility, and critical thinking.

The main contribution of peer review is to promote reflection, allowing individuals (students *and* instructors) to amplify their perception. The core of the peer review method for learning is the students' change, from passive and unquestioning receptors of information, to active and critic members of a community that constructs knowledge.

References

Association for Computing Machinery (1992). *ACM code of ethics and professional conduct.* Retrieved June 25, 2005, from http://www.acm.org/constitution/code.html

Bacchetti, P. (2002). Peer review of statistics in medical research: The other problem. *British Medical Journal, 324*(7348), 1271-1273.

Beck, K. (1999). *Extreme programming examined: Embrace change.* Reading, MA: Addison Wesley.

Cassel, L., & Reis, R. A. L. (2003). Preface. In L. Cassel & R. A. L. Reis (Eds.), *Informatics curricula and teaching methods* (pp. ix-x). Boston: Kluwer Academic Publishers.

Coad, P., LeFebrve, E., & De Luca, J. (1999). *Java modeling in color with UML*. Indianapolis, IN: Prentice Hall.

Cunningham, S. J. (1994). Using a computer conferencing system to support writing and research skill development. *SIGCSE Bulletin, 26*(4), 5-8.

Davies, R., & Berrow, T. (1998). An evaluation of the use of computer supported peer review for developing higher-level skills. *Computers & Education, 30*(1/2), 111-115.

Falchikov, N., & Goldfinch, J. (2000). Student peer assessment in higher education: A meta-analysis comparing peer and teacher marks. *Review of Educational Research, 70*(3), 287-322.

Gehringer, E. F. (2001). Electronic peer review and peer grading in computer-science courses. In *Proceedings of the 32nd SIGCSE Technical Symposium on Computer Science Education* (pp. 139-143). Charlotte, NC: ACM Press.

Gueldenzoph, L. E., & May, G. L. (2002). Collaborative peer evaluation: Best practices for group member assessments. *Business Communication Quarterly, 65*(1), 9-20.

Haddad, W. D., & Draxler, A. (2002). Are we there yet? In: W. D. Haddad & A. Draxler (Eds.), *Technologies for education: Potential, parameters and prospects* (pp. 198-202). Paris: UNESCO and the Academy for Educational Development.

Hafen, M. (1994). Developing writing skills in computer science students. *SIGCSE Bulletin, 26*(1), 268-270.

Hartman, J. (1989). Writing to learn and communicate in a data structures course. In R. A. Barrett & M. J. Mansfield (Eds.), *Proceedings of the 20th SIGCSE Technical Symposium on Computer Science education* (pp. 32-36). Louisville, KY: ACM Press.

The Joint Task Force on Computing Curricula—IEEE Computer Society and Association for Computing Machinery (2001, December 15). *Computing curricula 2001: Computer science*, final report. Retrieved June 28, 2005, from http://www.computer.org/education/cc2001/final/cc2001.pdf

Kern, V. M., Saraiva, L. M., & Pacheco, R. C. S. (2003). Peer review in education: Promoting collaboration, written expression, critical thinking, and professional responsibility. *Education and Information Technologies, 8*(1), 37-46.

Lehtinen, E., Hakkarainen, K., Lipponen, L., Rahikainen, M., & Muukkonen, H. (1999). Computer supported collaborative learning: A review. *CL-Net Project*. Retrieved June 26, 2005, from http://www.comlab.hut.fi/opetus/205/etatehtava1.pdf

Liu, E. Z., Lin, S. S. J., Chiu, C., & Yuan, S. (2001). Web-based peer review: The learner as both adapter and reviewer. *IEEE Transactions on Education, 44*(3), 246-251.

Moreira, D. A., & Silva, E. Q. (2003). A method to increase student interaction using student groups and peer review over the internet. *Education and Information Technologies, 8*(1), 47-54.

Mulder, F., & Van Weert, T. (Eds.). (2000). IFIP/UNESCO informatics curriculum framework 2000: Building effective higher education informatics curricula in a situation of change. *UNESCO, Paris*. Retrieved June 27, 2005, from http://poe.netlab.csc.villanova.edu/ifip32/ICF2000.htm

Nunes, L. E. P. (2005). *Trabalho colaborativo e avaliação por pares na aprendizagem de análise e projeto de sistemas* [Electronic version]. Unpublished master's dissertation, graduate program in production engineering, Federal University of Santa Catarina, Florianópolis, Brazil.

Organization for Economic Co-operation and Development (2001, December 4). *Executive summary: Knowledge and skills for life, First results from PISA 2000*. Programme for International Student Assessment. Paris: OECD.

Pernigotti, J. M. (2004). *Tensões e torções na operação pedagógica por um povoamento em EAD*. Unpublished doctoral thesis, graduate program in psychology, Pontifical Catholic University of Rio Grande do Sul, Porto Alegre, Brazil.

Riggs, T., & Wilensky, R. (2001). An algorithm for automated rating of reviewers. In *Proceedings of the first ACM/IEEE-CS joint conference on digital libraries* (pp. 381-387). Roanoke, VA: ACM Press.

Rotter, J. B. (1966). Generalised expectancies for internal versus external control of reinforcement. *Psychological Monographs, 80*(1), 202-210, 609.

Saraiva, L. M. (2002). *Proposta metodológica de aplicação da revisão pelos pares como instrumento pedagógico para a educação ambiental* [Electronic version]. Unpublished doctoral thesis, graduate program in production engineering, Federal University of Santa Catarina, Florianópolis, Brazil.

Shackelford, R., Cross, II, J. H., Davies, G., Impagliazzo, J., Kamali, R., LeBlanc, R., et al. (2005, April 11). The overview report, a cooperative project of The Association for Computing Machinery (ACM), The Association for Information Systems (AIS), and The Computer Society (IEEE-CS). *Computing Curricula 2005*, (p. 57). Retrieved June 28, 2005, from http://www.acm.org/education/Draft_5-23-051.pdf

Sitthiworachart, J., & Joy, M. (2003). Web-based peer assessment in learning computer programming. In *Proceedings of the 3rd IEEE International Conference on Advanced Learning Technologies (ICALT '03)* (p. 5). Los Alamitos, CA: IEEE Computer Society.

Smith, A. J. (1990). The task of the referee. *IEEE Computer*, *23*(4), 65-71.

Snodgrass, R. (1999). *Summary of conference management software.* Retrieved June 28, 2005, from http://www.acm.org/sigs/sgb/summary.html

Stehbens, W. E. (1999). Basic philosophy and concepts underlying scientific peer review. *Medical Hypotheses*, *52*(1), 31-36.

Talbott, S. (1995). *The future does not compute: Transcending the machines in our midst* (1st ed.). Cambridge, MA: O'Reilly & Associates.

Topping, K. J. (1998). Peer assessment between students in colleges and universities. *Review of Educational Research*, *68*(3), 249-276.

Trautmann, N. M., Carlsen, W. S., Yalvac, B., Cakir, M., & Kohl, C. (2003, March 22-26). *Learning nature of science concepts through online peer review of student research reports*. Paper presented at the annual meeting of the National Association for Research in Science Teaching, Philadelphia.

Van der Geest, T., & Remmers, T. (1994). The computer as means of communication for peer-review groups. *Computers and Composition*, *11*(3), 237-250.

Chapter IV

Learning Management Systems:
An Overview and Roadmap of the Systemic Application of Computers to Education

William R. Watson,
Indiana University - Purdue University Indianapolis, USA

Sunnie Lee, Indiana University, USA

Charles M. Reigeluth, Indiana University, USA

Abstract

This chapter discusses learning management systems (LMS) as a technology necessary for supporting the educational needs of the information age. It defines LMS and argues that the move from the mechanistic, sorting-oriented paradigm of the industrial age to the customized, learning-oriented paradigm of the information age requires the application of LMSs to succeed. The history of LMS is presented and the definition further clarified by comparing and contrasting LMS with course management systems (CMS), learning content management systems (LCMS) and learning objects. Several major K-12 LMSs are presented, evaluated, and their features compared. Finally, the current trends of LMS are discussed, and goals for further development are offered. A better understanding of LMS, its role in the new paradigm, and the areas where it needs to improve and continue to grow are essential to improving the effectiveness of education in the information age.

Introduction

The potential impact of computers on learning has been recognized since well before the widespread adoption of the technology itself. With a history dating back to the 1950s, computers have been used to assist with or even directly provide instruction to learners (Reiser, 1987). Learning management system (LMS) is a relatively recently coined term that refers to computer systems that incorporate providing instruction, tracking achievement, and managing resources for individual students and an organization as a whole. This chapter defines LMS, discusses the pressing need for LMS technology in the emerging knowledge-based paradigm of education, and examines the history of LMS and how it has developed from, and differs from, past computer learning technologies. LMS is then compared to other computer learning technologies and related concepts, after which four popular K-12 LMS products are described and evaluated. The chapter concludes with a discussion of the current state of LMS, what trends exist in the further development of LMS, and what needs LMS must meet in order to satisfy the requirements of the information-age paradigm of education.

Definition of LMS

Learning management system (LMS) is a generic term often used to describe a number of different types of computerized training and instructional systems. Essentially, an LMS is an infrastructure that supports the delivery and management of instructional content, the identification and assessment of individual and organizational learning goals, and the management of the progression toward meeting those goals, while providing data for the supervision of the organization as a whole (Szabo & Flesher, 2002). To differentiate LMS from the sea of acronym-driven computer learning technologies in the literature, it is important to understand the systemic scope of LMS. An LMS, as Gilhooly (2001) states, "goes beyond basic content delivery to offer course administration, registration, tracking, reporting and skills gap analysis" (p. 52). General characteristics include the following:

- instructional objectives are specified with individual lessons;
- lessons are integrated into the standardized curriculum;
- courseware extends several grade levels in a consistent manner;
- a management system collects and records the results of student performance; and
- lessons are provided based on individual students' learning progress. (Bailey, 1993)

Need for LMS

There have been a substantial number of publications discussing the shift of society from the Industrial Age into what many call the Information Age (Reigeluth, 1994; Senge, Cambron-McCabe, Lucas, Smith, Dutton, & Kleiner, 2000; Toffler, 1984). In order for our schools to meet the needs of today's learners, the way in which the schools function must also change dramatically and systemically to focus on individual learners' needs (Reigeluth, 1994; Reigeluth & Garfinkle, 1994; Senge et al., 2000).

The current educational system was built to fit the image of the industrial-age society, in which learning is highly compartmentalized into subject areas and students are "treated as if they are all the same and are all expected to do the same things at the same time" (Reigeluth, 1994, p. 204). Furthermore, much of the onus for learning is laid at the feet of teachers rather than the students themselves, and students do not take an active role in either their own learning or the school community as a whole. The current industrial model of education places an emphasis on sorting students rather than developing their knowledge. A fixed amount of content is presented in a fixed amount of time, and students must move on, whether they have learned it or not. Students are divided into grade levels with classes in which they learn the same things at the same time. This forces "achievement to vary among students, with the consequence that the low-achieving ones gradually accumulate deficits in learning that handicap them in their future learning endeavors" (Reigeluth, 1997, p. 204), while high-achieving students are held back and lose interest. The system is not designed to promote student learning; it is designed to select students. In the industrial age, it was important to separate the laborers from the managers, and educating the common laborers was not economical and, indeed, was not desired, for they would not be content doing the repetitious and dull tasks that their jobs at the assembly lines would require (Joseph & Reigeluth, 2002).

However, today the mechanistic, unthinking jobs of the assembly line have largely disappeared, and employers are now looking more and more for problem-solving employees with initiative and a variety of skills to work effectively as a part of a team. These requirements reflect a need, in the information age, for expanded mental capabilities, which greatly increases the importance of student learning. The focus of education must shift from student sorting to student learning, and therefore, certain changes are required to truly help students learn. Since it is known that children learn at different rates and have different learning needs, even from the first day of class, it does not make sense to hold time constant and thereby force achievement to vary. Apart from not meeting the needs of society at large, it is an inhumane treatment of the children to not focus on helping all children to reach their potential. The alternative to holding time constant is to hold achievement constant at a mastery level, and allow children to take as much time as needed to reach that level. This requires the educational system to move from a process of standardization that results in high failure rates to a completely new paradigm that supports customization in order to meet all learners' needs.

This new paradigm for information-age-appropriate education will require significant changes in the use of time, talent, and technology (Schlechty, 1991). The changes in use of time entail not only allowing each student as much time as needed to achieve mastery, but also allowing each student to move on as soon as he or she reaches a mastery level. This means that the pace of instruction will be customized to help meet each student's needs.

Schlechty (1991) also argues that the use of talent will need to be altered. Talent refers to the roles that both students and teachers play. The role of teachers will change substantially as instruction moves to a more learner-centered approach (McCombs & Whisler, 1997). Teachers will become facilitators of knowledge acquisition by acting as guides, coaches, and motivators for students. No longer will the teacher be the primary source of knowledge, a talking head, but instead the teacher will help each student to find appropriate materials for acquiring the desired knowledge. This shift in roles will also place new demands on the student. Students will be required to be active learners, assuming the responsibility to take initiative and be more self-directed as they gain knowledge.

The third shift that Schechty (1991) argues will be necessary in the new paradigm of education involves the use of technology. First, with learner-centered, custom-paced instruction, technology is needed to track what each learner has mastered. This will allow teachers to easily keep records of each student's progress and thereby provide appropriate guidance to each student. Second, decisions about what to learn next (i.e., the sequencing of instruction) for each student will also be important, and technology will need to play a central role in helping student and teacher decide what should be learned next. Third, as teachers move from being the sole source of instruction to being guides or coaches, technology will be needed to help instruct the students by providing content, often in more interactive ways than have traditionally been used. Simulations and instructional games can provide interactive content, give immediate feedback, diagnose student needs, and provide effective remediation. Fourth, technology will also be needed to help in the assessment of student knowledge to certify student mastery and store examples of student work that represent their attainments (e.g., portfolios). Finally, technology will need to provide a systemic integration of all of these features.

In essence, an information-age, learner-centered paradigm of education cannot be effectively implemented without technology, and by the same token, technology cannot approach its potential contribution to education and learning without a learner-centered paradigm of education.

Fortunately, computing is becoming more ubiquitous every day, and a major part of the information-age classroom will be the use of advanced technology to meet the five needs just listed. Instructional technology has shown promising results in evaluation studies conducted during the 1960s to 1980s, and technology is widely used in schools these days. In envisioning the information-age school, "technology will play central roles in teaching, assessment, and keeping track of learner progress..." (Reigeluth & Garfinkle, 1994). LMSs promise an integrated tool for serving the five major functions that are needed for technology in information-age schools.

History of LMS

LMS has evolved through a history of various applications of computer technology to instruction. These applications have been described with various terms, many of them generic. Computer-based instruction (CBI), computer-assisted instruction (CAI), and computer-assisted learning (CAL) are all generic terms that have been used to describe different applications of computers to instruction. While there are not specific definitions for these terms, Parr and Fung report that generally, CAI is typically used to describe drill-and-practice programs, CAL includes more sophisticated tutorial instruction, and CBI places more emphasis on individualized instruction (Parr & Fung, 2001). More differentiated from these other terms are integrated learning system (ILS) and computer-mediated instruction (CMI) which include such additional functionality as a management and tracking system on top of the instructional content, integration across the system, and greater focus on personalized instruction (Bailey, 1993; Becker, 1993; Brush, Armstrong, Barbrow, & Ulintz, 1999; Szabo & Flesher, 2002).

In the early 1980s, many classroom teachers and administrators turned away from ILSs because they appeared to be the same old products in new packaging. Most of these educators were primarily skeptical about how individualized instruction and computer-assisted instruction came and went with other educational trends of the 1960s and 1970s. But as more sophisticated ILS software began to address problems associated with individualizing instruction, it began to show greater potential to improve learning and teaching, and it evolved into a more holistic learning and data management system. Now, LMS takes these additional components even further in helping to "manage the entire instructional program and learning process" of an organization (Szabo & Flesher, 2002). Further, LMS is systemic in nature, covering both learning and e-learning programs and processes. It is this systemic nature that differentiates LMS from much of the other educational software available, in that it is neither simply a collection of instructional software nor only a student assessment tracking platform, but is instead truly systemic in addressing all aspects of the instructional process.

LMS' Relation to Course and Content Management Systems and to Learning Objects

While we have addressed the definition of LMS and further detailed this definition by looking at the history of LMS and its relation to past computer learning technologies, it is important to also discuss the role of LMS amongst other related advancements in computer learning technologies. These include course management system (CMS), learning content management system (LCMS), and learning object (LO). While LMS is often used synonymously with CMS and LCMS and is conceptually seen as having equivalent goals as LO, LMS is again differentiated by its scope, and this section explores how LMS is related and impacted by these technologies due to its systemic incorporation of them.

Course Management System

One technology that is often confused with LMS is CMS. The systemic nature of LMS previously discussed differentiates LMS from CMS. A CMS is a tool that focuses on the management of one or more courses, typically by an instructor, and is usually used for distance education or hybrid (both face-to-face and distance) courses. As defined by the EduTools[1] Web site, a CMS excludes:

Single function software like stand-alone assessment tools, synchronous tools or authoring packages that do not also have many other features or act as part of a larger suite that delivers online education courses, and course content materials and course content bundled with its own online delivery system. (Leslie, 2003[2])

A CMS is a tool that just helps an instructor to manage individual courses, rather than also providing a system-wide tool. Its function is defined as: "it provides an instructor with a set of tools and a framework that allows the relatively easy creation of online course content and the subsequent teaching and management of that course including various interactions with students taking the course" (EDUCAUSE Evolving Technologies Committee, 2003, p. 1). Examples of a CMS include Blackboard, WebCT, Angel, and Oncourse.

Learning Content Management System

LCMS is often used either synonymously with LMS or touted as a newer version of LMS. However, the focus on content is the key to understanding the difference between these two technologies and seeing how they relate. Oakes (2002) reports that the IDC defines LCMS as a system that is "used to create, store, assemble and deliver personalized e-learning content in the form of learning objects" (p. 73). So, the focus with LCMS is on content: "it tackles the challenges of creating, reusing, managing, and delivering content" (Oakes, 2002, p. 74). While LCMS focuses on content, an LMS is "learner and organization focused: It's concerned with the logistics of managing learners, learning activities, and the competency mapping of an organization" (Oakes, 2002, p. 74). Connolly (2001) echoes this, stating that while LMS and LCMS complement each other, the "LMS provides the rules and the LCMS provides the content" (p. 58).

Learning Object

Learning object has become a highly visible buzz-word in education recently and is taking its place as the favored technology for the future, based on its promise for reusability (ability for instruction to be reused in multiple contexts), generativity (the ability to generate instruction), adaptability (ability to be adapted to individual learners), and scalability (ability to be extended to both larger and smaller audiences without a substantial increase in cost) (Gibbons, Nelson, & Richards, 2002; Hodgins, 2002; Wiley, 2002).

While learning object is fairly consistent in its promise of instructional design that reduces costs and produces instruction that is adaptable to individual learners and contexts, the actual definition of learning object remains unclear. Learning object has been used to describe everything from a textbook to a computer image to an instructional simulation or video game. Furthermore, terms other than learning object are sometimes used to describe what appear to be learning objects, such as MERLOT's use of "online learning materials," or Merrill's use of "knowledge objects" (MERLOT, 2005; Merrill, 2002). Parrish (2004) notes that the Institute of Electrical and Electronics Engineers (IEEE) provided the vague definition of a learning object as "any entity, digital or nondigital, that may be used for learning, education, or training" (p. 52). Wiley (2002) notes how this definition does not exclude anything related to instruction of any type. He therefore proposes his own definition of a learning object as "any digital resource that can be reused to support learning" (2002, p. 3).

This definition seems to be more on par with the general definition of a learning object as a reusable digital artifact that can be used in learning. However, Parrish (2004) argues that this definition does not eliminate software tools a student might use, such as a calculator or word-processing program. He instead argues for defining learning object in terms of its use or function: "instructional content becomes a learning object when it is used as a learning object" (p. 52).

While Parrish's arguments have some merit, and it is certainly unclear whether Wiley intends to include instructional tools in his definition as well as instructional content, it seems that Parrish's approach might result in more confusion in the long run among those unfamiliar with object-oriented concepts. However, Wiley's use of the term "resource" to describe the object itself could cause some confusion. The key elements of learning objects that lie behind much of the discussion would seem to be the ideas of learning and reusable artifacts. These artifacts would not typically include tools; therefore, Wiley's definition would be more precise if it referred to digital "media" rather than digital "resource." This clarification seems to capture the key concepts and the general understanding of learning objects and their benefits without requiring a more expert understanding of the object-oriented design process that Parrish's definition calls for. Furthermore, Parrish (2004) admits that, while the concept of breaking instructional systems intro smaller reusable objects and methods is related to learning object creation, he points out that learning is different than computer programming, and the concepts of object-oriented programming are not a perfect fit to the instructional design of learning objects.

It should be clear that learning object, while related to LMS, certainly exists at a much narrower scope than LMS. While the key component of LMS is its systemic nature, a key feature of learning object is its modularity, discreteness, and reusable nature.

The Interconnectedness of Learning Object, CMS, LCMS, LMS, and Associated Challenges

This section has shown the close relationship between learning object, CMS, LCMS, and LMS. The role of LMS as a systemic manager of the included technologies places a focus on scope when seeking to understand the differences among these kinds of tools. Furthermore, just as the LMS encompasses the other technologies, learning objects by definition exist as the smallest discrete components of all of these technologies; they make up the reusable instructional content that is managed by an LCMS and are plugged into the courses managed by a CMS, both of which are pieces of the larger, systemic LMS. To be reusable, learning objects by nature need to be distinct. Therefore, to better understand how all of these technologies tie together to form an LMS, it is important to also examine the challenges that exist with the creation, sharing, and use of learning objects.

There are several current challenges to the implementation of learning objects. Foremost among these problems is the need for standards to allow learning objects to be reusable and searchable across different educational systems. A key component in this search for standards is meta-data, which is used to describe the learning object and make it accessible. Without a standard for meta-data, even if a learning object is made to be reusable, it is unlikely to be reused, simply because access to it is severely limited by the lack of meta-data. Unfortunately, there are many current standards being applied to the creation of learning objects, including LOM, CanCore, and SCORM. The lack of standards for learning objects causes a trickle down effect which negatively impacts LMSs.

Just as there are many standards for learning objects, there are also several standards "for evaluating interoperability between LMSs and content" (Connolly, 2001, p. 57), mainly SCORM and the Aviation Industry CBT Committee (AICC) standard. Furthermore, there is also no agreement as to exactly what LMSs must do to be compliant with the standards that exist, as each of these standards has multiple levels of compliance (Alexander, 2001). Ultimately, confusion aside, one large problem with applying standards is the inherent cost. Much of the content being used by LMSs was developed well before standards existed or have never had standards applied. Furthermore, content providers have their own proprietary software development tools that do not support standards, so the cost of converting old content to meet standards, and acquiring industry development tools which support compliance with standards, can be prohibitive.

Finally, there is the issue of what kind of instruction is promoted by learning objects and LCMS. Parrish (2004) cites Wilson's 2001 discussion of the spectrum in distance education where one trend focuses on automation, standards, and control (the old practice of "drill and kill" software), while the other end of the spectrum points toward open systems and learner-centered approaches. If a strong reason for the use of computers in the classroom is to use the processing and tracking power they offer in order to help customize learning, then perhaps the learning objects being created should be modifiable by students or their instructors in order to help establish learning environments that allow for exploration and the building of knowledge, as opposed to the limited interactivity of assessing the ability to regurgitate static facts (Parrish, 2004).

Much of the learning software used today promises personalization but does not deliver outside of the barest sense of students being able to move through static instruction at their own pace, while the system assesses their progress. LMSs today are based somewhat on the concept of learning objects, in that they present digital instruction that can be tailored to state and federal educational standards and therefore can be sold to schools across the world. The reusable nature of these learning objects shows the successful promise of learning objects while at the same time going against the notion of an open environment by charging schools for access to the objects. Many of the current LMSs available to schools in the United States are offered by companies with a long history of creating digital instructional modules for their customers. These modules are essentially composed of the learning objects that the LMSs are reusing. The LMS then provides additional features, to support students' learning such as assessing the student's performance and customizing the sequencing of additional objects. While LMS and its various components face challenges, it also holds a great deal of promise, and some applications offer features that are well-suited for a learning-focused paradigm of education. A better understanding of the nature of existing LMSs can be reached by examining the various features currently offered by the major K-12 LMS products available in the United States, as well as looking at existing research into their application.

Comparison and Evaluation of Existing LMSs

This section presents and compares the major features of a number of LMSs available today for K-12 schools, and it provides a general overview of the evaluative research that has been conducted on those LMSs. Since these LMSs are highly complex systems, the number of features they possess is so large as to be unmanageable in a review such as this. Therefore, a conceptual framework of major features is presented to facilitate this description and comparison of features. Table 1 shows the features identified from our analysis of LMSs that seem to be the most important for understanding them.

It is helpful to note the features that are particularly well-suited to meeting the needs of the information age, for some of the LMSs were developed to meet the needs of the sorting-focused paradigm of education. However, it is likely that these products will continue to develop and move toward providing true, systemic, integrated, learner-centered features such as: customizable, unique instructional content, individual pacing, assessment of individual learning gaps, addressing those gaps, and further involving students and their parents in learning.

The LMSs examined are some of the largest LMSs available in the United States: PLATO, Pearson Digital Learning, SkillsTutor, and Co-nect. The sheer number of educational programs under the umbrella of a larger product system makes the comprehension of what each product offers daunting. Pack (2002) states that one of the first hurdles to implementing a new program is "sifting through the multitude of proffered solutions" (p. 23). He references e-learning analyst Bryan Chapman, who states that, at that time, there were more than 650 vendors of e-learning products. While the trend has been the merger and absorption of products into the larger LMS companies, it can still be very confusing trying to sort out what each product actually does. Pack (2002) quotes Healy, a research analyst for education and training, who describes the market: "It's just a big mess... There are way too many platforms and solutions right now. There's a lot of confusion on the buyer's side" (p. 23). Further complicating this is the focus on industry buzz-words and the use of marketing language common in the literature of these companies, which makes it difficult to determine if the products truly offer, or to what degree they offer, certain features, such as customizable instruction. This section reports the results of a determined attempt to sift through the morass of information and present a comparison of several of the major current LMSs for K-12 schools.

PLATO

PLATO is currently one of the largest LMSs used in K-12 schools and governmental institutions in the United States. The LMS PLATO was initially designed as a CMI system for use with PLATO, which was at the time a mainframe system completely devoted to the delivery of instruction and training. This system was designed to work with other curricula and to manage other courseware in the corporation. Another CMI system was custom-developed for

Table 1. Major features of LMS

Features (grayed features support information-age needs)		
Instructional Method	Standard features	Content presentation
		Curriculum standards
		Direct instruction
		Bilingual
		Self-paced learning
		Project-based work
		Group work
		Authentic, real-world problems
		Individualized instruction
	Teacher customizability	Adaptive sequencing
		Adaptive lesson plans
		Customizable instructional content
		Prescription of lessons
	Outside school	Online message center
		Online discussion board
		Project-based work
		Activities/homework with parent involvement
		Community relations and support
		Online lesson plan management for teachers
Data management		Attendance
		Health information
		Parent/guardian information
		Enrollment
		Class schedule
		Record of attainments mastered
		Mastery progress
Assessment		Post test / Pre test
		Formative tests
		Practice tests
		Diagnostic tests
		Mastery-level tests
Reporting		Summative test report to teachers/ parents
		Formative test report to teachers/ parents
		Student information report to teachers/ parents
		Record of attainments report to teachers/ parents
		Mastery progress report to teachers/ parents
		Customizable reporting for teachers

the University of Illinois PLATO system, which later became the original system of CDC PLATO (Szabo & Flesher, 2002).

The PLATO system provides a wide variety of instructional programs, as well as district software and assessment and reporting tools. The products are organized into three categories: accountability solutions, assessment solutions, and instructional solutions (PLATO, Inc., 2005).

PLATO's accountability solutions include data warehousing and synchronization tools, standards and curriculum integration tools, and a collection of communication tools and resources called the PLATO Network. Together, these tools allow local standards to be defined; assessments to be associated with specific standards; student, school, district, and professional data to be collected, stored, and managed; and communication to be promoted among members of the learning community (including students and their families) through the sharing of information and resources.

PLATO's assessment solutions provide a wide variety of testing products, many of which are tied directly to PLATO instructional products. Students may take practice tests, have their learning assessed and learning gaps identified, and either have a PLATO curriculum path automatically generated or have a customized path developed for them by their teacher. PLATO also provides teachers a way to create their own assessments in addition to providing practice for such tests as the National Writing Test, the GED, and the Pre Professional Skills Test, as well as a practice test for helping paraprofessionals meet the testing requirements of the No Child Left Behind Act of 2002.

The instructional programs are for elementary, secondary, and post-secondary grade levels. Subjects include reading, writing, mathematics, science, social studies, and life and career skills, as well as interdisciplinary and ESL/ELL curriculum in Spanish. Plato focuses on providing self-paced, individualized learning environments with tutorials and practice opportunities that are highly integrated with curriculum standards. With a 30-year heritage of research and development, PLATO claims that it strives to constantly evolve and grow to realize learner-centered, information-age education (Foshay, 1998). In summary, Table 2[3] shows the features that PLATO seems to offer, though we advise that these ratings be interpreted with caution, and many features are a matter of degree rather than yes-no.

PLATO has a large body of evaluation studies, mostly conducted by PLATO's own evaluators and evaluation consultants from research laboratories. Foshay conducted a meta-analysis of 13 PLATO evaluation research studies conducted from 1993 to 2001. The study's target populations included urban, suburban and rural, underachieving, low-income populations in elementary, secondary, and post-secondary education settings. The analysis showed improvements up to 60% on achievement of standards. The pass rates on state exit exams ranged up to 85% in English and 100% in math.

Kulik (2003) also conducted a meta-analysis on 20 studies of PLATO based on Foshay's analysis conducted in 2002. The evidence reviewed in this report provides support for the effectiveness of PLATO learning products, both as supplementary and as the only instruction compared to low-tech, traditional instruction alone. However, there were eight studies using a control group which

Kulik identified as providing the most reliable data. In these studies, which used an experimental group receiving solely PLATO instruction and a control group receiving only conventional instruction, the average effect size Kulik found was 0.43, which suggests positive effects of PLATO. However, as Foshay (2002) points out, the relationships between achievement and time on task with PLATO are complex, and the effects of PLATO were never measured in isolation from

Table 2. Major features of PLATO

Features (grayed features support information-age needs)			PLATO
Instructional Method	Standard features	Content presentation	✓
		Curriculum standards	✓
		Direct instruction	
		Bilingual	✓
		Self-paced learning	✓
		Project-based work	
		Group work	
		Authentic, real-world problems	
		Individualized instruction	✓
	Teacher customiz-ability	Adaptive sequencing	✓
		Adaptive lesson plans	
		Customizable instructional content	
		Prescription of lessons	✓
	Outside school	Online message center	
		Online discussion board	
		Project-based work	
		Activities/homework with parent involvement	✓
		Community relations and support	✓
		Online lesson plan management for teachers	
Data management		Attendance	
		Health information	
		Parent/guardian information	
		Enrollment	
		Class schedule	
		Record of attainments mastered	✓
		Mastery progress	✓
Assessment		Post test / Pre test	✓
		Formative tests	
		Practice tests	✓
		Diagnostic tests	✓
		Mastery-level tests	✓
Reporting		Summative test report to teachers/ parents	✓
		Formative test report to teachers/ parents	✓
		Student information report to teachers/ parents	
		Record of attainments report to teachers/ parents	✓
		Mastery progress report to teachers/ parents	✓
		Customizable reporting for teachers	

these various influences; therefore, it is hard to evaluate the independent effectiveness of the PLATO system.

Pearson Digital Learning

Pearson Digital Learning is another large LMS currently widely used in schools. It provides a number of instructional programs as well as district-wide reporting software, assessment tools, and reporting tools. The broadly used instructional programs are Waterford, SuccessMaker, KnowledgeBox, and Novanet. Pearson Digital Learning offers a series of programs for student data, which include SASI, Pearson Centerpoint, and CIMS. Pearson Digital Learning also has a new division, Pearson School Systems, which produces enterprise software covering everything from student data and assessment, to decision support systems, to human resources and finance tools.

Waterford. Waterford focuses on the pre-kindergarten to 2 age group with reading, math, and science instruction adapted to each learner. It provides year-long instruction, from beginner to mastery, for classroom activities and take-home assignments. It also provides multimedia instruction. The Waterford Early Reading Program is a software-based curriculum currently serving over 13,000 sites and 350,000 students with three levels of full-year instruction. The Waterford Early Math and Science Program also serve three levels of full-year, computer-based curriculum aligned to the National Council for Teachers in Mathematics and National Science Education standards (Pearson, Inc., 2005).

Several studies have been conducted by independent evaluators on the effectiveness of the Waterford program. The Education Commission of the States (1999) reported evaluation results stating that overall Waterford had a positive impact on student performance, particularly with limited or low performing students, compared to traditional instruction. Studies conducted on the Waterford Reading program at Rutgers University in New Jersey and the Dallas Independent School District in Texas both showed results for the Waterford classes outperforming the control group by highly significant differences.

SuccessMaker. SuccessMaker incorporates subjects such as English language development/ESL, mathematics, science, and social studies into the curriculum. SuccessMaker focuses on individualized, adaptive instruction for standards-based curriculum by adapting sequences for individual students and presenting instruction based on previous student assessment. SuccessMaker also provides flexible group work, authentic literature, bilingual options, and parent involvement (Pearson, Inc., 2005).

Quite a few evaluation studies have been conducted on SuccessMaker. The Education Commission of the States (1999) had a large-scale research evaluation conducted on the impact of SuccessMaker, which by and large did not show clear advantages of this program. The most emphasized aspects were that the program could not be a stand-alone intervention, but needed to be integrated within a traditional curriculum and other activities, and without this integration the program was not as effective. However, several evaluations have indicated that SuccessMaker can result in moderate gains in reading in schools. A number of school districts have shown better scores in reading, and Kulik's meta-analysis reported that SuccessMaker resulted in significantly better scores on standardized testing (Kulik, 1994). Miller, DeJean, and Miller (2000) observed that the embedded curricula in SuccessMaker did not complement existing curricula, instructional sequences, and teaching methods, but the teachers who were using the program thought that it was still a benefit to students because they were exposed to more content and strategies.

KnowledgeBox. KnowledgeBox is a K-6 lesson development tool. The program helps teachers customize existing lessons by combining engaging video, interactive software, Internet links, and electronic text resources into their curriculum. It also supports varied instructional approaches: direct instruction, small group, or independent work. The distinguishing feature is that teachers can choose pacing and target instruction for specific students and also collaborate and mentor, or be mentored by, other teachers (Pearson, Inc., 2005). However, we were unable to find any significant literature on the evaluation of KnowledgeBox.

NovaNet. NovaNet is a comprehensive software suite designed for grades 6-12. It includes an online courseware system that is integrated with assessment and student management tools. Students work at their own pace in completing the online course content and assessments. The student tracking and management tools then allow students to progress in meeting school standards. This suite allows individual students to either remediate or progress at a faster pace in completing course credits and preparing for state and other standardized tests.

Student Information Series. The Pearson Student Information Series includes three different products: SASI, Pearson Centerpoint, and CIMS student. SASI is a student management system that collects and manages student records, enrollments, scheduling, and attendance data. It includes such features as scheduling, parent collaboration, a grade book, and the creation of registration forms. Pearson Centerpoint is a Web-based student information communications tool. It handles student attendance and grade recording, while also supporting student and teacher calendars, automated alert emails to parents, student and class discussion boards, assessments construction, online assignment posting, reports generation, and announcements. CIMS Student maintains a great deal of student data, including home information, discipline records, emergency information, immunizations, course requests, and others. Student and academic information is automated by the system, which captures student grades and teacher comments and generates GPAs and class rankings in multiple formats that can be provided to students, parents, or other educational institutions. Likewise, CIMS tracks attendance and generates efficient attendance reports.

In summary, Table 3[4] shows the features that Pearson Digital Learning seems to offer, though again we advise that these ratings be interpreted with caution, and many features are a matter of degree rather than yes-no.

Table 3. Major features of Pearson Digital Learning

Features (grayed features support information-age needs)			Pearson
Instructional Method	Standard features	Content presentation	✓
		Curriculum standards	✓
		Direct instruction	✓
		Bilingual	✓
		Self-paced learning	✓
		Project-based work	✓
		Group work	
		Authentic, real-world problems	✓
		Individualized instruction	✓
	Teacher customiz-ability	Adaptive sequencing	✓
		Adaptive lesson plans	✓
		Customizable instructional content	✓
		Prescription of lessons	✓
	Outside school	Online message center	✓
		Online discussion board	✓
		Project-based work	✓
		Activities/homework with parent involvement	✓
		Community relations and support	✓
		Online lesson plan management for teachers	✓
Data management		Attendance	✓
		Health information	✓
		Parent/guardian information	✓
		Enrollment	✓
		Class schedule	✓
		Record of attainments mastered	✓
		Mastery progress	✓
Assessment		Post test / Pre test	✓
		Formative tests	✓
		Practice tests	✓
		Diagnostic tests	✓
		Mastery-level tests	✓
Reporting		Summative test report to teachers/ parents	✓
		Formative test report to teachers/ parents	✓
		Student information report to teachers/ parents	✓
		Record of attainments report to teachers/ parents	✓
		Mastery progress report to teachers/ parents	✓
		Customizable reporting for teachers	✓

Achievement Technologies, Inc.

Achievement Technologies is a company offering an LMS with over one million users (SkillsTutor, 2005). While their primary software product is SkillsTutor, a true LMS, they also offer a number of additional products for different grade levels, workplace training, and instructional content alone. These include K-2 Learning Milestones, SkillsBank, CornerStone, and a number of Workforce Education products,

SkillsTutor. SkillsTutor is an LMS for grades 2 to adult. It provides age-specific instruction in language arts, math, science, and workforce readiness skills. The product includes more than 1,000 activities, and each subject area contains 40 to 70 lessons that help students to learn major concepts and skills mostly needed in standardized tests (Felix, 2003). These lessons take around 20 minutes each to complete. Some of these lessons have components of higher-order thinking skills as well. The lessons begin with the introduction of concepts, and students are given opportunities to practice skills with explicit feedback. Pretests and post-tests, tracking student progress, and tests that are in a similar format to standardized tests are provided. Diagnostic tests are also provided in the program in order to identify each student's weak areas. This helps the system to provide the appropriate lessons to help all students reach the achievement level. As a whole, the management system essentially assesses students' skills, prescribes their lesson assignments, monitors the students' progress, reports results to teachers and parents, and generates accountability reports (SkillsTutor, Inc., 2005).

K-2 Learning Milestones. K-2 Learning Milestones is Achievement Technologies' product for lower grade levels. It includes pre-reading, phonics, and math skills for young students. Learning offers pre-instruction, diagnostic tests and customizable, printable workbook activities. It also offers customizable assessment tests that it grades automatically and a reporting utility for tracking achievement. Learning Milestones is also appropriate for supporting ESL students with audio instructions available in both English and Spanish.

SkillsBank. SkillsBank is a scaled-down offering of SkillsTutor. SkillsBank offers the instructional content of SkillsTutor without the additional features that SkillsTutor offers. Content is available both online and through CD-ROMs.

CornerStone. CornerStone focuses on strengthening students' key skills of language arts, reading vocabulary, reading comprehension, and math. CornerStone is designed to supplement the classroom instruction for grades 2-4, 3-4, 5-6, and 7-8. It offers interactive lessons, tutorials, and practice tests along with a management system for teachers that allows for individualized lesson plans. CornerStone also offers a reporting feature for tracking student achievement and practice worksheets for students to take home.

Workforce Education. Achievement Technologies also offers software to help adults or students about to enter the workforce. The Workforce Education suite is divided into the following components: employability and work maturity skills, work based learning, and citizenship skills.

In summary, Table 4[5] shows the features that Achievement Technologies seems to offer, though we again advise that these ratings be interpreted with caution, and many features are a matter of degree rather than yes-no.

Table 4. Major features of Achievement Technologies

Features (grayed features support information-age needs)			Achievement Technologies
Instructional Method	Standard features	Content presentation	✓
		Curriculum standards	✓
		Direct instruction	
		Bilingual	✓
		Self-paced learning	✓
		Project-based work	
		Group work	✓
		Authentic, real-world problems	✓
		Individualized instruction	✓
	Teacher customizability	Adaptive sequencing	✓
		Adaptive lesson plans	✓
		Customizable instructional content	✓
		Prescription of lessons	✓
	Outside school	Online message center	
		Online discussion board	
		Project-based work	
		Activities/homework with parent involvement	✓
		Community relations and support	
		Online lesson plan management for teachers	
Data management		Attendance	
		Health information	
		Parent/guardian information	
		Enrollment	
		Class schedule	
		Record of attainments mastered	✓
		Mastery progress	✓
Assessment		Post test / Pre test	✓
		Formative tests	
		Practice tests	
		Diagnostic tests	✓
		Mastery-level tests	✓
Reporting		Summative test report to teachers/parents	✓
		Formative test report to teachers/ parents	✓
		Student information report to teachers/ parents	
		Record of attainments report to teachers/ parents	✓
		Mastery progress report to teachers/ parents	✓
		Customizable reporting for teachers	

Compared to the larger LMSs, there were very few independent studies available that reviewed SkillsTutor or the other Achivement Technologies products. The Achievement Technologies studies that were primarily available were effectiveness reports on using SkillsTutor as an intervention tool for low and high achieving students. One independent study (Felix, 2003) was conducted in Jones Middle School in Marion, Indiana. The school used the online version of SkillsTutor as an intervention tool for students who did not pass the Indiana Statewide Testing for Educational Progress (ISTEP) test. The teacher there described the use of SkillsTutor as "a major contributor to overall improved academic performance" (p. 50) and "SkillsTutor helped cover the basics, and if the kids don't know the basics, they will never reach the higher level" (p. 50). The program was also being used as a homework program for accelerated students to practice for the ISTEP test at home. The school had tracked scores for the past three years, and the study showed considerable improvement in this student population. Overall, math scores were enhanced 40%, and scores for the Language Arts class improved 145% (Felix, 2003).

Co-nect

The Co-nect model was established in 1992 and has been working with schools to incorporate an individualized, systemic, whole-school reform effort that is focused on improving student performance through the restructuring of educational environments. The efforts are focused toward organizational restructuring, building community relations and support, and classroom-level changes. In classroom activities, Co-nect promotes a standards-based approach in project-based learning that is based on authentic "real-world" problems (Co-nect, Inc., 2005).

The overall structure of the Co-nect model is demonstrated in the five benchmarks adopted by the design team of Co-nect to produce high-quality teaching and learning. They are (1) shared accountability for results, (2) use of project-based learning for understanding and accomplishment, (3) comprehensive assessment and reporting for continuous improvement, (4) team-based and cluster-based school organization for continuous improvement, and (5) use of technology integration in the curriculum (Co-nect, Inc., 2005). In summary, Table 5[6] shows the features that Co-nect seems to offer, though again we advise that these ratings be interpreted with caution, and many features are a matter of degree rather than yes-no.

Ross and Lowther (2003) conducted a large-scale study in five inner-city schools relative to a matched comparison sample of four schools in the same district. The study examined five Co-nect schools in an inner-city school district on the aspects of (a) school climate, (b) teaching methods, (c) teacher buy-in, (d) level of design implementation, and (e) student achievement. Results of this study showed the following differences between Co-nect schools and similar schools.

Co-nect's effects on instruction, particularly in the direction of suggesting active learning, were more apparent at the lower-SES than higher-SES schools. Co-nect engendered use of student-centered teaching strategies and use of technology as a learning tool, appeared to create a positive climate, and was well-

Table 5. Major features of Co-nect

Features (grayed features support information-age needs)			Co-nect
Instructional Method	Standard features	Content presentation	✓
		Curriculum standards	✓✓
		Direct instruction	
		Bilingual	✓
		Self-paced learning	✓
		Project-based work	✓
		Group work	✓
		Authentic, real-world problems	✓
		Individualized instruction	✓
	Teacher customizability	Adaptive sequencing	✓
		Adaptive lesson plans	✓
		Customizable instructional content	✓
		Prescription of lessons	✓
	Outside school	Online message center	
		Online discussion board	
		Project-based work	✓
		Activities/homework with parent involvement	✓
		Community relations and support	✓
		Online lesson plan management for teachers	
Data management		Attendance	
		Health information	
		Parent/guardian information	
		Enrollment	
		Class schedule	
		Record of attainments mastered	✓
		Mastery progress	✓
Assessment		Post test / Pre test	✓
		Formative tests	
		Practice tests	
		Diagnostic tests	✓
		Mastery-level tests	✓
Reporting		Summative test report to teachers/ parents	✓
		Formative test report to teachers/ parents	✓
		Student information report to teachers/ parents	
		Record of attainments report to teachers/ parents	✓
		Mastery progress report to teachers/ parents	✓
		Customizable reporting for teachers	

received by teachers and principals. However Co-nect schools showed mixed results in raising achievement on district and state norms. Achievement outcomes were mixed, showing positive results relative to the state and district norms for three of the Co-nect schools but negative outcomes for two of the schools. Also, by the time the study was completed, Memphis City Schools announced that all of its 165 schools would be required to discontinue implementation of Co-nect (Ross & Lowther, 2003).

Others

Although these are some of the most representative LMSs, there are many others available, such as Sylvan Learning, Renaissance Learning, Riverdeep Learning, and American Education Corporation, among others. These LMSs should also be examined and evaluated in the near future to investigate what they can offer to K-12 classrooms. However, given the number of products on the market, it is beyond the scope of this chapter to examine them.

Potential for Information Age

This section has described several of the major LMS products available to K-12 schools in the United States. It is important to note that many of these products are the latest in a long history of products that were first developed many years ago, over 50 years in some cases. Furthermore, these companies have been in constant flux as they purchase and absorb competitors. This has sometimes resulted in a fragmented and confusing collection of products and features, and some of these features were developed to meet the needs of the sorting-focused model of education, rather than placing a true focus on learner-centered instruction. Furthermore, as can be seen in the description of these LMSs, many of them are composed of multiple products and therefore do not seamlessly blend together to create a true, systemic, LMS. However, these products will continue to evolve toward providing true, systemic, integrated, learner-centered services, and some of the features currently available are already well-suited for the information-age paradigm. Table 6[7] presents a summary and comparison of the various features that the reviewed LMSs offer and indicates which features are well-suited to information-age needs. Again, we advise that these ratings be interpreted with caution, and many features are a matter of degree rather than yes-no.

Current Trends in LMS

With a history in CAI and ILS, LMSs currently still incorporate much of the drill-and-practice approach that was designed to serve the needs of the industrial-age, time-based, sorting-focused, teacher-centered, standardized paradigm. Many ILSs focus on remedial learning and instruction of basic knowledge (Foshay, 1998; Sherry, 1993). LMSs are continuing to evolve and are slowly moving toward supporting various approaches of instruction, including a focus on customizable and personalized instruction and assessment (Sherry, 1993). Taylor (2004) identifies customizing assessments, analyzing student progress, evaluating student performance, tracking academic achievement, and identifying areas for additional scaffolding or assistance as some of the areas where technology can offer significant contributions to schools and classrooms, and these features are being integrated into LMSs. It is therefore important that LMSs continue to develop toward better serving the needs of the information-age paradigm, which will be attainment-based, learning-focused, learner-centered, and customized. LMSs also need to continue to teach more higher-level thinking skills and support a more student-directed, self-motivated learning process, which will help develop critical-thinking and problem-solving skills and encourage a life-long love of learning. LMSs should develop stronger support for appropriate methods to accomplish this, such as integrated, thematic, authentic problem-based learning.

Furthermore, the continued growth and availability of computers and computer networks is guiding LMSs toward a more network-based structure. The U.S. Department of Education announced that the number of computers in schools has been growing over the last 10 years, and 99% of American schools now have a 5:1 student to computer ratio (U.S. Department of Education, 2004). With the increasing numbers of computers and Internet connections available in classrooms, LMS is starting to play a more critical role in learning. Furthermore, with the increasing spread of wireless networking, LMSs will be able to leave the physical bounds of the classroom and better support learning outside of the school. Students will have their learning better supported at home and in the community as they interact with real problems and become more involved in service learning. Parents will find better support in working with their children and being involved in out-of-school learning activities. The collection of student learning artifacts in the form of student portfolios will also have a place in LMS.

LMSs and the continued research on reusable learning objects and their management are also putting pressure on LMSs to support the use of learning objects on multiple platforms of instructional software.

Table 6. Comparison of major features of LMS products

Features (grayed features support information-age needs)			PLATO	Pearson Digital Learning	Achievement Technologies	Co-nect
Instructional Method	Standard features	Content presentation	✓	✓	✓	✓
		Curriculum standards	✓	✓	✓	✓
		Direct instruction		✓		
		Bilingual	✓	✓	✓	✓
		Self-paced learning	✓	✓	✓	✓
		Project-based work		✓		✓
		Group work			✓	✓
		Authentic, real-world problems		✓	✓	✓
		Individualized instruction	✓	✓	✓	✓
	Teacher customiz-ability	Adaptive sequencing	✓	✓	✓	✓
		Adaptive lesson plans		✓	✓	✓
		Customizable instructional content		✓	✓	✓
		Prescription of lessons	✓	✓	✓	✓
	Outside school	Online message center		✓		
		Online discussion board		✓		
		Project-based work		✓		✓
		Activities/homework with parent involvement	✓	✓	✓	✓
		Community relations and support	✓	✓		✓
		Online lesson plan management for teachers		✓		
Data management		Attendance		✓		
		Health information		✓		
		Parent/guardian information		✓		
		Enrollment		✓		
		Class schedule		✓		
		Record of attainments mastered	✓	✓	✓	✓
		Mastery progress	✓	✓	✓	✓
Assessment		Post test / Pre test	✓	✓	✓	✓
		Formative tests		✓		
		Practice tests	✓	✓		
		Diagnostic tests	✓	✓	✓	✓
		Mastery-level tests	✓	✓	✓	✓
Reporting		Summative test report to teachers/ parents	✓	✓	✓	✓
		Formative test report to teachers/ parents	✓	✓	✓	✓
		Student information report to teachers/ parents		✓		
		Record of attainments report to teachers/ parents	✓	✓	✓	✓
		Mastery progress report to teachers/ parents	✓	✓	✓	✓
		Customizable reporting for teachers		✓		

Reflections and Recommendations for Future LMS and Research

While the LMS examples discussed in this paper illustrate the continued growth of computer technology toward systemic, customizable, and adaptive interchangeable packages, the literature on the evaluation of LMSs clearly points out that improvements are needed. The results of the studies discussed indicate that LMSs assist learning more than traditional instruction alone. It is important that more design-based research (Brown, 1992; Collins, 1992) and formative research (Reigeluth & Frick, 1999) be conducted to identify specific aspects of LMSs that do and do not work well and, more importantly, to identify ways they can be improved.

It is clear that much work remains to be done before LMSs fully answer the needs of the information-age learner. Whether these LMSs continue to develop or new, alternative LMSs appear, this process will require much research work on LMSs. The following ideas detail what the LMS of the near future needs to support, and also what kind of research is needed for the improved design of LMSs in the future.

- Providing more constructivist-based instruction that focuses on personalized and flexible approaches to meet learner-defined goals in the future (Reigeluth & Garfinkle, 1994).
- Supporting collaborative and cooperative learning inside and outside of the classroom and providing students with a seamless learning environment between school and *home*, allowing *parents* to be more engaged in their child's learning (Taylor, 2004).
- Addressing personalized assessment, progress tracking, reporting, and responsiveness to learner needs in the future (Reigeluth & Garfinkle, 1994).
- Truly integrating systems that allow for improved collaboration across systems and among stakeholders (Sherry, 1993).
- Improving support for professional diagnosis and development for teachers and other stakeholders.
- Improving cost effectiveness and maximizing efficiency in leveraging existing resources that are already available in schools and LMSs (Szabo & Flesher, 2002).

These are some of the current trends and issues of LMSs, and they should be examined and evaluated through more in-depth research.

Summary

In summary, a learning management system (LMS) is a computer system that incorporates providing instruction, tracking achievement, and managing resources for individual students and an organization as a whole. This paper focused on the examination of previous research studies on LMS by discussing the need for integrated computer systems in the schools, providing an overview of past terminology used to describe the use of computers for instruction and how LMS relates to these terms, presenting an analysis and comparison of four current LMSs for K-12 schools, reviewing evaluation studies on those LMSs, and concluding with a reflection on LMS trends and issues.

References

Advanced Distributed Learning. (2003). *Advanced distributed learning* [Homepage of Advanced Distributed Learning]. Retrieved March 13, 2005, from http://adlnet.org/

Alexander, S. (2001). Learning curve. *InfoWorld, 23*(23), 59-61.

Bailey, G. D. (1993). Wanted: A road map for understanding integrated learning systems. In G. D. Bailey (Ed.), *Computer-based integrated learning systems* (pp. 3-9). Englewood Cliffs, NJ: Educational Technology Publications.

Becker, H. J. (1993). A model for improving the performance of integrated learning systems. In G. D. Bailey (Ed.), *Computer-based integrated learning systems* (pp. 11-31). Englewood Cliffs, NJ: Educational Technology Publications.

Bracey, G. W. (1993). The bright future of integrated learning systems. In G. D. Bailey (Ed.), *Computer-based integrated learning systems*. Englewood Cliffs, NJ: Educational Technology Publications.

Brown, A. L. (1992). Design experiments: Theoretical and methodological challenges in creating complex interventions in classroom settings. *The Journal of Learning Sciences, 2*(2), 141-178.

Brush, T. A., Armstrong, J., Barbrow, D., & Ulintz, L. (1999). Design and delivery of integrated learning systems: Their impact on students achievement and attitudes. *Educational Computing Research, 21*(4), 475-486.

Collins, A. (Ed.). (1992). *Toward a design science of education*. New York: Springer-Verlag.

Co-nect, Inc. (2005, May 2). *Our approach: Data-driven solutions to improve instruction.* Retrieved May, 2, 2005, from http://plato.com/products_all.asp

Connolly, P. J. (2001). A standard for success. *InfoWorld, 23*(42), 57-58.

Deubel, P. (2002). Selecting curriculum-based software. *Learning & Leading with Technology, 29*(5), 10-16.

Dunkel, P. A. (1999). Considerations in developing and using computer-adaptive tests to assess second language proficiency. *Language Learning & Technology, 2*(2), 77-93.

EDUCAUSE Evolving Technologies Committee. (2003). *Course management systems (CMS)*. Retrieved April 25, 2005, from http://www.educause.edu/ir/library/pdf/DEC0302.pdf

Felix, K. (2003). In the spotlight. *MultiMedia Schools, 10*(6), 49-50.

Foshay, R. (1998). *Instructional philosophy and strategic direction of the PLATO system.* Technical paper. Bloomington, MN: PLATO Learning, Inc.

Foshay, R. (2002). *An overview of the research base of PLATO*. Bloomington, MN: PLATO Learning, Inc.

Friesen, N., Roberts, A., & Fisher, S. (2002). Metadata for learning objects. *Canadian Journal of Learning and Technology* (Online version)*, 28*(3), 43-53. Retrieved July 10, 2005, from http://www.cjlt.ca/content/vol28.3/friesen_etal.html

Getting up to speed on learning management systems. (2002). Retrieved April 3, 2005, from http://www.brandonhall.com/public/execsums/execsum_gutsonlmss.pdf

Gibbons, A. S., Nelson, J. M., & Richards, R. (2002). The nature and origin of instructional objects. In D. A. Wiley (Ed.), *The instructional use of learning objects: Online version*. Retrieved March 13, 2005, from http://reusability.org/read/chapters/gibbons.doc

Gilhooly, K. (2001). Making e-learning effective. *Computerworld, 35*(29), 52-53.

Hodgins, H. W. (2002). The future of learning objects. In D. A. Wiley (Ed.), *The instructional use of learning objects: Online version*. Retrieved March 13, 2005, http://reusability.org/read/chapters/hodgins.doc

Joseph, R., & Reigeluth, C. M. (2002, July-August). Beyond technology integration: The case for technology transformation. *Educational Technology*, *42,* 9-12.

Kulik, J. A. (2003). *Instructional technology and school reform models*. Ann Arbor: Office of Evaluations & Examinations, University of Michigan. Retrieved March 10, 2005, from http://www.schooldata.com/mdrtechhilites.asp

Leslie, S. (2003). *Important characteristics of course management systems: Findings from the Edutools.info project*. Retrieved April 15, 2005, from http://www.edtechpost.ca/gems/cms_characteristics.htm

McCombs, B., & Whisler, J. (1997). *The learner-centered classroom and school*. San Francisco: Jossey-Bass.

MERLOT. (2005). *Multimedia educational resource for learning and online teaching Web site*. Retrieved March 13, 2005, from http://www.merlot.org/

Merrill, M. D. (2002). Knowledge objects to support inquiry-based, online learning. In D. A. Wiley (Ed.), *The instructional use of learning objects: Online version*. Retrieved March 13, 2005, from http://reusability.org/read/chapters/merrill.doc

Miller, L., DeJean, J., & Miller, R. (2000). The literacy curriculum and use of an Integrated Learning System. *Journal of Research in Reading, 23*(2), 123-135.

Oakes, K. (2002). E-learning: LCMS, LMS—They're not just acronyms but powerful systems for learning. *T+D, 56*(3), 73-75.

Pack, T. (2002). Corporate learning gets digital. *EContent, 25*(7), 22-27.

Parr, J. M., & Fung, I. (2001, September 28, 2004). *A review of the literature on computer-assisted learning, particularly integrated learning systems, and outcomes with respect to literacy and numeracy*. Retrieved April 2, 2005, from http://www.minedu.govt.nz/index.cfm?layout=document&documentid=5499&indexid=6920&indexparentid=1024

Parrish, P. E. (2004). The trouble with learning objects. *Educational Technology Research & Development, 52*(1), 49-57.

Pearson, Inc. (2005, May 2). *Pearson Digital Learning: All products and services*. Retrieved May, 2, 2005, from http://www.pearsondigital.com/products/

PLATO, Inc. (2005, May 2). *Products and services: All products and services*. Retrieved May, 2, 2005, from http://plato.com/products_all.asp

Reigeluth, C. M. (1994). The imperative for systemic change. In C. M. Reigeluth, & R. J. Garfinkle (Eds.), *Systemic change in education* (pp. 3-12). Englewood Cliffs, NJ: Educational Technology Publications.

Reigeluth, C. M. (1997, November). Educational standards: To standardize or to customize learning? *Phi Delta Kappan, 79*(3), 202-206.

Reigeluth, C. M., & Frick, T. W. (1999). Formative research: A methodology for creating and improving design theories. In C. M. Reigeluth (Ed.), *Instructional-design theories and models: A new paradigm of instructional theory* (Vol. 2, pp.633-651). Mahwah, NJ: Laurence Erlbaum Assocates, Publishers.

Reigeluth, C. M., & Garfinkle, R. J. (1994). Envisioning a new system of education. In C. M. Reigeluth & R. J. Garfinkle (Eds.), *Systemic change in education* (pp. 59-70). Englewood Cliffs, NJ: Educational Technology Publications.

Reiser, R. A. (1987). Instructional technology: A history. In R. M. Gagne (Ed.), *Instructional technology: Foundations* (pp. 11-48). Hillsdale, NJ: Lawrence Erlbaum Associates.

Ross, S. M., & Lowther, D. L. (2003). Impacts of the Co-nect school reform design on classroom instruction, school climate, and student achievement in inner-city schools. *Journal of Education for Students Placed at Risk, 8*(2), 215-246.

Schlechty, P. C. (1991). *Schools for the 21st century: Leadership imperatives for educational reform.* San Francisco: Jossey-Bass Inc.

Senge, P., Cambron-McCabe, N., Lucas, T., Smith, B., Dutton, J., & Kleiner, A. (2000). *Schools that learn: A fifth discipline fieldbook for educators, parents, and everyone who cares about education.* Toronto, Canada: Currency.

Sherry, M. (1993). Integrated Learning Systems: What may we expect in the future? In G. D. Bailey (Ed.), *Computer-based Integrated Learning Systems* (pp. 137-141). Englewood Cliffs, NJ: Educational Technology Publications.

Shore, A., & Johnson, M. F. (1993). Integrated Learning Systems: A vision for the future. In G. D. Bailey (Ed.), *Computer-based Integrated Learning Systems* (pp. 83-91). Englewood Cliffs, NJ: Educational Technology Publications.

SkillsTutor, Inc. (2005, May 2). *Why choose products developed by achievement technologies?: Instructional, supplemental, practical and effective.* Retrieved May, 2, 2005, from http://skillstutor.com/index.cfm?fuseaction=products.home

Successmaker. (1999). Educational Resources Information Center (ERIC ED447436). Retrieved April 28, 2006, from http://www.eric.ed.gov/ERICDocs/data/ericdocs2/content_storage_01/0000000b/80/23/c1/41.pdf

Szabo, M., & Flesher, K. (2002). *CMI theory and practice: Historical roots of learning management systems.* Paper presented at the E-Learn World Conference on E-Learning in Corporate, Government, Healthcare, & Higher Education, Montreal, Canada.

Taylor, F. P. (2004). Education technology helps unite school communities, improve academic achievement. *T.H.E. Journal, 31*(10), 46-48.

Toffler, A. (1984). *The third wave*. New York: Bantam.

U.S. Department of Education, O. o. E. T. (2004). *Toward a new golden age in American education: How the Internet, the law and today's students are revolutionizing expectations*. Washington, DC: U.S. Department of Education, Office of Educational Technology.

Van Dusen, L. M., & Worthen, B. R. (1994). The impact of Integrated Learning System implementation on student outcomes: Implications for research and evaluation. *International Journal of Educational Research, 21*, 13-24.

Waterford early reading program. (1999). Educational Resources Information Center (ERIC ED447438). Retrieve April 18, 2006, from http://www.eric.ed.gov/ERICDocs/data/ericdocs2/content_storage_01/0000000b/80/23/c1/86.pdf

Wiley, D. A. (2002). Connecting learning objects to instructional design theory: A definition, a metaphor, and a taxonomy. In D. A. Wiley (Ed.), *The instructional use of learning objects: Online version*. Retrieved March 13, 2005, from http://reusability.org/read/chapters/wiley.doc

Endnotes

1. An online database of individual reviews of different CMSs by the Western Cooperative on Educational Telecommunications (WCET).
2. Web page without page number.
3. PLATO Learning, Inc. was contacted to review the features attributed to them for accuracy but declined comment.
4. Pearson Digital Learning was contacted to review the features attributed to them for accuracy.
5. Achievement Technologies was contacted to review the features attributed to them for accuracy.
6. Co-nect was contacted to review the features attributed to them for accuracy.

7 The authors would like to acknowledge the contribution of Dr. Tom Brush at Indiana University for his support in reviewing and providing advice on the development of this table of features.

Chapter V

Integrating Computer-Supported Learning into Traditional Distance Courses

Cengiz Hakan Aydin, Anadolu University, Turkey

Mehmet Emin Mutlu, Open Education Faculty, Turkey

Marina S. McIsaac,
Educational Media & Arizona State University, USA

Abstract

This chapter describes how a traditional distance education provider, Anadolu University of Turkey, integrated computer-supported learning into its traditional distance courses. Anadolu University has been struggling with offering quality education to their large body of distance learners (approximately 1 million). To do so, the university tries to integrate computer-supported learning environments into its traditional correspondence programs. Building supplementary e-learning portals, through which learners can access videos, textbooks, audio books, computer-assisted instruction materials, self-tests, pedagogical and managerial support is one of the important steps taken. The authors hope that those who are interested in distance learning and computer-supported learning in different contexts will benefit from the efforts of Anadolu University explained in this chapter.

Introduction

Distance education, the structured teaching-learning process that is not limited by time and place, is one of the fastest growing fields of practice and study. Advances in computers and computer related technologies have fostered this growth and have provided distance learners better opportunities and freedom to determine when, where, what, and how to study. Not only new providers, but also traditional distance education programs, have had to adapt their services according to these advances.

Anadolu University of Turkey, as one of the largest distance education providers (Daniels, 1996), has started to integrate computers into its distance courses, as well. However, transferring a textbook-based (correspondence type) self-paced learning system into computer-supported learning system was not an easy job, and required a thorough planning due to large number of students, technological infrastructure, access issues, and so forth.

This chapter mainly focuses on how a traditional distance education provider, Anadolu University, integrated computer-supported learning into its traditional distance courses. The chapter consists of three parts: the first part covers the related literature about computer-supported learning and traditional distance education programs, while the second part gives details about traditional distance higher education programs of Anadolu University, and the last part introduces how the university attempts to integrate computer-supported learning into its traditional distance programs. The last part also includes the results of selected studies in which effects of integrating computer-supported learning into the traditional distance courses were investigated.

Computer-Supported Learning

The computer is a technology written and talked about frequently in the literature on education. Although its roots can be traced back to the 1960s or even 1950s, the widespread applications of and studies on using computers in the learning processes were started in the early 1980s right after the invention of microcomputers (Niemiec & Walberg, 1989). Since then, quite a large body of literature has been built up about various aspects of instructional computing.

On the other hand, this extensive literature shows that the terms in the field of instructional computing are not standardized. One of the main reasons, we have observed, is that computers can play different roles in various learning contexts, and experts tend to offer various names for the same or similar roles. Therefore, we thought it would be beneficial to briefly clarify what we mean by using the term "computer-supported learning." We use "computer-supported learning" as a general term that represents the use of computers and computer-based technologies in any learning environments, such as classroom, televised learning, and online learning for the purpose of fostering human learning.

The roles of computers are varied and extensive in computer-supported learning environments. The following information describes three categories representing the different roles computers can play in computer-supported learning environments. Although these categories have been previously introduced by Wilson (1996) for explaining the use of computers in constructivist learning environments, they can also be adapted to describe the roles of computers in learning over a broad-spectrum.

Computer-based learning represents instructional contexts in which computers provide all the necessary actions for learners to master the content or accomplish the instructional goals. These actions may include presenting information, guiding the learners, practicing, and assessing learning. In computer-based learning environments, the learner usually interacts only with the computer. Commercially available multimedia and computer-based training software are good examples for this category.

In *computer-assisted learning* context, computers are used to support classroom or any other technology-based learning experience. The computer may function as a tool to provide one or more of the following or similar instructional events: presenting information, guiding the learners, practicing, assessing learning. For instance, after receiving instruction in the classroom, learners may be asked to complete the practices either individually or within small groups in front of computers. Wilson (1996) gives the Jasper Woodbury problem-solving series as a good example of a classroom-based computer-supported learning environment.

Virtual learning environments are also considered as one of the computer-supported learning contexts. In contrast to previous categories, computers offer learners more open systems in which they can interact not only with software (content and interface) but also with other learners, resources, and presentations. E-mail, listservs, electronic bulletin boards, shared whiteboards, text-based chat environments, and computer-based video conferencing represent some of the more common computer-based tools that can be used in virtual environments. Some of the online learning applications and virtual learning communities are regarded as open, virtual environments.

The literature includes different categories as well (e.g., Simonson & Thompson, 1997). However, the categories listed are the ones directly related to the human learning processes rather than management or other aspects of education. Since others do not directly involve the learner, we do not include them in this chapter. For example, computer-managed instruction is a category that can be included in the above list. It refers to the instructor's use of the computer to manage instruction. Since its relation with learning is not as direct as the above ones, we do not consider computer-managed instruction as a category representing the role of computers in computer-supported learning environments.

On the other hand, one can easily come across an application in which use of the computer falls in two or all three of the above categories. In particular, the latest e-learning environments promise a combination of all three categories. In these environments, learners may work alone or with their peers to master the content presented by the computer, they may join the classroom-based practice activities, and they may collaborate online with other participants. These environments can be regarded as good examples of how computers have blurred the gap between face-to-face education and distance education.

Distance Learning

Distance education refers to the structured teaching-learning process that is not limited by time and place. Access to continuous education and meeting the huge demand for education as a result of increasing population seems to be the main driver of the growth of distance learning all around the world. Moreover, advances in computers and computer related technologies have fostered this growth and have provided distance learners better opportunities and freedom to determine when, where, what, and how to study. For many (e.g., Gunawardena & McIsaac, 2003; Harrasim, 1990; Schrum, 1998), advances in computer networks opened new doors to distance education providers due to their unique characteristics such as speed of delivery and increased interaction. These two characteristics helped distance education providers reach more geographically and physically separated individuals, offer more interactivity among learners, employ current instructional approaches, and above all, bring the distinction between distance education and traditional education closer. Figures, such as cited in work of Duffy and Kirkley (2004), about the growth of distance learning courses and programs support the impact of computers.

However, this expansion threatens the traditional distance learning providers all over the world—particularly in emerging countries. Bollag (2001) reports the experts' comments on what happened when American and European universities came to China, South Africa, India, and Latin American countries. According to those experts, learners in these countries often choose to pay more for the Western institutions because they assume those institutions are better than what they have in their countries. Huge demand attracts many private and public American and European institutions that try to offer distance programs either by themselves or with local partners.

This situation, advances in the practice of distance learning and the main goals of any distance learning initiative (improvement of access, enhancement of quality, improvement of efficiencies, etc.), forces traditional distance education providers to modify their programs in a way that allows them easy integration of new technologies (particularly computers and computer-based ones) into the programs and/or to offer new computer-supported learning programs. Reports (e.g., Farrell, 1999) uncover that almost in all parts of the World, policy makers are trying to integrate computer-supported learning into their educational systems without questioning its effectiveness, and efficiency. The World of Open and Distance Learning, a work of Reddy and Manjulika (2000), shows that this integration into distance learning appears to be in forms of either creating completely new virtual learning environments for a relatively limited number of learners or establishing computer-based support services for the available programs that aims at large numbers. Successful implementations in developed countries encourage traditional distance education providers to foster efforts of integrating computer-supported learning into their systems (Farrell, 1999, 2001). On the other hand, especially cost and availability of technology (access) for learners and some other reasons, such as learners' goal orientations, shortage of know-how and human resources, initial cost of integrating advanced technology, seem to be forces opposing the integration of computer-supported learning in not only emerging countries but also in developed ones (Farrell, 1999).

Turkey is one of those emerging countries that struggle with building new "brick-and-mortar" universities to keep up with population growth, not to mention handling expanding enrollment. So, distance learning has been a major solution for meeting the higher education demand in Turkey since the early 1980s. Anadolu University is the largest distance higher education provider in Turkey. It offers distance learning to more than one million Turkish citizens. That makes it one of the mega universities of the world (McIsaac & Murphy, 1988; Ozkul, 2001). However, the opposing forces mentioned above play an important role in the process of integrating computer-supported learning into its traditional distance programs.

Turkish Higher Education

As an emerging country with a relatively young population (total 63 million), education has the utmost priority for Turkey. The schooling rates are 99.7% for primary school, 69.3% for middle school, 53.4% for high school, and 22.4% for higher education including open education. About 35% of the country's higher education population is in the Anadolu University distance education system. The Ministry of National Education is responsible for all educational services in the country, excluding higher education. The Council of Higher Education is the planning, coordinating, and policy making body for higher education. Higher education is defined as all post-secondary programs with duration of at least two years. The system consists of universities (53 public and 22 private) and non-university institutions of higher education (police and military academies and colleges). Each university consists of faculties (four-year colleges or schools) offering bachelor's level programs, and two-year vocational schools offering associate level programs of a strictly vocational nature.

Admission to higher education in Turkey's centralized system is based on nationwide, yearly examinations administrated by the Student Selection and Placement Centre (OSYM), a government agency. There is severe competition for university entrance, causing a bottleneck in the initial process of acceptance to higher education institutions. For example, in 2004, 1,902,250 students (high school graduates) applied to take the university entrance exam, but only 543,035 (28%) were placed in the higher education institutions. Among the placed students, 274,474 (approximately 50%) entered Anadolu University's distance programs. Figure 1 gives details about placement ratios in higher education.

As can be observed in Figure 1, Anadolu University has been filling quite a large portion of the higher education demand in Turkey since the early 1980s.

Anadolu University and its Distance Programs

According to the World Bank, Anadolu University is the world's largest university due to its student body (Potashnick & Capper, 1998). The university actually is not an open university. It has a dual mode education system. The on-campus education is offered though its nine colleges (or faculties—"faculty" is a term used in Turkey instead of "college" or "school"), 10 vocational schools, 18 research centers, and the state conservatory (school of music and theatrical

Figure 1. University placement ratios in higher education in Turkey

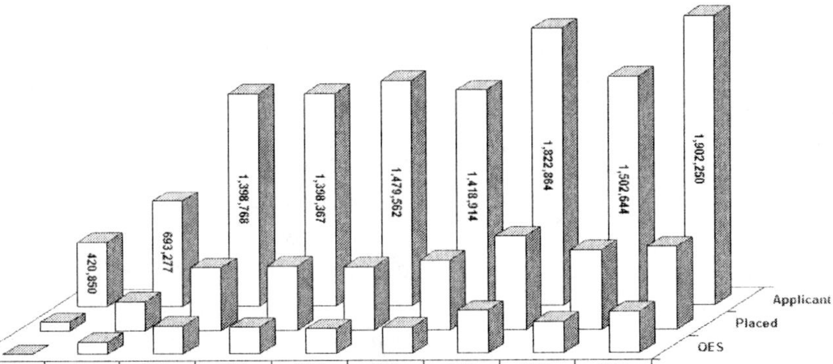

	1981	1988	1989	1997	1999	2001	2002	2003	2004
□ OES	0	81,356	185,136	178,766	166,175	173,771	285,395	211,346	274,474
□ Placed	54,818	188,183	412,207	421,372	414,372	455,913	614,125	522,844	543,035
□ Applicant	420,850	693,277	1,398,768	1,398,367	1,479,562	1,418,914	1,822,864	1,502,644	1,902,250

acting). The distance education programs are organized under three faculties: open education, business administration, and economics.

Anadolu University was established in 1981 from an older institution, the Academy of Eskisehir, Economics and Commercial Sciences (EAECS). In accordance with the Higher Education Act of 1981, it was also authorized to provide distance education in Turkey on a national scale. As a result, in 1982 the former Faculty of Communication Sciences of the EAECS was transformed to become the Faculty of Open Education, or, as it is called commonly, the Open Education Faculty (OEF). This faculty was an outgrowth of the newly established Anadolu University because at that time, it was the only institution that had experience in the technical and theoretical aspects of distance education. The first educational television pilot project of Turkey was undertaken here during the 1970s under the auspices of the Educational Television department of the EAECS (McIsaac, Murphy, & Demiray, 1988).

In the 1982-1983 academic year, the OEF started to offer two, four year undergraduate distance education degree programs in business administration and economics. That year 29,478 students enrolled in the programs. By 2004-2005, the number of enrolled distance students at Anadolu University reached approximately one million. Today, the OEF, along with the other two distance education faculties, is offering eight different bachelor's degree and 22 associate degree programs to students in Turkey, the Northern Cyprus Turkish Republic, and some of the European countries such as Germany, The Netherlands, and France. The programs vary from business administration to preschool teacher education. Recent figures show that the majority of the distance learners of the university have jobs (78%). Among these students 30% live in villages and small towns, 62% are over 24 years old, and 45% are married. Moreover, 40% of them are female.

The distance programs of Anadolu University are primarily textbook-based and require self-study. In other words, students are expected to study their textbooks at their own pace, alone, and to take scheduled centralized exams administered at remote locations. Textbook-based instruction is also supported with several services including broadcast television programs aired by a state channel throughout the country, video and radio programs distributed on cassettes, CDs or DVDs, remote evening classes, and computer-supported learning environments. The rationale behind this sort of an instructional approach is common to all open and distance learning initiatives in emerging countries. These are based on (1) outreach to as many learners as possible in cost effective ways, and (2) providing alternatives for learners' limited access to the other technologies including VCRs, computers, and even television broadcasts. Figure 1 reveals that distance learning is a necessity for Turkey rather than a convenience owing to the shortage of higher education institutions and the increasing demand for education. Since printing and mailing do not cost as much as advanced technologies, Anadolu University is able to accept thousands of learners every year into its programs. In addition, recent figures show that the majority of distance students cannot access computers and other technologies, despite the improvements in technology distribution. For instance quite a number (30%) of the current distance learners of the university live in rural areas where they have difficulties receiving television broadcasts, especially the channel that airs the university's programs. Also, the percentage of students who own a computer and have Internet connection at home is even lower. This situation is related to the home computing ratio in Turkey. In general figures show that only around 12.5% of the population has computers at home and only 7% have an Internet connection (TUBITAK, 2000). Although the number of students who are able to access the Internet at work or in Cyber Cafés is growing, students are having difficulties (such as heavy work conditions and high costs) using the Internet for learning. Thus, the majority of Anadolu University's distance programs are still textbook-based. The number of learners in online (only 2% of all learners) and hybrid (10%) programs is quite limited despite the improvements.

Currently there are about 400 textbooks used at the programs. All are designed and produced in-house. The university has modern printing facilities where these textbooks and other print materials are printed. The total number of textbooks printed at the beginning of the 2004-2005 academic year was more than three million copies.

Anadolu University also has its own television program production and broadcasting facilities. Around 4,300 television programs have been designed and produced in the Educational Television Centre (ETV) since it was first establishment in 1982. The Centre, supported with editing and post-production units, has two production studios and a mobile production vehicle. Currently 165 technical and administrative staff are employed in the Centre. The university just recently launched its own television channel, entitled TVA. However, it is a local channel and is not eligible to air the programs according to the legislations. So, the university broadcasts nationwide six hours of programming every day (total around 900 hours of broadcasting every academic year) on Channel 4 of the Turkish Radio and Television (TRT4) Corporation. Learners in Turkey may also acquire videocassette or VCD/DVD formats of these programs with a minimum charge for shipping expenses, while those in Europe get this service free owing to the fact that they cannot watch TRT4 where they are. In addition, Anadolu University in collaboration with the TRT4 offers live broadcasting three times in a year just before the centralized exams. During those live broadcasts, learners may reach the instructors in the studios via phone and ask their questions.

For certain courses, academic support is also provided via face-to-face lecture sessions. The university has agreements with local universities (currently 38 universities) in 59 provinces of the country to hire their personnel and facilities to offer these lectures to its learners. The lectures are given during the evenings (after work hours) and weekends. Every year approximately 20,000 learners regularly attend those lectures.

Student success is determined by multiple choice tests. Each academic year, a midterm, a final, and a makeup exam are centrally administered to the students to evaluate their performance in the courses. The weights of these tests for the final grade are 30% and 70%. An average score of 50% is required in order to "pass" a course. The students who fail are given an opportunity to recover their final test score at a makeup exam. Exam papers are graded by computer, and the results are delivered either by mail or through the Internet. The Centre for Research in Testing of the university is responsible for the preparation and maintenance of a question data bank for the exams. Tests are prepared at this Centre by a joint committee of authors/editors, field experts, technical consultants, and scientific assessment specialist. Those scheduled exams are administered in 88 provinces in Turkey and 11 centers in Europe. The university usually uses 55,000 classrooms in 4,000 buildings and hires 50,000 personnel (local teachers, school staff and administrators, transporters, etc.) to administer the exams.

Furthermore, Anadolu University provides administrative support to its distance learners through its 84 offices in 77 provinces of the country. Those offices are run by the university's own staff (total 335 staff), and almost all the properties of the offices are owned by the university. In addition, learners may reach the university via e-mail and phones to receive help for their administrative and technical problems. In terms of social support, the university encourages the learners to attend graduation ceremonies and local events organized by the administrative offices. Moreover, the university has an online weekly newspaper that gives news and recent developments in the university.

On the other hand, critics of Anadolu University's distance programs essentially focus on its centralized structure and the number of the learners (e.g., Cagiltay, 2001). The assessment system, fixed programs, lack of interaction, and a widely felt sense of isolation are the most frequently criticized aspects of the programs. Also, the credit given to the distance learning programs is still low in Turkey. Askar (2005) reports the results of a study in which she interviewed learners and faculties about distance learning. She found out that both learners and faculties regard distance learning as a chance for those who have no other options, and that it is not an alternative but a supplement to conventional universities. Moreover, high drop out rates as a common characteristic of distance education learners prevails also in Anadolu University distance programs. The overall drop out rate of the system is 40%, and most of the dropouts are observed in the first year of study.

Anadolu University takes these or similar criticisms into consideration and so, has always been in search of bringing new technology into its programs. Therefore, since the early 1990s, the university has been trying to integrate computers and computer-based technologies into its distance programs. As a result of this continued search, authentic ways of technology utilization for distance learning have been generated over time. These have been elaborated in the following sections.

Computer-Supported Learning in Anadolu University's Distance Programs

Anadolu University has great potential for contributions to the Turkish Higher Education System through distance learning. The administrators of the university are aware that computer-supported learning can provide vast opportunities to overcome the problems of the distance learning system and to transform it from being traditional to being innovative. Therefore, the university has been in search of integrating computer-supported learning into its programs since the late 1980s. As the authors of this chapter, we thought it would be beneficial to follow a chronological approach to explain how Anadolu University is trying to integrate computer-supported learning into its distance programs (Figure 2).

Establishment of the Computer-Based Learning Centre can be regarded as the first serious attempt of Anadolu University in terms of computer integration. The Computer-Based Learning Centre was first established in 1989 to produce computer-supported learning courseware and to conduct research studies about effective use of computers into various instructional settings including open and distance learning. During the first year, 12 experts including instructional designers, programmers, and graphic artists started to work on designing and producing computer-based instructional materials for different audiences. In 1990-1991 the Centre designed and produced 300 hours of instructional software for primary science education in collaboration with the Ministry of National Education and IBM. In 1992, a series of software for mentally retarded learners, for "using the mouse," "object recognition," and "object matching" was developed.

Figure 2. Chronology of integrating computer-supported learning into Anadolu University's traditional distance courses

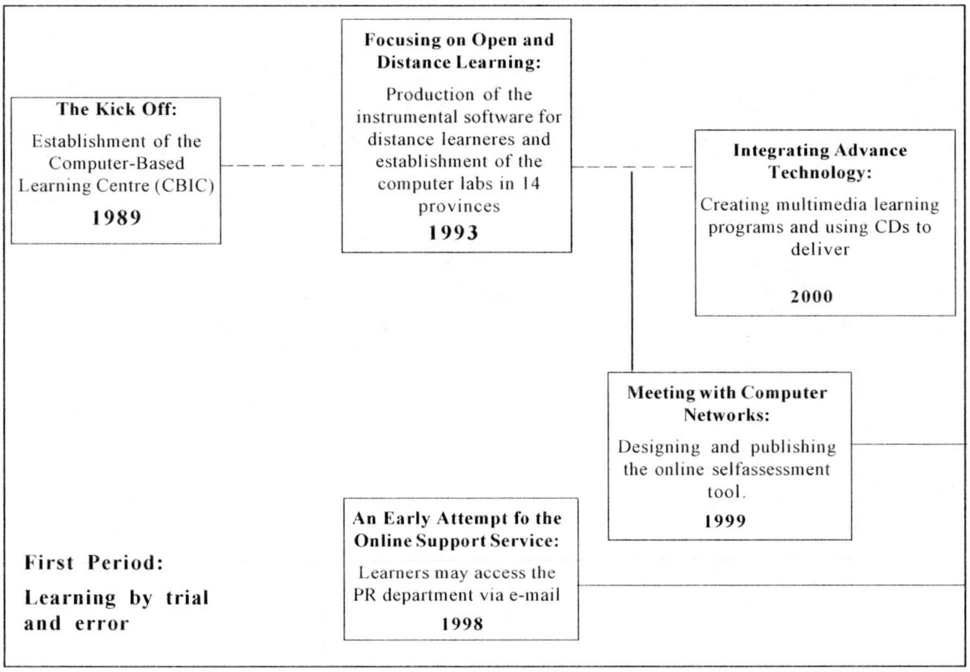

Figure 2. continued

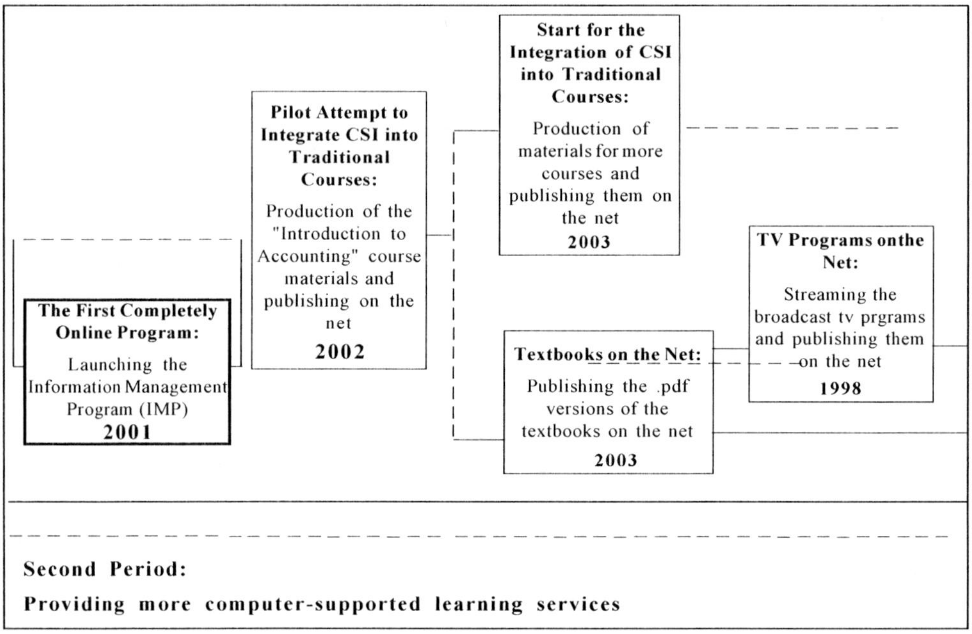

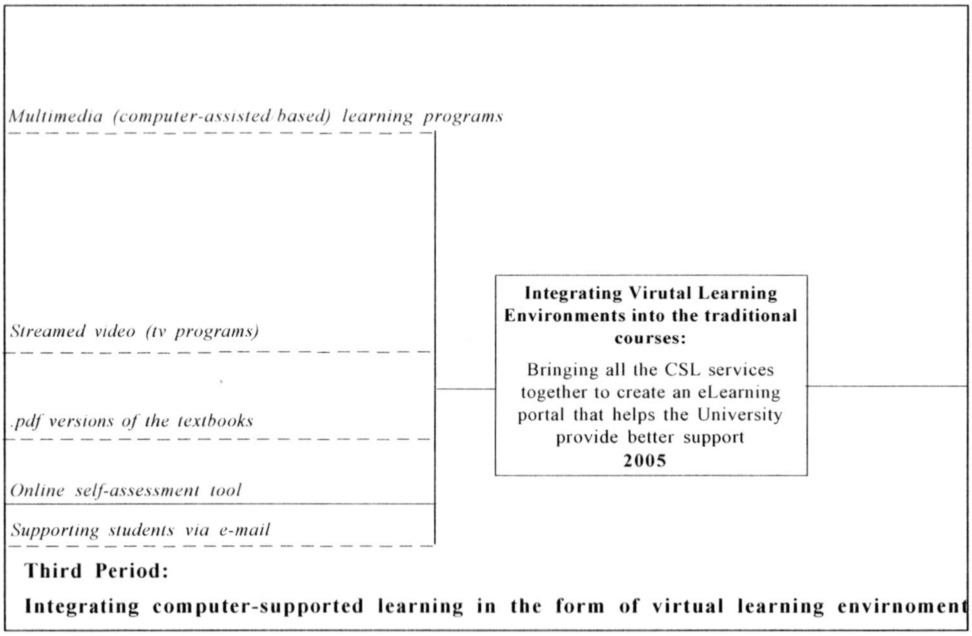

In 1993, the Centre started to focus on distance learning. In the first year, instructional software for three distance courses, "Introduction to Mathematics," "Statistics," and "English" were produced. This software was planned to be used in a computer-assisted learning context, in which computers were used to support textbook-based learning. In other words, the learners were still responsible for reading their textbooks in order to be successful in the exams, but they could voluntarily study the software that was produced to help learners comprehend better and reinforce what was written in the textbooks. The software also aimed to prepare the students for the exams. So, the software for each course included interactive content presentations, drill and practice sessions, and on-screen tools such as calculator, notepads, dictionary, and so forth. They were first developed for MS Windows 3.1 by using Asymetrix's Toolbook authoring system. The problem with using the instructional software was a managerial one, and continues to be one of the main issues of computer-supported learning in Turkey: learners' access to technology. To address this problem, Anadolu University planned to build computer labs through the country. During 1994-1995, 15 labs, each containing 20-30 personal computers, were established in 14 provinces of the country. Any distance learner who wanted to use the labs was able to reserve a computer for a designated time period, usually for two to three hours. A decade after the first courseware, the Computer Based Learning Centre has designed, produced, and revised 25 programs to be used in the labs. During this period, technology and the software used in the production have changed a lot, but the role of computers in instructional contexts has remained computer-assisted learning.

Although those labs are still functioning, several problems occurred over time. Keeping the hardware and software up to date, managing the labs, escalating cost of maintenance, and so forth, along with advances in access to computers and increasing demand for the computerized instruction forced administrators of the university to find new means of delivery. Thus, in 2001, the computer-supported learning software was revised, and multimedia components were added and published on CD-ROMs. For each course around 250,000 copies of these CD-ROMs were prepared and distributed to learners along with the textbooks. Therefore, the university provided an opportunity for those learners who have access to computers at homes, at work places, or at the Internet cafes to use the multimedia software.

Advances in computer-mediated communications have helped the administrators of Anadolu University offer different computer-supported learning services to the distance learners. For example, the Computer-Based Learning Centre has prepared an online self-test tool for the learners to assess their readiness for the exams. This tool allows learners to test themselves in any course they want to. The learners can log on to this tool with their student IDs from any location. In addition, each time a learner logs on the system, the tool recognizes the learners and presents a different set of questions. These questions are randomly selected by the tool. Experts in the Centre for the Research in Testing take a part in construction and revisions of the questions. The Computer-Based Learning Centre revises and updates the questions and the tool every year. The records show that an increasing number of learners are using this tool. In the 1999-2000 academic year, a total of 60,000 learners used the tools one million times, while in 2001-2002, the number of learners reached nearly 200,000. These learners logged on to the tool 4,000,000 times in 2001-2002. Since the kick off, approximately 450,000 learners used this tool to test themselves 22,000,000 times.

Demographic data about the distance learners have shown that quite a number of the learners who often use the online tools the university provides are working in information technology or related sectors and seeking a university degree. This phenomenon gave the administrators of the university the idea of offering a new program specially designed for the needs of these and similar sorts of learners. Because these learners already possess basic computer skills and the demand is related to the IT sector, knowledge about computer networks opens new dimensions for students. As a result, the university decided to offer a virtual learning environment particularly for those who work in IT related jobs. So, the first completely online degree program of the university, the Information Management Program (IMP), was launched in 2001.

IMP is an associates degree (two-year) program that requires the use of online technologies in instructional processes. This program is also the first online undergraduate level degree program in Turkey. It aims to help learners (1) gain the necessary skills to use required business software effectively and efficiently, (2) acquire the concepts and experience of Information Management in business, (3) attain the collaborative working experience and institutional communication through an Internet environment, and (4) acquire the necessary experience for the enterprise and management of the Internet environment.

After registering the program either through the Internet or through the Anadolu University's Offices, the learners receive instructions on learning processes as well as licensed software and instructional materials. The instructional materials are Web sites and tools, licensed software, textbooks, and video CDs. The Web sites and tools help learners learn the content. The Computer-Based Learning Center has produced 25 modules of online learning environments that provide interactive presentation of information, examples, and practices. The information is presented in different verbal and visual formats such as text, narration, and animation. The majority of the practices include multiple choice items with immediate feedback and links to the related content. These environments have been designed in a way that enables self-paced learning and easy navigation.

The online tools serve the need for synchronous and asynchronous interactions among learners, between learners and facilitators, as well as between learners and organizational and technological support staff. The learners are able to interact synchronously (chat) four hours a day for each course with the facilitators. They can also use asynchronous tools (e-mail) to get help from the facilitators and other staff. There are 60 facilitators (academic advisors) employed primarily for providing the learners academic (instructional) support. Each facilitator is an expert in one course content. For each course there are five facilitators. They do not only answer the learners' questions but also evaluate the assignments. In addition, for every course there is a coordinator whose main responsibility is to help and supervise the facilitators. The facilitators sometimes provide organizational and technical supports, too. However, there are staff that help to solve the learners' technical and organizational problems online as well as via phone.

The learners are also able to use video CDs produced by the CBIC. These CDs generally include around 40 hours of animated demonstrations about how to use the software. The videos on these CDs are also available online for the ones who have faster Internet connections. In addition, a series of textbooks are provided to learners as supplementary materials. Textbooks are the products of a private company and can be bought in any bookstore in Turkey. Anadolu University pays a fee to the publishing company for these textbooks. Also, an online environment called "Ders Arasi" (break time, as in schools) is provided for social interactions among students. In the Ders Arasi, students can come together and share their ideas, feelings, and experiences with each other without any monitoring. Additionally, students can have these kinds of interactions with mentors and staff, as well as course coordinators and administrators during synchronous and asynchronous online communications. Besides, IMP gives Web domain and space for students to build their own individual Web sites. Students are also able to join the student clubs in Anadolu University and meet with their on-campus counterparts.

The learners must take midterm and final exams. These exams must be administered face-to-face according to the Higher Education Council. So, the exams are held in 11 different provinces of the country. The course coordinators and the university representatives are sent to those provinces to monitor the exams. During and right after the exams the learners have the opportunity to meet face-to-face with the course coordinators. These meetings help the course coordinators get feedback about different issues and problems the learners face.

Previous experiences, especially in the multimedia production, the IMP, and integration of the online tool for self-test encouraged Anadolu University to use the Internet to deliver the multimedia (computer-assisted) learning materials. First of all, one of the previously produced multimedia courses about "Introduction to Accounting" was revised and reproduced by using Macromedia Flash in 2002. After having learners' positive remarks on this sort of use, the Computer-

Based Learning Centre focused on transforming other multimedia materials to online format and developing new ones for other courses. In the 2003-2004 academic year, online multimedia learning materials for 10 courses and in 2004-2005, materials for total 24 courses were available to the distance learners. In 2006 it is planned to add 26 more course materials to the already available 24 courses. Those courses that learners usually have difficulty understanding were given priority to be transformed to virtual environments. During 2002-2005, more than 150,000 learners logged on to these virtual environments more than one million times.

In addition to multimedia (computer-supported) learning materials, FlashPaper and/or Portable Document Format (PDF) versions of the textbooks have also been presented in these virtual environments since 2003. This service, actually, was the result of a critical incident (a delay during the distribution of the textbooks) that occurred during the beginning of the 2003-2004 academic year, but the learners requested the same service for the following years. In 2004-2005, 115 textbooks were transformed to FlashPaper and/or PDF formats and published in the virtual environments of the courses. Up to June 2005, more than 500,000 downloads of these materials were reported.

Moreover, experiences in transforming textbooks to e-book format along with diffusion of ADSL usage throughout the country has promoted the idea of using these virtual environments to distribute digitized versions of the television programs originally produced for broadcasting. So, the television programs produced in the ETV were streamed in the Computer-Based Learning Centre to be integrated into virtual environments of the courses in 2004. Until May 2005, 421 television programs, belonging to 46 different courses, have been streamed and published in the virtual environments. Approximately 100,000 learners executed two million downloads. The numbers reveal that this service helped the learners who have difficulty watching television programs.

Furthermore, since 1998 the learners have had the opportunity to reach the administrators of the distance programs via e-mail. Every year the university receives 15,000-20,000 e-mails from learners. The majority of these e-mails are related to managerial issues, and only a small portion is about requesting pedagogical support. Before May 2005, the public relations department of the Open Education Faculty was receiving, categorizing, responding, and/or forwarding mail to the students. In May 2005, a pilot project was initiated to improve the effectiveness and efficiency of this service. For the project, a moderator and a content specialist were assigned for each course. Also, a virtual forum environment was established for each course so that learners can see each others' questions and the content specialists' responses. Moderators first categorize the messages posted in the environment and forward them to either the content specialist or the related staff. Later, moderators receive the specialist's or other staff's responses and post them in the forum. The administrators hope this pilot project will provide an insight about possible pros and cons of implementing fully interactive computer-supported learning in the distance programs. Initial results are quite promising. So, this service is planned to be extended to 50 courses.

On the other hand, the university has decided to bring all these services together and present them to the learners as a learning support package rather than stand alone services. Therefore, in the first half of 2005, the Computer-Based Learning Centre specialists focused on design, development, utilization, and management of an online portal, titled as "e-Learning Portal of Open Education Faculty." Any learner may use her/his personal identity number to log on the portal and choose a course to study and use these components embedded into this virtual environment. Since its launching in May 2005, 108,330 learners logged on to the portal 1,123,804 times, and sometimes, around 5,000 learners simultaneously used it.

The e-learning portal includes e-television, e-book, e-exam, e-practice (multimedia learning materials), and e-tutoring components. The e-television part of the portal contains streamed format (MPEG4) of broadcast television programs. Their average size is around 22 MB and can be downloaded in 10-50 minutes according to the connection type. Similarly, e-book consists of PDF—or Flash Paper—format of the textbooks, and learners can easily download these files onto their hard disks. The e-exam part of the portal provides randomized self-test for midterm, final, and makeup exams. The e-practice part helps learners access the multimedia self-paced learning materials. Usually drill and practice type of an instructional strategy is employed in these materials. However, they also include brief explanations about the topic, short quizzes, and some other tools like notepad, calculator, and dictionary. The main reason for choosing the drill and practice is learners' expectations and needs. In other words, unfortunately, the Turkish education system is very instructive, and the assessment of the achievement depends only on the exam scores in every level of the system. So, almost all learners enter the distance programs as well as others with a performance-based goal orientation. Getting a good grade is more important than learning. Therefore, instructional designers found the drill and practice method as being the most appealing strategy for the learners. Evaluation studies support this decision. E-tutor is actually not a new service the university provides its distance learners. But, before the portal, communication was one-to-one. In the portal, learners can see other learners' questions and answers of the tutors to these questions. So, it saves time and energy for both learners and tutors. However, the portal does not allow learner-to-learner interaction currently due to large number of learners. The server and the Internet bandwidth do not allow this sort of an interaction.

The portal and the included tools were all created in house. The programmers used MS Visual Studio applications (e.g., ASP.net) to create the environment. The portal was located on an IBM445 server with 4 GB RAM and around 1 TB hard disk capacity. Its uplink speed is currently 34 MB. Their technical support personnel keep the server running 24 hours a day and seven days a week.

In sum, Anadolu University's story about integrating computer-supported learning into its distance programs has started with computer-based instruction context; later, computer-assisted instruction context was employed, and now it is in the process of a transition to a virtual learning environment context. However, in every context and almost in every distance program of the university, the computers have been playing a support role. In other words, textbooks are still the main instructional media, and the learners are responsible for the content of these textbooks. So, they must study them in order to be successful in the exams that are constructed according to the content of the textbooks. On the other hand, using computer-supported learning materials is a voluntary activity, and the learners are not responsible for the content of these materials. In addition, computers cannot be used for assessing the learners' achievement in any program, except the Information Management Program. Also, interaction among learners via computer networks is very limited.

Among the main motives for this sort of use of the computers are learners' limited access to technology, infrastructure restrictions, shortage of basic computer skills among learners, limited number of experienced instructors and instructional designers, and, above all, enormous number of enrolled learners in every course. Unfortunately, as mentioned before, the home computer ownership percentage is still around 12.5% of the whole population (approximately 70 million), and only 7% of these have Internet connection. People usually access computers at work places and Internet cafés. But studies have shown that learners hesitate to use computers for learning purposes in these environments owing to inappropriateness of the environments for learning (noise and lack of privacy). Also, computers are still new to many people in Turkey, especially for those who live in rural and underdeveloped regions. So the majority of the population still has a lack of basic computer skills. Similarly, technology-based/supported teaching is quite new for the majority of university faculties. Many professors still prefer to lecture without the use of technology. In addition, the field of instructional design is still in an infancy stage. The number of experienced instructional designers, who either hold a degree or are experienced in effective use of technology in the learning process, is extremely limited (less than 20). Finally, it is difficult to manage the large number of learners (in the freshman courses the number reaches 250,000, and the total is around one million). Although Anadolu University is aware of the significance of interaction in distance learning and the capacity of computer networks, the large number of distance learners restricts the university's ability to transform education into a more interactive learning experience. Even now, during the peek hit hours, the servers and the bandwidth create problems. Although a government agent provides the Internet services to the Universities as well as other institutions and individuals and the university gets one of the biggest bandwidths (70 Mbps ULAKNET and 38 Mbps TTNET) from Turkish Telecomm, it is still not enough. Despite the shortcomings of the model that Anadolu University employs, a limited number of studies conducted to examine the effects and the efficiency of the model suggest promising results. For instance, Mutlu, Ozogut, and Yilmaz (2004) investigated the relationship between frequency of students' visits to these environments and their exam scores. They found out that there is a positive relationship between these two constructs, meaning that students who visit the course open learning environments more often and spend longer times there have better scores in the exams than those who do not or seldom use these environments. Other studies (e.g., Mutlu, Ozogut-Erorta, Kara, & Aydln, 2005; Ozkul, 2003) have also shown similar results favoring the use of computer-supported learning in their studies.

Therefore, the university is trying to improve the computer-supported learning integration into its distance programs. For instance, the Computer-Based Learning Centre of the University is working on preparing audio for the textbooks. Learners who have a reading disability might benefit from having MP3 format of their audio textbooks. These audios will be published in the e-learning portal and will be available to all learners. Additionally, the university is working with Turkish Telecomm to double and triple its bandwidth. Therefore, the learners will be able to use the e-learning portal more effectively. In addition, the university is also focusing on how to establish a system that facilitates building virtual learning communities among its distance learners as well as tutors.

Finally, Anadolu University has been working on transforming its traditional distance programs to up-to-date advanced systems by integrating computer-supported learning into these programs. In that way, the university may provide a better, more democratic and equal learning opportunity to those who need a higher education and those who want to improve their knowledge and skills.

Future of Computer-Supported Distance Learning

Before summarizing what we predict about the future of computer-supported learning in open and distance learning, we would like to remind our readers how a well-known telegraph company evaluated the telephone technology a century ago: "This telephone has too many shortcomings to be seriously considered as a means of communication. The device is inherently of no value to us" (cited in Time, July 1996, p. 54). Making assumptions in any field involving some sort of technology is very risky. However, past experiences, current developments, and research studies help us make predictions about computer-supported learning and distance learning. Here are some of them:

- Integration of computer-supported learning, especially in open or virtual learning environments context, in traditional distance learning programs will speed up, but correspondence type of or textbook-based study will survive at least for a while because of its capacity to provide instruction to masses at lesser cost.
- Hybrid courses and programs will be widespread. Computer-supported learning blurs the gap between distance and classroom learning. Distance learning providers, especially those who offer e-learning in corporate settings, try to integrate some sort of same time same place components to make their instructions more "classroom-like" (e.g., blended learning), while an increasing number of educators use computers to support in-class learning. Soon, we will not see so many differences between distance and classroom learning.
- More and more institutions will invest in education to make a profit. Actually, education has been a good sector to invest in for some time. So, educational institutions have been looking for new marketplaces to sell their products—courses, instructional materials, and so forth. Computer-supported learning helps these institutions to reach those markets. We will most probably observe more for-profit institutions in the field of education and more educational institutions trying to market their goods and services to make a profit.
- As a consequence of the above development, global/international education (multinational, multi-cultural education) will be a hot topic. More studies will focus on investigating effective methods of teaching and using various media in multi-cultural environments.
- Additionally the same development will force institutions to work collaboratively. Institutions that want to extend their target learners are looking for partners from all over the world. So, we will come across more cooperation among institutions from different nations.
- There will be computer-based tools that combine audio, video, and communication technologies. While the sizes get smaller, these new tools will have advanced capabilities and will be available to greater numbers of people. Personal digital assistants (PDAs) or pocket PCs and cell phones are good examples of these tools. These tools will facilitate the m-learning (mobile-learning) applications.

- Multimedia-based communications will replace current text-based instructional communications. In almost all advanced e-learning initiatives, communication among learners and between learners and facilitators is essentially text-based (e-mail, chat, forum, etc.). However, soon learning environments will include more tools that will help participants feel like they are in the same place at the same time.

These are just some of our predictions. There will undoubtedly be more changes. The task ahead for distance learning providers such as Anadolu University is trying to foresee the developments before they are widely diffused and integrated into programs.

Conclusion

Advances in computer-supported learning have fostered the growth of open and distance learning. Traditional distance education providers have been feeling pressure to integrate some form of computer-supported learning into their programs in order to be able to survive. Anadolu University of Turkey is one of these mega universities of the world. It has been providing open and distance higher education to a great number (approximately one million) of Turkish citizens who live in Turkey, Europe, and Northern Cyprus. Although the majority of its distance programs are traditional, textbook-based, the university has been trying to transform these traditional programs in accordance to the current and future trends via computer-supported learning. Efforts toward this transformation started in the form of computer-based instruction during the beginning of the 1990s and now are focusing on building virtual learning environments. One of these environments, titled "e-Learning Portal," was launched in May 2005. Actually this portal is an interface that brings all the previous stand alone computer-supported learning applications together for easy access to these resources. The portal includes an electronic version of the textbooks, ready to download versions of the broadcast television programs, instructional software in the context of computer-assisted instruction, tools for learners to test their development (self-test), and a communication tool to get pedagogical and managerial support.

However, transferring a traditional, textbook-based, self-paced learning system into a computer-supported learning system was not an easy job, and required a thorough planning due to the large body of learners, lack of sufficient technological infrastructure, the majority of learners' limited access to computers and computer related products, and some legislative problems. Therefore, all the efforts of Anadolu University including the e-Learning Portal have had to be a supplement to correspondence study, or an extra resource for learners. The question was "if we build it, will they come?" On the basis of results of a few studies and figures derived form logs, the answer is YES; a large number of the university distance learners have benefited from the computer-supported learning materials.

The next step will be to make these supplementary services integral to the entire distance program, in other words, completing the e-transformation from providing instruction via traditional media to building learning with technology environments. E-transformation is not easy, but Anadolu University as well as other traditional distance education providers should work toward greater progress in integrating technology into learning environments in order to offer more effective, efficient, appealing, flexible, equal, and democratic learning opportunities.

References

Askar, P. (2005). Distance education in Turkey. In C. Howard, J. Boettcher, L. Justice, K. Schenk, P. L. Rogers, & G. A. Berg (Eds.), *Encyclopedia of distance learning* (Vol. 2, pp. 635-640). Hershey, PA: Idea Group Reference.

Bollag, B. (2001, June 15). Developing countries turn to distance education. *The Chronicle of Higher Education* (p. A29).

Cagiltay, K. (2001). *Uzaktan eitim: Ba_arlya giden yol teknolojide mi yoksa pedagojide mi?* [Distance education: Does the road to success in technology or in pedagogy?] Retrieved February 2, 2005, from http://www.teknoturk.org/docking/yazilar/tt000037-yazi.htm

Daniel, J. S. (1996). *Mega universities and knowledge media: Technology strategies for higher education*. London: Kogan Page.

Duffy, T., & Kirkley, J. (2004). Introduction: Theory and practice in distance education. In T. Duffy & J. Kirkley (Eds.), *Learner-centered theory and practice in distance education: Cases from higher education* (pp. 3-13). Mahwah, NJ: Lawrence Erlbaum.

Farrell, G. M. (2001). Introduction. In G. M. Farrell (Ed.), *The development of virtual education: A global perspective* (pp. 1-11). Vancouver, Canada: The Commonwealth of Learning.

Farrell, G. M. (2001). Introduction. In G. M. Farrell (Ed.), *The changing faces of virtual education* (pp. 1-9). Vancouver, Canada: The Commonwealth of Learning.

Garrison, D. R., & Archer, W. (2000). A model of meaningful learning activities in higher education: Thinking ahead to desired learning outcomes. In *Proceedings of the 30th Annual Conference of the Canadian Society for the Study of Higher Education* (pp. 42-45).

Gunawardena, C. N., & McIsaac, M. S. (2003). Distance education. In D. H. Jonassen (Ed.), *Handbook of research in educational communications and technology* (2nd ed., pp. 355-395). Mahwah, NJ: Lawrence Erlbaum Associates.

Harasim, L. (1990). Online education: An environment for collaboration and intellectual amplification. In L. Harasim (Ed.), *Online education: Perspectives on a new environment* (pp. 39-66). New York: Praeger Publishers.

McIsaac, M. S., & Murphy, K. L. (1988). *Turkey: Does distance education meet national educational priorities*. Paper presented at the 14th ICDE World Conference, Oslo, Norway.

McIsaac, M. S., Murphy, K., & Demiray, U. (1988). Examining distance education in Turkey. *Distance Education, 9*(1) 106-114.

Mutlu, M. E., Cetinoz, N., & Avdan, H. (2004). *Internete dayali alistirma yazilimlarinin etkinligi [Effectiveness of Internet-based practice software]*. Paper presented at the 4th International Symposium on Educational Technologies, Sakarya, Turkey.

Mutlu, M. E., Ozogut-Erorta, O., Kara, E., & Aydln, S. (2005, April). *E-Ogrenme hizmetlerinin basariya etkisi [Effects of e-learning services on achievement]*. Paper presented at the 2. Polis Bilisim Sempozyumu, Ankara, Turkey.

Mutlu, M. E., Ozogut-Erorta, O., & Y1lmaz, U. (2004 October). *Efficiency of e-learning in open education*. Paper presented at the First International Conference on Innovations in Learning for the Future: E-Learning, Istanbul, Turkey.

Niemiec, R. P., & Walberg, H. J. (1989). From teaching machines to microcomputers: Some milestones in the history of computer-based instruction. *Journal of Research on Computing in Education, 21*, 263-276.

Ozkul, A. E. (2001). Anadolu University distance education system from emergence to 21st century. *The Turkish Online Journal of Distance Education 2*(1). Retrieved November 5, 2003, from http://tojde.anadolu.edu.tr/tojde3/2/ekremtxt.htm

Ozkul, A. E. (2003, March). Distance education in Turkey: Anadolu University. Paper presented at *the 2nd Conference on Distance Learning*, Patras, Greece: Hellenic Open University.

Potashnik, M., & Capper, J. (1998). Distance education: Growth and diversity. *Finance & Development, 35*(1). Retrieved November 5, 2003, from http://www.imf.org/external-/pubs/ft/fandd/1998/03/index.htm

Reddy, V. V., & Manjulika, S. (Eds.). (2000). *The world of open and distance learning.* New Delhi, India: Viva Books.

Schrum, L. (1998). Online education: A study of emerging pedagogy. In B. Cahoon (Ed.), *Adult learning and the Internet* (Vol. 78, pp. 53-61). San Francisco: Jossey-Bass.

Simonson, M. R., & Thompson, A. (1997). *Educational computing foundations*. Columbus, OH: Merrill/Prince Hall.

TUBITAK-BILTEN (2000). *Bilgi teknolojileri yayginlik ve kullanimi arastlrma raporu [Report on diffusion and use of information technologies].* Ankara, Turkey.

Wilson, B. G. (1996). *Constructivist learning environments: Case studies in instructional design*. Englewood Cliffs, NJ: Educational Technology Publications.

Section II

Main Issues and Trends in CSL

Chapter VI

E-Learning: Trends and Future Development

Bernhard Ertl, Bundeswehr University Munich, Germany

Katrin Winkler, Ludwigs-Maximilians-University Munich, Germany

Heinz Mandl, Ludwigs-Maximilians-University Munich, Germany

Abstract

During the last several years, high expectations have surrounded e-learning initiatives in companies, universities, and schools. Presently, however, this optimism has often given way to disillusionment. In this paper, we will postulate three central theses to help counteract both this process of disillusionment and the problems that were encountered during the initial euphoric phase of e-learning. The theses provide a framework for realizing the potential of e-learning in a beneficial and meaningful way. Firstly, this new technology should be applied to learning only when its use reflects a new culture of learning. Secondly, e-learning has to be integrated into the existing training culture of an organization. Thirdly, the implementation of e-learning should focus on the learner rather than on technology. To substantiate these theses, we will provide examples that illustrate sustainable implementations of e-learning.

Introduction

During the last decade, there have been significant developments in computer technology. With the increased use of modern computer and communication technologies, a new buzzword was also born: e-learning. The term e-learning is used as a label for learning that takes place using new electronic media. This kind of learning, which relies heavily on information and communication technologies, is a hot topic in the field of corporate learning. According to eLearningNews (2005), many implementations of e-learning can be found in companies that are dedicated to providing further on the job training for the company's employees. However, educational institutions, such as schools or universities, were also highly optimistic about the potential of this new kind of learning. There was the hope of being able to deliver courses of higher quality to more students at less expense. In short, e-learning was associated with *very* high expectations. It was considered to be a flexible, efficient, and relatively cheap style of learning. Consequently, just two years ago, many journals had headlines such as "Learners can access learning material anytime and anywhere, whether at home or on the road." Currently, there are questions about the degree to which these expectations can be satisfied.

This chapter aims to answer these questions. To this end, we will firstly define the concept of e-learning. Based on the latest research studies, we will analyze the degree to which e-learning can satisfy the expectations that have come about in recent years. We will then postulate three theses that provide a framework for the beneficial and meaningful realization of the potentials of e-learning. We will substantiate these theses using three particular examples of e-learning within university and business settings.

E-Learning

The term of "e-learning" seems to be derived from word creations like "e-mail" and means learning with support of electronic media—in particular with the support of computers and the Internet. There are many scenarios for realizing e-learning, which include computer-based trainings (CBT), Web-based trainings (WBT), and different styles of online learning, for example, virtual lectures, virtual seminars, or virtual tutorials. Computer-based trainings (CBTs) describe programs for individual learning with computers (Learnframe, 2005), which have been used since the early 1980s. This kind of e-learning is widely used for training on the job. The term Web-based trainings (WBTs) is used for learning in network environments like the Internet or a company's intranet. WBTs rely on information systems, for example, databases, and learning programs with, for example, exercises and tests. From this point of view, WBTs are technically higher developed CBTs, which rely on network technologies but use still the same instructional design methods as CBTs. When using the term "online learning," one often imagines a virtual classroom, which is the space or platform in which a virtual course teaches the learning material. In this scenario, teachers and learners are based at different locations and enter one virtual classroom. Online courses rely on an e-learning platform, which is often just called the learning platform. This platform is a system that allows the creation and realization of a virtual learning center within an institution or company. As a minimum, this platform supports the administration of e-learning courses. The platform can provide different kinds of learning media and keeps track of user data. Furthermore, many learning platforms have sophisticated features. For example, they may provide media libraries, enable virtual communication between learners, offer search functions, and often supply an individual workspace for each learner (Volery & Lord, 2000). Learning platforms often reflect the particular needs of an organization or company and are developed further on this basis.

When examining the technological aspects of different e-learning scenarios, one can distinguish between distributive, interactive, and collaborative technologies (Back, Seufert, & Kramhöller, 1998). Distributive technologies are aimed at information transfer and focus mainly on the teacher, who is providing the information. These technologies make use of traditional learning paradigms, which means that the teacher transmits information to the learners, for example, by making lecture contents available online. Interactive technologies focus on the learner's individual acquisition of knowledge and skills. They can be characterized as learner centered, because they allow interactions between the learner and the learning environment, for example, when completing tests in a WBT. In contrast, collaborative technologies support team-centered learning. In this scenario, the learning environment supports the interaction of the learners with one another. Their learning process consists of content-specific discussions and collaborative reflections. The main focus lies on the learners' exchange of knowledge and experiences and on collaborative problem solving. These activities take place in virtual classrooms, and the learning environment provides discussion boards and chat rooms for this purpose.

High Expectations for E-Learning

The expectations of companies regarding e-learning were varied and reflected the optimism companies had when this new technology was launched. The opportunity for flexible learning, which is independent of time and space, was rated the highest in terms of the companies' expectations (Haben, 2002). The second priority was the potential for applying e-learning as a timesaving mechanism. E-learning's ability to facilitate self-directed learning was ranked third. This was ranked even higher than the optimism concerning a reduction in training costs when using e-learning. However, the advantage of a higher quality of learning had the lowest priority in the ranking of companies' expectations. In sum, the expectations regarding e-learning were quite high. Despite these high expectations, a recent study disclosed that only a third of the major companies used e-learning (Harhoff, & Küpper, 2002). Furthermore, the expectations regarding e-learning were only satisfied to a moderate degree (Bernard, et al. 2004). To date, only the aspects of flexible learning and the reduced time needed have received positive scores (Haben, 2002; Harhoff, & Küpper, 2002).

Reservations about e-learning stem from problems with the manner in which this new kind of learning was implemented. Besides underestimating of the expense of e-learning, the lack of employee acceptance was one of the biggest problems (Bürg, Kronburger, & Mandl, 2004). A further reason cited by the companies was the lack of high quality e-learning courses offered by external providers. Furthermore, the courses available mainly covered IT applications, specific business topics, foreign languages, and trainings for particular products and did not fulfill companies' needs (Haben, 2002). A further obstacle to the success of e-learning is the lack of integration within the existing culture of training. In the common use of e-learning courses, they are viewed as being of an additive nature rather than playing a substantial part in the companies' training culture. Problems often arise when planning the implementation of e-learning due to the complexity of some projects and due to the incorrect estimation of the time required for such projects. However, despite these obstacles and problems, most companies plan to increase their application of e-learning, even if assigning reduced budgets for these projects.

The situation is similar with respect to schools and universities. In contrast to recent years during which much money was available for the foundation of virtual universities and e-learning initiatives, current optimism has decreased, and the budgets have decreased (Mandl, & Winkler , 2004). The problems are similar to those encountered within companies. Time has shown that simply adding new technologies to traditional classrooms provides few benefits for the education in schools and universities (Scardamalia, & Bereiter, 1994). Many approaches for implementing e-learning are still technology driven and lack relevance for the user.

With respect to the opportunities and limitations of e-learning, we postulate three central theses, which should be considered when implementing e-learning. Using these theses as a framework for the introduction of e-learning could counteract the problems, which were encountered in the first euphoric phase of e-learning. Furthermore, the theses could help to build courses that are able to satisfy these expectations. Our theses are:

1. The application of new technologies and e-learning is only beneficial for learners when it is based on a new philosophy of learning and teaching.
2. E-learning has to be integrated in the existing training culture of an organization. To achieve this, integrative approaches should be applied, such as blended learning.
3. Professional strategies of implementation are prerequisite to the beneficial realization of e-learning in schools, universities, and companies. These strategies should be learner-centered instead of technology driven.

In the following section, we will elaborate upon these theses and illustrate them using examples.

Thesis 1: A New Culture of Learning

In many learning scenarios, the teacher plays an active role, and the learner simply acts as a passive recipient of the knowledge presented. This mechanism can be found in many different institutions for education and also reflects the experiences of many learners (Reinmann-Rothmeier & Mandl, 2001a). Such scenarios provide a very systematic and controlled kind of learning, which is based on two main assumptions:

1. the development of knowledge results from learning facts and routine; and
2. knowledge is an entity, which can be transferred from one person (the teacher) to another person (the learner).

Applying these assumptions in the context of teacher-centered approaches often generates inert knowledge. This can be defined as knowledge that has been learned theoretically and without any situational context. Therefore, learners often are unable to apply this knowledge to a real world situation (Renkl, Mandl, & Gruber, 1996). In an attempt to counteract this problem, a new constructivist philosophy of learning and teaching has recently emerged. The aim of this new culture of learning is to allow for the generation of applicable knowledge to fill the gap between knowledge acquisition and knowledge application (Reinmann-

Rothmeier & Mandl, 2001a). The core of this new philosophy is active knowledge construction, which means that knowledge does not result from passive reception. In contrast, learners acquire knowledge through an active process mediated by the individual's prior knowledge, motivation, and learning prerequisites. This view of knowledge construction implies a change in basic assumptions about learning. Knowledge can no longer be considered an entity, which can be passed from one person to another. According to this viewpoint, learning is an active, constructive, situated, social, and emotional process (Reinmann-Rothmeier & Mandl, 2001a). Learning can be described in detail as follows:

- **Learning is an active process:** Only the active involvement of the learner enables learning.
- **Learning is a self-directed process:** Within the context of learning, the learner takes active control and responsibility for his/her own learning activities.
- **Learning is a constructive process:** A learner can only acquire and use new knowledge if he/she can embed the new knowledge within existing knowledge structures and interpret it on the basis of individual experiences.
- **Learning is a social process:** Learning is mainly an interactive event and is influenced by social components.
- **Learning is a situated process:** Knowledge acquisition takes place in a specific context and is linked to this context. Therefore, learning has to be viewed as a situated process.
- **Learning is an emotional process:** Emotions with respect to social values and achievement greatly influence learning. The emotional component is particularly important for the motivation of the learners.

Realizing learning environments according to these principles has shown that learners also need a certain amount of instruction to learn effectively (Mandl, Gräsel, & Fischer, 1998; Mandl, Gruber, & Renkl, 1996). This instructional support is necessary even if learners take an active role in the learning process and differs depending on individual learner prerequisites and skills (Kollar & Fischer, 2004; Renkl, Gruber, & Mandl, 1999; Weinberger, Ertl, Fischer, & Mandl, 2005). Highly self-directed learning often results in cognitive overload (Sweller, Van Merrienboër, & Paas, 1998) for the learners (Mandl, Ertl, & Kopp, in press). Learners need support when questions arise and when they encounter problems, for example by receiving feedback from a tutor (Zumbach & Reimann, 2003).

Designing problem-based learning environments (Dochy, Segers, Van den Bossche, & Gijbels, 2003; Lave & Wenger, 1991) can be a pragmatic method for

Figure 1. Construction and instruction in the problem-based learning approach (Reinmann-Rothmeier & Mandl, 2001a)

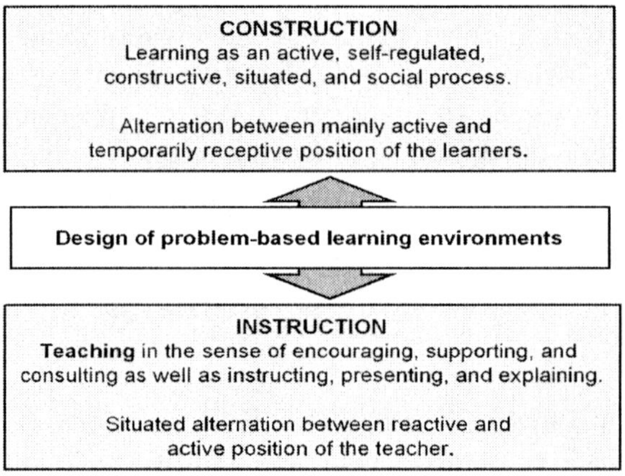

implementing this new culture of learning and teaching. The basis for problem-based learning environments is a balance between construction and instruction (Figure 1). Thus, the core of this philosophy is that an active learner receives assistance throughout the learning process by instructional design (Reinmann-Rothmeier & Mandl, 2001a). This implies that a learner has the opportunity to use self-directed learning, which promotes active knowledge construction. However, this learning takes place in a designed learning environment, which provides learning material and instruction. Problem-based learning environments are highly dependent on context, described in detail as follows:

- **Learning in an authentic context:** Learning stems from authentic problems, which are meaningful and relevant for the learners. The use of realistic problems and authentic cases provides a strong link to the situations in which this knowledge can be applied. Furthermore, authenticity increases the students' interest in the subject matter.
- **Learning in multiple contexts:** Learners find themselves in different authentic situations and are encouraged to apply the knowledge learned when dealing with different problems. To this end, the learning process may integrate different sample applications of the subject matter. Multiple contexts can support the acquisition of knowledge that can be flexibly rehearsed, applied, and developed in different situations.

- **Learning in a social context:** Learning and working collaboratively is an essential part of the learning process, for example, when the learners collaboratively solve an authentic case.
- **Learning with instructional support:** Learners receive valuable resources for their learning activities and can contact an advisor or coach when they encounter problems.

The power of problem-based learning results from two sources: collaborative learning and self-directed learning. The features of the new information and communication technologies offer great potential for the implementation of problem-based learning and for the realization of collaborative and self-directed learning scenarios. When comparing problem-based learning to traditional classes that offer only a limited opportunity for each learner to play an active role in the learning process, one can get a sound appreciation for the potential of problem-based learning. In traditional courses, the learning environment, the learning duration, and the path through the learning process are preset. In such environments, the learner only occasionally has the opportunity to be active, for example, when answering a question. Furthermore the effectiveness of such actions is very limited with respect to the time this action takes and the benefits for the learner. Moreover, there are only limited opportunities for active and constructive learning. New media offer various opportunities that can have beneficial effects on the learner's motivation, for example, the ability to choose one's own learning path through a learning environment (Deci & Ryan, 1992). Furthermore, the learner can often proceed at his/her own pace through the learning process and chose the duration and the speed of learning.

However, studies regarding the acceptance of e-learning show that the design of many learning environments is qualitatively lacking with respect to these criteria (Haben, 2002). Many learning environments lack a sound didactic structure and do not consider new learning philosophies. They often apply a systematic approach of knowledge transfer in virtual learning environments exactly as used in traditional lectures. There are many "long-winded" learning environments, which can be distinguished from a book only with respect to the method of turning pages, which is done by a mouse click. Other learning environments try to make up for the absence of any kind of didactic approach by using multimedia fireworks and animations (Mayer, Hegarty, & Mayer, 2005). However, the application of adapted didactics is essential for considering e-learning as a future approach to education.

Example: An Introductory Course in Media Didactics

As an example for the introduction of a new culture of learning and teaching and the problem-based learning approach, we will describe a university course about the didactic design of multimedia learning environments. This course was provided by the Virtual University of Bavaria (VHB) and offered to teachers, who wished to acquire specific knowledge in the area of didactics with new media. The course was designed according to the problem-based learning approach (Dochy et al., 2003; Reinmann-Rothmeier, & Mandl, 2001a) and includes virtual and co-present phases. The conception of this course has three main goals with respect to content and didactics. Participants should:

1. **become familiar with different styles** of applying problem-based learning with new media in the classroom;
2. **acquire theoretical knowledge** about problem-based learning and learning with new media; and
3. **acquire skills for planning** their own projects for applying problem-based learning with new media in the classroom.

This introductory course to media didactics starts with a kickoff workshop, which provides a general course overview, an overview of the course contents, and an introduction to the learning platform used for hosting the course. A further goal of this workshop is for students to get to know their tutors. Furthermore, students have the chance to form small groups for collaboration during the virtual phases.

These small groups work on five cases during the virtual phase. These multimedia cases show the application of new media in the classroom with respect to different subject areas. The example of "learning stages" gives an exemplary glimpse at the conception of these cases.

"Learning stages" has its origins in a classroom project about the self-directed learning of mathematics in higher education. It was developed by a school in Germany and founded by a governmental project for applying new media in the classroom. The "learning stages" project aims at disclosing an individual view on mathematics to students, which provides insights for solving practical problems by applying mathematics. Furthermore, "learning stages" should help learners through its problem-based design and by using self-directed learning with new media. "Learning stages" is directed at students of the 11th grade (secondary education). In a manner

similar to "circle training", students work on different tasks in 21 stages, which are realized by learning programs on the computer (Altenburg, Arnold, & Schürmann, 2003). Core characteristics of the project are different content-specific views on mathematics, different levels of task difficulty and problems, which are closely related to students' daily experiences. In the "learning stages" environment, it is mandatory for students to work on some of the stages. In addition, they may choose to work on the other stages. This project supports self-directed and collaborative learning with new media, and learners can independently control the results of their work. As the case of "learning stages" shows, the content-specific focus of the course on introduction to media didactics emphasizes self-directed and collaborative learning and the specific support of these skills for learners in the classroom.

When collaborating on the cases, students use discussion boards for their collaborative negotiation. During the entire online phase, a tutor helps learners with questions or when problems are encountered. Furthermore, learners may also benefit from using a content-specific learning unit about problem-based learning, which contains the theory and possible applications of this approach. This unit provides a background for the students when solving the cases. In addition to working on the case solutions, learners also work collaboratively on a transfer task to increase the applicability of their knowledge. In this task, the students design a framework for applying problem-based learning in the classroom by collaborative negotiation in small groups. The course ends with a closing workshop, which allows learners to present the frameworks they have designed and encourages them to discuss these frameworks. This introductory course to media didactics realizes several aspects of problem-based learning:

- **Authentic context:** The authentic context of the course involves the integration of five example cases, which are derived from realizations in the classroom. The description of such pilot projects, which already have been realized in the classroom, is therefore the basis for acquiring knowledge about the didactic realization of new media in the classroom.
- **Multiple contexts:** Cases relating to different subjects and different grades provide learning within multiple contexts. Furthermore, the didactic procedure is different in each of the cases. The discussion of these cases in newsgroups also provides different perspectives for the learners and supports them in discussing the case solutions and the project specifics.
- **Social context:** For integrating the social context, learners meet at the kickoff workshop and form small groups of four for the collaborative

negotiations that take place during the online phase. When the work on a case is finished, learners have to engage in individual or group assignments. These group assignments are discussed and solved through a shared discussion board, which is provided by the learning environment. In this way, students reflect on their own case solution and also consider the other group's solutions.

- **Instructional support:** The learning environment also provides a newsgroup for questions and problems encountered by the students. The tutors use this newsgroup for quickly providing feedback to the learners. Furthermore, the learning environment provides some cues for working on the task solution. These cues may be either a reference to literature or short summaries of the contents of the particular case. Learners and groups receive detailed feedback on their task solutions. This feedback contains evaluations of the solutions and of the group's collaborative procedure.

Results of an evaluation show that the acceptance of this course was rather high (Hasenbein, 2003). Learners particularly valued the comprehensibility of the learning material and the didactic design. Learners stated that the cases aided comprehension and that the authenticity helped illustrate the learning material. Furthermore, they valued the ability to navigate their way through the learning material in a self-directed manner. These attitudes are reflected in high learner motivation and also in the learner's high estimation of their own learning outcomes.

Now we will move from the example of a problem-based learning environment and will focus on our second thesis concerning a specific implementation of blended learning.

Thesis 2: Blended Learning

Experience has shown that learners in online courses appreciate having face-to-face meetings alongside their work in virtual learning environments (Reinmann-Rothmeier & Mandl, 2001b). This integration of e-learning and face-to-face learning also facilitates a beneficial embedding of virtual learning units into the traditional culture of training within companies and organizations. Blended learning is based on the integration of virtual phases and phases of physical co-presence, which offer learners the chance to meet and talk face-to-face. When learning in blended learning scenarios, learners find themselves using a combination of co-present courses and different types of net-based learning, for example, WBTs, CBTs, virtual learning environments, newsgroups, or virtual

Figure 2. A sequence of co-present and virtual phases in a blended learning course

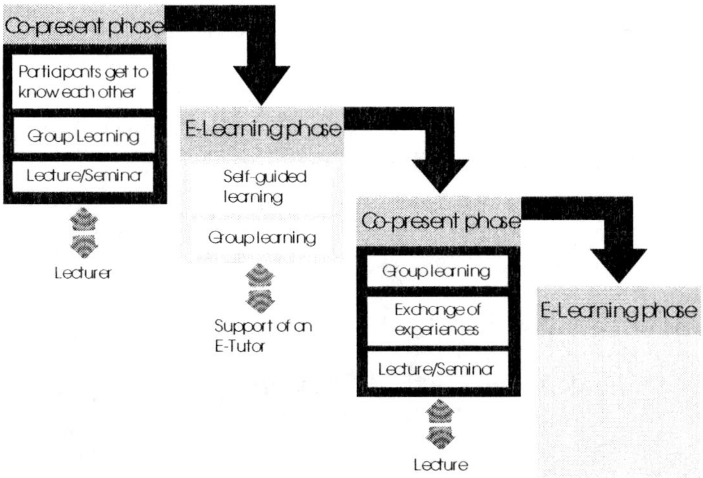

classrooms. E-learning phases and physically co-present phases can be combined in many different ways. For example, learners can work online to prepare for a co-present course, which links to the content of the e-learning unit. In a further step, learners can reflect on the meeting in another virtual phase. This sequence can be used repeatedly if necessary. Another method is to start with a co-present meeting, which is followed by an e-learning phase and again by a co-present meeting.

In summary, e-learning courses can help learners prepare topics for presence meetings through individual work or through discussions in virtual groups. Furthermore, the virtual units can trigger reflections on the contents of a co-present meeting. Figure 2 gives a schematic sketch of blended learning.

Example: The Knowledge Master

A course called the knowledge master illustrates an example of a blended learning scenario. The knowledge master is an interdisciplinary cooperation project of Siemens Qualification and Training (SQT) and the Ludwig Maximilian University in Munich (Erlach, Hausmann, Mandl, & Trillitzsch, 2002). The course was developed collaboratively by the departments of psychology, economics, and computer sciences. The half-year course provides on-the-job training with respect to knowledge management.

Goals of the knowledge master. Course participants are expected to acquire some basic knowledge in the area of knowledge management. In this course, learners focus particularly on knowledge communication and on tools for knowledge management. This focus also reflects the need for acquiring knowledge that is highly relevant to the practical problems experienced by the participants. The target group of the course includes employees at the intermediate management level, who possess only marginal knowledge in the area of knowledge management. The participants should also be interested in working within a virtual learning environment. Furthermore, a limited number of university students are accepted to the course, and thereby a limited number gain the opportunity to come into contact with practitioners.

Structure of the course. The knowledge master has a modular structure and implements the principles of problem-based learning. The didactic focus is on collaboration in small groups and on learning cases as a starting point for collaborative negotiation. The knowledge master relies on an Internet platform called the knowledge web. This knowledge web realizes the net-based communication and collaboration.

The knowledge master can be seen as hybrid learning environment, because it relies heavily on both co-present and e-learning phases, which are fundamentally linked. Within the period of half a year, learners collaborate on three different modules. There is a basic module, a module about communication and motivation, and a module about the integration of knowledge management (Figure 3). During the course, learners receive additional material and information on key knowledge management topics. This material is also discussed and explored further during the co-present workshops. These workshops take place at the beginning and at the end of each module (Figures 2 and 3). In the sequence of co-present and virtual phases, the first co-present phase plays a key role in allowing participants to get to know one another and in initiating virtual collaboration (kick off workshop). The other co-present meetings aim to support better coordination

Figure 3. Structure of the knowledge master

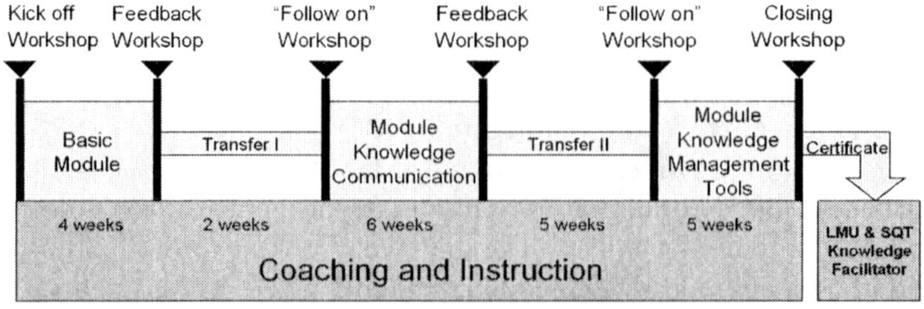

of the virtual collaboration between the members of the small groups and also aim to support face-to-face discussions. The workshops also allow participants to share their experiences with experts in the field, who are present at the meetings. Their presence often initiates reflections and discussions about concepts of knowledge management. Between the modules, there are so-called transfer phases. Transfer phases aim to relate the concepts learned to the individual's workplace. To this end, participants receive instructions and are encouraged to experience and to apply knowledge management concepts in "real life." The experiences gathered during the transfer phases can be shared, reflected, and discussed by the participants using the knowledge web.

The learning environment of the knowledge master realizes problem-based learning with respect to following aspects:

- **Learning with authentic contexts:** The course relies on authentic cases concerning knowledge management, which focus on psychological, business, and technical aspects of knowledge management. For example, one case deals with problems that can occur when companies merge.
- **Learning with multiple contexts:** In each of the first two modules, learners receive three cases on collaborative negotiation. One of them focuses on psychological, one on business, and one on computer-related aspects of knowledge management. Thus, learners are able to solve the cases from different perspectives, which also involve different backgrounds.
- **Learning in the social context:** Learners work collaboratively in small groups to solve the cases. They share and discuss their results using the knowledge web. Furthermore, the co-present meetings also focus on collaborative negotiation and on sharing experiences.
- **Learning with instructional support:** The learning environment provides literature and other material that is relevant for the collaborative case solutions. Furthermore, learners receive hints and strategies for virtual collaboration. A key element of instructional support is the provision of e-tutors, who support participants throughout the whole course. Learners can contact them easily when encountering problems in virtual collaboration and when they have questions regarding the cases or other content-specific aspects.

Evaluation. The learning environment is continuously evaluated for further improvement and for its adaptiveness to the needs of the learners. The acceptance of the learning environment, the learning outcome of the learners, and the learning process are evaluated using surveys, feedback panels, and by monitoring the virtual communication (Belanger, & Jordan, 2000; Scriven, 1980). Results show positive feedback from the learners with respect to all areas that were subject to evaluation. They support the acceptance of case-based learning and the combination of virtual and co-present phases (Erlach et al., 2002).

Thesis 3: Implementing E-Learning

The third thesis states that human aspects should be the driver for implementing e-learning, as opposed to technical feasibility. In general, when trying to integrate e-learning and blended learning courses in a company's training culture, the procedure for this integration should consider the needs of the prospective course users. The following five steps describe one possible procedure for introducing blended learning within companies and educational institutions (Figure 4; Tarlatt, 2001).

1. **Initiation:** The first step for implementing blended learning in organizations is the creation of a vision for the project. This vision needs to consider an organization's culture of training and must gain the support of the company's management. This vision should be the basis for the development of strategic goals and for the development of a business case for the project. In addition, a steering committee provides an important forum for counteracting a potential diffusion of responsibility within the project.

Figure 4. Process model for the implementation of blended learning

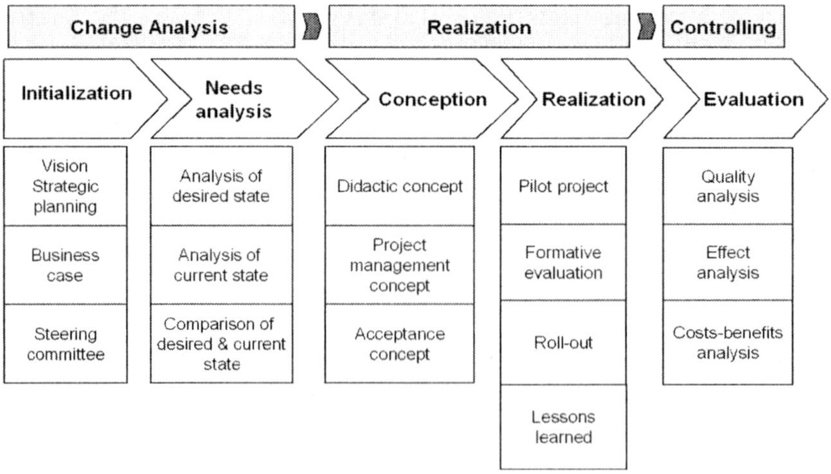

2. **Needs analysis:** As a second step, the analysis of the current situation takes place. The current situation is evaluated based on the vision established and on the strategic goals. This analysis deals with the availability and acceptance of existing courses, specific opportunities for improving existing courses, and on investigating which courses may be needed that are not yet offered. Analyzing the current situation should also involve the course participants. After this analysis, a desired state is defined in collaboration with the potential participants of future courses. This definition of the desired state should be driven by the employee's particular work-related problems. Comparing the current state with the desired state reveals the needs of the organization. These needs are the starting point for particular project decisions and for a subsequent definition of operative goals.
3. **Conception:** The conception phase is the core of the procedure of implementing e-learning. In this phase, the goals are translated into clearly defined processes on the basis of didactically meaningful concepts. Furthermore, a framework for the realization phase is defined with respect to project management and acceptance. In this context, a key activity is the selection of a target group and of the contents for a pilot project. Moreover, the selection and installation of a learning platform and the selection of available CBTs and WBTs takes place.
4. **Realization:** The realization phase starts with a first pilot project for implementing the concept of e-learning or blended learning. A particular project team should be responsible for the success of this implementation. In this phase, it is essential to have a clear definition of responsibilities. A formative evaluation of the pilot project, which is the basis for continuous improvement, is crucial for the success of the whole project. Lessons learned from the implementation of this pilot project can be a model for further realizations of similar concepts in the organization. Depending on the results of the evaluation, the main project may start immediately or commence after some problems are resolved (roll-out).
5. **Evaluation:** The continuous evaluation of the project is essential for improving the processes and for ensuring a fit to users' needs. This evaluation should comprise an analysis of quality as well as an analysis of effects. Furthermore, a cost-benefit analysis can illustrate aspects for further improvement and can form a basis for the internal marketing of the new concept of learning.

In connection with our third thesis, we will illustrate some additional aspects of ensuring participant acceptance. Reservations regarding e-learning and blended learning often result from problems related to the implementation of this new style of learning. These problems have their origins in an underestimation of the costs for e-learning courses and in the lack of acceptance of these courses by the target group (Davis, 1989; Goodhue, 1995). In this context, the issue centers on determining the key for accepting e-learning. One indicator of acceptance is the usage of a course that has been implemented (Harhoff & Küpper, 2002). From this point of view, acceptance is the result of motivated action. This means that employees have to be motivated to use the course. Recent research names four target aspects for motivation (Tarlatt, 2001): organization, technology, participation, and qualification. These are described as follows:

- **Organization:** The key aspect regarding organization is that the company management supports a culture of training. An innovation has to be integrated into the strategic vision of the company, and the importance of the innovation has to be communicated to the employees (Gratton, 1996; Raimond, & Eden, 1990). Informing the employees comprehensively as well as continuously can further support innovations (Tarlatt, 2001). In addition, integration into the business processes has proven to be a key aspect for the successful implementation of innovations. This process can be further supported by material and ideological incentives (Tarlatt, 2001).
- **Technology:** The choice of adapted technology that is suited to the particular needs of the users is indispensable for achieving acceptance. The technology chosen has to fit the demands of the users from a usability perspective and has to be meaningful with respect to didactic aspects. In general, technology should just fulfill the didactic needs (Hinkofer, & Mandl, 2003).
- **Participation:** The participation of the users is indispensable for successful implementation. This participation should start as early as possible. Starting from the needs analysis, users should be involved to ensure that the planning and the decisions meet users' needs. User feedback is also important for the planning and conception phase (Hinkofer, & Mandl, 2003). This could be facilitated by a continuous formative evaluation. In general, users should participate in making changes, rather than only being affected by them (Alexander, 1985; Brehm, & Brehm, 1981).
- **Qualification:** Further qualification of the employees can support the implementation of an innovation. This qualification should take place during the process of implementation and should be aimed at technical and methodical aspects (Tarlatt, 2001).

These aspects of motivation are crucial for creating a culture of innovation in an organization and indicate that acceptance is a key aspect of the implementation of blended learning—no matter how sophisticated the implementation process may be planned.

Example: A Pharmacy Company

We will illustrate an exemplary implementation process based on the case of a pharmacy company. While trying to introduce a new product, the company management realized a need to apply knowledge management. This knowledge management should improve the knowledge exchange between the employees, namely the pharmaceutical representatives. The management of this company decided to initiate a knowledge management improvement project because they had experienced unknown challenges when launching new products. For the implementation of this knowledge management project, the company asked the Ludwig Maximilian University to coach them through the implementation process.

The business success of pharmacy companies in Germany relies heavily on pharmaceutical representatives. The knowledge of the representatives about products, markets, and about selling products is essential for the success of a product and consequently for the success of the whole company. However, this knowledge has to be kept up to date by continuous training. In this case, the management realized that the quality of the traditional co-present trainings and the individual preparations of the pharmaceutical representatives for these trainings were quite diverse. Furthermore, these co-present trainings were viewed as extremely time-consuming, particularly when new products had to be launched. Therefore, the company started to implement a blended learning environment for their pharmaceutical representatives. This implementation was comprised of the following steps:

1. **Change analysis:** Regarding change analysis, the company management initialized a vision of improved competitive ability. For a clear conceptualization, the management set up a steering committee and both worked collaboratively on a business case for estimating the project budget. Furthermore, the steering committee had the task of defining responsibilities for the particular subareas. The project started with a needs analysis to assess the current state of knowledge processes within the work of the pharmaceutical representatives. Furthermore, this analysis aimed to disclose further needs of the company. The needs analysis involved all the persons who might have been concerned with these changes. The results

of the needs analysis showed the need for improving the representatives' consulting abilities with respect to knowledge representation, knowledge generation, and knowledge communication.

2. **Realization:** On basis of the needs analysis, the realization focused particularly on knowledge representation, knowledge generation, and knowledge communication. Regarding knowledge representation, the main goal was to improve the preparation and distribution of information with respect to new products and related research results. The improvement of knowledge distribution was realized by a flexible knowledge management platform, which allowed a meaningful informational structure and easy access from anywhere. To address knowledge generation, blended learning courses were introduced, which included online and co-present phases. Knowledge communication was improved by discussion boards and online classrooms, which supported the exchange of general and course-specific ideas. The whole realization was accompanied by a concept for ensuring acceptance. This concept was supported by company management, user adapted technology, and active involvement and qualification of the employees.
3. **Controlling:** An evaluation of the pilot project took place with respect to a formative analysis of quality and effects. The evaluation focused on the usability and acceptance of the platform and the WBTs used. Experts continuously analyzed the quality of the program with respect to content and didactics. A summative evaluation focused on acceptance, participation, learning outcomes, integration into the workflow, management support, and technology.

The evaluation of this implementation revealed that job relevance and the level of information provided by the management were highly correlated with acceptance (Bürg, & Mandl, 2005). Furthermore, the freedom in the workplace to work with e-learning, the usability, and the support of the learners also had a substantial impact. Users who accepted the learning environment also expended more effort working with the learning environment (Bürg, & Mandl, 2005; Bürg et al., 2004).

Conclusion

The initial optimism regarding e-learning as a new style of learning in schools, universities, and companies has often changed to disillusionment. In the context of this paper, we have shown that missing didactic concepts and unprofessional implementation strategies of e-learning courses can be considered the main causes for this disillusionment. For exploiting the potentials of new media in the future, it is clear that indispensable prerequisites include the application of learner-centered didactic concepts and holistic implementation strategies.

We have stated three theses with respect to the didactic structure (thesis 1), the course organization (thesis 2), and the implementation of e-learning (thesis 3). The theses focus on different aspects of e-learning, but together they can be seen as a framework and as prerequisites for successful e-learning. This means that the theses cannot be seen discretely: ensuring users' acceptance implies that the course fits into the organization's culture of training, and it implies also that the learners acquire knowledge they can apply on their workplace.

We have illustrated three examples of the implementation of e-learning in higher education and in organizations. Each example featured the intention of the particular thesis quite distinctly. However, besides these features, each example also comprised several aspects of the other theses. Therefore, each example could illustrate the road to the future of e-learning, which is based on need-driven didactic concepts and facilitated by the technological support of a learning environment. Such e-learning scenarios encourage motivated, application-oriented learning and achieve user acceptance on the basis of a professional implementation process.

References

Alexander, D. L. (1985). Successfully implementing strategic decisions. *Long Range Planning, 18*(3), 91-97.

Altenburg, E., Arnold, G., & Schürmann, A. (2003). *Stationenlernen im fächerübergreifenden Sachunterricht.* Donauwörth: Auer.

Back, A., Seufert, S., & Kramhöller, S. (1998). Technology enabled management education. *iomanagement, 21*(3), 36-40.

Belanger, F., & Jordan, D. H. (2000). *Evaluation and implementation of distance learning: Technologies, tools and techniques.* Hershey, PA: Idea Group Publishing.

Bernard, R. M., Abrami, P. C., Lou, Y., Borokhovski, E., Wade, A., Wozney, et al. (2004). How does distance education compare with classroom instruction? A meta-analysis of the empirical literature. *Review of Educational Research, 74*(3), 379-439.

Brehm, S. S., & Brehm, J. W. (1981). *Psychological reactance—A theory of freedom and control.* New York: Academic Press.

Bürg, O., Kronburger, K., & Mandl, H. (2004). Implementation von e-learning in unternehmen—Akzeptanzsicherung als zentrale Herausforderung (Forschungsbericht Nr. 170). München: Ludwig-Maximilians-Universität, Department Psychologie, Institut für Pädagogische Psychologie.

Bürg, O., & Mandl, H. (2005, August). *Fostering acceptance as a central challenge for the implementation of e-learning into companies. The meaning of personnel-related and organizational measures as well as technical conditions.* Paper presented at the 11th Biennial Conference of the European Association for Research on Learning and Instruction (EARLI), Nicosia, Cyprus.

Davies, F. D. (1989). Perceived usefulness, perceived ease of use and user acceptance of information technology. *MIS Quarterly, 13*(3), 319-339.

Deci, E. L., & Ryan, R. M. (1992). The initiation and regulation of intrinsically motivated learning and achievement. In A. K. Boggiano & T. S. Pittman (Eds.), *Achievement and motivation: A social-developmental perspective* (pp. 9-36). Cambridge: Cambridge University Press.

Dochy, F., Segers, M., Van den Bossche, P., & Gijbels, D. (2003). Effects of problem-based learning: A meta-analysis. *Learning and Instruction, 13*(5), 533-568.

eLearningNews.net. (2005). *Survey predicts transatlantic increase in blended learning.* Retrieved September 8, 2005, from http://www.elearningnews.net/view_news.php?news_id=505

Erlach, C., Hausmann, I., Mandl, H., & Trillitzsch, U. (2002). Knowledge Master—A collaborative learning program for Knowledge Management. In T. H. Davenport & G. J. B. Probst (Eds.), *Kowledge management case book. Siemens best practicesi* (pp. 208-227). Erlangen: Publicis KommunikationsAgentur GWA.

Goodhue, D. L. (1995). Understanding user evaluations of information systems. *Management Science, 41*(12), 1827-1844.

Gratton, L. (1996). Implementing a strategic vision—Key factors for success. *Long Range Planning, 29*(3), 290-303.

Haben, M. (2002). E-learning in large German companies—Most of the concepts are not effective. *Computerwoche, 30*(22), 12-16.

Harhoff, D., & Küpper, C. (2002). *Akzeptanz von E-Learning. Eine empirische Studie in Zusammenarbeit von Cognos und dem Institut für Innovationsforschung, Technologiemanagement und Entrepreneurship.* München: INNOtec.

Hasenbein, M. (2003). *Evaluation einer Webbasierten lernumgebung: Das lernmodul "Mediendidaktik" für lehramtsstudierende im aufbaustudie-*

ngang medienpädagogik. Unpublished term paper, Ludwig-Maximilians-Universität, München.

Hinkofer, L., & Mandl, H. (2003). *Implementation von e-learning in einem pharmaunternehmen* (Praxisbericht Nr. 28). München: Ludwigs-Maximilians-Universität, Lehrstuhl für Empirische Pädagogik und Pädagogische Psychologie.

Kollar, I., & Fischer, F. (2004). Internal and external cooperation scripts in Web-based collaborative inquiry learning. Effects on the acquisition of domain-specific and general knowledge. In P. Gerjets, P. Kirschner, J. Elen, & R. Joiner (Eds.), *Instructional design for effective and enjoyable computer-supported learning. Proceedings of the first joint meeting of the EARLI SIGs Instructional Design and Learning and Instruction with Computers* [CD-ROM] (pp.37-47). Tuebingen: Knowledge Media Research Center.

Lave, J., & Wenger, E. (1991). *Situated learning: Legitimate peripheral participation.* New York: Cambridge University Press.

Learnframe.com. (2005). *About e-learning.* Retrieved September 8, 2005, from http://www.learnframe.com /aboutelearning/

Mandl, H., Ertl, B., & Kopp, B. (in press). Cooperative learning in computer supported learning environments. In L. Verschaffel, F. Dochy, M. Boekaerts, & S. Vosniadou (Eds.), *Instructional psychology: Past, present and future trends. Fifteen Essays in Honor of Erik De Corte* (pp. 165-182). Amsterdam, The Netherlands: Elsevier.

Mandl, H., Gräsel, C., & Fischer, F. (1998). Faciliating problem-orientated learning: The role of strategy modeling by experts. In W. Perring & A. Grob (Eds.), *Control of human behaviour, mental processes and awareness. Essays in honour of the 60th birthday of August Flammer.* Mahwah, NY: Erlbaum.

Mandl, H., Gruber, H., & Renkl, A. (1996). Communities of practice toward expertise: Social foundation of university instruction. In P. B. Baltes & U. Staudinger (Eds.), *Interactive minds. Life-span perspectives on the social foundation of cognition* (pp. 394-411). New York: Cambridge University Press.

Mandl, H., & Winkler, K. (2004). E-Learning—Trends und zukünftige entwicklungen. In K. Rebensburg (Ed.), *Grundfragen multimedialen lehrens und lernens* (pp. 17-29). Norderstedt: Books on Demand.

Mayer, R. E., Hegarty, M., & Mayer, S. (2005, April). *Does animation improve learning?* Paper presented at the 86th Conference of the American Educational Research Association (AERA), Montréal, Canada.

Raimond, P., & Eden, C. (1990). Making strategy work. Long Range Planning. *International Journal of Strategic Management, 32*(5), 97-105.

Reinmann-Rothmeier, G., & Mandl, H. (2001a). Unterrichten und lernumgebungen gestalten. In A. Krapp & B. Weidenmann (Eds.), *Pädagogische Psychologie* (pp. 601-646). Weinheim: Beltz.

Reinmann-Rothmeier, G., & Mandl, H. (2001b). *Virtuelle seminare in hochschule und weiterbildung: Drei beispiele aus der praxis.* Bern: Huber.

Renkl, A., Gruber, H., & Mandl, H. (1999). Situated learning in instructional settings: From euphoria to feasibility. In J. Bliss, R. Saljö, & P. Light (Eds.), *Learning sites: Social and technological resources for learning* (pp. 101-109). Amsterdam, The Netherlands: Elsevier.

Renkl, A., Mandl, H., & Gruber, H. (1996). Inert knowledge: Analyses and remedies. *Educational Psychologist, 31*(2), 115-121.

Scardamalia, M., & Bereiter, C. (1994). Computer support for knowledge-building communities. *Journal of the Learning Sciences, 3*(3), 265-283.

Scriven, M. (1980). *The logic of evaluation.* Iverness: Edgepress.

Sweller, J., Van Merrienboër, J. J. G., & Paas, F. G. W. C. (1998). Cognitive architecture and instructional design. *Educational Psychology Review, 10*(3), 251-296.

Tarlatt, A. (2001). *Implementierung von strategien im unternehmen.* Wiesbaden: Gabler.

Volery, T., & Lord, D. (2000). Critical success factors in online education. *The International Journal of Educational Management, 14*(5), 216-223.

Weinberger, A., Ertl, B., Fischer, F., & Mandl, H. (2005). Epistemic and social scripts in computer-supported collaborative learning. *Instructional Science, 33*(1), 1-30.

Zumbach, J., & Reimann, P. (2003). Influence of feedback on distributed problem based learning. Enhancing online communities in group functioning and well-being. In B. Wasson, S. Ludvigsen, & U. Hoppe (Eds.), *Designing for change* (pp. 219-228). Dordrecht: Kluwer Academic Publisher.

Chapter VII

Towards the Educational Semantic Web

Juan Manuel Adán-Coello,
Pontificia Universidade Católica de Campinas, Brazil

Carlos Miguel Tobar,
Pontificia Universidade Católica de Campinas, Brazil

João Luís Garcia Rosa,
Pontificia Universidade Católica de Campinas, Brazil

Ricardo Luís de Freitas,
Pontificia Universidade Católica de Campinas, Brazil

Abstract

The objective of this chapter is to discuss relevant applications of Semantic Web technologies in the field of education, emphasizing experiences that point out trends and paths that can make the educational Semantic Web a reality. The Semantic Web, through metadata, comes to make it possible that resources of every type could be localized, retrieved and processed without human intervention, helping to reduce the information overload of the current Web. The possibility of describing resources using metadata that can be processed by computers simplifies the creation of self-organizing networks of learners, information, authors, teachers, and educational institutions. The adoption of Semantic Web technologies in the e-learning field contributes to the construction of flexible and intelligent educational systems, allowing reuse, integration, and interoperation of educational and noneducational resources (content and services) distributed over the Web.

Introduction

In our society, everything—information mainly—changes very rapidly, resulting in a continuous cycle of relevant information gathering in order to produce knowledge. Individuals and organizations need mechanisms and processes that can help them to be involved in a constant learning engagement. Mizoguchi (2000) believes that e-learning is one of the keywords in this context.

During the last decade, the Internet and its most important application, the Web, have been the favorite platform for the construction of information objects and information services, including learning systems. The profusion of resources available in the Web and its constant increase offer several opportunities for a wide range of users and applications, but also big challenges for computer professionals.

Since the Web information space is huge, a precise search engine is not sufficient. It is necessary to make available accurate metadata about relevant pieces of information. Traditional search engines, based on keywords, usually retrieve large amounts of documents that have to be filtered by the user without support or with very limited support of automated tools. Moreover, the dynamic nature of the Web requires that the user periodically repeats this search-retrieve-filter process to localize new resources of interest and to update previous ones. This situation led to the development of information agents that continually browse the Web searching for resources of interest to its users.

The construction of information agents faces several obstacles, especially the enormous volume of distributed documents to be processed and the multimedia and unstructured or semi-structured nature of the documents, most of them prepared to be analyzed by people, not by programs.

The idea of a Semantic Web (SW) comes to tackle this problem of information overload. It should be possible that resources of every type could be localized, retrieved, and processed without human intervention.

Tim Berners-Lee, the "father" of the Web, foresees a SW that would allow automatic access to resources using semantic descriptions amenable to be processed by software agents (Berners-Lee, Hendler, & Lassila, 2001; Hendler, 2001).

Berners-Lee's vision of the SW is a stack system with seven layers. The base layer deals with representation schemes for characters and resource identification. The two following layers are concerned with basic languages, one for the creation of metadata languages for resource description, and the second for semantic statements about described resources. These three bottom layers are supported by consolidated W3C (World Wide Web Consortium) standards. Next there is an ontology layer oriented to represent information on categories of objects and the way objects are interrelated, for which there is an on-going standardization effort inside W3C. The three upper layers, Logic, Proof, and Trust, are not yet standardized. The Logic layer enables the writing of rules. The Proof layer allows evaluation of rules. The Trust layer depicts the ultimate goal for the SW: machines should be able not only to find and use relevant information, but also to assess the extent to which the information found is both accurate and trustworthy. Currently these three upper layers are subject of research, application demonstration construction, and standard submission.

The objective of this chapter is to present and discuss some of the main opportunities offered by the SW in the computer-supported learning (e-learning) field, pointing out ongoing projects that signal potential ways for realizing it.

The Background section presents the SW and its technologies. Next the educational SW is characterized, emphasizing some of the offered possibilities and current projects that are contributing to its construction. Representative project results are reviewed in order to give an idea of how much of the educational SW has been accomplished. The Future Trends section explores challenges that have to be addressed for the educational SW. The Conclusion section closes the chapter.

Background

In the SW, machines can understand, process, and reason about resources in order to provide support for humans. It is an evolution upon the current chaotic Web.

According to Fensel, Hendler, Lieberman, and Wahlster (2003), the achievement of an SW that provides solutions to the problems of the current Web requires:

- language development for expressing machine-understandable meta-information for information and knowledge objects;

- ontology development, using the above languages, and ontology availability on the Web;
- development of tools and new architectures that use languages and ontologies to provide support in finding, accessing, presenting, maintaining, and processing information; and
- application development that provides a new level of services to users (humans and computers).

SW Languages

There is a set of languages already standardized, some of which was available before the advent of the SW, and others developed for the SW. This language set constitutes the four base layers of the SW stack. In conjunction, all languages need formal syntax and semantics to enable automated processing of the content described through them. Ontologies (standard vocabularies) referring to real-world semantics are a cornerstone that enable humans and software agents to share information and knowledge.

URI and Unicode Language Layer

A uniform resource identifier (URI) (Berners-Lee, Fielding, & Masinter, 1998) is a string of characters for identifying an abstract or physical resource. An object or service to be part of the Web needs a URI.

Unicode provides a unique bit combination for every character, no matter the platform, no matter the program, no matter the language. Earlier versions of HTML allowed only the ISO Latin-1 character set. The current Web infrastructure supports a wide variety of languages by allowing the full range of Unicode characters.

XML Language Layer

XML (extensible markup language) (W3C, 2004a) is a standard for creating markup languages which describe the structure of data. It is not a fixed set of elements like HTML, but rather, it is like SGML (standard generalized markup language). In respect of that, it is a meta-language, or a language for describing languages. XML enables authors to define their own tags.

An XML schema is a type description for XML documents, typically expressed in terms of constraints on the structure and content, above and beyond the basic syntax constraints imposed by XML itself. An XML schema provides a view of the document type at a relatively high level of abstraction.

The XML language layer includes XML and XML schema (W3C, 1999, 2004d). In the current Web there is the use of syntactic rules specified by this layer, on top of which there are self-describing document languages, such as XHTML (W3C, 2002) and synchronized multimedia integration language (SMIL) (W3C, 2005). Virtual and real documents developed according to languages of this layer are self-described because they have a text-based syntax with markup meaningful to human readers.

RDF Language Layer

The general-purpose resource description framework (RDF) is used for exchanging descriptions of any Web resource that can be identified with a URI, even when it cannot be directly retrieved on the Web. Since an RDF description is written using an XML language, it can be supplied as a document on the Web. An RDF description can in turn be described by other RDF statements.

It is often useful to define a set of semantic concepts a given application should recognize using RDF, as well as the basic semantic relations among the concepts.

The fundamental building block in RDF is used to specify a resource property through a triple, consisting of the resource being described, the property name (an XML name), and the property value. RDF triples can be linked, chained, and nested. Together, they allow the creation of arbitrary graph structures.

Although RDF lets users encode complex metadata graphs, it does not associate specific semantics to the graphs other than the roles implied by the triples. It is often useful to define the set of semantic concepts a given application should recognize, as well as the basic semantic relations among the concepts. RDF schema (W3C, 2004e) defines a language on top of RDF that supports this definition process.

Ontology Language Layer

An ontology is used to represent and control the manipulation of terms and their relationships in a given domain. The control is provided through rules and constraints for manipulating and managing terms and relationships. An ontology can be regarded as an understanding of a domain. Once the understanding is formalized, it can be shared and communicated between people and computer applications.

WordNet (Fellbaum, 1998) and Cyc (Lenat & Guha, 1990) are two well known examples of available ontologies that illustrate the several degrees of formalism possible in ontology definition.

The same massive growth of documents in the Web is perceived in the use and development of ontologies. Reuse begins to be a major necessity, and tools for its support have been proposed as ontology engineering environments, such as Protégé (Gennari et al., 2003) and OntoEdit (Sure, Staab, & Angele, 2002), but there is no well grounded infrastructure to support search and retrieval of existing ontologies. OntoKhoj (Patel et al., 2003) is a recent attempt to rank citations of ontologies. Ontolingua (Gruber, 1993) is another example of effort that offers a distributed collaborative environment to browse, create, edit, modify, and use ontologies.

The Web ontology language OWL (W3C, 2004c) is a semantic markup language for publishing and sharing ontologies on the Web. OWL is developed as a vocabulary extension of RDF and is derived from the DAML+OIL Web ontology language (DAML, 2001). OWL is primarily aimed at representing information about categories of objects and how objects are interrelated. OWL can also represent information about the objects themselves.

Ontological Engineering Environments and Tools

Building ontologies manually is a difficult and time consuming task, what to say of a good one, it is a harder task. Ontology engineering is a successor of knowledge engineering that has the objective of building good ontologies. Ontology building requires a development methodology and an integrated environment that helps developers in every phase of the building process. There are several tools that can be used to construct ontologies. Mizoguchi (2004) evaluates four tools which cover the ontology development process rather than being single-purpose tools: OntoEdit (Sure, Staab, & Angele, 2002), WebODE (Corcho, Fernandez-Lopez, Gomez-Perez, & Vicente, 2002), Protégé (Crubérzy et al. 2003), and Hozo (Kozaki, Kitamura, Ikeda, & Mizoguchi, 2002). He concludes that ontology engineering environments are still in their early phase of development. Although some are powerful software tools, many are passive in the sense that they give few guidance or suggestions to ontology developers.

Following are some examples of tools oriented to the construction and maintenance of ontologies. They are presented by non-exhaustive categories.

Semiautomatic Construction of Ontologies

Semiautomatic tools to construct ontologies from available data are vital. They can be developed using machine learning, information extraction, natural language processing—for instance, ontological semantics (Nirenburg & Raskin, 2004)—and Web mining techniques. Their task is to extract concepts from data and determine hierarchies and relationships among concepts. Text-To-Onto (Maedche & Staab, 2000) is an example of an integrated environment for learning ontologies from available corpora of domain texts.

Reasoning Services

Reasoning services can be used to help in building ontologies and in using them for information access and navigation. They can be used, for example, to derive a value for an object attribute or to find the position for a new concept in a concept hierarchy.

Ontologies and reasoning services help to overcome many of the limitations of current information access and navigation tools. They enable the development of query-answering and information extraction services, integrating distributed information sources.

Annotation Tools

Annotation is the activity of annotating resources—such as services and documents written in plain ASCII or HTML—with tags related to concepts in an ontology. Marking resources can be also a very boring and time consuming task. Semantic annotation tools help in adding ontological annotation to documents.

Semantic Web Services

Web services are computational elements aimed at processing modeled resources. In the SW this modeling is conducted through RDF and ontologies.

Services are not considered in the stack vision for the SW. They are autonomous and platform-independent and are supposed to use some or all stack layers in order to be accessible (information on what they do, how they can be accessed, and where they are located), and to be distributed and interoperable (communication, synchronization, and control). They are oriented to the application domain.

Their platform-neutral and self-describing nature, and particularly their ability to automate collaboration between Web applications, makes them more than just software components.

A set of emerging standards oriented to Web services are already available, such as SOAP (Gudgin, Hadley, Mendelsohn, Moreau, & Nielsen, 2003), a protocol based on XML for information exchange among distributed applications, and WSDL (Web service description language) (Christensen, Curbera, Meredith, & Weerawarana, 2001) for describing how to interact intelligibly with services (accessibility).

Another on-going effort combining Web services and ontologies is OWL-S (W3C, 2004b), an OWL-based Web service ontology of general concepts to tackle automatic discovery, composition, and invocation of services.

The Educational Semantic Web

The SW for e-learning should support seamless understanding of information in order to allow knowledge acquisition for learning and training. Such information understanding ideally should happen disregarded of cultural and language barriers.

A vision for the educational SW is based on interoperability, reusability, and sharing of information and knowledge, in the form of objects and/or services, all necessarily described by semantic expressions with a standardized communication involving services (Aroyo & Dicheva, 2004).

According to Anderson and Whitelock (2004), the SW for e-learning is based on three capacities:

- the capacity for effective information storage and retrieval;
- the capacity for nonhuman autonomous agents to augment the power of human beings to learn, retrieve, and process information; and
- the capacity to extend human capabilities to communicate, using multimedia across bounds of time and space.

Toward this vision, it is possible to foresee one ad-hoc SW built inside the "global" SW. It is not a separate Web. Its main constituents are related to: educational ontologies; learning objects and their standard specifications; SW services for e-learning, especially those oriented to information management (retrieval, filtering, processing, and dissemination); and adaptive hypermedia educational systems.

Construction of Educational Ontologies

Ontologies are among the key technologies to accomplish the SW (Fensel, 2003; Gómez-Pérez & Corcho, 2002). Ontologies can be used in e-learning to formally describe educational organizations, courses, and people involved in the teaching and learning process, in addition to educational services. For instance, besides a learner model ontology, communication between educational agents requires a domain ontology to model objects and relations that exist in the domain. A learner model ontology is a kind of task ontology, that is, a vocabulary for modeling problem-solving structures.

Researchers at Mizoguchi Labs provide several good examples of research on educational ontologies and ontology based educational systems (Mizoguchi, 2003). For example, Chen and Mizoguchi (2004) exemplify the benefits of ontologies in educational systems through the development of a multi-agent architecture for learning support systems where learner-model agents based on ontologies exchange information with each other and with other pedagogical agents. This architecture includes interface agents, learning-material agents, learning-support agents, learner-modeling agents, and learner-model agents.

Metadata Standardization Efforts

Standards are, or should be, precise descriptions of design, representation, and implementation practices. They codify, or should codify, what is, could be, or should be common practice.

In the computational arena there is not one single standard, but many attempts to "standardize" a market share, as large as possible, by imposition or through agreement. The final picture is that of different organizations proposing incompatible "standards" and rarely some complementary ones. Following this same pattern, several groups around the world are doing work in different areas related to learning and training. They are producing specifications that are being developed to become standards. These groups cover far-reaching topics including courseware (learning object metadata and data), student profiles, course sequencing, computer managed instruction, competency definitions, localization, and content packaging (Hodgins & Conner, 2000). Software architectures, session management, and semantics are also focuses of work.

Although the number of standardization groups and their respective specifications are a recipe for incompatibility, several of these groups are working together to avoid incompatibilities and effort loss.

It is worth citing the following bodies that have been closely collaborating in the definition and specification of standards concerned with educational technology:

- **Dublin Core Metadata Initiative:** DCMI (http://www.dublincore.org)
- **Advanced Distributed Learning: sharable courseware object reference model:** ADL-SCORM (http://www.adlnet.gov/scorn)
- **The Aviation Industry CBT (Computer-Based Training) Committee:** AICC (http://www.aicc.org)
- **Alliance of Remote Instructional and Distribution Networks for Europe:** ARIADNE (http://www.ariadne-eu.org/)
- **IMS (Instructional Management Systems) Global Learning Consortium:** (http://www.imsproject.org/)
- **IEEE Learning Technology Standards Committee:** LTSC (http://ltsc.ieee.org)

The DCMI metadata can be used to describe any kind of resource, including various collections of documents and nonelectronic forms of media such as a museum or library archive. The DCMI aims the widespread adoption of interoperable metadata standards through specialized metadata vocabularies for describing resources to enable more intelligent resource discovery systems. Information categories were derived from an exploration of existing DCMI and LTSC metadata projects.

SCORM defines a Web-based learning "content aggregation model" and "runtime environment" for learning objects. It is a collection of specifications adapted from multiple sources to provide a comprehensive suite of e-learning capabilities that enable interoperability, accessibility, and reusability of Web-based learning content within a common technical framework.

ADL SCORM is built upon the work of AICC, IMS, IEEE, and ARIADNE. SCORM references the use of the IMS Content Packaging specification and the IMS Learning Resource Meta-data specification. Other IMS specifications may be included in future versions of SCORM, including: IMS Question & Test Interoperability, Learner Information Package, and Simple Sequencing specifications.

AICC develops guidelines for the aviation industry in the development, delivery, and evaluation of training objects and related training technologies produced for airlines. AICC wants to promote interoperability standards that software vendors can use across multiple industries. The scope of AICC specifications goes further than aviation, and the AICC works with IEEE, IMS, and ADL.

ARIADNE aims to solve two practical problems that arise when a metadata system is widely used: indexation (i.e., the creation of the metadata by human beings) should be as easy as possible; and exploitation of the metadata by users looking for relevant pedagogical material should be as easy and efficient as possible.

The most significant contribution of ARIADNE has been the development of a learning content metadata scheme recommendation that is based on LOM and harmonized with the IMS metadata specification.

IMS specifies a Content Package that "standardizes" the structure of a learning object and the physical resources it employs. Physical resources and the XML-based specification are bounded into a file for storage and retrieval reasons. IMS aims to obtain interoperable content packages. The IMS Metadata specification is based on the LOM specification.

IEEE Standard for learning object metadata (LOM) was the first learning content standard released by an accredited standard organization, in July 2002. LOM specifies a conceptual data schema that defines the structure of a metadata instance for a learning object. LOM makes it easier to find, evaluate, and share learning objects and ensures that objects in one system are understood readily in other systems.

LOM was developed by LTSC under the auspices of the IEEE Computer Society. IEEE LTSC was established as an attempt to harmonize results of initial independent efforts, especially from IMS and ADL but including ARIADNE, AICC, and DCMI.

Learning Objects

A learning object is an independent and self-standing digital learning resource developed to allow a learner to fulfill a single learning objective. Behind every learning object there is an implicit predisposition to reuse.

Learning objects are software or software results. They can present different formats: text documents, programs, figures, images, films, and so forth. One can treat them as static information objects or dynamic ones, some produced by information services.

In the SW, metadata must be considered for any information object or service. For the educational SW it should not be different; learning objects are very important Web objects. Thus, it is not possible to consider learning objects in the

SW detached from metadata standards. "Standards" such as LOM and SCORM have been used to specify metadata for learning objects, and usually are used as synonyms to learning objects.

In the LOM specification, a learning object is defined as any entity, digital or non-digital, that may be (re)used for learning, education, or training. But, considering non-digital objects, since LOM specifies metadata to these entities, a LOM object is always a digital entity that has a reference to the actual learning object.

Reuse presents a twofold importance. Learning objects and learning-object services are usually very expensive and time-consuming to develop. First, they can be treated as components, allowing the combination of ready and assessed learning objects into new ones or new courses. Second, they can be used, without modifications, in multiple and different educational contexts.

It is crucial, then, to have technologies that support leaning object discovery and retrieval, such as repositories.

A major problem with authoring educational material, especially learning objects, is the time-consuming procedure of filling many metadata fields. This problem can be tackled by using special authoring tools or "application profiles" as in CanCore (Mohan, 2004). Application profiles are the core to exploit customization of application reaction to user characteristics (see Adaptive Educational Systems).

The separation of learning objects from metadata facilitates indexing mechanisms that allow storage distribution of content. Another tendency is to produce portals for different repositories. These separation strategies are followed by several repository efforts. These include the Campus Alberta Repository of Learning Objects (CAREO—www.careo.org), the Multimedia Educational Resource for Learning and Online Teaching (MERLOT—www.merlot.org), the Digital Library for Earth System Education (DLESE—www.dlese.org), the National Engineering Education Delivery System (NEEDS—www.needs.org), and the national digital library for Science, Mathematics, Engineering and Technology Education (SMETE—www.smete.org/).

Several repositories are using the LOM standard, while others have chosen SCORM or even Dublin Core. In this scenario, interoperability appears as a must, imposing requirements to development efforts of services and even of "standards."

Another interesting storage strategy is a peer-to-peer (P2P) solution to share and reuse learning objects, such as the learning object metadata LOMster (Ternier, Duval, & Vandepitte, 2002).

It is likely that new repositories based on the P2P approach will emerge, mainly because of the appealing decentralized control that is considered. However, one problem with P2P repositories is the proliferation of metadata dialects. Approaches such as Edutella (Nejdl et al, 2002) (http://edutella.jxta.org/) are being used to interoperate P2P repositories, despite their metadata differences (Mohan & Brooks, 2003), offering connection to heterogeneous repositories together with query languages and metadata schema.

Finally, e-learning support for learning objects is expected to provide traceability as another functionality. The idea is to monitor human-computer interaction (HCI) in order to offer tutoring, mentoring, coaching, or other types of educational strategies. Thus, learning objects in the educational SW should be accessible, reusable, interoperable, and traceable.

Educational Semantic Web Services

In the traditional Web, users follow hypertext links manually. In the Web services model, users invoke tasks that facilitate some activity, for example, content-based discovery of learning material, fusion of similar educational material from multiple sites, course advertising, and registration.

Service-oriented architectures can improve the development of educational systems, since the systems can be built based on educational Web services even if these services are not yet available or are not known by the developers. This is possible because Web services are described using a service description language, discovered by applications that need to use them, and invoked through the retrieved interface.

A good example of service-oriented architecture for the integration of educational resources is given by the Smart Space for Learning mediation infrastructure, implemented in the Elena project (Simon, Miklos, Nejdl, Sintek, & Salvachua, 2003a; Simon, Nejdl, Miklos, Sintek, & Salvachua, 2003b). In a Smart Space for Learning, providers of educational services are connected within a learning management network, which is based on the peer-to-peer network Edutella. Using the learning network, personal learning assistants support learners in searching, selecting, and contracting learning services. They recommend learning services on the basis of a learner profile and implement rules that allow them to automatically perform several processes such as course registration.

One type of Web service that can contribute strongly in the educational SW is related to Semantic Web mining.

Web mining is the process of discovering potentially useful and previously unknown information and knowledge from Web data (Cooley, Mobasher, & Srivastava, 1997). It can be used in automatic resource discovery, automatic information extraction from Web documents, discovery of common patterns across different Web sites, and validation and interpretation of discovered patterns (Chakrabarti et al., 1999).

All categories of Web mining—content, structure, and use—are of interest for e-learning systems (Devedzic, 2004). Web content mining permits to collect content and knowledge from the Web and organize them into educational Web servers. The server in turn may mine its database trying to discover patterns that allow, for example, finding out new material of interest to the users (learners, instructors, pedagogical agents) based on their profiles. Newly discovered content may also be used to improve available ontologies. Web structure mining allows that an educational server continuously mine the Web and update its database of external educational resources and services available. This information can be used to help learners and pedagogical agents to automatically discover peers on the Web who are interested in the same topic, supporting the creation of communities of learners and of pedagogical agents. Web usage mining also offers several possibilities in educational systems, for example, permitting that educational servers select the most adequate pedagogical strategy for each known learner, based on learner profiles created using discovered usage patterns.

Adaptive Educational Systems

While McLoughlin (1999) considers the necessity to base learning design decisions not only on desired learning outcomes, but also on motivational, cognitive, and volitional views of learning from the learners' perspective, Nelson and Palumbo (1992) believe that computers present limited success as educational tools because learner profiles are usually not taken into consideration, that is, they are not adaptive systems, which could represent learning style, motivation, knowledge level of the domain, and attitudes.

According to Aroyo and Dicheva (2004), a class of adaptive Web-based educational systems forms the basis of the emerging educational SW in order to tailor the growing amount of information to the needs, goals, roles, and tasks of the learner.

Stephanidis and Savidis (2001) categorize adaptation behavior in two classes: one based on knowledge acquired prior to the initiation of interaction that is termed adaptability, and the other based on knowledge derived at run-time that is termed adaptivity. Adaptability and adaptivity can coexist in the same application (Kobsa, Koenemann, & Pohl, 2001). When adaptivity considers many different characteristics of a user, it is termed personalization.

Considering the stack vision for the SW, the functionality to the realization of adaptive systems is obtained on the logic layer, and constitutes a very fertile research area.

Adaptive systems comprise opportunities for adaptation considering three targets, which Brusilovsky and Maybury (2002) view as generations of adaptive systems and which Kobsa et al. (2001) view as distinctive types of data regarding adaptation:

1. the first target regards preferences, interests, and other personal information, considered individually or in groups—ideally this first target allows system personalization;
2. the second target regards goals and activities that are aimed by the user through the application; this second target allows the system to adjust itself according to the dialogue with human beings; it could comprehend content selection and recommendations, among other issues; and
3. the third target regards resource availability discovering and resource optimization, allowing the application of best-effort strategies during the use of computer resources; it could consist of bandwidth and absence of an output device, among other issues.

All three targets can be considered during design and development through the separation-of-concerns strategy, resulting in the following different data services: perception, navigation, interaction, query and retrieval, management, preparation, and authoring services (Tobar & Ricarte, 2005). With such strategy, it is possible to devise a rich ground for adaptation opportunities:

- the perception service is concerned with presentation issues, such as spatial structure, background, color, fonts, sound level, and media synchronization;
- the navigation service is one of the most explored, and it is concerned with link structure, overview map and location, resources already visited, bookmarks, and so forth;
- the interaction service is concerned with input and output devices for HCI, and adaptation can be applied to customization of devices, hot keys, tool control, control and query languages, and so forth;
- the query and retrieval service is concerned with information localization and gathering. It is possible to exploit adaptation through interest representation and updating, according to filtering parameters, and localization of information, according to personal intentions and task goals;
- the management service is concerned with policies for configuration, troubleshooting, security and privacy, and QoS (quality of service). In this service, there are interesting adaptation options to explore in mobile applications;

- the preparation service is concerned with rendering and modality processing. Adaptation can be exploited through selection of media and content (optional explanations, optional detailed information, hints, etc.);
- The authoring service is concerned with support to authoring in the adaptive application, such as with a graphical editor for CSCW (computer supported collaborative work).

Adaptation can be exploited with possession control, admission policy, election instrument, and so forth, and also with authoring tool preferences.

Adaptive technology provides opportunities to designers of educational systems, as any generic interactive system, to afford flexibility to what El Saddik, Fischer, and Steinmetz (2001) call changing user requirements, in order to allow:

- improved ways to people work, think, communicate, learn, critique, explain, argue, debate, observe, decide, calculate, simulate, and design through a computer (Fischer, 2001); and
- that learners personalize, assemble on the fly, and access e-learning on demand, and that development teams build content a single time, store it electronically, reuse it, and deploy it in different formats with a simple button click.

Empirical studies have proven the power and importance of adaptation. For instance, adaptive navigation support can increase the speed of navigation (Kaplan, Fenwick, & Chen, 1993) and learning (Brusilovsky & Pesin, 1998). It can also reduce the problems of information overloading (Thuring, Hannemann, & Haake, 1995), whereas adaptive presentation can improve content understanding (Boyle & Encarnacion, 1994).

There are several reported authoring systems that consider adaptive issues, such as AHA! (De Bra et al., 2003), InterBook (Brusilovsky, Eklund, & Schwarz, 1998), and NetCoach (Weber, Kuhl, & Weibelzahl, 2001). But they do not consider learning objects, avoiding the problem of assembling educational packages out of arbitrary learning objects scattered through the Web.

Ideally, it should be possible through information retrieval techniques to localize and retrieve learning objects (even unknown) in order to allow that the objects could be considered as information sources for content rendering, after preparation according to adaptive rules. An example of information retrieval as an extension to the authoring and processing adaptive system AHA! is the work by Aroyo, De Bra, and Houben (2004).

Representative Examples

Examples of application of SW technologies for e-learning are cited throughout this chapter. Generally, these examples cover one or two layers of the stack vision for the SW. As a matter of fact, building the SW with current available tools is much more complicated than it was to construct the original display-oriented Web. There are yet no complete practical or commercial applications of the SW (Anderson & Whitelock, 2004). However, a broader coverage can be observed in recent research prototypes such as those that compose the Elena project (Simon et al., 2003a; Simon et al., 2003b; Elena, 2005). The Personal Learning Assistant (PLA) (Dolog, Henze, Nejdl, & Sintek, 2004; Henze, Dolog, & Nejdl, 2004), part of the Elena project, is considered in order to overview a representative example of an educational SW application.

The PLA integrates personalization SW services, supported by services for retrieving learning resources and user information. Information about resources and participants involved in learning processes is represented in RDF, based on available metadata and standards, educational and domain oriented. An ontology on learning resources was constructed adopting attributes from the Dublin Core Initiative. Specific domain information is described by concepts and their mutual relationships in the domain. And an enhanced learner model was created by combining and extending IEEE and IMS proposals.

The PLA user interface is provided by a personalized search service. When users type free text, the personalized search service contacts an ontology service to get concepts similar to the ones provided in the typed text, which are then displayed to the user. The user can use the suggested concepts to refine the search. In doing that, the Personalized Search Service sends the refined query to the PLA.

The PLA uses a mapping service to generate a query from a concept list. In addition, the PLA contacts the query rewriting service to rewrite the query according to a learner profile, adding constraints to the query. In the sequence, the PLA sends a message with the rewritten query to the edutella query service, which propagates the query into the edutella P2P network.

The edutella query service returns all query results to the PLA that contacts the recommendation and link generation services, if desired by the learner, to derive recommendation information according to the learner profile or to a group profile. When the personalized results are available, the PLA notifies the personalized search service that displays them to the learner.

Query rewriting can be done through TRIPLE, a rule language for the SW that is based on Horn logic and borrows many basic features from F-Logic (Sintek & Decker, 2002).

The recommendation service can annotate learning resources according to their educational state for a user. One example of a recommendation rule is a rule determining that a learning resource is recommended if all its prerequisite concepts have been mastered by the user.

Predicates used in a query-rewriting rule can use knowledge on learning resource, concepts, users, observations, and learning states from metadata based on types taken from ontologies.

A link generation service connects a learning resource to a context, for example, within a course, links to previous and next steps, or to other resources that provide related examples of the learning resource content.

Similar to a Web portal, a semantic portal is an entry point to resources that may be distributed across several locations, through semantic services such as semantic browsing, semantic search, and smart question answering (Moreale & Vargas-Vera, 2004). Semantic browsing generates navigation pages from a combination of relevant information. Semantic search enhances current search engines with semantics, allowing the removal of non-relevant information. Smart question answering aims at providing answers to a specific question.

From a pedagogical perspective, semantic portals can be seen as an "enabling technology" allowing students to be in control of their own learning. They allow students to perform semantic querying for learning materials and construct their own courses, based on their own preferences, needs, and prior knowledge. This frees tutors from the task of organizing the delivery of learning materials, as soon as they describe the content and contexts in which each learning material can be used, for example using metadata that allow describing, indexing, and searching for the data.

INES (Devedzic, 2004) is an example of architectural proposal for constructing semantic portals. An INES-based portal aims at offering services to teachers, learners, and authors. These services are grouped into four categories: learning, assessment, reference, and collaboration. Learning services include course offering, integration of educational material, tutoring, and presentation. Assessment services support online tests, performance tracking, and grading. Reference services permit browsing and searching libraries, repositories, and portals. Collaboration services include group formation and class monitoring. Through agents and ontologies, INES also enables intelligent educational services to automatically self-delegate their functional roles to other services.

Vargas-Vera and Motta (2004) also propose an architecture for an educational semantic portal. The central component of the architecture is a broker that allows communication between service providers and requesters. It attempts to match a request for a service to the closest service that can provide that functionality. The offered services interact with a number of resources, including databases and documents published on the Web, and subscribe to relevant ontologies. Among the semantic services that an e-learning portal might include, the authors have implemented a question-answering service (AQUA) and a student essay service (SES).

Future Trends

Considering the same structure of this chapter, this section presents some comments, mainly research opportunities based on identified problems. They are by no means exhaustive.

Regarding the construction of educational ontologies, many ontology engineering environments are passive in the sense that they give few guidance or suggestion to ontology developers. A sophisticated development methodology is necessary. However, a methodology itself is not sufficient. Developers need an integrated environment to help them construct an ontology in every phase of the construction process. In other words, a computer system should allow developers navigate in the ontology construction process according to a methodology (Aroyo, Mizoguchi, & Tzolov, 2003a; Mizoguchi, 2003).

Dolog and Henz (Dolog et al., 2004; Henze et al., 2004) believe that the construction of semantic Web services requires the availability of high quality ontologies formally describing information sources. This means that it is essential to have tools that support the creation, maintenance, and consistency verification of information sources along with metadata that describe them. They also advocate that the construction and application of learner profile ontologies and protocols for learner-profile record exchange have to be better investigated.

Regarding standardization, there are efforts related to data and information models, in order to facilitate interchange of data, largely through the specification of metadata mainly for the construction, indexing, searching, and retrieval of learning objects. There are also ongoing proposals for ontologies and Web services. But, there are pressing needs to consider several issues involved in the educational SW, such as: open frameworks for interfaces and architectures so that different parts of an e-learning system can communicate with each other (Paris, 2004); or representations of user information and its sources that can make interoperability for adaptive systems a tractable problem.

Regarding learning objects, a next generation of e-learning environments is about to emerge no longer focusing on documents, but on objects that can be manipulated and executed (interactive—active semiotics) (Keil-Slawik, Hampel, & Eßmann, 2005). There is also the problem of populating digital repositories with learning objects. It may be related to the intrinsic difficulty of authoring metadata, pointing out to the necessity of automatic or semi-automatic tools mainly for annotation.

Regarding Web services, there are several efforts targeting integration of various educational systems and content providers. It is foreseen that learners and services will interact through educational service directories in future educational systems (Devedzic, 2003). For learning services to integrate resources and people, both have to be modeled, and mapping rules for interconnected systems have to be defined (Dolog et al., 2004; Henze et al., 2004). Educational servers will be based on standards, ontologies, and pedagogical agents to support interaction between authors and students and servers, hosting educational content and services.

Regarding adaptive systems, learner models used to the decision making of adaptation actions are uncertain, because their data came from observations and guesses, thus overt (direct control of the adaptive facilities by the user) and scrutable (provision of the current assumptions about the user with justifications) mechanisms should be offered to the student (Dimitrova, 2003). In order to obtain a real personalization, it remains an open research issue as to what is the proper type and number of dimensions to represent in a learner model. Additional dimensions will not always increase the accuracy of the user model but will always increase the complexity of the user model and the requirements to collect additional user information. Another key issue, previously discussed, is concerned with available learning objects that should be considered as information sources.

Besides the efforts for producing standards in the current Web and surely in the future SW, different ontologies, protocols, services, and process specifications will coexist, even within the same domain. Tools and architectures that reduce the high complexity of the process of mapping, integrating, and interconnecting different ontologies, processes, and services will play a major role in the construction of the future Web.

For instance, to discover appropriate learning objects for a particular educational context, ontologies must be defined for different disciplines and languages, and mappings must also be provided. SW mining can be one solution to be exploited in this context. The fusion of research results from the SW with those from Web Mining can help to improve the results of Web mining, using the new semantic structures in the Web, and to construct the SW using the Web, because it can help to discover structures for knowledge organization (ontologies) and to find instances of such structures (Berendt, Hotho, & Stumme, 2002).

Conclusion

In order to present a vision of what has been accomplished toward the educational SW, conceptualization and technologies for the SW are reviewed, and ontologies, metadata standards, learning objects, Web services, and adaptive systems are discussed as main constituents of a future educational SW.

Besides the interest and promises of the educational SW, there are many concerns among potential users that range from fundamental epistemological questions to practicality and implementation problems (Anderson & Whitelock, 2004).

Epistemological questions that cause suspicion in the educational context are not really new and did not show up by the advent of the educational SW. They are related to the capacity of machines and humans to deal with the same set of meaning-filled signs and to the roles that can be played by computers on education, seen as an intense human experience.

Individual differences in learning dictate that technology will facilitate learning for some, but will probably inhibit learning for others, while the remainders experience no significant difference (Russell, 1997).

The next-generation of e-learning systems, combining educational portals, ontologies, agents performing Web mining, and knowledge management to create, discover, analyze, and manage the information scattered on the Web, is a promising basis for constructing social networks. The notion of educational social networks is essential to some authors, when talking about Web-based educational systems. Such networks create a self-organizing structure of learners, information, authors, teachers, and educational institutions. Social relationships, such as friendship, coworking, and exchanging information about common interests, connect these entities (Devedzic, 2004).

The educational community is already using many of the technologies that are on the base of the SW, such as XML and RDF; however, the standards being defined are adopting their own formats and vocabularies, making it cumbersome to integrate educational content and systems with other content and systems. Several researchers, though, are showing their concern with this scenario and are working to simplify the integration of educational content and systems with other types of content and systems that will coexist on the SW (Aroyo, Pokraev, & Brussee, 2003b).

The Elena project and its PLA also raise several relevant points that have to be considered by e-learning practitioners and researchers interested in the educational SW (Dolog et al., 2004; Henze et al., 2004). For instance, the construction of semantic services requires the use of "low level" formalisms that cannot be expected to be mastered by most e-learning practitioners. Environments for service modeling are thus vital for the popularization of educational SW services. It will be convenient that those environments include dynamic service discovery and composition functionalities to simplify the reuse of available services.

But building Web services is not the only difficult problem. The same happens with ontologies, learning objects, and adaptive systems. Their manual construction is very difficult and time consuming, if compared with equivalent non-semantic counterparts. Therefore, automatic and semiautomatic tools to reuse available resources and to construct new ones are crucial. Common to all these building efforts is the semantic tag generation. The annotation problem is the most important to be addressed on the short term.

New tools for markup should make the task easy and natural to computer and educational professionals when developing new systems and agents that cross the (old) Web to automatically build and merge ontologies and tag resources, using Web mining techniques (Berendt et al., 2002; Han & Chang, 2002).

There are initiatives to standardize annotations using a common language, but how and who is going to markup semantically everything in the Web? Not many people are willing to annotate resources unless they can see an immediate gain in doing it (Moreale & Vargas-Vera, 2004).

Privacy in open e-learning environments is another relevant aspect that has received relatively little attention. Prevention of identity proliferation and identity theft, assuring address and location privacy, anonymity provision in databases, and privacy-enhancing authorization policies are also important questions that have to be the subject of further research (Elena, 2005).

Maybe the educational SW can bring real answers to requirements whose solutions have just been seen on movies and are being considered as necessary after terrorist threats begin to be ordinary, that is, automatic recognition of people who have computer chips inserted inside their bodies. These chips could be part of the Web and contain data about the persons who transport them. In order to take into account their interests, goals, and needs, the users could also be electronically recognized as physical individuals to receive personalized services.

References

Anderson, T., & Whitelock, D. (2004). The educational Semantic Web: Visioning and practicing the future of education. *Journal of Interactive Media in Education.* Retrieved April 6, 2006, from http://www-jime.open.ac.uk/2004/1

Aroyo, L., & Dicheva, D. (2004). The new challenges for e-learning: The educational Semantic Web. *Educational Technology & Society, 7*(4), 59-69.

Aroyo, L., De Bra, P., & Houben, G. (2004). Embedding information retrieval in adaptive hypermedia: IR meets AHA! *New Review in Hypermedia and Multimedia, 10*(1), 53-76.

Aroyo, L., Mizoguchi, R., & Tzolov, C. (2003a, December). Onto AIMS: Ontological approach to courseware authoring. In *International Conference on Computers in Education* (ICCE'03), Hong Kong, China. Retrieved April 13, 2006, from https://www.ei.sanken.osaka-u.ac.jp//pub/lora/icce03.pdf

Aroyo, L., Pokraev, S., & Brussee, R. (2003b, November). Preparing SCORM for the Semantic Web. In the *International Conference on Ontologies, Databases and Applications of Semantics* (ODBASE'03) (pp. 3-7). Catania, Sicily. Retrieved April 6, 2006, from http://doc.telin.nl/dscgi/ds.py/Get/File-33767/_113-ODBASE2003.pdf

Berendt, B., Hotho, A., & Stumme, G. (2002). Towards Semantic Web mining. In I. Horrocks & J. Hendler (Eds.), *International Symposium on Wearable Computers* (LNCS 2342, pp. 264-278). Seatle, WA.

Berners-Lee, T., Fielding, R., & Masinter, L. (1998). *Uniform Resource Identifiers (URI): Generic syntax, IETF RFC 2396*. Retrieved April 6, 2006, from http://www.ietf.org/rfc/rfc2396.txt

Berners-Lee, T., Hendler, J., & Lassila, O. (2001). The Semantic Web. *Scientific America, 284*(5), 34-43.

Boyle, C., & Encarnacion, A. O. (1994). MetaDoc: An adaptive hypertext reading system. *User Modeling and User-Adapted Interaction, 4*(1), 1-19.

Brusilovsky, P., Eklund, J., & Schwarz, E. (1998). Web-based education for all: A tool for developing adaptive courseware. *Computer Networks and ISDN Systems, 30*(1-7), 291-300.

Brusilovsky, P., & Maybury, M. T. (2002). The adaptive Web. *Communications of the ACM, 45*(5), 31-33.

Brusilovsky, P., & Pesin, L. (1998). Adaptive navigation support in educational hypermedia: An evaluation of the ISIS-Tutor. *Journal of Computing and Information Technology, 6*(1), 27-38.

Chakrabarti, S., Dom, B. E., Kumar, S. R., Raghavan, P., Rajagopalan, S., Tomkins, A., et al. (1999, August). Mining the Web's link structure. *IEEE Computer, 32*(8), 60-67.

Chen, W., & Mizoguchi, R. (2004). Leaner Model Ontology and Leaner Model Agent. In P. Kommers (Ed.), *Cognitive support for learning—Imagining the unknown* (pp. 189-200). Amsterdam, The Netherlands: IOS Press.

Christensen, E., Curbera, F., Meredith, G., & Weerawarana, S. (2001). Web Services Description Language, version 1.1, W3C note. Retrieved April 2006, from http://www.w3.org/TR/2001/NOTE-wsdl-20010315

Cooley, R., Mobasher, B., & Srivastava, J. (1997). Web mining: Information and pattern discovery on the World Wide Web. In D. Cooke (Ed.), *9th IEEE International Conference On Tools with Artificial Intelligence* (pp. 558-567). Piscataway, NJ: IEEE Press.

Corcho, O., Fernandez-Lopez, M., Gomez-Perez, A., & Vicente, O. (2002). WebODE: An integrated workbench for ontology representation, reasoning and exchange. In A. Gómez-Pérez & V. Richard Benjamins (Eds.), *Proceedings of 13th International Conference on Knowledge Engineering and Knowledge Management (EKAW 2002)*, (LNAI 2473 pp. 138-153). Heidelberg, Germany: Springer Berlin

DAML (2001). Reference description of the DAML+OIL. Retrieved April 7, 2006, from http://www.daml.org/2001/03/reference.html

De Bra, P., Aerts, A., Berden, B., De Lange, B., Rousseau, B., Santic, T., et al. (2003, August). AHA! The Adaptive Hypermedia Architecture. In H. Ashman & T. Brailsford (Eds.), *ACM Hypertext Conference*, Nottingham, UK (pp. 26-30).

Devedzic, V. (2004). Web intelligence and artificial intelligence in eucation. *Journal of Educational Technology & Society, 7*(4), 29-39.

Dimitrova, V. G. (2001). STyLE-OLM: Interactive open learner modelling. *International Journal of Artificial Intelligence in Education, 13*, 35-78.

Dolog, P., Henze, N., Nejdl, W., & Sintek, M. (2004). Personalization in distributed e-learning environments. In S. Feldman & M. Uretsky (Eds.), In *Proceedings of the 13th International World Wide Web Conference (WWW 2004)* (pp. 170-179). New York: ACM Press.

Elena (2005). Elena Final Project Report. Retrieved April 7, 2006 from http://www.elena-project.org/images/other/D73FinalReport.pdf

El Saddik, A., Fischer S., & Steinmetz, R. (2001, July-September). Reusable multimedia content in Web-based learning systems. *IEEE Multimedia, 6*(3), 30-38.

Fellbaum, C. (Ed.). (1998). *WordNet: An electronic lexical database.* Cambridge, MA: MIT Press.

Fensel, D. (2003). *Ontologies: A silver bullet for knowledge management and electronic commerce.* Berlin: Springer-Verlag.

Fensel, D., Hendler, J. Lieberman, H.,& Wahlster, W. (Eds.). (2003). *Spinning the Semantic Web.* Cambridge, MA: MIT Press.

Fischer, G. (2001). User modeling in human-computer interaction. Contribution to the 10th Anniversary Issue of the *Journal User Modeling and User-Adapted Interaction (UMUAI), 11*(1/2), 65-86.

Gennari, J., Musen, M., Fergerson, R., Grosso, W., et al. (2003). The evolution of protégé: An environment for knowledge-based systems development. *International Journal of Human-Computer Studies, 58*(1), 89-123.

Gómez-Pérez, A., & Corcho, O. (2002, January-February). Ontology languages for the Semantic Web. *IEEE Intelligent Systems, 17*(1), 54-60.

Gruber, T. T. (1993). A translation approach to portable ontology specifications. *Knowledge Acquisition, 5*(2), 199-220.

Gudgin, M., Hadley, M., Mendelsohn, N., Moreau, J-J., & Nielsen, H. F. (2003). *W3C recommendation. SOAP Version 1.2 Part 1: Messaging framework*. Retrieved April 7, 2006, from http://www.w3.org/TR/soap12-part1/

Han, J., & Chang, K.C-C. (2002, November). Data mining for Web intelligence. *IEEE Computer, 35*(11), 64-70.

Hendler, J. (2001). Agents and the Semantic Web. *IEEE Intelligent Systems, 16*(2), 30-37.

Henze, N., Dolog, P., & Nejdl, W. (2004). Reasoning and ontologies for personalized e-learning in the Semantic Web. *Educational Technology & Society, 7*(4), 82-97.

Hodgins, W., & Conner, M. (2000). Everything you ever wanted to know about learning standards but were afraid to ask. *LineZine*. Retrieved April 7, 2006, from http://www.linezine.com/2.1/features/wheyewtkls.htm

Kaplan, C., Fenwick, J., & Chen, J. (1993). Adaptive hypertext navigation based on user goals and context. *User Modeling and User-Adapted Interaction, 3*(3), 193-220.

Keil-Slawik, R., Hampel, T., & Eßmann, B. (2005). Re-conceptualizing learning environments: A framework for pervasive e-learning. In M. Kumar (Ed.), *Proceedings of the 3rd International Conference on Pervasive Computing and Communications Workshops (PerCom 2005)* (pp. 322-326). Piscataway, NJ: IEEE Press.

Kobsa, A., Koenemann, J., & Pohl, W. (2001). Personalized hypermedia presentation techniques for improving online customer relationships. *The Knowledge Engineering Review, 16*(2), 111-155.

Kozaki, K., Kitamura, Y., Ikeda, M., & Mizoguchi, R. (2002). Hozo: An environment for building/using ontologies based on a fundamental consideration of "role" and "relationship." In A. Gómez-Pérez & V. Richard Benjamins (Eds.), *Proceedings of the 13th International Conference Knowledge Engineering and Knowledge Management* (LNAI 2473, pp. 213-218). Heidelburg, Germany: Springer Berlin.

Lenat, D. B., & Guha, R. V. (1990). *Building large knowledge-based systems: Representation and inference in the Cyc project*. Boston: Addison-Wesley.

Maedche, A., & Staab, S. (2000, October 2-6). *Mining ontologies from texts* (LNCS 1937, pp. 189-202). Heidelberg, Germany: Springer Berlin.

McLoughlin, C. (1999). The implications of the research literature on learning styles for the design of instructional material. *Australian Journal of Educational Technology, 15*(3), 222-241.

Mizoguchi, R. (2000). IT revolution in learning technology. In *Proceedings of the SchoolNet2000* (pp. 46-55). Pusan, Korea. Retrieved April 7, 2006, from http://www.ei.sanken.osaka-u.ac.jp/miz/Pusan.pdf

Mizoguchi, R. (2004). Ontology engineering environments. In S. Staab & R. Studer (Eds.), *Handbook on Ontologies* (pp. 275-295). Heidelberg, Germany: Springer Berlin.

Mohan, P. (2004). Reusable online learning resources: Problems, solutions and opportunities. In E. Sutinen (Ed.), *IEEE International Conference on Advanced Learning Technologies (ICALT '04)* (pp. 904-905). Piscataway, NJ: IEEE Press.

Mohan, P., & Brooks, C. (2003). Learning objects on the Semantic Web. In K. Kinshuk, & D. G. Sampson, (Ed.), *3rd IEEE International Conference on Advanced Learning Technologies (ICALT '03)*.

Moreale, E., & Vargas-Vera, M. (2004). Semantic services in e-learning: An argumentation case study. *Journal of Educational Technology & Society, 7*(4), 112-128.

Nejdl, W., Wolf, B., Qu, C., Decker, S., Sintek, M., Naeve, A., et al. (2002). Edutella: A p2p networking infrastructure based on rdf. In D. Lassner, (Ed.), *Proceedings of the 11th International World Wide Web Conference* (pp. 604-615). New York: ACM Press.

Nelson, W. A., & Palumbo, D. B. (1992). Learning, instruction and hypermedia. *Journal of Educational Multimedia and Hypermedia, 5*(1), 287-299.

Nirenburg, S., & Raskin, V. (2004). *Ontological semantics.* Cambridge, MA: MIT Press.

Paris, M. (2004). Reuse-based layering: A strategy for architectural frameworks for learning technologies. In E. Sutinen (Ed.), *IEEE International Conference on Advanced Learning Technologies* (ICALT04, pp. 455-459). Piscataway, NJ: IEEE Press.

Patel, C., Supekar, K., Lee, Y., & Park, E. K. (2003). OntoKhoj: A Semantic Web portal for ontology searching, ranking and classification. In R. Chiang,

A. H. F. Laender, & E. Lim (Eds.), *Proceedings of 5th ACM International Workshop on Web Information and Data Management (WIDM)*, New Orleans, LA (pp. 58-61). New York: ACM Press.

Russell, T. (1997). Technology wars: Winners and losers. *Educom Review, 32*(2), 44-46. Retrieved April 8, 2006, from http://www.educause.edu/pub/er/review/reviewArticles/32244.html

Simon, B., Nejdl, W., Miklos, Z., Sintek, M., & Salvachua, J. (2003a, May 20-24). Smart space for learning: A mediation infrastructure for learning services. In *Proceedings of the 12th International World Wide Web Conference (WWW 2003)*, Budapest, Hungary. Retrieved April 8, 2006, from http://www.dbai.tuwien .ac.at/staff/miklos/p616-simon.pdf

Simon, B., Nejdl, W., Miklos, Z., Sintek, M., & Salvachua, J. (2003b, May 20-24). Elena: A mediation infrastructure for educational services. In *Proceedings of the 12th International World Wide Web Conference (WWW 2003)*, Budapest, Hungary. Retrieved April 8, 2006, from http://kbs.uni-hannover.de/Arbeiten/Publikationen/2002/elena_draft_simon.pdf

Sintek, M., & Decker, S. (2002). TRIPLE—A query, inference, and transformation language for the Semantic Web. In *1st Intermational Semantic Web Conference* (NLCS 2342, pp. 364-378).Heidelburg, Germany: Springer Berlin.

Stephanidis, C., & Savidis, A. (2001). Universal access in the information society: Methods, tools, and interaction technologies. *Universal Access in the Information Society (UAIS), 1*(1), 40-55.

Sure, Y., Staab, S., & Angele, J. (2002). OntoEdit: Guiding ontology development by methodology and inferencing. In R. Meersman, Z. Tari, et al. (Eds.), *Proceedings of the Confederated International Conferences CoopIS, DOA and ODBASE* (LNCS 2519, pp. 1205-1222). Heidelberg, Germany: Springer Berlin.

Ternier, S., Duval, E., & Vandepitte, P. (2002, June). *Proceedings of the 14th World Conference on Educational Multimedia, Hypermedia & Telecommunications (EDMEDIA 2002),* Denver, CO. Retrieved June from http://www.cs.kuleuven.ac.be/~stefaan/LOMster/papers/LOMster_long.pdf

Thuring, M., Hannemann, J., & Haake, J. M. (1995). Hypermedia and cognition: Designing for comprehension. *Communications of the ACM, 38*(8), 57-66.

Tobar, C. M., & Ricarte, I. L. M. (2005). The extended abstract categorization map (E-ACM). In S. Cheng & G. Magoulas (Eds.), *Adaptable and adaptive hypermedia systems* (pp. 59-79). Hershey, PA: IRM Press.

Vargas-Vera, M., & Motta, E. (2004). *AQUA—Ontology-based question answering system.* (LNCS 2972, pp. 468-477). Heidelberg, Germany: Springer Berlin.

W3C. (1999). *XML namespaces.* World Wide Web Consortium. Retrieved January 14, 1999, from http://www.w3.org/TR/REC-xml-names

W3C. (2002). *XHTML™ 1.0 The Extensible HyperText Markup Language* (2nd ed.). A reformulation of HTML 4 in XML 1.0. W3C Recommendation. Retrieved August 1, 2002, from http://www.w3.org/TR/xhtml1

W3C. (2004a). *Extensible Markup Language (XML) 1.0* (3rd ed.). W3C Recommendation. Retrieved February 4, 2004, from http://www.w3.org/TR/REC-xml

W3C. (2004b). *OWL Web Ontology Language for Services (OWL-S)*. Retrieved April 8, 2006, from http://www.w3.org/Submission/2004/07/

W3C. (2004c). *OWL Web Ontology Language Reference.* W3C Recommendation. Retrieved February 10, 2004, from http://www.w3.org/TR/owl-ref/

W3C. (2004d). *XML Schema Part 0: Primer* (2nd ed.). W3C Recommendation. Retrieved October 28, 2004, from http://www.w3.org/TR/xmlschema-0

W3C. (2004e, February 10). *RDF Vocabulary Description Language 1.0: RDF Schema. W3C Recommendation.* Retrieved April 14, 2006, from http://ww w.w3.org/TR/rdf-schema/

W3C. (2005). *Synchronized Multimedia Integration Language (SMIL 2.0)* (2nd ed.). W3C Recommendation. Retrieved January 7, 2005 from http://www.w3.org/TR/smil20

Weber, G., Kuhl, H., & Weibelzahl, S. (2001). *Developing adaptive Internet-based courses with the authoring system NetCoach.* (LNAI 2266, pp. 226-238). Heidelburg, Germany: Springer Berlin.

Chapter VIII

Using Semantic Web Technologies within E-Learning Applications

Wilson Castello Branco Neto,
University of Planalto Catarinense, Brazil

Abstract

This chapter reveals how the Web has improved e-learning as well as some of the problems that came along with it. It argues that the main problem is the gap between two groups involved on Web-based learning. The first group spent its energy studying learning processes, although they are not concerned with reducing the costs and the work necessary for the development and management of such systems. On the other hand, the second group aims at facilitating the construction and management of the courses, without turning its efforts toward learning subject. In this chapter, the union of technologies developed by both groups, such as intelligent tutoring systems, adaptive hypermedia, learning management systems, and learning objects, is discussed. The proposal to put together the four technologies is based on Semantic Web technologies, aiming to solve problems faced by developers, teachers, and learners of Web-based learning.

Introduction

The terms e-learning and computer-supported learning (CSL) are used to refer in general to the use of technologies of information and communication to make available instructional modules. One form of e-learning is the Web-based learning (WBL), in which the instructional contents are accessed through Internet or intranets. The term came from the integration of the Web and the systems of e-learning, developed in the '70s and '80s, which were locally carried out at the students' computers.

Two large groups of researchers were developed, with the birth of WBL. While the first one's purpose was to facilitate the students' learning process, the second aimed at studying methods and tools able to facilitate the courses' construction and management. Studies carried out by the members of the first group helped to create technologies such as intelligent tutoring systems (ITS) and adaptive hypermedia systems (AHS). Researchers from the second group were responsible for the birth and progress in learning management systems (LMS) and learning objects (LO).

Although the progress obtained by both groups is significant and useful, it is known the lack of consolidated results from the union of the benefits reached in each one of them. It is clear that the means offered by LMS and LO to the people responsible for building and managing courses do not improve the students' learning. On the other hand, it is noticed that the benefits provided to the students by ITS and AHS make courses construction and management an arduous task. This prevents these technologies from being incorporated in the majority of the systems existent today, due to the difficulty to reuse instructional and adaptive techniques present in ITS and AHS.

This chapter's objective is to identify and discuss the main advantages and problems related to each of the technologies used in WBL. In addition, some proposals based on the Semantic Web (SW) to solve such problems are presented. We intend to show that SW can be the key to combining the advantages obtained by LMS, LO, ITS, and AHS with a view in developing the adaptive learning systems based on Semantic Web.

Background: E-Learning and Web-Based Learning

In the last decades it was noticed the insertion of the computer as a supportive tool to learning as well as the terms computer-supported learning and e-learning.

Such terms are used to define a new way of teaching/learning, distinguished at first by the use of instructional programs disposed in floppy disks and CD-ROMs.

The Internet and the Web have revolutionized e-learning in the nineties and have also stated the Web-based learning term. It was through Web resources that the transmission of knowledge took place as a wider process, which makes a better instruction of students possible, thus minimizing a crucial problem: the lack of interactivity. Technologies involved in WBL at present can be divided into two large groups, each with different objectives and results as follows.

Adaptive Learning Systems

Since the seventies, there has been intensive research aiming to improve conditions for e-learning students and to develop systems able to adapt the available content to different students. Among other methods, it is important to highlight the intelligent tutoring systems and the adaptive hypermedia systems.

ITS researchers aim to create systems with the ability and knowledge as similar as possible to human teachers. Its main purpose is to offer the students a personalized environment in the interface as well as in the content. It also aims to overcome one of the biggest difficulties of traditional and computer-supported teaching by adapting the content to each student's own characteristics and learning difficulties (Self, 1990).

There are three main questions regarding ITS: what should be taught; who will be taught; and how will it be taught. The answer to the first question defines the subject to be taught by the system (Domain Model); the second answer defines for what kind of student this subject will be taught (Student Model); and, finally, the third answer indicates the way in which the subject must be structured (Tutoring Model). According to Self (1999), these answers have formed the research on ITS in the seventies and have constituted their classic architecture.

Domain model is composed by the material, which describes the subject to be introduced to the students. It can contain texts, images, videos, exercises, and so forth. Individual characteristics and knowledge about the students are stored in student model. According to its data, an ITS defines the best teaching strategy to be used, among the strategies contained in tutoring model (Vicari & Giraffa, 2003).

AHS are another kind of system used to support learning process. AHS were formed joining hypermedia and techniques of user's modeling, due to the limitations of the static hypermedia pages. AHS build a model with objectives, preferences, and knowledge of the users, which is used during the interactions, so that the system can adapt itself to the user's needs. With the Web-based learning arising, AHS have become primordial in the development of ITS interfaces. With its methods, it is possible to customize the presentation of instructional contents through the Web, according to the user's knowledge and previous experience.

To solve problems such as user's disorientation in hyperspace or overloaded information, AHS acts in two areas: adaptive presentation and adaptive navigation support. Brusilovsky (1996) showed technologies that support these two great areas, which are reviewed and updated in Brusilovsky (2001), originating the taxonomy presented in Figure 1.

The technologies related to the adaptive presentation's objective is to adapt the content of a page according to the knowledge, objectives, and any other individual characteristics of the user. Adaptive navigation support aims at helping users to find their paths in hyperspace at local or global levels. Furthermore, it allows users to have access to different views from the system, based on their own characteristics.

Figure 1. Adaptation technologies in adaptive hypermedia

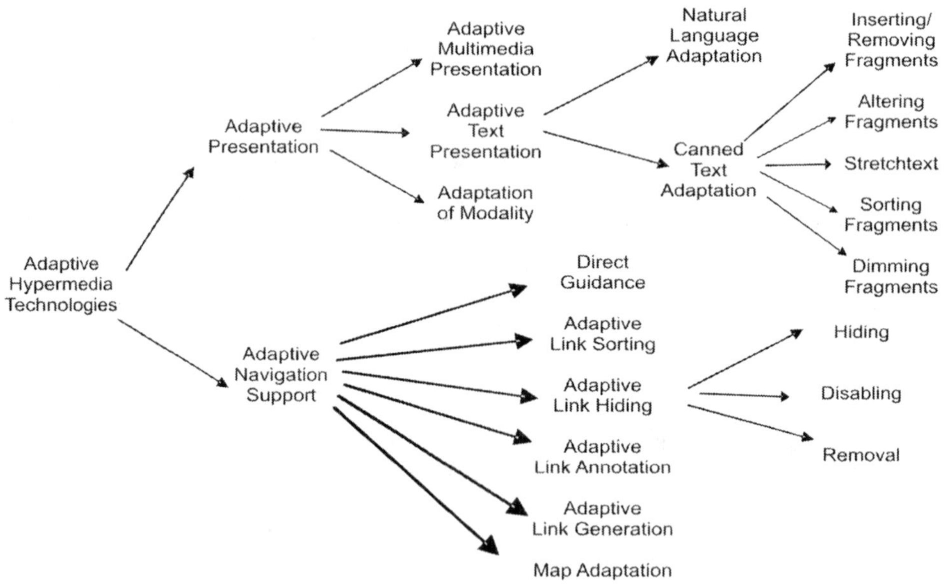

Learning Management Systems and Learning Objects

The first Web-based learning systems (WBLS) were adapted directly from instructional programs distributed in CD-ROM. During that period, it was necessary to create the whole base structure for each new developed course. Then, it was necessary to improve the process of construction and management of WBLS as well as to create structures capable of performing their basic functions, which could be applied in different courses. Then came along the learning management systems (LMS) concept to separate the instructional subject from administrative functions (registration of students, teachers, subjects, evaluations, etc.).

LMS are specialized learning technology systems based on the state-of-the-art Internet and Web technologies in order to provide education and training, following the open and distance learning paradigm (Avgeriou, Papasalouros, Retails, & Skordalakis, 2003). LMS allow teachers to develop and publish the instructional materials and exercises and be able to communicate with students. For the students, LMS should provide access to the materials, besides making tools available for communication among them. With LMS emerging, a faster development occurred on WBLS, as they were not designed for any specific course or area. Among well-known LMS are WebCT (www.webct.com) and Blackboard (www.blackboard.com).

There was a growth on the learning objects (LO) concept following the search for a mechanism able to ease the WBLS development. IEEE Learning Technology Standards Committee (2002) defines LO as an entity, digital or non-digital, which can be used, reused or referenced during technology-supported learning. They can be constituted by instructional subjects (text or multimedia); learning objectives; instructional software; people; tools; and other mentioned entities during the teaching and learning process.

According to Longmire (2001), some characteristics are common to all LO, despite applications, such as:

- **Modularity:** An LO is a small part of a course, which can be formed by other LO;
- **Flexibility:** As LO are built in order to have beginning, middle, and end, they are flexible, and can be reused without any kind of maintenance;
- **Interoperability:** Creating standards to store LO allow its reuse at learning systems and in other applications;
- **Increase of knowledge significance:** When an LO is reused many times in several specializations, its consolidation gets spontaneously better as time passes; and

- **Indexation and search:** Standardization facilitates the search for a required LO.

Beyond any doubt, the greatest advantage in LO is reusing them. After they are created and made available, they can be used by any LMS, which has enough support for searching and linking to those resources. Thus, the creation of Web-based courses has become an easier task, as teachers do not need to prepare all material. They should only integrate the LO related to their courses.

Problems with E-Learning and Web-Based Learning

Following the analysis of technologies presented in the previous section, it is clear the presence of different objectives about e-learning or Web-based learning among groups of researchers. This section's aim is to discuss the main problems in each approach, and some given solutions are presented.

Problems with Adaptive Learning Systems

ITS main contribution to e-learning is the architecture divided in: domain model; tutor model; and student model. Such division allows the contents to be personalized to the characteristics of each student while using the system, facilitating learning. Nevertheless, many difficulties arose with the use of ITS to solve problems such as the lack of personalization in e-learning.

These difficulties are related to the fact that tutor models and student models are strongly dependent on domain models. Knowledge of the problems faced by students when learning the chosen subject is important in order to create aid mechanisms (tutor model). That is why the information used to define a better strategy to teach a student should be based or even be part of the domain model. These factors hamper the reutilization of courses or part of them; tutorial strategies and information about students, causing the construction of an ITS to be slow and expensive.

Another issue is that the majority of professionals in education do not see ITS and some other e-learning systems with good eyes. According to them, ITS are not well founded in theories of Instructional Sciences or Learning Sciences. The lack of support in these theories is already serious, as ITS are created by people who spend months studying in order to model the domain, the tutorial strategies, and information about the students. It is worse when authoring tools are used to create ITS with a view in reusing the contents, activities, and strategies (Murray, 1999). Mizoguchi and Bourdeau (2000) list many current problems in ITS and in their development process:

- there is a deep conceptual gap between authoring systems and authors;
- authoring tools are neither intelligent nor user-friendly;
- building an ITS requires a lot of work as it is always built from scratch;
- knowledge and components embedded in ITS are rarely sharable or reusable;
- it is not easy to make shareable specifications of functionalities of components in ITS; and
- many of the ITS are unaware of the research results of instructional sciences and learning sciences.

Besides ITS, another research area has contributed to improving WBL. AHS have been an important link to the development of Web-based adaptive learning. Their purposes are the same as ITS ones; they look for the development of systems capable to adapt themselves to the students' personal characteristics and needs. With their methods and techniques it is possible to expand the application of traditional ITS to Web-based ITS, making WBL more interactive and efficient. However, just like the ITS, AHS are strongly based on information from student models; therefore, they suffer the same problems in relation to reusing components in different domains.

According to the information presented, it is clear that adaptive learning systems still present a number of limitations. As the lack of bases in learning theories is the main fault from an educational point of view, the difficulty to reuse information during the construction of ITS and AHS seems to be the major problem from a computational point of view.

Problems with LMS and LO

Some of the problems found in old e-learning systems were solved with LMS. Among these problems is the difficulty to manage and make available various courses simultaneously. However, in some aspects the situation has worsened, like the pedagogic support for the build up of a course and the content not adapting to each student's needs. These aspects were seriously damaged by LMS for being generalist and independent of knowledge domain. Students find them equal or even worse than traditional classes as they are not able to adapt contents and instructional activities to each student's needs. LMS are alike the teachers that administrate a class with many students. They do not consider the diversity of learning styles.

In general, students feel frustrated and put off by LMS. According to Pittinsky (2003), the main reasons are the lack of orientation caused by the excess of information, the lack of feedback concerning the result of their activities, and the fact that they feel isolated when facing the task to learn a new content. LMS have not followed progresses in the teaching-learning area, and they do not allow instructional contents to adapt to students.

Despite all problems presented, LMS are clearly dominant over intelligent and adaptive learning systems today. Nagy (2004) highlighted their success by mentioning that the technology section for Web-based learning is under the control of such supplier systems. However, according to Brusilovsky (2003), this is a surprising control as for every function carried out by a LMS, there is another system able to perform it better. For instance, Interbook (Brusilovsky, Eklund, & Schwarz, 1998) and NetCoach (Weber, Kuhl, & Wiebelzahl, 2001) allow the construction of adaptive materials, which provide a quicker learning than any LMS. Furthermore, specific tools for students' monitoring and for learning collaborative, such as shown in Oda, Satoh, & Watanabe, 1998), are also more efficient than LMS.

Considering that there are applications performing the same functions as LMS that obtain better results, there is only one way to explain the success of this technology: the integration of many functions in a single system. People who do not use LMS to build and make available their courses will need tools for the creation and organization of instructional material, others to control and make available students' access, others for progress monitoring, and so forth. Having to use various tools hardens the work of the teacher, who will need to know various technologies, and the students will need to manipulate different systems. Another characteristic found in LMS that makes them more useful than other tools is the modularity, which allows each person to use only the desired resource.

It can be said that LMS with the LO concept brought advantages, diminishing time and effort needed to build up courses; however, some problems remained unsolved. A teacher wishing to build up a course, for instance, should know which LO will be used and where they are stored. Such limitations still happen because the way the information is currently organized on the Web does not allow more elaborated searches. Pages written in natural language only allow searches by keyword from the text, making undesired results to return while relevant ones are discharged.

When creating a statistic course, for instance, a teacher can look for an LO that tackles the "Mean" subject, but requires materials for working adults, who are very interactive, have a high level of difficulty, and present the content with examples related to the work field of the students. It is very unlikely that this teacher will be able to get a precise search with all the parameters on today's Web. According to Koper (2004), finding, sharing, and reusing LO are still very hard duties due to the lack of semantic descriptions about them.

Toward the Solution

A number of proposals have been presented to solve given problems. Many of them are a combination of ITS, AHS, LMS, and LO technologies, creating intelligent learning management systems (iLMS). However, the way used today to structure knowledge on the Web makes it more difficult to come up with more elaborated solutions. As there are no precise and semantically rich definitions about learning systems, pedagogic techniques, adaptive techniques, students, and LO, it is then not possible to develop WBL systems and courses to provide better results to students or that are easier to construct.

The Semantic Web can contribute significantly to this by allowing the storage of structured information about any entity involved in learning process. Thus, it will be possible to create LO, student models, adaptive techniques, and so on, described semantically, which can be used by different LMS that understand these descriptions, in order to generate adaptive courses founded on learning and instructional theories.

Web-Based Learning in the Semantic Web Era

Previous sections presented the technologies used nowadays on Web-based learning, as well as some problems concerning them. In this section, some proposals are introduced aiming to solve such problems through the use of the SW technologies. First, the SW objectives and structure are described, so that related works and the proposal presented later can be understood.

The Semantic Web

Semantic Web is the name given to a project coordinated by W3C (World Wide Web Consortium), which "gives information a well-defined meaning, better enabling computers and people to work in cooperation" (Berners-Lee, Hendler, & Lassila, 2001, p. 1). While AI tried to enable computers to understand human language, the SW has looked for forms to represent the human knowledge in a way that it can be easily understood and manipulated by computers. The main purpose of the SW is to allow software agents to execute more and more complex tasks on behalf of people, without their intervention. It will facilitate the increase of services available on the Web, and the creation of many others still not thought of.

According to Berners-Lee (1999), the SW development requires:

- languages to express meta-information on documents, which can be processed by computer;
- standard terminology on the most different domains; and
- tools and structures able to make use of such languages and terminology to provide support for information search, access, presentation, and maintenance.

To satisfy those requisites, the SW project was structured with layers with different functions, as seen in Figure 2. While low layers correspond to the basic structure for data transmission, high ones contemplate semantic definitions, which will allow their automated process by computers.

The inferior layers (URI and UNICODE) are responsible for making possible, respectively, the identification of the resources in a univocal form (World Wide Web Consortium, 2001), and standardize the codes to represent characters independently from platform (Unicode Inc., 2004). Above Unicode and URI are Extensible Markup Language (XML) (Fallside & Walmsley, 2004; Holzner, 2000) and namespaces (Bray, Hollander, & Layman, 1999). XML provides elements to describe the syntax and the basic semantic definitions of the documents, making them independent of application. Namespaces constitute a mechanism to create unique names to elements and features of the XML documents.

The SW layer immediately above XML and namespaces is formed by resource description framework (RDF). It is defined by Manola & Miller (2004) as a language to denote resources information one the Web through metadata and consequently satisfying the first requirement stated by Berners-Lee (1999).

Figure 2. Semantic Web layers

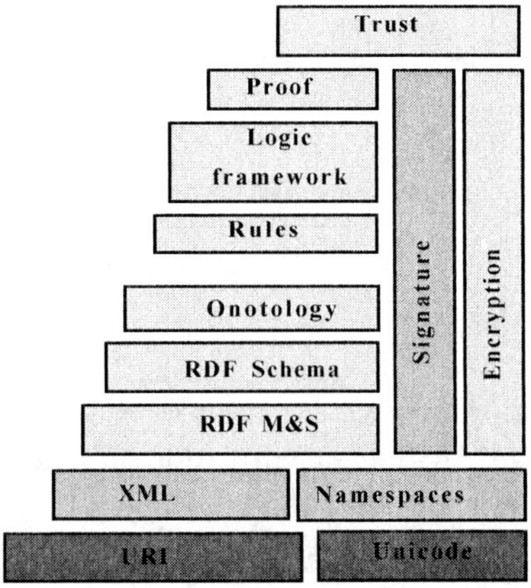

Klyne and Carroll (2004) highlight some reasons why RDF has become a W3C recommendation for the SW:

- Its capacity of providing information about Web resources (metadata);
- RDF can do for computer processable data just as the Web did for hypertext: allow them to be processed out of the private environment in which they were created; and
- its power to get new information by combining different sources, by providing them with a single language, and allowing Web content to be processed by software agents.

RDF is based on statements that establish a value for a property associated to any resource, and can be represented through triples or graphs (Klyne & Carroll, 2004). When considering XML advantages, W3C opted to use it as a base for RDF documents construction, creating the normative syntax called RDF/XML, defined by Beckett (2004).

It is important to highlight that the XML and RDF languages described previously allow metadata to be joined to documents. However, these technologies have not standardized how the metadata names should or should not be used, and do not even explain their meaning. To satisfy the second requisite stated by Berners-Lee (1999), it is necessary to create vocabularies that standardize the terms used on different domains. Both RDF schema (RDFS) (Brickley & Guha, 2004) and ontology are used for such task, although the latter has more representative power.

Some concepts increase the understanding of ontology role, when the term refers to engineering knowledge:

- an ontology is an explicit specification of domain concepts and the relation between them, providing a formal vocabulary for information exchange (Noy, Sintek, Decker, Crubézy, Fergerson, & Musen, 2001);
- "an ontology is an explicit specification of a conceptualization. Conceptualization means a simplified and abstract view of the world which is intended to represent for some purpose" (Gruber, 1993, p. 1).

In short, ontology's objective is to make possible the formalization, reutilization, and sharing of knowledge. When document information needs to be processed by applications, ontology should be used, in opposition to situations where the content should only be shown to humans. Currently, Ontology Web language (OWL) is the most frequent language used to create ontology on the SW (Dean & Schreiber, 2004; McGuinness & Harmelen, 2004; Smith, Welty, & McGuinness, 2004).

The highest point reached within limits of knowledge representation, sharing, and reutilization is expressed by ontology. However, for SW to occur, there is a need to build programs able to exchange data on the Web and to make decisions without constant people intervention. These are the characteristics of Web services, which satisfy the third requirement necessary for SW development. Web service is a technology, which has been opposed to the barriers imposed by proprietary solutions to the interoperability and integration of the applications. Daconta, Obrst, and Smith (2003, p. 58) define them as "software applications which can be discovered, described and accessed through XML protocol as well as other Web standard protocols in intranets, extranets and in the Internet."

This section has demonstrated the SW through technology descriptions that support it, aiming to understand learning systems presented later. It is important to emphasize that some SW upper layers, like rules, logical framework, validation, and confidence mechanisms were not approached due to their few consolidated results and also because most applications built for the SW so far, use only inferior layer resources.

Related Work

Some works that have already applied SW technologies in the WBL are presented in this section aiming to identify their main characteristics, advantages, and disadvantages. Initially, a proposal of an iLMS called Multitutor developed by Simic, Gasevic, and Devedzic (2004) is presented, which is divided in three modules:

- **Expert:** allow teachers to create the content of their courses;
- **Student Model:** where the students' personal data and their results are stored; and
- **Tutoring:** the module that contains pedagogic strategies.

This structure seems to present an unimportant innovation in relation to what is already known about ITS. However, its differential is in the way that each module is implemented, with metadata and ontology. The system uses ontology to represent course information and the student model. A course is divided into chapters, which are divided into several lessons. LO are associated to each lesson, and it has a concept, an explanation, several tests, and learning contents. The ontology of the students includes their basic data, stereotype, real skills, and the skills estimated by the system. By using this information, tutoring module will determine the next contents to be presented to the student and how to present them.

Due to its capacity to represent the student model and the subject of the courses through ontology, Multitutor allows metadata to link to those resources and then facilitates its reuse. However, some important characteristics have not been shown in this system. One is the lack of interoperability with other systems. As ontology used to describe knowledge domain, and student models do not follow metadata standards defined by international entities such as IEEE or IMS, other systems may not adopt them to describe their information. Therefore, reusing information can only occur among courses built in Multitutor. The language used to represent ontology is another area for improvement. Multitutor uses XML schemas to fulfill this task. Due to their higher semantic representativeness, languages such as RDFS and OWL could be used instead.

Ontology and metadata are also used in another WBL system, presented by Devedzic (2004), named intelligent educational systems (INES). According to INES, WBL should be completely distributed as shown in Figure 3.

The author's intention is to offer a distributed structure, where LO are stored in different servers and are accessed in a transparent way. Teachers use it during

Figure 3. Semantic Web-based learning structure

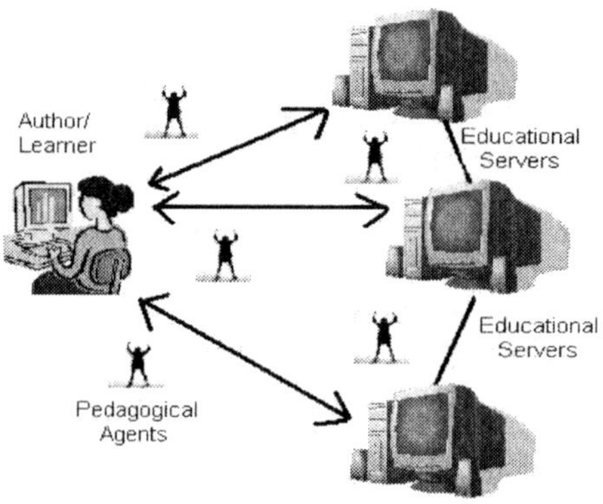

course construction, and students access it to learn subjects. This transparency should be assured by pedagogic agents, which are responsible for locating educational servers where the LO are stored. Educational servers should also be able to search for necessary materials to complement information that will be shown.

Another characteristic of the educational servers is that they should perform as ITS, by using pedagogic knowledge, domain knowledge, as well as information about the students to determine the best order and form for content presentation. Besides, the server should offer services common to any LMS, such as content presentation, exercises and tests accomplishment, support to consultation of materials, group organization, and communication among their participants. Besides the use of pedagogical agents, every educational server should be connected to some ontology. By using ontology, educational servers can delegate tasks to other servers, as well as search for information in order to accomplish its tasks. Thus, a network of educational servers properly described and interlinked through ontology, can interact on behalf of a common objective, which is to maximize the students' learning.

Even though the INES proposal was very promising, it only reached a few practical results. According to the author of this proposal, there should be much more research in the areas such as intelligent Web services, social networks, ontology, and Web mining until the proposal is fully developed.

Based on presented work, we notice that the construction of educational ontology as well as the description of resources through metadata occurs in order to improve WBL. However, we also notice that ontology is being built by isolated groups and many times not following the accepted international standards. This way, researchers may perpetuate the problem, which follows the development of adaptive learning systems, for more then three decades.

During all these years, only the people who actually developed them are using intelligent and adaptive techniques, because of the difficulty to suit them and to reuse them in different domains. If research on applying SW in WBL carries on in the way that each group defines their own ontology without following a standard, it is possible that created systems and courses will remain being used only by their creators as ontology applied by them is unknown by others, who also have their own "private" ontology.

To make vocabularies (ontology) be really useful, it is necessary that they represent the involved community's consent. In the educational area, some organizations are leading studies about standards to represent information on educational process, namely: IEEE Learning Technology Standardization Committee (LTSC), Advanced Learning Technology (ADL), and IMS Global Learning Consortium. It is paramount to follow these standards to facilitate interoperability of the developed systems with other systems, once terminology recommended by international entities will be used.

Among the main standards already developed are IEEE Learning Object Metadata (LOM) (IEEE Learning Technology Standards Committee, 2002) and IMS Learning Resource Meta-data Information (IMS—Global Learning Consortium, 2001a), which specify conceptual schemas with the structure defined for a group of metadata of the LO. In addition to those standards, other ones were also suggested describing information on students using Web-based learning systems, as follows: IEEE Learning Technology—Public and Private Information for Learners (PAPI Learner) (IEEE Learning Technology Standards Committee, 2000) and Learner Information Packaging (LIP) (IMS—Global Learning Consortium, Inc., 2001b).

Completing the group of standards, some were suggested in order to define from content organization aspects, such as IMS Content Packing (IMS—Global Learning Consortium, Inc., 2004) and SCORM Content Aggregation Model (Advanced Distributed Learning, 2004a), to matters referring to the instructional process, which is IMS Learning Design (IMS—Global Learning Consortium, Inc., 2003a), as well as the sequence and navigation of the content, like SCORM Sequencing and Navigation (Advanced Distributed Learning, 2004c) and IMS Simple Sequencing and Behavior Model (IMS—Global Learning Consortium, Inc., 2003b).

Figure 4. Systems involved in courses construction and availability

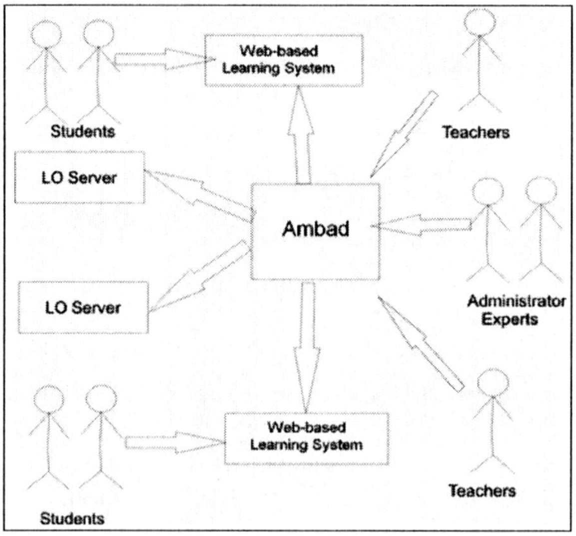

Ambad

Some of the standards previously described are used to allow the development of Ambad. It is a computational system for creating and running adaptive courses by Web, which adopts SCORM standards. Basically, two kinds of computational entities interact with Ambad: Web-based learning systems and LO servers, as shown in Figure 4. WBLS should have the basic functions of LMS, such as content presentation, students' registration, and communication among participants. LO servers should store LO described through LOM standard to be used and reused during courses construction.

Ambad administrators and experts on the domain, learning and adaptive techniques are responsible for creating and updating ontology. This ontology describes the knowledge about the domain to be taught, pedagogic knowledge to be used during the course construction, and the adaptation rules. Information provided by them is stored in domain, pedagogic, and adaptive ontology presented in Figure 5, which describes the internal structure of Ambad, as well as the modules that are accessed by each kind of user.

Building a Course

Teachers and course designers interested in building a course through Ambad should define some information, which is manipulated together with the informa-

Figure 5. Adapting system structure and its relations

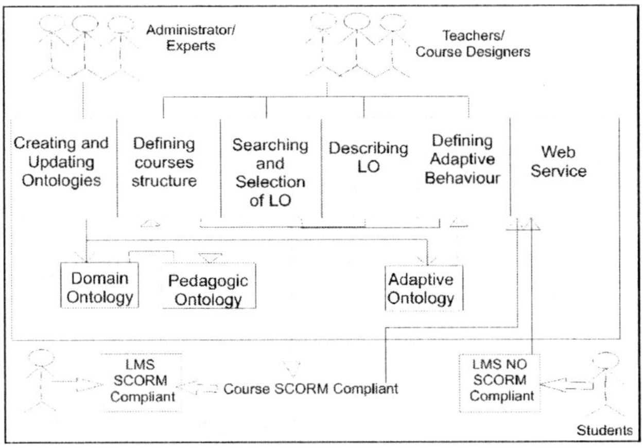

Figure 6. Domain ontology main classes

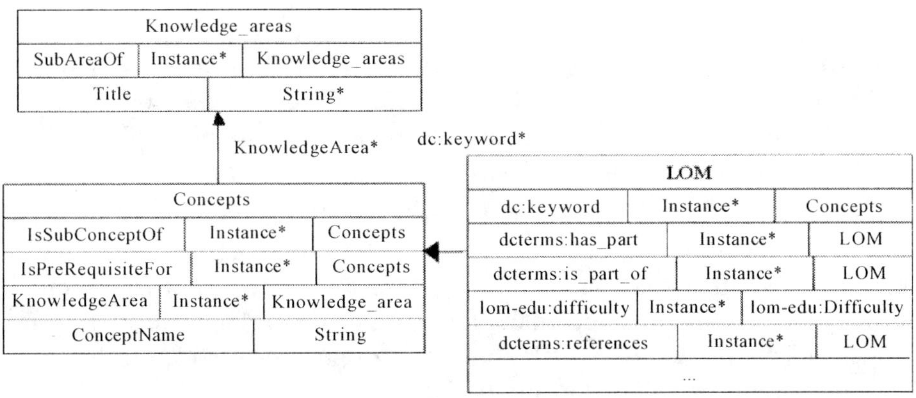

tion from ontology, in order to define the course structure, its contents (LO), and adaptive behavior. Aiming to facilitate course creation and the reuse of learning activities and LO, a domain ontology was built, allowing the standardization of the terminology used to describe concepts associated to a subject, as well as the metadata associated to LO stored on servers. The main ontology classes are knowledge areas, concepts, and LOM (Figure 6), whose instances represent subjects or concepts that can be approached in a certain domain, and the LO that approach these concepts.

Based on domain ontology classes, a conceptual map with instances from concepts and knowledge areas classes can be drawn, so that people responsible for creating a new course can select the concepts to be used, based on a

Figure 7. Domain ontology instances

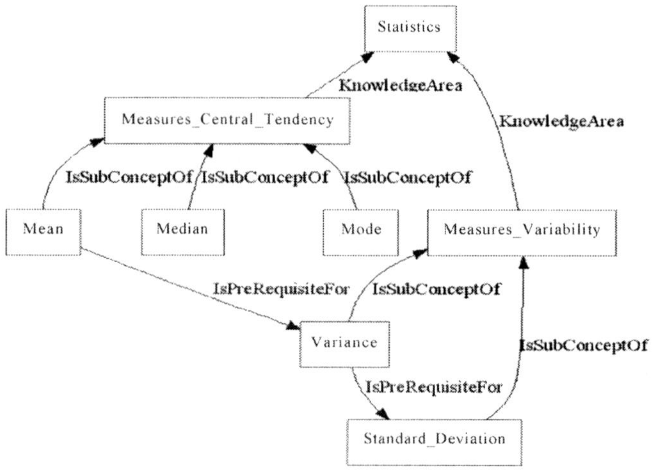

standardized terminology. Those instances are related to each other through associations such as SubAreaOf, KnowledgeArea, isSubConceptOf, or isPrerequisiteFor, to make easier the selection of relevant concepts for a course. Figure 7 presents a conceptual map built for Statistics with some concepts.

Selecting the instances of the class "concepts" from domain ontology, the person in charge of creating the course will be defining which concepts will be approached. To help with structure and organization of the activities responsible to allow students to learn selected concepts, rules that relate information from the user with information from pedagogical ontology are used in a similar way to what is done today by ITS authoring tools.

The pedagogic ontology includes educational terms definition. Its classes (bold) and instances (italic) presented next were obtained from Blomm (1956), Gagnè (1985), and Gagnè, Briggs, and Wager (1992) studies:

- **Instructional Strategies:** *Independent Study, Indirect Instruction, Direct Instruction;*
- **Instructional Objectives Types:** *Knowledge, Comprehension, Application, Analysis, Synthesis, Evaluation*;
- **Type of Knowledge**: *Verbal Information: Names and Facts; Intellectual Skills: Discrimination, Defined Concept, Concrete Concept, Rule, High-Order Rule*; *Cognitive strategy*;
- **Instructional Events**: *Gaining Attention, Informing the Objective, Recall of Prerequisites, Presenting the Material, Providing Guidance,*

Eliciting the Performance, Providing Feedback, Assessing the Performance, Enhancing the Retention and Transfer;

- **Didactic Resources**: *Example, Lecture, Narrative Text, Exercise, Simulation, Diagram, Figure, Exam, Problem Statement, Figure, Experiment.*

Providing the system with information such as the kind of student that will take the course, which instructional strategy will be used on the course, and so on, teachers allow the system to reason and define which activities should be planned so that students can reach their objectives and the best order of activity. At present, only a few rules to help with structuring the course have been established. An example is the rule that verifies the kind of instructional strategy the user wishes to apply. If "Independent Study" is chosen, activities are organized following the same sequence in which the concepts were selected, so the academic will have the freedom to navigate between them any time.

When choosing "Indirect Instruction" or "Direct Instruction," the system will create an activity for each concept, and the sequence will be based on the kind of relation between the concepts (isSubConceptof or isPrerequisiteFor). The difference between these strategies is that in the Indirect Instruction the system generates the sequence explained previously, but allows the student to break the passage straight to other activities whenever he/she pleases. Unlikely, in Direct Instruction the generated course does not allow skipping from an activity to another that is not directly related (Previous and Next).

Knowledge available in pedagogic ontology may also help in the following stage, which is the association of LO to be used in teaching each concept, by indicating what kind of LO should be associated to each part of the course. One or more instance of class LOM can be associated to each instance of class concept, and they represent LO used to build the course. Each instance is not only associated with a concept but also has a physical location of the LO and a set of information defined in the LOM standard such as difficulty, interactivity level, learning resource type, and so forth.

Instances of class LOM that represent the LO stored on the servers are also related to each other through associations such as isPartOf, hasPart, Requires, isRequired by,and so forth, in order to make the search of LO easier to compose a learning activity.

When selecting LO, which will be part of the course, it is important to observe that more than one about the same content is chosen to compose the same activity whenever possible, although with distinct characteristics. Through defined information in the adaptive ontology, the user can create the rules in charge of defining the adaptive behavior of the course. These rules define the possible ways for sequencing the contents and selecting which of these LO will be presented to the student, based on the student's personal characteristics as well as on his/her results during the course. This module is still being constructed, and its structure is based on the work of Dolog, Henze, Nedjl, and Sintek (2003).

After defining activities, structure, LO, and adaptive behavior used in the resulting course, it should be available in a way that the WBLS are able to run it. As a process result, a course built in agreement with SCORM standards is obtained, which will be stored in a SCORM Content Package and can be run in any LMS that adopts this standard.

A SCORM Content Package contains an XML file, named IMSManifest, which defines its structure, resources used by it as well as the rules determining how it should make content sequencing and navigation. The union of the IMSManifest file with other files used in the course (LO) builds a Content Package, which is made available through LMS to the students.

Figure 8. IMSManifest file with a SCORM standard course structure

```
<?xml version="1.0" encoding="UTF-8" ?>
- <manifest ...>
+ <metadata>
-<organizations default="DMCE">
 -<organization identifier="DMCE">
 <title> Example </title>
 +<item identifier="A1" identifierref="r1">
 +<item identifier="A2" identifierref="r2">
 -<imsss:sequencing>
   <imsss:controlMode flow="true" />
  </imsss:sequencing>
 </organization>
</organizations>
-<resources>
-<resourceidentifier="r1" href="A1/i01.html"
  adlcp:scormType="sco" type="webcontent">
     <file href="A1/01.html" />
     <file href="A1/02.html" />
</resource>
-<resource identifier="r2" href="A2/f01.html"
  adlcp:scormType="sco" type="webcontent">
     <file href="A2/01.html" />
     <file href="A2/02.html" />
 </resource>
 </resources>
</manifest>
```

Figure 8 shows an IMSManifest of a course with two modules, denominated respectively, Activity_1(A1) and Activity_2(A2), about "mean" and "variance" that illustrate the course generated by Ambad.

As domain ontology defines that "mean" concept is prerequisite for "variance," Ambad defined that it should be addressed in activity 1, while "variance" concept is addressed in activity 2. During Activity_1, the student will access the content of two HTML pages (A1_01.html and A1_02.html), which present, respectively, the concept of "mean" and some exercises concerned. In Activity_2, learner will accesses the pages A2_01.html and A2_02.html, which also contain the concept and the applications of "variance"(A2_01.html) and some exercises (A2_02.html).

Although that is the sequence for information exhibition, users can access them in the sequence they wish, since the option "controlMode flow" is defined with the "true" value. It allows the access to all pages at any time, despite the student having already visited or not visited the previous ones. Such flexibility is possible due to the option of indirect instruction when choosing instructional strategy during course creation.

The code shown in Figure 8 is quite simple and helps to understand the result generated by Ambad. It is a similar file, and together with all the resources referenced by it that forms the Content Package sent to LMS SCORM compliant to be made available to the students. With this proposal, the intention is to solve the already mentioned problem of high cost to develop adaptive learning courses founded in learning and instructional theories because it allows the incorporation of defined knowledge in pedagogic ontology without its creator having to deeply dominate it.

Course Availability

WBL systems represented in Figure 4 that are used to run the courses can be any LMS, despite adopting or not adopting SCORM standard, as seen in Figure 5. The difference is the fact that LMS SCORM compliant are able to run the generated course without needing to interact again with Ambad, once they know the rules defined in advanced distributed learning (2004a, 2004b, 2004c). However, as it is expected not to impose many barriers in the LMS development process, another module was developed in Ambad, which is implemented by a Web service, capable of simulating the behavior of an LMS SCORM compliant.

According to Figure 5, LMS that does not adopt the SCORM standard can make requests to the Web service sending some data, such as student characteristics and the content presented at a given moment. Ambad will access the information of the course created by itself, run the rules defined in Advanced Distributed Learning (2004b, 2004c), and forward to the LMS the contents that should be presented next to the student. These resources will adapt the contents presented to the students because even if not altering the contents of LO, WBL systems will be able to guide the student through adaptive navigation techniques.

Future Trends

A student comes home and decides to study more about the contents of object-oriented programming lecture he has just attended. After connecting his computer, he runs his educational assistant and asks to elaborate a lecture of approximately two hours about classes and instances. After a couple of seconds searching the Web, the educational assistant presents the lecture proposed. As the assistant knows the student gets easily discouraged when reading long conceptual definitions, he draws up a lecture containing three sections: quick reading of concepts; analyzing examples; and exercises solving (...). When noticed that the user was reading the concepts and examples for a longer period than expected, the educational assistant interrupts and asks if there are any problems. The user's reply is that he cannot see the relation between concepts and given examples.

The assistant that has never planned an OOP lecture before realizes his strategy was not suitable to provide student learning. He immediately returns to the Web and interacts with other WBLS with courses available on the same subject. After sending the user's characteristics to the WBLS, the educational assistant will be sent a new lecture proposal with a different structure and resources than the one it had created. As the lecture was sent by a system with more experience in the subject than the user's assistant, it then decides to trust the proposal and to present it to the student.

When the assistant identifies that the user has fulfilled all activities given in the new lecture, it informs the WBLS that supplied the lecture about the results reached by the user. Studying the information, the WBLS identifies the main user's characteristics in relation to OOP and suggests a series of activities to the assistant, which can be presented the next time the user requests a lecture on the same subject. It also points to another WBLS where other students with similar characteristics and knowledge are undertaking a course so that the user can interact with them. At last, the WBLS asks the user's educational assistant where the material is used in the first lecture so that it can use them again in future lectures.

This story illustrates how WBL will be in the future. It will be a reflection of what takes place in the classrooms today but with more efficiency. We can tell that computers will be able to: exchange information in order to reach shared objectives; search for knowledge about questions related to teaching and learning; and allow the change in teacher focus to the student. If computational entities involved in the example, that are educational assistant and WBLS, were substituted by human teachers, we would have a well-known situation of a teacher who asks for help to another one with more intensive knowledge of the subject to elaborate his lecture. This example also shows that WBL becomes even better than traditional learning as the lecture is not planned for a group of students, but for a specific student who will have several teachers available to him/her at any time.

Even though it will take some time for this to occur, the direction undertaken by many researchers in the field leads us to believe in possibilities. The main tendencies found in WBL research are unfolding in three major aspects: standardization of information aiming at interoperability; building of systems based on instructional and learning theories; and building pedagogic and adaptive techniques independent of domain.

Initially, WBL will go through a standardization phase, because with the arising of SW and the increase of ontology researches, the knowledge is no longer restricted only to human beings. Knowledge can now be shared with computers aiming to make them perform several duties in peoples' names without their intervention. Nevertheless, for the computers to have full autonomy they should be able to share standardized and consensual information about the teaching and learning process.

Although people related to teaching and learning do not support standardization of information, they will render to the countless benefits reached when standardizing the terms, like the facility to reuse LO, instructional activities, instructional strategies, and information about students. Standardization is fundamental to WBL development as it was for other areas of computing. For example, if it was not for the standardization of protocols, the built of TCP/IP and HTTP among others, Internet would not have the number of users like it does.

Furthermore, an idea already presented many years ago and that still constitutes in future trends is the wish to build learning systems well founded in instructional and learning theories. Programmers' team and domain experts no longer construct tools on their own. Professionals linked to learning are fundamental to the development of systems, which allow academics to reach their instructional objectives in the easiest and quickest manner. Therefore, the union between researchers of artificial intelligence, multimedia, learning science, and instructional design science will be stronger.

Another important point is a research that has been carried out to generalize instructional and adaptive techniques from current systems so they can be used and reused easily in any system. At last, it is pointed out that e-learning and Web-based learning will become synonyms in the 21st century as the learning systems stand-alone will be no longer adequate due to the expanding and improvement in communication technology. Any developed system shall follow the computer supported collaborative learning paradigm.

Conclusion

It is a general consent that content adaptation to the student's characteristics is the key to improving the Web-based learning process. Also, it is clear that the cost for the development of adaptive learning systems is the great barrier that hampers the creation of more elaborate tools. It justifies the importance of research accomplished with the intention of facilitating and reducing costs in the construction of Web-based adaptive learning systems.

This chapter has shown that SW technologies can assist in solving these problems, allowing a standardized way of description of resources involved in learning such as LO, instructional strategies, instructional activities, students, and so forth. Certainly, the link of Web-based learning, metadata, and ontology is a non-trivial process, which involves creation of standards that can be used by different providers of learning systems, in order to guarantee the interoperability requested by the SW.

The first steps toward that interoperability have already been taken with the creation of several standards of educational metadata. Besides the definition of these standards, some necessary changes have been made in adaptive techniques, as they are based on the knowledge domain to be shown. Based on metadata standards and on ontology construction for standardizing the knowledge domains, adaptation techniques and pedagogic knowledge, it will be possible to solve, at least partially, the mentioned problem about the high cost for the adaptive educational applications development, due to the reutilization of LO and the information described on ontology.

There are still just a few results consolidated from this link. Just like the Ambad system presented in this chapter, the majority of Semantic Web-based learning systems are still not being used in large scale so that more crushing conclusions about its efficiency can be established.

Ambad has been currently used only to build courses in two domains, statistics and computer programming, even though the domain ontology easily allows it to be expanded to other areas through the creation of new instances. Furthermore, the influence of pedagogic ontology data in the resulting course is still small, thus significant according to professionals of learning area involved in the project. At present, deeper studies have been carried out in the instructional design area to improve the performance of the module in charge to assist in the definition of the course structure and of the LO that compose it.

The evaluation of the course generated by students still has not been done because the main objective of the system is to facilitate the construction of courses based on the Web, a duty that requires more involvement of teachers. Nevertheless, as soon as the adaptive module is concluded, the course will be available to students so that it is possible to evaluate whether the adaptation mechanisms are assisting in learning the contents.

References

Advanced Distributed Learning. (2004a). *Sharable Content Object Reference Model—SCORM® Content Aggregation Model. v. 1.3.1.* Retrieved March 7, 2005, from http://www.adlnet.org/index.cfm?fuseaction=DownFile&libid=648&bc=false

Advanced Distributed Learning. (2004b). *Sharable Content Object Reference Model—SCORM® Run-Time Environment. v 1.3.1.* Retrieved March 7, 2005, from http://www.adlnet.org/index.cfm?fuseaction=DownFile&libid=648&bc=false

Advanced Distributed Learning. (2004c). *Sharable Content Object Reference Model—SCORM® Sequencing and Navigation. v.1.3.1.* Retrieved March 7 ,2005, from http://www.adlnet.org/index.cfm?fuseaction=DownFile&libid=648&bc=false

Avgeriou, P., Papasalouros, A., Retails, S., & Skordalakis, M. (2003). Towards a pattern language for Learning Management Systems. *Educational Technology & Society*, *6*(2), 11-24.

Beckett, D. (2004). RDF/XML syntax specification (revised). In *World Wide Web Consortium Recommendation*. Retrieved June 10, 2004, from http://www.w3.org/TR/rdf-syntax-grammar

Berners-Lee, T. (1999). *Weaving the Web.* London: Orion Business.

Berners-Lee, T., Hendler, J., & Lassila, O. (2001, May 17). The Semantic Web. *Scientific American, 284*(5) 34-43.

Bloom, B. S. (1956). *Taxonomy of educational objectives, Handbook I: Cognitive domain*. New York: David McKay.

Bray, T., Hollander, D., & Layman, A. (1999). Namespaces in XML. In *World Wide Web Consortium Recommendation*. Retrieved May 22, 2004, from http://www.w3.org/TR/1999/REC-xml-names-19990114/

Brickley, D., & Guha, R. V. (2004). RDF Vocabulary Description Language 1.0: RDF Schema. In *World Wide Web Consortium Recommendation*. Retrieved June 10, 2004, from http://www.w3.org/TR/2004/REC-rdf-schema-20040210

Brusilovsky, P. (1996). Methods and techniques of adaptive hypermedia. *User Modelling and User-Adapted Interaction, 6*(2-3), 87-129.

Brusilovsky, P. (2001). Adaptive hypermedia. *User Modelling and User-Adapted Interaction, 11*(1-2), 87-110.

Brusilovsky, P. (2003). A distributed architecture for adaptive and intelligent Learning Management Systems. In R. A. Calvo & M. Grandbastien (Ed.), *Proceedings of Workshop on Towards Intelligent Learning Management Systems* (pp. 5-13). Artificial Intelligence in Education Conference, Sydney, Australia.

Brusilovsky, P., Eklund, J., & Schwarz, E. (1998). Web-based education for all: A Tool for developing adaptive courseware. *Computer Networks and ISDN Systems, 30*(1-7), 291-300.

Daconta, M. C., Obrst, L. J., & Smith, K. T. (2003). *The Semantic Web—A guide to the future of XML, Web services, and knowledge management*. Indianapolis, IN: Wiley Publishing Inc.

Dean, M., & Schreiber, G. (2004). OWL—Web Ontology Language Reference. In *World Wide Web Consortium Recommendation*. Retrieved September 21, 2004, from http://www.w3.org/TR/2004/REC-owl-ref- 20040210/

Devedzic, V. (2004). Web intelligence and artificial intelligence in education. *Educational Technology & Society, 7*(4), 29-39.

Dolog, P., Henze, N., Nejdl, W., & Sintek, M. (2003). Towards the adaptive Semantic Web. In F. Bry, N. Henze, & J. Maluszynski (Ed.), *Lecture Notes in Computer Science, Vol. 2901* (pp. 51-68). Mumbai, India. Springer.

Fallside, D. C., & Walmsley, P. (2004). XML Schema Part 0: Primer. In *World Wide Web Consortium Recommendation*. Retrieved May 22, 2004, from http://www.w3.org/TR/2004/REC-xmlschema-0-20041028/

Gagne, R. M. (1985). *The conditions of learning and theory of instruction*. New York: Holt, Rinehart & Winston.

Gagne, R. M., Briggs, L. J., & Wager, W. W. (1992). *Principles of instructional design* (2nd ed.). Orlando, FL: Harcourt Brace Jovanovich College Publishers.

Gruber, T. R. (1993). A translation approach to portable ontologies. *Knowledge Acquisition, 5*(2), 199-220.

Holzner, S. (2000). *Inside XML*. Berkeley, CA: New Riders.

IEEE Learning Technology Standards Committee. (2000). *IEEE draft standard for learning technology—Public and private iInformation (PAPI) for learners (PAPI Learner)*. Retrieved September 10, 2004, from http://ltsc.ieee.org/wg12

IEEE Learning Technology Standards Committee. (2002). *IEEE standard for learning object metadata*. Retrieved June 15, 2004, from http://standards.ieee.org/

IMS—Global Learning Consortium, Inc. (2001a). *IMS Learning Resource Meta-data Information Model v1.2*. Retrieved April 24, 2004, from http://www.imsglobal.org/metadata/index.html

IMS—Global Learning Consortium, Inc. (2001b). *IMS Learner Information Package - Information Model v1. 0*. Retrieved March 7, 2005, from http://www.imsglobal.org/profiles/lipinfo01.html

IMS—Global Learning Consortium, Inc. (2003a). *IMS Learning Design—Information Model v1.0*. Retrieved March 7, 2005, from http://www.imsglobal.org/specificationdownload.cfm

IMS—Global Learning Consortium, Inc. (2003b). *IMS Simple Sequencing Information and Behaviour Model. v 1.0*. Retrieved March 25, 2005, http://www.imsglobal.org/simplesequencing/ssv1p0/imsss_infov1p0.html

IMS—Global Learning Consortium, Inc. (2004). *IMS Content Packing—Information Model. v1.1.4*. Retrieved March 7, 2005, from http://www.imsglobal.org/content/packaging/cpv1p1p4/imscp_infov1p1p4.html

Klyne, G., & Carroll J. J. (2004). Resource description framework (RDF): Concepts and abstract syntax. In *World Wide Web Consortium Recommendation*. Retrieved June 10, 2004, from http://www.w3.org/TR/

Koper, R. (2004). Use of the Semantic Web to solve some basic problems on education: Increase flexible, distributed lifelong learning, decrease teachers' workload. Special Issue on the Educational Semantic Web. *Journal of Interactive Media in Education, 6,* 1-23.

Longmire, W. (2001). *A primer on learning objects.* VA: American Society for Training & Development.

Manola, F., & Miller, E. (2004). RDF Primer. In *World Wide Web Consortium Recommendation*. Retrieved June 10, 2004, from http://www.w3.org/TR/rdf-primer/

McGuinness, D. L., & Harmelen F. (2004). OWL—Web Ontology Language Overview. In *World Wide Web Consortium Recommendation*. Retrieved September 15, 2004, from http://www.w3.org/TR/2004/REC-owl-features-20040210/

Mizoguchi, R., & Bourdeau, J. (2000). Using ontological engineering to overcome common AI-ED problems. *International Journal of Artificial Intelligence in Education, 11*(2), 107-121.

Murray, T. (1999). Authoring intelligent tutoring systems: An analysis of the state of the art. *International Journal of Artificial Intelligence in Education*, *10*, 98-129.

Nagy, A. (2004). *E-learning*. (E-Content Report 6). ACTeN—Anticipating Content Technology Need. Retrieved April 11, 2006, from http://www.acten.net/uploads/images/423/e-learning.pdf

Noy, N. F., Sintek, M., Decker, S., Crubézy, M., Fergerson, R. W., & Musen, M. A. (2001). Creating Semantic Web contents with Protege-2000. *IEEE Intelligent Systems*, *16*(2), 60-71.

Oda, T., Satoh, H., & Watanabe, S. (1998). Searching deadlocked Web learners by measuring similarity of learning activities. In *Proceedings of Workshop WWW-Based Tutoring, 4th International Conference on Intelligent Tutoring Systems,* San Antonio, TX.

Pittinsky, M. S. (2003). *The wired tower: Perspectives on the impact of the Internet on higher education,* Englewood Cliffs: Prentice Hall.

Self, J. (1990). Theoretical foundations for intelligent tutoring systems. *International Journal of Artificial Intelligence in Education, 1*(4), 3-14.

Self, J. (1999). The defining characteristics of intelligent tutoring systems research: ITSs care, precisely. *International Journal of Artificial Intelligence in Education*, *10*, 350-364.

Simic, G., Gasevic, D., & Devedzic, V. (2004). Semantic Web and Intelligent Learning Management Systems. In *Proceedings of International Workshop on Applications of Semantic Web for E-Learning,* Maceio, Brazil.

Smith, M. K., Welty, C., & McGuinness, D. L. (2004). OWL Web Ontology Language Guide. In *World Wide Web Consortium Recommendation*. Retrieved June 10, 2004, from http://www.w3.org/TR/2004/REC-owl-guide-20040210/

Unicode Inc. *What is Unicode*. Retrieved May 28, 2004, from http://www.unicode.org/standard/WhatIsUnicode.html

Vicari, R. M., & Giraffa, L. M. M. (2003). Fundamentos dos sistemas tutores inteligentes. In D. Barone (Ed.), *Sociedades artificiais: A nova fronteira da inteligência das máquinas* (pp. 155-208). Porto Alegre: Artmed.

Weber, G., Kuhl, H. C., & Wiebelzahl, S. (2001, September 1). Developing adaptive Internet based courses with the authoring system NetCoach. Lecture Notes in Computer Science, Vol. 2266. In S. Reich, M. M. Tzagarakis, & P. M. E. De Bra (Ed.), *Proceedings of Third Workshop on Adaptive Hypertext and Hypermedia*(pp. 226-238). Sonthofen, Germany.

World Wide Web Consortium (2001). URIs, URLs, and URNs: Clarification and recomendations 1.0. Retrieved May 25, 2004, from World Wide Web: http://www.w3.or/TR/uri-clarification

Chapter IX

Using Open Archives and Learning Objects for Reusing CSL Contents: The SCORM – Sharable Content Object Reference Model

Rogério Patrício Chagas do Nascimento,
Universidade do Algarve, Portugal

Abstract

In this chapter the SCORM standards as a mean of creating skills to support the conception and development of e-learning devices (contents and systems) are introduced. It is shown how the SCORM, combined with new technologies/techniques as metadata harvesting, XML family, RSS, and feedreaders, offers a potentially substantive approach to understanding the dissemination of open archives initiatives and learning objects repositories in a variety of contexts. Furthermore, understanding the underlying assumptions and theoretical constructs through the use of the

SCORM Model will not only teach the researcher a better way to design and develop CSL contents, but also help in the understanding of storing, distributing, sharing, and reusing CSL contents made by themselves or by other institutions abroad.

Introduction

In the last decade, e-learning has been a widespread matter of interest both for entities (institutions) and people. In particular, the discussion focused on the way to guarantee the e-learning systems effectiveness and efficiency. What supports this reflection is essentially the identification of adequate mechanisms to guarantee the consistency of the learning processes supported by the information and communication technologies.

On the other hand, other fundamental questions regarding the content of such learning processes appeared. Can we share our knowledge? Moreover, can we share our work? Can we distribute the work? What do we get in advantage with all this? If we have interest in sharing our work, how do we achieve such a goal? In this context, references are to be found to support not only the conception and development of e-learning devices (contents and systems), but also the reuse of these devices. In this aspect, the SCORM (sharable content object reference model) can bring decisive contributions in the learning objects and in the institutional initiatives that promote "open archive" systems and metadata harvesting.

In next section, we will define a learning object repository. Moreover, the XML family and RSS (really simple syndication) format will be defined. In our opinion, such technologies can promote the learning objects repositories. In this section, the reader will find a list of the main international institutions and relative norms for the creation of institutional repositories. It will be boarded the innovative institutions and organizations that spread the use of open archives and free software. These organizations essentially aim to the sharing and use of metadata and systems that deal with Learning Objects storage and distribution.

The following section will detail the SCORM standards. It will describe the architecture model and the main standards involved. It begins with an introduction to the SCORM norms, later justifies the SCORM CAM (SCORM content aggregation model), the SCORM RTE (SCORM run-time environment), and, finally, talks about the SCORM SN (SCORM sequencing and navigation).

In the second to last section, you can see examples of learning objects repositories. In particular, it will describe the proposal of a repository elaborated to manage the *Projecto Sabiá* intellectual production. The *Projecto Sabiá* is a humanitarian and intercontinental project supported by the *Caravela Digital* project. The author of this chapter idealized the *Caravela Digital* to deal with the scientific and pedagogical productions of the *Projecto Sabiá*.

Finally, in the last section, there is a compilation of some proposals and conclusions that can be drawn from this work.

Learning Objects Repositories

We are living in a revolutionary time for information and knowledge in academic institutions. As the researchers develop their work in a global contribution, they are constantly searching more efficient (however less expensive) platforms to share their own products: the scientific data and its publications.

The aim of this chapter is to motivate the reader to exercise its social responsibility in the current knowledge society. This does not mean the information society defined by Toffler (1984). Information does not lead necessarily to the knowledge, and the increase of the amount of information without an integration method tends to increase the confusion and the difficulties of data processing. Through the spreading and propagation of the use of learning objects repositories, this chapter aims to stimulate the use of new tools to diminish this gap between Information and Knowledge.

Following pioneering works as the Arxiv, Ginsparg (1996) declared at Los Alamos National Laboratory that institutions and communities in the whole world were constructing institutional repositories of its digital archives. In addition, these archives were open sources because they would like to share their works in the academia.

On the one hand new elements appear as the digital libraries (or catalogued resources), the resources institutional repositories (repositories with homologated technologies like JPG, MPEG, etc.), the metadata virtual repositories (or libraries) with simultaneous functions of library and distributed repositories, and the cataloguers (or search engines) that take care of resources indexation and localization. On the other hand, new ways of interaction that make use of those elements get immense popularity. They are the weblogs, the feedreaders, the podcastings, the Web portals with contents syndication, the new chat tools, Web communities, and digital repositories.

Transversely to this conjuncture, appears the learning objects. Wiley (2000) defines them as any digital object that it can be used to give support to the learning activity. However, in this definition, learning object can be confused with learning resource. A learning resource and a markup document (that associates metadata to the resource) compose a learning object. In a simple way: RESOURCE + METADATA = LEARNING OBJECT.

In turn, institutional repositories are used to capture, to store, to index, to preserve, and to redistribute the intellectual production of an institution in a digital format (Lynch, 2003). Diverse sources of multimedia data (text, images, audio, and video) compose this production to supply necessities in several areas. The institutional repositories supply physical storage for a long time. They facilitate the digital management of items in a safe way, including standard services for search and data recovery, security copies, replication of data, and updating of stored documents.

In the context of this work, digital institutional repositories that make use of learning objects define a learning objects repository.

Open Archive

Dedicated organizations motivate the current *momentum* to decide interoperability problems among digital documents, repositories, and libraries. These organizations help to establish automatic interchange between Digital Libraries through the definition of technologies, standards, and methodologies. They promote the creation of simple protocols such as, for example, the protocols used in the metadata interchange. Hence, communication nets formed by institutional repositories making possible the information exchange, the knowledge dissemination, the "pairs" communication, and the scientific knowledge development, among others.

Among these organizations, it distinguishes OAI—Open Archive Initiative (Lagoze & Sompel, 2001), PKP—Public Knowledge Project[1], InterPARES[2], the BOAI[3], and the OAIster (Wilkin et al., 2003). These initiatives promote the implantation and dissemination of digital repositories with open archives. Such archives are "open" because they are collected for other added-value services. What this means is that a process named "metadata harvesting" creates databases, and the main systems do not hold back documents stored in the distributed bases but make "links" to the same ones. Currently, the most famous metadata harvesting protocol is the OAI-pmh—Open Archives Initiative Protocol for Metadata Harvesting (Nelson & Warner, 2002).

Metadata and Free Software Systems

Appraised research centers start to develope free software to support open archives organizations. Developed in England by the University of Southampton, the GNU EPrints[4] is distinguished amongst the main systems that support the implementation of an institutional repository with open archives. Other important free systems are the OJS—Open Journal System[5] (produced in Canada by the University British Columbia)—and the DSpace (Bass & Branschofsky, 2002), resultant of a partnership between the HP—Hewlett-Packard Company—and the MIT—Massachusetts Institute of Technology—in the United States.

In turn, these systems are supported by primary metadata standards like the DCES—Dublin Core Metadata Element Set[6], the Marc-21[7], and for several other standards. For example, systems that aim to manage papers, abstracts, journals, e-magazines, or thesis can use these standards for document indexations.

In Brazil, three important initiatives are in progress. The first one is the *Plataforma Lattes*[8], which created the LMPL—*Linguagem de Marcas da Plataforma Lattes*[9] (Lattes Platform Markup Language). Among others, LMPL indexes the information about the professors' and researchers' *curriculum vitae*. The second one is the IBICT—*Instituto Brasileiro de Informação em Ciência e Tecnologia*[10] (Brazilian Institute of Information in Science and Technology)—established in 1976. The IBICT recently created the SEER—*Sistema Electrónico de Editoração de Revistas* (Electronic System of Magazines Editoring)—which is an OJS adaptation for publication of electronics magazines. The IBICT also created another tool for approval framework named DICI—*Diálogo Científico em Ciência da Informação* (Scientific Dialogue in Information Science). The DICI uses the Eprints, and it is a space of free access to store different types of digital documents. Furthermore, IBICT created the BDTD—*Biblioteca Digital de Teses e Dissertações* (Thesis and Dissertations Digital Library). This latter tool aims to integrate the existing thesis information systems of all Brazilian educational institutions. Finally, the third most important Brazilian initiative is the SciELO—Scientific Electronic Library Online[11]. This virtual e-library comprehends a selected list of Brazilian scientific magazines.

In Portugal, the main initiative launched in 2004, the b-On—*Biblioteca do Conhecimento Online*[12] (Online Knowledge Library)—congregates the main publishers of international scientific magazines. It intends to offer a vast set of online scientific articles for the participant universities. An example of Portuguese institutional repository is the RepositoriUM[13]. Developed by the University of Minho, the MIT DSpace system supports it.

Adjacent Technologies

The following subsections describe the adjacent technologies that will be able to offer benefit to learning objects repositories. They describe XML language, XML Schema, RSS format, and feadreaders.

XML Family

The XML is a description language based on text that allows software developers to describe, distribute, and change data between applications[14]. Developed by the W3C—World Wide Web Consortium—XML is a robust language for information modelling that quickly emerged as the standard for metadata (auto-description of data) interchanged via Web by mainframes and client-server applications. The XML facilitates the data transference between servers.

The main advantage in the use of an XML document consists of the complete separation between data and its formatting. Differently of the HTML, the XML uses marks (or tags) to delimit pieces of data and leaves the applications that will read the XML document in charge of the data interpretation. XML is also a way to describe data independently of the platform used. It is legible in such a way for human beings as for machines (Chester, 2001). XML data also are independent of language. The XML solutions are much more flexible because it is possible to express data in a literal format (opposed to a binary codification).

Nowadays, some incompatible databases distribute vast repositories of legacy information. The XML family allows the identification, changes, and processing of these data in a way that they can understand each other. If necessary, it is possible to normalize new formats for particular applications.

The XML is a family of technologies. The XML 1.0 (Bray et al., 2000) is a specification that defines tags and attributes of an XML element. Around of XML 1,0, an increasing set of optional modules that supplies a set of tags and attributes also exists, such as XML Schema, XSL, CSS, XSLT, XSL:FO, XML Namespaces, DOM, Xlink, Xpointer, and so forth.

A DTD (document type definition) or an XML schema[15] can be used to state structures and relationships between data. This ability allows the computer programs to validate XML data. This occurs to certify whether the system can use such data. A DTD specifies and validates the types of tags an XML document can enclose. Anyway it is difficult to specify a DTD for a complex document in a way that it prevents all invalid combinations and only allows the valid ones (Armstrong et al., 2003). For example, it is impossible to specify with a DTD that the tag <heading> described for one <book> must have the <title> and the <author>, while the <heading> described for one <chapter> only needs the <title>. Therefore, DTD does not have sensitivity to the context.

To attenuate these disadvantages some proposals of "hierarchic" schemas appeared. Known as XML Schema, the W3C proposal became the standard *de facto*. This complex standard has two parts. The biggest and more complex part specifies the structure relationships. The other part states mechanisms to validate XML elements content, defining a Datatype for each element.

RSS and Feedreaders

RSS (really simple syndication) is a document format. As XML, RSS is W3C-based too. An RSS reader (or Feedreaders) calls documents named RSS Feeds or aggregators. Lately, some Web browsers incorporated aggregators' functions. For example, the Mozilla Firefox™ (www.mozilla.org) comes with this characteristic.

Usually, RSS (or content syndication) can be used to publish Web pages, news headings, blogs, and other information. New uses continuously emerge, especially in the education world. In this field, RSS files can be used to syndicate modules of learning, jobs, new publications, scientific works, and so forth. As informative resources, RSS files can create a new generation of Web portals for students, professors, and educational managers. Thus, the access to particular areas of interest became easier (Harrsch, 2003).

Some previsions state that a second Internet age is arriving with nets development that open access to information and, therefore, to knowledge. At this time, we can have notice, information, articles, new features, and entertainment without browsing Web pages to look for its updates. With RSS, it is possible to subscribe a notice server and new features with a Feedreader[16], which automatically verifies all the Web pages that are indicated and shows the new contents that had been added.

E-Learning Standards

During the decade of 1990, great investments in different e-learning technologies appeared. The race in the e-learning market led to the proliferation of different products with different quality standards. Technologies such as authors' tools, synchronous contribution, and contents management are still in an immature state; such situation can cause frustration for the final users. The suitable content development lacks in interactivity. The creation of norms in the production of such products can promote the interoperability and consequently the integration of technologies.

However, what had greater influence on the quality was the creation of interoperability norms that improve the compatibility between the content and the LMS—Learning Management Systems. Gradually, all of the industry accepted the e-learning standards. Table 1, extracted from SRIC-BI[17], describes this e-learning evolution supported by quality norms. It is possible to distinguish two phases of evolution: the first phase up to 2004 and the second phase with a prognostic up to 2008.

Table 1. E-learning evolution supported by quality norms

1998-2004	2002-2008
Content and closed LMS architectures	Norm and open LMS architecture content-based
Course orientation	Learning object orientation: information consisting of independent media elements, reused like construction modules blocks
Static and text-based content	Learning based in simulations and synchronous collaboration tools
Separated e-learning components	Integration of LMS, LCMS, mobile components and synchronous collaboration tools
LMS as a separate application	LMS integrated like a application component (ERP, CRM, HRIS, etc)
Orientation for formation and development costs reduction	Orientation towards the reduction of costs, and the increase of productivity, optimization of the human capital and strategic advances
To form the work force	Formation available for all members of the company, from staff to suppliers and customers

Nevertheless, before the term "e-learning" appeared in the formation market, many organizations had already started to work toward the creation of a set of technological and pedagogical specifications. They aim to normalize the use of metadata in the CSL (computer-supported learning contents) to use the user's profiles definition, contents sequencing, Web courses structure, and the way of contents management.

The following groups, listed in alphabetical order, developed the aforementioned initial works: AICC—Aviation Industry CBT (computer-based training) Committee; ARIADNE—Alliance of Remote Instructional Authoring and Distribution Networks will be Europe; DCMI—Dublin Core Goal-Dates Initiative; IEEE—Institute of Electrical and Electronics Engineers; and, IMS—Global Learning Consortium, Incorporation, among others.

First, these groups appoint to different norms application areas, working simultaneously, but not in a coordinate way. Later, the ADL (advanced distributed learning) decided to coordinate a process with the aim of creating a reference model: such process is known as SCORM (sharable content object reference model). The ADL is an organization composed by the North American Defence Department, the Department of Work, and American National Guard.

Thus, the SCORM is a unified set of specifications and norms for e-learning contents, technologies, and services. Nowadays, the groups presented above are working together to set the SCORM in a collaborative way.

SCORM – Sharable Content Object Reference Model

The SCORM (sharable content object reference) model is an interrelated set of specifications techniques mainly established in the previous work of the AICC, IMS and IEEE. The SCORM aims at the creation of a "Content Model." Different "books" deal with the mentioned specifications:

- **SCORM Overview[18]:** Presents the ADL initiative and the summaries of the guidelines of specifications techniques contained in other sections.
- **SCORM CAM[19]:** Supplies the specifications to identify and add resources in structuralized CSL contents (that means in learning objects).
- **SCORM RTE[20]:** Supplies specifications to run the applications, to establish communication, and to control the CSL content.
- **SCORM SN[21]:** Describes how the CSL content, in compliance with the SCORM, can be sequenced through a set of navigation events initiated by the system or by the user.

SCORM Overview

SCORM is a set of specifications and guidelines that establish the levels of accessibility, interoperability, durability and reuse of the Web-based CSL contents and systems. Presently, the SCORM already knew four versions. It is the best reference model in the international market, because it integrates different norms from different organizations in diverse scopes.

The SCORM is not a norm, but a reference model that serves a set of norms and individual specifications. The SCORM works with bodies of norms as the AICC, the IMS, and the IEEE to integrate its specifications in a holistic model. Thus, it defines key interrelationships between norms.

Therefore, the SCORM is a *de facto* model. Since a body of norms approval does not map SCORM, it became a model that governments and the learning industry adopted voluntarily. Thus, SCORM defines a CSL content aggregation model. Indeed, SCORM defines the run-time environment to call such contents. The specifications allow the Web-based CSL contents reusing, through multiple platforms and products. Three basic pillars support the SCORM:

- **Representation of XML-based courses structures:** The courses can be shared by different LMSs.

- **Set of specifications related with the run-time environment:** Include an API (application programming interface), a data model for CSL contents communicate with LMS, and a CSL contents specification to publish contents and call them online.
- **Specification used to create courses metadata and its respective CSL contents:** It uses specifications form the description of physical resources to the description and cataloguing of structuralized objects (the learning objects).

SCORM CAM (Content Aggregation Model)

The content aggregations model, or simply CAM, represents a neutral way to add SCO (sharable content objects) to an LMS. An SCO (or a learning resource) is any representation of information used in a learning experience. An electronic resource supports (or not) activities that compose learning experiences. One of the activities in the process of creation and distribution of learning experiences involves the creation of simple resources (text, images, etc.). In addition, they call Content Aggregations for the integration (or aggregation) of these resources in more complex learning resources (SCOs), organized in a sequence of distribution.

Figure 1. SCORM CAM *graphical representation*

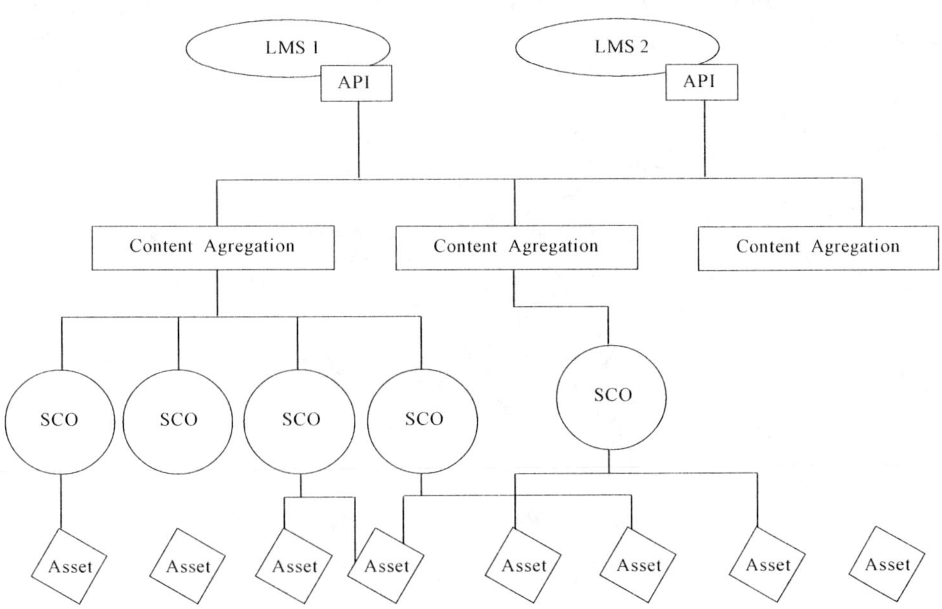

According to Figure 1, the following elements compose the CAM: assets, SCO, and content aggregations. When these elements are associated with metadata documents, they receive the denomination of learning objects.

Assets

The assets are the most basic way of CSL content. They are media electronics representations (text, images, animations, sound, Web pages, questions for evaluation, etc.). It is possible to describe an asset through metadata. This allows the research of assets in CSL contents repositories for reuse.

In essence, the assets are homologated digital documents (DOC, JPG, MPEG formats, etc.). For example, Figure 2 can be part of a course package as an image in JPG format.

SCO

An SCO represents a collection of one or more assets. It includes a specific resource of execution, using the SCORM run-time environment to communicate to LMS. Run-time environment is the mechanism that detects, initiates, and/or communicates with the SCO in a typical Web environment. The LMS and the SCO carry this communication.

Figure 2. Image of Alvor beach (Algarve, Portugal) in JPG format (Example of an Asset)

An SCO represents the most granular level of learning resources that LMS can control. For reusing, the SCO must be independent of the learning context. For example, in different learning experiences to achieve different aims of learning.

Content Aggregations

A content aggregation is a map (or a contents structure) that is useful to add SCOs in an instruction unit, applying structures, and associating learning taxonomies. In fact, metadata is the way to describe a content aggregation. This allows the content aggregation to be searchable in repositories for reusing.

The content aggregation establishes the structure and the mechanisms to define the sequencing in which the learning resources (SCO and assets) are presented to the user (see Figure 1). The learning resources navigation and sequencing will be defined in the book SCORM NS, using prerequisites for each learning resource. The LMS is responsible for interpreting the intended sequencing (described in the map). The LMS also is responsible by the control of sequencing in run-time.

For an effective aggregation of simple resources in more complex learning resources, the following elements compose the CAM:

- **Content model:** The nomenclature used to define the components of learning experience content.
- **Metadata components:** The mechanisms to describe specific instances of the contents model components.
- **Contents package:** Defines how to represent the behavior of a learning experience (contents structure) and how to pack the resources in a way that learning is placed in different environments.

Metadata Components

The SCORM metadata model describes the elements used to construct metadata registries in compliance with SCORM. Such registries can contain additional elements of information.

The model has nine categories. IMS Metadata Model supports these nine categories, as follows:

- **General.** It groups general information that describes the whole resource.

- **Lifecycle:** It groups the characteristics related to the history and the current state of a resource. It also groups the characteristics that influence the resource during its evolution.
- **Metametadata:** It groups information related to the metadata registries.
- **Technical:** It groups the technical requirements and resource characteristics.
- **Educational:** It groups the educational and pedagogical resource characteristics.
- **Rights:** It groups the intellectual property laws and the conditions about the resource using.
- **Relation:** It groups the characteristics that define the resource relationship.
- **Annotation:** It makes possible the existence of commentaries to the pedagogical use of the resource. It lists information about "when" and "who" created the resource.
- **Classification:** It describes where the resource fails in one defined system of classification.

To generate XML documents from SCORM Metadata in three different formats it may use the SCORM MdG (meta-data generator [22]): "Raw Media" to describe assets, "Course" to define SCO or "Content" for Content Aggregation.

Content Package

The content package aims to normalize the way to exchange learning resources between different LMS and Web authoring tools. The content package is a software program that allows creating e-learning courses in a personalized way. The types of Web authoring tools are the instructional, programming, and authorship tools. These tools create standards documents called template-focused authoring tools and knowledge capture systems.

The content package defines the structure and the intended behavior of a specific set of learning resources. The content package also defines how a **manifest file** and the guidelines to pack the Manifest and all files should be created. A ZIP format file or a CD-ROM may pack them. A manifest file contains package metadata, a list of references to the package resources, and an optional section called organizations that defines the contents structure and behavior.

The SCORM content package is a sub-set of the IMS content package. It works as the IMS content package supplying additional guidelines on packing learning resources (assets, SCOs, and content aggregation). In the SCORM, the content package comprises:

- **Content structure:** It is the map of sequencing/navigation through the learning resources defined in the Content Package. It must not only contain the learning resources structure, but also the behaviors applied to the learning experience. The content structure drifts from the management of instructions in computers defined by the AICC. The AICC specifications define the information model for the course structure, properties, and aims. Three parts define the content structure, each one defining specific aspects of a learning resources collection: contents hierarchy, content specific metadata, and sequencing/navigation.
- **IMS package description:** IMS content package contains two main components: the XML Manifest document (**imsmanifest.xml**) and the physical files referred to in this document. Manifest describes the organization of the contents and the resources of the package. In this way, a content package represents a unit of usable content. A part of a course, a complete course, or a collection of courses constitutes the Content Package.
- **Information model for content package:** Such as the metadata component, SCORM CAM presents a table with the information model for the content package.
- **XML binding for content package:** It exists, such as XML binding, a linking for the content package information model. However, two rules must be satisfied: the linking must respect the XML 1.0 specifications and it must keep the structure defined for the information model for SCORM content package. ADLNet supports a XML project (XML schema – XSD) that implements this concept.

SCORM RTE (Run-Time Environment)

SCORM RTE specifies the run-time environment. It allows the learning resources to demonstrate interoperability between multiples LMSs. For this to be possible, a common way to initiate these resources, a common mechanism to communicate them with a LMS, and a predefined language to support this communication must be created. These three basic aspects are described as follow.

Launch Mechanism

It defines a common way to LMS initiate Web learning resources. For establishing communication between learning resources and LMS launch mechanism is used. It defines the procedures and responsibilities. The use of a common API normalizes the communication protocols.

An LMS may call the two SCORM content models: assets and SCOs. There are different requirements to run them according the type of learning resource intended to execute. The execution mechanisms define the way that LMS will call assets and SCOs. Thus, the type of resource defines the procedures and responsibilities to establish the communication between the LMS and the learning resources.

API Common Mechanism

The SCORM API is the communication mechanism that informs the state of the learning resource (started, finished, etc.) to the LMS. It may use the SCORM API to exchange data (classifications, time limits, etc.) between LMS and SCOs. The run-time environment functionality supports the SCORM API. AICC—Aviation Industry CBT American Committee (www.aicc.org)—and defines the SCORM API through the CMI (computer managed instruction). It uses the SCORM API to get and to transmit data values defined by an external data model. The AICC specifications define one of these models.

Data Model

Data model is a set of normalized elements. Defined in the SCORM run-time environment, it describes elements that LMS and SCO must know. Data model drifts from the CMI data model, created in the AICC. The reason to choose this model is because of its successful implementation. To identify the data model in use, the elements' names described in the SCORM data model specification start with the letters "cmi."

SCORM SN (Sequencing and Navigation)

The SCORM SN describes how the assets and SCOs can be sequenced for the user through a set of navigation events started by the system or by the user. Thus, a set of predefined activities can describe the assets and SCOs flow.

Content structure defines the learning contents sequencing that are external to the proper learning contents. This concept is important because the learning resources reusing will not work if resources contain embedded information that specific determined contexts. If a learning resource (asset, SCO, or content aggregation) contains specific links to another SCO, a different course cannot use that learning resource because it cannot be applicable or available.

The SCO reuse depends on its autonomy in terms of not being connected to a specific aggregate. However, SCORM recognizes that learning resources can contain internal logic for the accomplishment of one determined task (related to the user interactivity), and that normally it is not visible for the LMS. Examples of this internal logic are the *Play, Stop, Rewind,* and *Pause* buttons used to control a video clip inside of an SCO. This is an important indication that the developers must be in mind to determine which learning resources to use and how add an asset, an SCO, or a content aggregation.

In addition, the study of terminologies and concepts of navigation and sequential organization is important. Learning activities, activity trees, and clusters are some of them.

Sequential Definition Model

The sequential definition model supplies technical details about learning resources sequencing. To describe the sequential strategies during the content development, each part of the sequential information explained in the Sequential Definition Model may be used.

SCORM Navigation Model

The SCORM Navigation Model describes a data model in run-time. It makes it possible for learning resources consulting an LMS to know the sequential state, and, after, to indicate to the LMS the desired order of navigation. This model also supplies LMS guidelines to provide appropriate navigation controls to its users.

Proposal of a SCORM-Based Learning Objects Repository

The proposal of the *Caravela Digital* project (Nascimento, 2004) was born to provide the informatics support to *Projecto Sabiá* intellectual production.

Projecto Sabiá understands a navigation program into a scholar tall-ship. A group of university alumni and mentally impaired young people compose the crew. Researchers from psychology, pedagogy, biology, educational, and computer sciences areas will guide the crew. In addition, Portuguese, Spanish, French, and Brazilian post-graduating students will also help.

Supporting production and management of all information (literal and iconographic) produced by the scholar tall-ship crew, *Caravela Digital* assists the assets, SCOs, and Content Aggregations production. These learning resources come from the activities of the crew related to on-board scientific researches, TV programs, digital movies, photos, and so forth. The crew will discover common learning mechanisms together. Diverse elements like history, geography, biology, culture, and ethology will feed the learning contents. Ocean ecological environment and physical effort in the sails manipulation will also contribute to contents productions. Besides, Portugal, Spain, France, and Brazil institutions will use ubiquitous learning services to create learning contents. Pedagogical activities and telecommunications infrastructure will generate the following "opportunities" into the scholar tall-ship:

1. Test the proposal telematics architecture so that it can be used in other scholar tall-ship or confined environments;
2. Compose a Digital Library from the crew intellectual production (literal and iconographic contents);
3. Create individual blogs concerning crew member multimedia diaries;
4. Analyze the ubiquitous learning pedagogical contributions offered by educators and students crew;
5. Allow sea-based productions: elaborate articles for periodicals and scientific magazines in the education, ethology, informatics engineering, and telematics areas; produce technical tutorial, digital documents (DVDs, multimedia CD-ROMs, presentations, books, etc.).

Caravela Digital Architecture

Caravela Digital uses ubiquitous learning and computation studies to compose two basic pillars: *Caravela Digital* portal (www.caraveladigital.org) and the telematics system into the scholar tall-ship (see Figure 3).

The telematics system should work efficiently in African, American, and European coasts. It should provide an innovative u-learning (ubiquitous learning) system among Brazilian, French, Spanish and Portuguese institutions.

*Figure 3. Telematics Architecture and main ubiquitous computer devices: The Fleet System (*Sistema Fleet*), the Inmarsat F Service, the Wireless Internet Server (*Servidor de Internet Sem Fio*), the Video Edition Server (*Servidor de Edição de Vídeo*), and the* Cibercafé *and* Media Lab *environments*

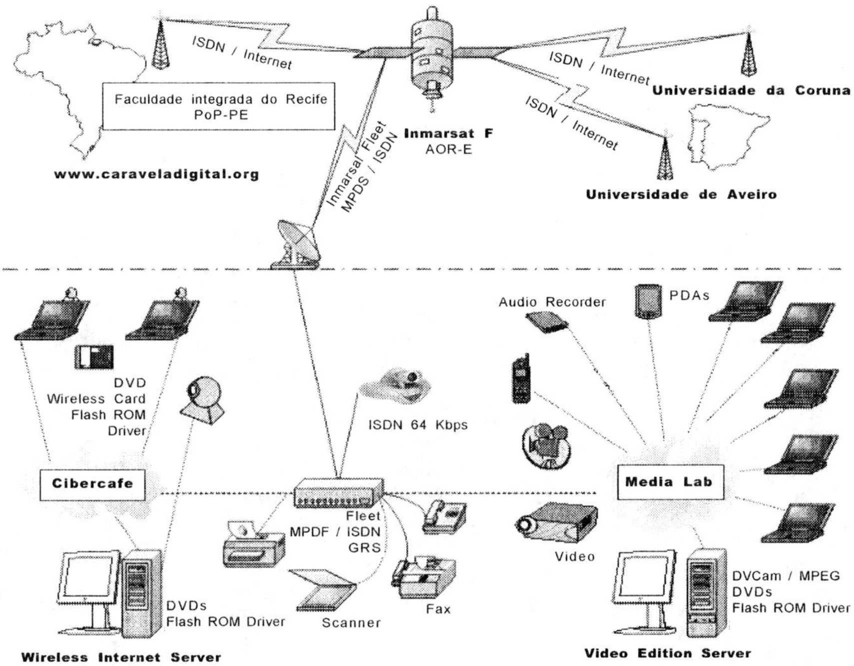

Caravela Digital Library

Projecto Sabiá will develop a digital library to deliver the knowledge produced by the scientific and educative activities into the scholar tall-ship. Such library will be an institutional repository that will use open archives and free Web access. It will allow the storage, indexation, preservation, and dissemination of all multimedia production in a digital format. A set of learning objects will compose the repository. Later, it will serve as a research source for studies in computation, education, psychology, communication, and sociology areas, among others.

Because of *Projecto Sabiá*'s large scale and its multi-discipline role, the international contribution and multi-institutional work from diverse teams of different learning institutions and social solidarity associations becomes necessary. These teams compose the community responsible by the learning objects production that will feed the Caravela digital library. Thus, a coherent logical organization should exist, independent of technologies and platforms used in the Library implementation. In this way, it will be possible to contemplate the different learning resources composed in the Community intellectual production.

Creating Learning Objects

Learning objects composes *Projecto Sabiá*'s "digital memory." In turn, diverse activities into scholar tall-ship will inspire the creation of new multimedia documents. The experiences of the crew will motivate this creation environment. Edition Video Server (see *Servidor de Edição de Vídeo,* in Figure 3) and the Caravela digital library will store the learning objects produced. In addition, there will be a backup site (or mirror) in the Internet Service Provider PoP-PE in Brazil. This mirror exists because *Caravela Digital* Portal needs to provide high-speed connections to access some learning contents (videos, audios, images) through

Figure 4. Some XML elements of a Caravela digital learning object based on the SCORM standards

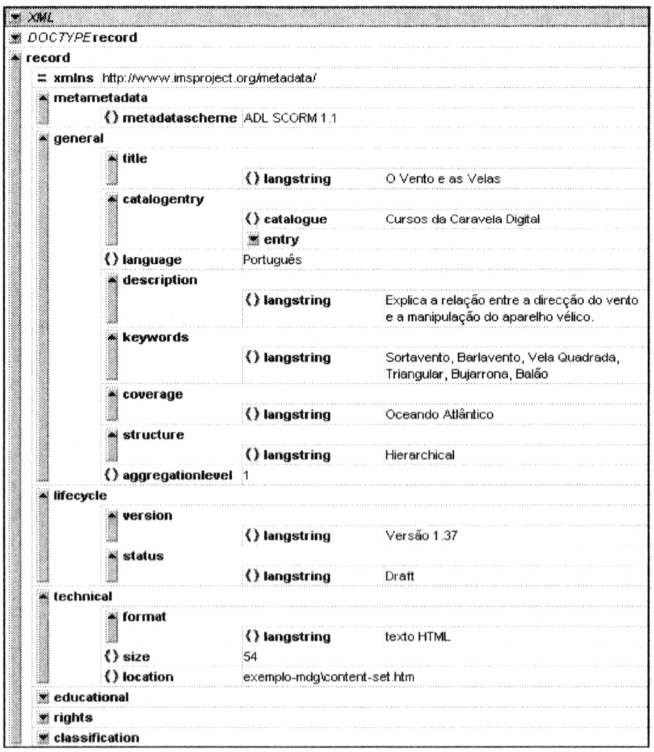

the RNP2 (*Rede Nacional de Pesquisa 2*) (Brazilian National Research Network 2).

The SCORM Metadata Model is used to index the stored information. For example, Figure 4 shows a partial vision of XML elements that could belong to a *Caravela Digital* learning object. Therefore, each learning object stored will keep a list of information that describes data about creator, date, heading, used language, and document digital format, among others.

Caravela Digital project promoters (FIR—*Faculdades Integradas de Recife in* Brazil—and UA—*Universidade de Aveiro in* Portugal) decided to follow different technological development platforms concerning learning objects library implementation. They intend to develop a hybrid system based on previous experience of each institution.

FIR will use open-source software based on the Linux operative system. Its options are DSpace, Eprints, and DICI solutions. UA will use Microsoft's SharePoint Portal development tool. They (FIR and UA) will use XML Web services for communication among these different solutions. Consequently, they will be able to interchange similar XML documents based on the SCORM standards.

Learning Objects Logical Organization

On the other hand, different collections will compile learning resources according to Learning Objects subjects. Initially, five collections will group these archives:

- **Geopolitical collection:** This collection categorizes Learning Objects about visited regions, popular cultures and their geographic relationships with the world.
- **Navigation collection:** This collection manages Learning Objects about techniques and instruments of navigation, use of maritime maps, astronomical studies, reading of nautical letters, and so forth.
- **Pedagogical collection:** This collection organizes all scientific-cultural-playful-creative crew production.
- **Press collection:** This is a compilation of news, articles, releases, and documents produced by the *Projecto Sabiá* press staff.
- **Scientific collection:** This collection treats all academicals information and scientific production generated through scientific expeditions on board of the scholar tall-ship.

Edu-Blogs and Learning Objects

Another innovative way of using new technologies for education is the creation of collective Weblogs (Barbosa & Granado, 2004). Weblogs—or simply blogs—are Web pages frequently updated with the new material placed in the top of the page. Personal reflections, a variety of texts, and a list of links may compose the Weblog content. In addition, diverse commentaries and links to resources such as images, audio, videos, other Weblogs, Web pages, and so forth, may be added. Among others, ubiquitous Web devices (Dede, 2004; Light et al., 2002) may feed this content.

In the *Caravela Digital* project, courses for personal Web pages, multimedia documents, video, audio and images edition, and for construction of Weblogs will be presented. The student crew will discuss subjects chosen by the educator crew. Their points of view and their personal experience will be evaluated. Reading will be stimulated, identifying the particular interests of each one. The binary archives will come from the creative composition on manipulation of the documents produced by the members of the crew.

As a result, a living book produced by its own characters will be implemented and will be named *Blog Tripulantes* (Crew Blog). In this blog, student and educator crews will talk about their experiences, discoveries, and emotions during all the boat expeditions. There will be hundreds of individual blogs referring to each other and reacting to diverse bred opinions. It will be an innovative learning universe to perform ubiquitous learning, either with crew or people browsing the *Caravela Digital* Web portal.

Other Learning Objects Repositories

The Universia.Net[23] learning resources library can be shown as an emblematic example of a learning objects repository that can work well. Created from a private foundation initiative, at present it counts with a contribution of more than 800 Latin American institutions. Resultant of this synergy, this library contains more than 930,000 learning resources distributed in 33 collections.

You can see other resources library examples listed in Keenoy and Papamarks (2003), as follows:

- CAREO http://careo.netera.ca
- EdNA http://www.edna.edu.au: Australian educational net.
- ETB (European Treasury Browser) http://etb.jrc.it

- IMS DRI Spec. http://www.imsglobal.org/digitalrepositories/
- Learning Matrix http://thelearningmatrix.enc.org: Repository revised among "pairs"
- MERLOT http://www.merlot.org
- SMETE http://www.smete.org: It uses LOM metadata
- UBP http://www.educanext.org: Resources commercialization platform
- Canada SchoolNet http://schoolnet.ca: More than 7,000 resources, including a metadata search system
- GEM http://www.thegateway.org: Search engine for educative materials with more than 26,000 resources

Conclusion

The use of learning object technology and the SCORM standards simplifies the interchange of universities and research institutions LMS or scientific production systems. Using interchangeable standards, it allows the interoperability between those systems. Thus, a learning object repository can function as an intelligent teaching resources catalogue belongs to the institutions: its digital collections and individual productions.

In consequence, the author of this chapter wishes that digital learning object repositories obey model SCORM and publish its contents in RSS format for professors and students. Moreover, they have to share the same contents with other OAI-based repositories.

However, what lacks for this utopia to come true? It lacks tools to manipulate the learning objects, structures for learning objects functioning, knowledge of the informatics aspect of the learning objects, and time to generate dynamism with learning objects.

In this context, Denominato (2004) considers that some actions could be taken to disseminate learning objects. First, initiatives of spreading and sensitization of the distance learning normalization should be created. Second, efforts should be made in the improvement and development of the interoperability and reuse of CSL contents. Third, courses personalization and CSL contents standardization into the LMS should be promoted. Technical formation for the implementation of SCORM standards should also be promoted.

The author of also wishes that this work might contribute to the understanding of SCORM standards, description of SCORM components, and applications in the real world. For this, metadata harvesting, XML family, and RSS format was illustrated as key elements for dissemination of open archives initiatives, and creation of learning objects institutional repositories.

The information compiled here not only assists with a better development design of learning resources, but also with a better understanding of the storage, distribution, sharing, and reuse of these CSL contents.

References

Armstrong, E., Ball, J., Bodoff, S., Carson, D., Evans, I., Green, D., et al. (2005). The J2EE 1.4 Tutorial. *Sun Microsystems.* Retrieved March 5, 2004, from http://java.sun.com/j2ee/1.4/docs/tutorial/doc/

Barbosa, E., & Granado, A. (2004). *Weblogs: diário de bordo (Weblogs: on board diary).* Porto: Porto Editora.

Bass, M., & Branschofsky, M. (2002). *DSpace internal reference specification—A sustainable solution for institutional digital asset services.* Massachussets: MIT Libraries.

Bray, T., Paoli, J., Sperberg-McQueen, C. M., Maler, E., & Yergeau, F. (2000). *Extensible Markup Language* (XML) 1.0 (2nd ed.). W3C Recommendation. Retrieved May 5, 2001, from http://www.w3.org/TR/REC-xml

Chester, T. M. (2001, September-October). Cross-platform integration with XML and SOAP. *IEEE Computer Society, IT PRO.* Retrieved February 25, 2003, from http://computer.org

Dede, C. (2004). *Handheld devices for ubiquitous learning.* Cambridge: HGSE News. Retrieved March 5, 2004, from http://www.gse.harvard.edu/news/features/dede02012004.html

Denominato, R. (2004). *A qualidade do e-learning em Portugal* (The e-learning quality in Portugal). SAF/Novabase S.A. ISBN: 972-8252-01-3.

Ginsparg, P. (1996). Winners and losers in the global research village. In Sir R. Elliot & D. Shaw (Eds.), *Electronic Publishing in Science I Conferência.* Paris: ICSU Press/UNESCO. Retrieved April 7, 2006, from http://fisika net.lipi.go.id/utama.cgi?cetakartikel&976554000

Harrsch, M. (2003, July-August). RSS: The next killer app for education. *The Technology Source.* Retrieved November 5, 2004, from http://ts.mivu.org/default.asp?show=article&id=2010

Keenoy, K., & Papamarks, G. (2003). *SeLeNe Report: Learning management systems and learning object repositories.* Birkbeck College, University of London.

Lagoze, C., & Sompel, H. (2001). *The open archives initiative: Building a low-barrier interoperability framework.* JCDL—Joint Conference on Digital Library (ACM + IEEE), Roanoke, VA. Retrieved June 30, 2004, from http://www.openarchives.org/documents/jcdl2001-oai.pdf

Light, D., McDermott, M., & Honey, M. (2002). *The impact of ubiquitous portable technology on an urban school project Hiller.* New York: Center for Children and Technology, Education Development Center. Retrieved March 5, 2004, from http://www.edc.org/CCT

Lynch, C. (2003). Institutional repositories: Essential infrastructure for scholarship in the digital age. *ARL Bimonthly Report 226, The Association of Research Library.* Retrieved April 22, 2004, from www.arl.org/newsltr/226/ir.html

Nascimento, R. (2004). Projecto Sabiá: Experiência inédita 'navega' rumo à integração (Sabiá Project: Innovate experience 'sail' toward social inclusion). *Magazine Linhas, Revista da Universidade de Aveiro, 1*(1) 36-39.

Nelson, M., & Warner, S. (2002). *The open archives initiative protocol for metadata harvesting—Protocol Version 2.0.* Retrieved June 30, 2004, from http://www.openarchives.org/OAI/2.0/openarchivesprotocol.htm

Toffler, A. (1984). *The third wave.* New York: Bantam Books.

Wiley, D. (2000). *Learning object design and sequencing theory.* Unpublished doctoral thesis, Brigham Young University. Retrieved January 2, 2004, from http://davidwiley.com/papers/dissertation/dissertation.pdf

Wilkin, J., Hagdorn, K., & Burek, M. (2003). *Creating an academic hotbot.* OAI Harvesting Project final report at University of Michigan. Retrieved June 30, 2004, from http://oaister.umdl.umich.edu/o/oaister/mellon-harvesting-final.doc

Endnotes

1 PKP (2001). PKP–Public Knowledge Project. http://www.pkp.ubc.ca/index.html (15/06/04)

2 InterPARES–International Research on Permanent Authentic Records in Electronic Systems, 1999. http://www.interpares.org/ (15/06/04)

3 BOAI (2001). BOAI–Budapest Open Archive Iniciative. http://www.soros.org/openaccess/index.shtml (15/06/04)

4 GNU (2002). EPrints Archive Software. http://software.eprints.org/ (30/06/04)

5 OJS (2003). OJS–Open Journal Systems. http://pkp.ubc.ca/ojs/ (30/06/04)

6 DC-Lib AP (2003). Dublin Core Metadata Element Set, Version 1.1: Reference Description. DCMI–Dublin Core Metadata Iniciative, Libraries Working Group, Recommendation. http://www.dublincore.org/documents/dces/ (4/27/2004).

7 MARC Standards (2003). Library of Congress, Network Development and MARC Standards Office. http://www.loc.gov/marc/ (30/06/04)

8 Plataforma Lattes (1999). http://www.cnpq.br/plataformalattes/index_novo.htm (30/06/04)

9 LMPL–Linguagem de Marcação da Plataforma Lattes (Plataforma Lattes Markup Language). http://lattes.stela.ufsc.br/lmpl/?go=cv.jsp (06/06/04)

10 IBICT (1976). Instituto Brasileiro de Informação em Ciência e Tecnologia (Brazilian Institute of Information in Science and Technology). http://www.ibict.br/ (05/06/04)

11 SciELO (2002). SciELO–Scientific Electronic Library On-line. http://www.scielo.br/ (10/06/04)

12 b-On (2004). b-On–Biblioteca do Conhecimento Online (On-line Knowledge Library). http://www.b-on.pt (30/06/04)

13 RepositoriUM (2003). https://repositorium.sdum.uminho.pt/index.jsp (30/06/04)

14 Confer Software Inc. (2000). Confer Web XML Plataform. White Paper. www.confer.com (05/05/2001)

15 W3C Consortium (2001). Xml schema part 0: Primer. W3C Recommendation, May. http://www.w3.org/TR/xmlschema-0/ (03/03/2004)

16 Google Directory (2005). Relevant list of News Readers. http://directory.google.com/Top/Reference/Libraries/Library_and_Information_Science/Technical_Services/Cataloguing/Metadata/RDF/Applications/RSS/News_Readers/ (25/05/2005)

17 SRIC-BI (2002). Quality and Efectiveness in eLearning: views of industry experts and Practicioners. Learning on Demand (LOD) Program Report. SRI Consulting Business Intelligence.

18 SCORM ® Overview (2004). 2nd Edition Overview © Advanced Distributed Learning http://www.adlnet.org/ (24/05/2005)

19 SCORM ® CAM (2004). Content Aggregation Model (CAM) Version 1.3.1 © Advanced Distributed Learning. http://www.adlnet.org/ (24/05/2005)

20 SCORM ® RTE (2004). Run-Time Environment Version 1.3.1 © Advanced Distributed Learning. http://www.adlnet.org/ (24/05/2005)

[21] SCORM ® SN (2004). Sequencing and Navigation (SN) Version 1.3.1 © Advanced Distributed Learning. http://www.adlnet.org/ (24/05/2005)

[22] SCORM ® MdG (2004). Version 1.1 Meta-data Generator Version 1.1. ADL Technical Team. http://www.adlnet.org/downloads/35.cfm (25/05/2005)

[23] Universia (2004). Biblioteca Universia: recursos de aprendizagem (Universia Library: learning resourses). http://biblioteca.universia.net (25/05/2005)

Chapter X

Implementing Computer-Supported Learning in Corporations

Doris Lee, Pennsylvania State University, USA

Steve Borland, Temple University Health Systems, USA

Abstract

In this chapter, the use of computer-supported learning (CSL) in a corporate setting is defined as the delivery of learning modules or lessons containing knowledge and/or skills to employees via the Internet or a company's intranet. Thus, effective CSL may include multimedia, streaming video, e-mails, job aids, an electronic performance support system, electronic bulletin boards, or chat rooms. With CSL, learning is independent from time and location, and therefore, learners gain a greater degree of flexibility to acquire knowledge and skill needed. This chapter further reviews the many challenges facing the design, development, implementation, and evaluation of CSL. Possible solutions along with future trends and critical research questions concerning CSL in the corporate world are also presented.

Introduction

Corporations considering computer-supported learning are faced with numerous options that can manage and deliver training customized for their specific needs. The major issues and recommendations discussed here include cost, content, and administration. Many different definitions and categorizations exist for the various forms of technology-based learning, including e-learning, Web-based learning (WBL), computer-based learning (CBL), or computer-supported learning (CSL) (Chalmers & Lee, 2004; Lee, Chalmers, & Ely, 2005; Trombley & Lee, 2002). All of these terms are used to represent the use of a computer, a public computerized network such as the Internet, a private computer network, or a company's intranet, to deliver a learning module or lesson. Specifically, some researchers maintain that CSL or e-learning is primarily delivered via the Internet but includes conference calls, e-mail, teleconferencing, and additional video technology and can be synchronous or asynchronous (Fry, 2001). Others limit their definitions to learning modules solely delivered via the Internet or a private intranet (Fichter, 2002).

In this chapter, CSL, or e-learning, does not simply refer to a particular list of computer technologies, features, or functions. Limiting the definition of CSL or e-learning tends to lock the meaning and functionality of this learning method into a single technologic box. Rather, CSL refers to the delivery of a learning module or lesson via various kinds of technologies judged appropriate to successfully achieve individualized or group-based transfer of skills and knowledge. Thus, it may be delivered through a compact disk, the Internet, or an intranet; it may include technologies such as streaming video, e-mails, job aids, an electronic performance support system, electronic bulletin boards, chat rooms, or additional multimedia and can be asynchronous or synchronous. CSL is also commonly used in blended training solutions where electronic delivery is teamed with classroom face-to-face delivery.

Background

Traditionally, the process of transferring knowledge and skills in either a corporate or an academic setting is similar: an employee or a student learns the content that is presented by an instructor or a trainer and is generalized for a relatively large group of employees or students. Such a process is mostly knowledge-based and instructor-centered, making the learner a knowledge receiver while the instructor is the content presenter. This process has boundaries of time, space, content, and orientation. In contrast, learning or training via

CSL or e-learning is an entirely different paradigm and is not contained by the boundaries listed above. Through this paradigm, learning content is packaged in small, reusable modules that may be organized in any sequence chosen by the learner and is aligned with needs the learner defines. Learners gain more freedom and are always encouraged to actively seek and construct knowledge or solve problems (Chalmers & Lee, 2004; Lee, Chalmers, & Ely, 2005; Khan, 1997; Trombley & Lee, 2002).

Historically, the major appeal of using CSL in the corporate sector is the cost savings of time and travel (Macpherson, Homan, & Wilkinson, 2005; Nisar, 2004). The benefits can be enormous. Up to two thirds of the cost of training can be attributed to travel and lodging. For example, in 2001, IBM claimed to save 350 to 400 million dollars by delivering their Basic Blue course for new managers online. Consulting firm, Deloitte & Touche, reported a 40% budget reduction in their first year of using e-learning. General Motors claimed that through offering over 1,300 online courses, their training budget was reduced by approximately $4 million. Circuit City reduced per employee training hours from 200 per year to 60. What these examples have in common is a large employee population dispersed across time and space. In each of these cases, the savings are entirely attributed to salary, travel, and lodging. The savings in travel and lodging alone are not the only reason to generate an electronic learning effort. Geisinger Health System now delivers, tracks, and reports mandatory training on over 8,500 employees in 38 counties in Pennsylvania. Jack Latshaw, Assistant Director of Technical Education, explained the reason for using e-learning in his company in an interview: "The bottom line is we're heavily regulated, and the ability to demonstrate compliance is where we get our return on investment, although it's a soft return and you can't always put a dollar amount on it" (Crosman, 2004, p. 37).

Unfortunately, not many companies are measuring the effectiveness of their CSL or e-learning initiatives. For instance, the *Financial Times* of London sponsored the annual Corporate University XChange Excellence Awards and reported that in 2001, only a few companies entered in the category of measuring outcomes, and most of them reported that they did not even monitor their training programs. This indicates that companies are implementing e-learning for the easily measured savings in time, salary, and travel while avoiding evaluating business or learning results (Authers, 2001; Schneider, 2001; Swanson, 2000).

Obviously, many challenges concerning CSL remain. This chapter reviews and synthesizes pertinent literature on CSL, presents reasons, criteria, examples, and results of using CSL specifically in the corporate sector. This chapter further discusses the many challenges facing the design, development, implementation, and evaluation of CSL and presents possible solutions to overcome the challenges discussed. Finally, the future trends and pertinent research issues concerning CSL in corporations are also discussed.

The Use of CSL in the Corporate World

The issues regarding why and whether or not CSL should be used in the corporate world need to be addressed before detailing the status, examples, and results of using it.

Reasons and Criteria

Why do companies use CSL or e-learning? Wentling, Waight, Strazzo, File, La Fleur, and Kanfer (2000) all agreed that e-learning provides "strategic prominence" (p. 3) for needed tasks such as managing organizational competency, offering employees a competency roadmap, delivering latent knowledge, and skills and aligning business goals with employees' learning objectives.

Specifically, regarding the reasons for using the Internet as the delivery medium, Wentling et al. (2000) listed the following: (a) Internet access can be obtained both at home and the workplace; (b) the advancement of the Internet technology has increased the level of interactivity and content quality provided by the Web; (c) increasing bandwidth helps e-learning become more viable; (d) more options have become available for the selection of e-learning development tools; and (e) technology standards that assist the issues of compatibility and usability of e-learning products are emerging (pp. 3-4).

In comparison, from a learners' perspective, most of the cited reasons for using CSL or e-learning included (a) enabling employees to engage in self-directed learning; (b) not being solely restricted to text only; (c) adding a more sophisticated level of interactivity, color, and depth to coursework and the learning process; (d) enhancing cyber collaboration between instructors on site and instructors at other companies; (e) making up-to-date information available and faster; (f) using embedded assignments and assessments to monitor employees learning progress and/or difficulties; (g) reducing duplication of effort; (h) having documents and other training sites cross-referenced with hyperlinks; and (i) having e-books and hence reducing printing costs. In contrast, reasons listed for not using CSL included lack of management buy-in, employee motivation, Internet access, and technical support (Bonk, 2002; Croft-Baker, 2001; Kiser, 2001; Trombley & Lee, 2002).

Status and Examples

Currently, a great number of companies are either converting the existing instructor-led, face-to-face learning into CSL or are conducting an e-learning initiative. For example, companies including IBM, Cisco Systems, Procter & Gamble, and Lockheed Martin are among those that reported the use of e-learning for employee training or learning (Barbian, 2002; Trombley & Lee, 2002). Trombley and Lee reported that a relationship existed between the size of a company, the type of business sectors, and the use of e-learning. Companies with more employees used CSL more frequently for a longer period of time than companies with fewer employees. Business sectors dealing with financial services, information technology, and consulting use more e-learning than other sectors (Bonk, 2002).

According to Trombley and Lee (2002), online self-paced courses have been commonly employed to deliver learning for computer and technical skills, but these courses were rarely used for covering interpersonal or sales skills. However, there are some companies that use e-learning extensively for various kinds of learning purposes. For example, PricewaterhouseCoopers, a consulting firm, has programs that allow employees to form virtual professional communities based on areas of interest, abilities, or client relations (Koonce, 1998). IBM, Xerox, Siemens Business Communications, and Eli Lilly Corporation all used a variety of strategies including individual assignments, group discussions, and projects in their asynchronous courses to enhance employee performance (Chalmers & Lee, 2004; Frieswick, 1999; "IBM builds its manager training," 2000; "Siemens saves $2000," 2000). Cisco also has an expanded e-learning system to place their employees, partners, and end-user customers in touch with more than 8,000 learning resources, including online learning courses, class scheduling information and additional paper-based and video-based resources (Galagan, 2001).

Results

Systematic, rigorous studies investigating the results or effects of using CSL in corporations is very limited. In the study by Strother (2003), the results showed that compared to other media, e-learning did not produce better results. Information from the academic community that compares student achievement in classroom versus CSL modalities is also very limited. In a study published by the University of Central Florida in 2004, student success in fully online courses rose slightly to be about the same as in face-to-face classroom courses (as cited in Dziuban, Hartman, & Moskal, 2004). However, many managers had observed that their employees, when using online learning, accomplished better post-test performance, produced more sales, and achieved a higher quality of customer satisfaction. In a report by Galagan (2001), Tom Kelly, Vice President of the Internet Learning Solution Group of Cisco, pointed out that based on his experiences, e-learning had produced equal or better retention results among

Cisco employees, compared to face-to-face type learning. Kelly maintained that such a result was primarily due to the nature of e-learning in providing timely and pertinent learning experiences to his employees.

Many Challenges and Possible Solutions

The Initial Planning and Design Phases

Prior to the design of a CSL module, a company needs to consider if the module should be built in-house or purchased through a vendor. Purchasing a pre-packed CSL module may be more cost effective if it is applicable for the learning needs. Once a decision is made for an in-house project, the company must realize that it could take months, if not years to complete the project. For better planning and documentation, a style book is recommended. A style book is a team reference detailing every procedure or decision for a CSL module from file naming conventions, to font sizes, Web page format, and navigation issues, along with team processes, criteria, and quality review procedures ("SCORM Best Practices Guide for Content Developers," 2003). Storyboards that visually present and specify the design, layout, and locations of every object in each and every screen are also suggested.

A number of challenges exist during the initial planning and design phases for a CSL project. The first challenge would very likely come from the selection of a proper instructional design model. Traditional instructional models including components like analysis, design, development, and evaluation are created mostly for the design of instructor-led, face-to-face learning. Thus, it would be beneficial for a CSL design team to select a model that is conducive to cyberspace learning. A number of emerging instructional design models have become available, and most of them expanded on the traditional models to include a maintenance component to take care of the technological issues and to allow rapid prototyping and beta testing of the prototype (Schoenfeld & Berge, 2005; Tomlinson, 2005). However, new or innovative models that are derived from the paradigm behind e-learning should be considered.

The second challenge is related to the technology used for a CSL lesson. In recent years, it has become relatively easy for a programming specialist to include dynamic audio and video effects into CSL. However, technology should not drive the learning, and the special technological effects should not distract learners' attention from the learning content. Further, by using the Internet, learners are no longer restricted by the specific learning or progressive path set up by an instructor. Therefore, it is suggested that learning through a CSL lesson, a learner should be allowed to devote maximum concentration on the critical learning content, not the never-ending navigations in the Internet.

Additional challenges come from the design of content, file, browser, and Web page standards. Regardless of how the content of CSL is developed, it is important to stay focused on the purpose of learning, and content should be presented and organized in a way that ensures learners' concentration. Whether developed new or converted from traditional training packages or modules, content of a CSL should conform to sharable content object reference modules (SCORM) standards as much as possible. SCORM documents a set of content guidelines developed by the Department of Defense through the advanced distributed learning (ADL) initiative. These evolving standards are supported through an association of organizations with an interest in furthering the SCORM mission by coordinating their efforts. The ADL has taken the lead in this effort because the U.S. Government is the largest player in the e-learning market. The major organizations include the Aviation Industry CBT Committee (AICC), the IMS Global Learning Consortium, the Institute of Electrical and Electrical Engineers (IEEE), and the Customized Learning Experiences Online Lab Project (CLEO). Through SCORM, these organizations are cooperating on the same mission: to reduce training costs by producing content that is reusable, durable, accessible, and interoperable. The main concept of SCORM is that much content can be used across audiences that have common interests. For example, a lesson to teach cardiopulmonary resuscitation to nurses could also be useful for ambulance crews, police, and firefighters. By creating reusable content, the cost of development is reduced. In addition, SCORM refers to durability as content that continues to function as environments mature and are upgraded ("SCORM Best Practices Guide for Content Developers," 2003).

Content is accessible when all potential users can locate it through a common convention known as metadata. Metadata provides a means of organizing and keeping track of each object and asset. It refers to a series of database fields primarily developed by the IEEE for each object and contributed to SCORM. SCORM recommends packaging content into the smallest logical units called objects. Generally, each object is a learning unit addressing a single objective. The object contains, or has links to, all necessary media including documents, audio, and video files. Essentially, an object is a plug and play training module that is not dependent on context. Objects may also include embedded and summative testing. If the object will be shared with another organization, then tests could alternatively be created as a separate object ("SCORM Best Practices Guide for Content Developers," 2003).

Standard browser functions and features should also be written into the style book. Many corporations struggle to keep all employees on the same version of hardware and software so it is important to insure the site functions properly across browsers and various browser versions. Once version conflicts are under control, Moertl (2002) suggests opening a new window for outside links so that users have an easy way to return to the corporate site. He also suggests that the page background should complement the foreground, and the amount of animations should be limited. Excessive use of animated graphics is not only distracting; it takes the page longer to load. The Hong Kong Polytechnic Institute (as cited in Chan & Simon, 2002) described a good standard structure for e-learning Web sites to include an introduction (including the goal and terminal objective), the course modules and material, an assessments section, and a section for contacts and support. Desirable features include book markings so the student can resume where they left, a print feature, key word searches, a glossary (or mouse over pop up definitions), a hyperlinked site map, and the ability to communicate feedback and questions to the team by both e-mail and phone. The trainee is provided a measure of comfort if there is a way to opt out for more support. Use a printable word processed document when lengthy reading is required. It is easier to read hard copy. An Adobe Acrobat (.PDF) is often used as it requires less bandwidth and provides good security to prevent manipulation by the users. It is tempting to include sound, animations, and movies. All multimedia should be scrutinized as to how it supports the instructional goal or maintains the student interest.

Site design that acknowledges the physically disabled should be an important quality check in the process. If the e-content is for use by the U.S. Government, then accessibility by the physically disabled is required under the Americans with Disabilities Act. Joe Landsberger recommends numerous sites available to assess Web pages for accessibility of the physically challenged, including W3C HTML Validation Service, Dr. Watson, Bobby World Wide Web Design Group WDG Validator, and Usability.gov (Landsberger, 2002). Developers should incorporate ALT tags in the HTML coding. This coding replaces graphics with a text description if the user turns off browser graphics in order to speed loading or are visually impaired or if the graphic just fails to display.

In addition to the above challenges, it is also critical to make the participating employees remain engaged (Lee, Chalmers, & Ely, 2005). Learning through CSL, employees may feel alienated, not "belonging" and simply turn off the computer prematurely. A great number of researchers and practitioners have suggested the following to overcome this difficulty: (a) a certain degree of self-control, meaning that with an appropriate design, employees should be able to choose their own navigational paths for the desired content; they should be allowed to stop, pause, or repeat a segment, especially a video or audio, and review, correct, or repeat missing or difficult content; (b) group activities such as debates and panel discussion and presentations should be used to raise employees' sense of obligation to their group; (c) an interactive forum for the employees to pose questions and share reflections should be made available; and (d) appropriate user interface design including clear and speedy page transitions, hyperlinks and placement indicators should be provided to reduce learner frustration; and (e) the site functions should be properly presented across browsers or different browser versions; a new window for outside links may be beneficial for returning to the company's site (Bearman, 1997; Curtin, 1997; Furnas, 1997; Henke, 1997; Jones & Okey, 1995; Kilby, 1997; Kruse & Keil, 2000; Moertl, 2002; Strandberg, 1999; Williams, 1998).

Finally, flexibility and convenience are strong motivators for learners to choose online training. Learners also noted that boredom, lack of time, interactivity with the module, real work simulations, animation, and navigational control as factors and qualities that motivated them to either stay or drop out of the module. The lack of human interactivity was a negative motivator for students but not for working adults (Kim, 2004).

The Development Process

One of the immediate challenges to develop a CSL lesson is that a strong team is required. With instructor-led learning, a single instructor usually assumes most of the development tasks to create and deliver the content. However, developing CSL could be comparable to assembling a jigsaw puzzle; it has to be a team effort due to the various skill sets needed. The team may include a subject matter expert, a content author, a programmer, and a graphic artist. Other skill sets should be included on an as-needed basis; these skills may include a database designer, a network engineer, and a specialist in network and Internet security (Horton, 2002). The solution to this challenge is for a company to allow sufficient time and budget to identify, recruit, and retain all of the necessary and competent personnel for the team. The goal is to develop a lesson that is aligned with the needs of the learners and to achieve a business objective. The trainers/ instructional designers should assume leadership of the team to assure that the goal remains the driving force. The role of technology is to develop media and methods that support the management and delivery of the lesson content.

For example, in order to maintain the instructional goal as the project driver, the model used by the California State University Center for Distributed Learning (CDL, n.d.) emphasizes that the development process should begin with defining the learning problem by stating the need or problem objectives. Then formulate requirements based on assumptions, followed by evaluating similar alternative requirements. Design solutions should include scenarios and assignments in order to meet objectives. Issues that need to be considered when formulating performance measures include prioritizing by function and prioritizing by technical difficulty. The design document should include a description of the functions, screen sketches, and assumptions, as well as a concept map. Then evaluate the design and match it to the requirements, objectives, and other criteria. After the evaluation, make a prototype, and develop user documents for the prototype. Evaluate the prototype to ensure that it iterates the process used in formulating requirements and follows the performance measures. In addition, the core of the development team structure consists of two content experts: a designer and a programmer. The team responsible for managing the project and testing it for usability should monitor the core team. When needed, consultants are hired for specialty work, instructional design, and media productions. The advising body takes the software developed by the three subgroups and defines the topic area, tests for requirement validation, performs beta testing, and facilitates the adoption of the software by local companies.

The second challenge is to make sure all of the technologies needed are present. For example, the network technicians will need to ensure that the network and the destination computers are all functioning well prior to the actual coding. Next, it is crucial to be sure that sufficient bandwidth is available. Bandwidth determines the amount of information and the speed for sending the information across the Web. Bandwidth problems often result in slow and delayed transmission of information and response time. The most common bandwidth problem occurs when the data-carrying capacity of the computer-to-computer delivery channel, the "pipeline," is small, which often slows transmission of data-intensive multimedia such as videos, complex audio, live transmissions, or animation (Bassi, Cheney, & Lewis, 1998; Chalmers & Lee, 2004; Filipczak, 1997a; Kurtus, 1997; Schaaf, 1997, 1999a; Williams, 1998). Adding data-intensive multimedia features will increase the traffic in cyberspace and, if accessed during a busy part of the business day, could significantly slow response times on the network.

To overcome the challenge from bandwidth, separate, smaller programs, called applets should be created that execute within the primary application. Applets can be downloaded from the Web and can be launched by the primary application to support data-intensive features without adding to the size of the primary program. A master file can be created with other smaller files and should be stored separately to reduce the download time. In addition, digital subscriber lines (DSL), satellite transmission systems, and cable modems can all be used as alternatives to overcome bandwidth limitations ("Applets," 2000; Bassi et al., 1998; Beer, 2000; Chalmers & Lee, 2004; Wiley, South, Bassett, Nelson, Seawright, Peterson, & Monson, 1999).

Implementation and Evaluation

Major challenges facing the implementation stage include support from the management, issues related to cost-effectiveness, the use of learning management and content management systems, and employees' acceptance. Support from the key manager or a decision maker is critical for the successful implementation of a CSL module. To obtain management support, the design team needs to justify the investment with a projected return; data needs to be collected to demonstrate that the implementation of CSL can satisfy a compelling learning need of employees and can further result in better productivity or other tangible gains (Lustig, 2002). Stronger management support is not limited to marketing and budget allocation; it could include the support of a flexible working schedule, the preparation of employees' technical or psychological readiness for online learning, merit raise, and proper recognition for outstanding learning results (Sloman, 2002). For instance, at Dell Computer Corporation, a sense of "official completion and shared success" (p. 62) has been invented by having an official graduation ceremony where the participating employees of e-learning can share their learning achievements, as indicated by John Cone, vice president of Dell Learning at Dell Computer Corporation (Galagan, 2000).

The next challenge concerns cost. A quality CSL is one that meets the needs of the learners and is economical. Regarding the cost, in an instructor-led type of learning, the cost per employee is reduced as the class size gets bigger. Similarly, CSL would become economically viable when the number of participating employees is large, and they are separated by time and/or locations. To justify the cost, the number of the participating employees should be sufficiently large so that the cost per learner approximates the cost of face-to-face learning. This is why among those corporations noted previously, most of them delivered CSL or e-learning to a large group of employees who work across the globe. However, if a company can reduce cost by contracting an outside provider for their CSL lessons, the following procedures are suggested to avoid mistakes: (a) requiring potential providers to provide detailed justification for the charge and every important feature included in the lesson; and (b) making sure that the provider(s) can customize for corporate branding and the participating employees can receive an anytime, anywhere type of service. The Sloan Consortium recommends starting a cost analysis by defining the scope with: (a) The size of the target population and whether it is internal or external, (b) Metrics that specify the measurement outcomes such as increasing throughput, reducing cost, or generating surplus and (c) How the results will be measured as a return on the investment. A recommended method is to use an Activity Based Costing model where costs are allocated across the budgets for marketing, designing, developing, and delivering online content (Geith, 2005).

Two important challenges are the administration of trainee information and managing the access and development of the training content. Many companies are using, and will continue to use, a learning management system (LMS) coupled with a learning content management system (LCMS). An LMS is a learning/training administrative application, which manages learners and monitors their learning performance and progress (Hall, 1997). It often has a graphical user interface that serves as a portal for employees and managers to register for an online learning or training session and may include a feature that automatically notifies employees regarding learning/training tasks and assignments. It can contain specific information including time, place, and format, including classroom, online, downloadable documents, and virtual classroom deliveries. A keyword search capability is a standard feature included for the participating employees to identify available content. It can also store a profile of each participant. Data in the LMS may be collected through an interface with other corporate applications including data from the human resources office, customer service, employee reviews, or new product rollouts.

An LCMS is a content management application and is designed to include features that help create, reuse, locate, deliver, and manage learning content and supporting materials. Since LCMS can be employed to conduct a more detailed tracking of content use of each participating learner, it can be used to recommend remedial content. An important feature to look for is the ability to report on module abandonment as a feedback mechanism for the design/development team. In addition, the LCMS can provide the design team and managers with the capacity to track and lock content under development to avoid design mistakes. Specifically, in an LCMS, content is generally included in small self-contained packages called sharable content objects (SCO), and SCO can be in various formats including documents, Web pages, video, or audio. In comparison, most of the features and functions of an LMS and an LCMS overlap; in fact, they complement each other. Together, the use of an LMS and an LCMS can help manage the development of learning content, track employees' learning progress and status, maintain a comprehensive management and reporting system, and prescribe individualized learning plans.

Over 50 commercial LMSs are currently competing in the marketplace. The cost of a combined LMS/LCMS is usually structured as either a per user or site license fee and could take up to two years to install. Due to the wide difference in pricing structures, comparison across vendors is difficult. Crosman (2004) reported that, "Depending on the number of seats and the complexity of the e-learning applications, initial costs range from $5,000 to more than $1 million" (p. 37). Recent prices in Europe are reported to be between 20,000 and 50,000 euros and ranging up to 100,000 euros if new servers and database software are included (Paulsen, 2003). According to Bersin (2005), while evaluating an LMS, it is recommended that a company (a) considers a hosted LMS to take advantage of the vendor's support staff and reduce reliance on internal resources; (b) simplifies an LMS implementation by distributing modules one module at a time; (c) uses a methodological procurement; (d) asks for and reviews references for organizations of similar size and structure; (e) avoids multiple LMSs in the enterprise to avoid competing for scarce resources; (f) selects an LMS vendor that is well capitalized with mature products and services; (g) avoids internally developed LMSs due to the fact that they rank low in satisfaction and high in demand for resources; (h) selects a feature rich LMS, including strong reporting and content development tools to simplify upgrades; (i) favors an LMS with the ability for integration with human resources (HR) applications; and (j) addresses organizational issues before making a selection.

Finally, the challenge for evaluating CSL is about allocating sufficient time and resources for a thorough job. The design team needs to convince the managers that piloting and evaluation are worthy of investing the time and resources needed. Piloting refers to gathering a small number of intended users to go through every step involved in the lesson. These measures can help identify gross mistakes both in the learning content and in the log on procedure. These mistakes may include confusing, erroneous content or examples, redundant or inappropriate practices and assessments, typographical and procedural errors, and navigational functions or hyperlinks that do not work as intended.

Future Trends

A number of possible future trends concerning CSL or e-learning in the corporate sector have emerged. These trends may include the advancement of computer and networked technologies for the creation of virtual learning environments and the continuous use of powerful LMS and LCMS to track learning progress and the search and identification of the best "blend" of different learning methods to maximize employees' learning results.

For the continuous use of e-learning in the future, Wentling et al. (2000) employed the research methodology of scenario building, which involves scenario building sessions for subjects to imagine the possible future of e-learning in their workplaces. The essence of the results unveiled by the study across both the corporate and the academic perspectives are: (a) wireless, highly interactive, and integrative e-learning will continue to happen due to advances in technology; e-learning will continue to be easily accessible and will allow performers to have verbal and visual contacts through enlarged computer screens; (b) e-learning will be transformed into a more humanized environment where the focus of the learning will be on meeting the needs of learners and performance improvement by using constructive learning activities such as problem-based scenarios, interactive case studies, virtual simulations, e-books, and projects; (c) as e-learning becomes more common in organizations, organizational structures will continue to flatten, and outsourcing and telecommuting will continue to increase; (e) e-learning will be designed to be more sensitive and responsive to learner differences in age, learning styles and languages, nationality, ethnicity, educational, and intellectual levels; (d) learners of e-learning will be more technologically competent and will be motivated to engage in life long learning; however, they may perceive e-learning as a potential threat to collaborative work due to issues concerning intellectual property and security; and (e) global partnerships between corporate and academics will increase because of the unique versatile and integrative features of e-learning.

Wentling et al. (2000) seemed to be prescient about the use of wireless communication. One of the exciting qualities of new technologies is how they are transformed from their original market or intent. Corporations should pay attention to trends in the educational arena as they offer examples beyond established CSL methods of Web pages, virtual classrooms, or live chats. Podcasting, Weblogs, video blogs, instant messaging, and wikis are developing technologies and are simultaneously being transformed in creative ways by children as early as elementary school age. For these technologies, specifically, podcasting, as defined by Weinberger (2005), is a program published via a RSS feed to the host, or corporate, Web site. RSS (Rich Site Summary, or Really Simple Syndication, or RDF Site Summary) is a syndication format that uses metadata items to make content aware to a news aggregator program. The aggregator application then automatically alerts Podcast listeners of the new posting. The program can then be downloaded to the listener's MP3 player, such as an iPod. A Weblog, or blog, is a personal online journal of dated entries, usually addressing a specific topic. However, Weblogs are evolving into a source of knowledge management through group blogs where there is give and take among a community of readers. In a corporate world, they can foster knowledge sharing in all corporate levels from an individual team to across the enterprise and, as opposed to e-mail, can archive the conversation string. Wikis, from the Hawaiian term for quick, uses simplified hypertext markup language that allows users to define for themselves how their processes and groups will develop, usually by making things up as they go along. For example, employees can use wikis to support meeting planning: when a provisional agenda becomes available and the URL is distributed to the participating employees, who can comment or alter the agenda add items (Lamb, 2004).

The use of LMS and LCMS will continue to grow. There are features and functions of LMS that vendors should bring to market. Heo and Joung (2004) predicted advancement in LMS systems with the ability to adapt to the unique needs of individual learners automatically. They propose that, with a self-regulation mechanism integrated in an LMS, expert learners will structure and manage their own experience. Learners will establish their own goals and identify the tasks, effort, and time required. Adaptive qualities include multiple representations in response to learning preferences with feedback that has more robust and tutorial loops.

The options for learning modules, or content, include internal development or purchasing from a vendor either off-the-shelf or customized. It is important to note that the cost of content is in addition to the expense for an LMS. Outsourcing is an option if the organization does not have sufficient human and hardware resources to maintain the system in-house. Development of content is significantly higher for CSL, which can range as much as 20 hours to 40 hours per contact hour compared to classroom programs (Parks, 2004).

The various ways to combine technology and content is both a strength and challenge that presents corporations with a spectrum of choices. An LMS/LCMS system is not necessarily a requirement to deliver CSL. The simplest and least expensive way is to provide learners with a menu of content that can be accessed and launched directly. The content is primarily presentation with a minimum of media, interactivity, testing/evaluation, curriculum advising, or automated administration. The content could begin as classroom material transcribed for electronic delivery. The most complex and highest cost solution is to install an LMS/LCMS system that automates administration and recommends groups of modules to form an individualized curriculum for every participant. It is important to remember that cost and human support resources increase with an increase in technology. Corporations should analyze cost versus benefit to determine their own best solutions.

Next, the use of a live, synchronous learning environment in cyberspace for employee learning is desirable. With the inclusion of online discussions, real-time audio, videoconferencing, and/or application sharing where two or more employees can simultaneously work on the same file, such as a shared electronic whiteboard or a spreadsheet, the employees can interact with each other via the Web in a "real-time" context. Such an environment is employed when real time, instantaneous class interaction is necessary. Again, within WIKI, which might be thought of a tabla rasa cyberspace environment, employees are able to edit, update, or post information in real time. Meeting planning and agenda distribution are common ways for the use of WIKI in corporations. It can be designed to expand on employee learning or training to create an instantaneous virtual professional community based on areas of interest, abilities, or client relations to enhance communication, interaction, and even friendship among employees.

As the corporate sector continues to search for the best possible solution for employee learning, blended or hybrid learning is on the rise, which combines two or more learning delivery methods for employees. While different definitions of blended learning exist, however, most express that blended learning is the combined use of face-to-face and technology-based, e-learning (Voci & Young, 2001). The key factor for considering blended learning is whether the selected learning methods can be interwoven and complement each other for the covered content. E-learning is best suited for knowledge or skills that can be simulated by the computer and/or the Internet. Face-to face learning is necessary for content that requires live modeling, practicing, rehearsing, and discussing or that entails immediate, specific, corrective feedback from an instructor (Young & Young, 2002; Zenger & Uehlein, 2001).

It needs to be noted that the aforementioned challenges and possible solutions will remain the same for the design and production of a virtual classroom or a blended learning module. The results revealed by the study of Wentling et al. (2000) confirmed that more powerful e-learning will continue to happen in the corporate world. However, this study only involved a small number of subjects, and therefore the results may not be as valid as those shown by extensive and rigorous studies. Finally, more evidence that proves e-learning substantiates employee learning and performance is needed to support the claim that e-learning will continue to occur in the corporate world.

Conclusion

To be justifiable, CSL should relate to a business need to close a known learning gap of employees and can result in a more positive return on investment when there are a large number of participating employees across distant locations. A company could choose to purchase an existing CSL module; however, the to-be-purchased module must fulfill the learning needs of the employees, can be used smoothly in a company's network system, and meet all the necessary quality design criteria. For a company to have an in-house CSL lesson, the key success factor is to align the goal of the lesson with the learning intent and the business need. A well designed CSL lesson would not let the integration of the computerized features overshadow the learning purposes.

Additional challenges come from participating employees' technological competencies and their motivation to stay engaged. Some of the possible solutions are having a very thorough design, development, implementation, and evaluation process for all learning content, file, browser, Web page browser standards, and the interface. For the future, CSL or e-learning will continue to grow, and the corporate sector will continue to improve their systems to check employees' learning progress. Finally, virtual classrooms that can be used to expand online learning functions for an instantaneous, communicative, and interactive learning community continue to gain popularity in corporations.

However, many issues concerning the emerging models, the learners, the content, the learning results, and the cost to an organization that uses CSL or e-learning remain. First of all, data is necessary to prove the effectiveness of applying the emerging instructional design models that were created primarily for instructor-led learning. Innovative models should be considered based on the reality that CSL is wireless and requires constant modifications and change due to advances in technology. A research-based formula could be helpful in determining the quantitative relationship between the scope or length of a CSL lesson and the size of a design team. A systematic comparison between e-learning versus face-to-face learning in the areas of learning effects and transfer is necessary to identify the potential strengths and limitations of each method.

Regarding the participating employees, it is imperative that they feel comfortable and ready for CSL. This leads to the demand for establishing standard technology literacy or competencies for CSL participation. In addition, effective strategies are needed for employees to adapt to CSL where an instructor is not present, and a structured, learning path may not be required. More evidence is required to explore how certain motivational factors such as salary increases, job security, or personal growth affect employees' attitude toward CSL. Evidence confirming ways that enable employees to experience gratification and pride in using CSL is highly desirable. Furthermore, the impact caused by many design factors in CSL needs to be determined, and these factors include, the nature of the content (knowledge, skill, or problem-based), the navigational possibilities provided, the special audio and video effects, the graphics and multimedia integrated, and the level of interaction required.

Finally, critical organizational issues need to be considered. Stronger evidence is needed for CSL in the areas of cost savings and return-on-investment. Given that CSL, online learning, or education as a whole is expanding rapidly, it is critical to have research models that will help managers of these programs understand best business practices and benchmark costs and other key business performance metrics (Sloan-C, 2003, 2004). Corporations also need to assure their employees that the continuous growth of e-learning will not jeopardize job security; rather, participating in CSL to improve performance will be rewarded. Clearly, in order to ensure an effective and efficient delivery of CSL, all these complex issues, concerns, and questions need to be resolved or answered by consistent, systematic, and rigorous research. Results unveiled by rigorous research certainly will shed light on the most effective design, development, implementation, and evaluation of CSL, e-learning, or any other type of technology-based learning in the corporate world.

References

Applets. (2000, February 19). Retrieved August 7, 2000, from http://webopedia.internet.com/TERM/a/applet.html

Authers, J. (2001, May 7). Learning curve for business training: Corporate university awards. *The Financial Times Limited*, 12.

Barbian, J. (2002). Blended works here's proof. *Online Learning Magazine, 6*(6), 26-31.

Bassi, L., Cheney, S., & Lewis, E. (1998). Trends in workplace learning: Supply and demand in interesting times. *Training & Development, 52*(11), 62-66.

Bearman, M. (1997). *Why use technology?* Retrieved November 20, 1998, from http://www.monash.edu.au/informatics/teachme/whyuse.htm

Beer, V. (2000). *The Web-learning field handbook: Using the World Wide Web to build workplace learning environments.* San Francisco: Jossey-Bass Pfeiffer.

Bersin, J. (2005, April). *Evaluating LMSs? Buyer beware.* Retrieved August 18, 2005, from http://web.lexis-nexis.com/universe/printdoc

Bonk, C. J. (2002, January). *Online training in an online world.* Retrieved May 26, 2002, from http://www.publicationshare.com/docs/corp_survey.pdf

Carnegie Mellon University Learning Systems Architecture Lab. (n.d.). *SCORM Best Practices Guide for Content Developers* (1st ed.). (2003). Retrieved September 20, 2005, from http://www.lsal.cmu.edu/lsal/expertise/projects/developersguide/index.html

CDL development process map. (n.d.). Retrieved September 3, 2005, from http://www.cdl.edu/resources/developmentmap.gif

CDL development team structure. (n.d.). Retrieved September 3, 2005, from http://www.cdl.edu/resources/devteam.gif

Chalmers, T., & Lee, D. (2004). Web-based training in corporations: Organizational considerations. *International Journal of Instructional Media, 31*(4), 345-354

Chan, C., & Simon L., (2002). Development of an online taxation course: From design to evaluation. *The International Tax Journal, 28*(4), 23-50.

Croft-Baker, N. (2001, April). Eight companies keep e-learning from e-scaping. *The New Corporate University Review, 9*(2). Retrieved June 20, 2002, from http://www.traininguniversity.com/tu_pi2001ma_4.php

Crosman, P. L. (2004, July). *E-learning for short attention spans.* Retrieved August 18, 2005, from http://Web.lexis-nexis.com/universe/printdoc

Curtin, C. (1997). Getting off to a good start on intranets. *Training & Development, 51*(12), 41-46.

Dziuban, C. D., Hartman, J. L., & Moskal, P. D. (2004). Blended learning. Education Center for Applied Research. *Research Bulletin, 7*(7), 5.

Fichter, D. (2002, Jan/Feb). Intranets and e-learning: A perfect partnership. *Online, 26*(1), 68-70.

Filipczak, B. (1997, December). Are you wired enough? *Training, 34*(12), 25-39.

Frieswick, K. (1999). The online option. *CFO, 15*(12), 89-92

Fry, K. (2001). E-learning markets and providers: Some issues and prospects. *Education & Training, 43*, 233-239.

Furnas, G. (1997). *Effective view navigation.* Retrieved April 27, 2000, from http://www.acm.org/sigchi/chi97/proceedings/paper/gwf.htm

Galagan, P. A. (2000, May). Getting started with e-learning. *Training & Development, 54*(5), 62-64.

Galagan, P. A. (2001, February). Mission e-possible: The cisco e-learning story. *Training & Development, 55*(2), 46-56.

Geith, C. (2005). Cost analysis: A valuable decision support tool. Retrieved September 5, 2005, from http://www.sloan-c.org/publications/view/v4n1/pdf/v4n1.pdf

Hall, B. (1997). *Web-based training cookbook.* New York: John Wiley & Sons.

Henke, H. (1997). Evaluating Web-based instructional design. Retrieved November 14, 1999, from http://scis.nova.edu/~henkeh/story1.htm

Heo, H., & Joung, S. (2004). *Self-regulation strategies and technologies for adaptive learning management systems for Web-based instruction.* Paper presented at the conference of Association for Educational Communications and Technology, Chicago.

Horton, W. (2002, July). *Building the e-learning team.* Learning Circuits. Retrieved December 2, 2002, from http://www.learningcircuits.org/2002/jul2002/horton.html

IBM builds its manager training program with learning space 4.0 Lotus Development Corporation. (2000). Retrieved June 27, 2000, from http://www9.software.ibm.com/mindspan/distlearning.nsf/wdocs/5EE5DODC064CAD03852568DA00655551?Open Document

Jones, M. G., & Okey, J. R. (1995). *Interface design for computer-based learning environments.* Retrieved November 14, 1999, from http://hbg.psu.edu/bsed/intro/docs/idguide/

Khan, B. H. (1997). Web-based instruction (WBI): What is it and why is it? In B. H. Khan (Ed.), *Web-based instruction* (pp. 5-18). Englewood Cliffs, NJ: Educational Technology Publications, Inc.

Kilby, T. (1997). *What is Web-based training?* Retrieved November 1, 1999, from http://www.filename.com/wbt/pages/htm

Kim, K. J. (2004). *Motivational influences in self-directed online learning environments: A qualitative case study.* Educational Resources Information Center (ERIC ED485041). Retrieved April 18, 2006, from http://www.eric.ed.gov/ERICDocs/data/ericdocs2/content_storage_01/0000000b/80/2b/c7/1c.pdf

Kiser, K. (2001, October). The road ahead: Our first annual state of the industry report. *Online Learning Magazine*, 17-24. Retrieved May 26, 2002, from http://www.onlinelearningmag.com/onlinelearning/images/pdf/2001state_of_industry.pdf

Koonce, R. (1998). Where technology and training meet. *Technical Training, 9*(6), 10-15.

Kruse, K., & Keil, J. (2000). *Technology based training.* San Francisco: Jossey-Bass Pfeiffer.

Kurtus, R. (1997). *Authoring Web-based training.* Retrieved November 1, 1999, from http://www.ronkurtus.com/wbt/wbtauthoring.htm

Lamb, B. (2004, September/October). Wide open spaces: Wikis, ready or not. *EDUCAUSE Review, 39*(5), 36-48.

Landsberger, J. (2002, September/October). Accessibility: How easy, or even possible... *TechTrends, 46*(5), 65.

Lee, D., Chalmers, T., & Ely, T. (2005). Web-based training in corporations: Design issues. *International Journal of Instructional Media, 31*(4), 345-354.

Lustig, D. (2002, December). Creating a hassle-free training program. *Pharmaceutical Executive, 22*, 1-4.

Macpherson, A., Homan, G., & Wilkinson, K. (2005). The implementation and use of e-learning in the corporate university. *Journal of Workplace Learning, 17*(1/2), 33-48.

Moertl, P. (2002, November). 2002 PSA Web site contest. *PSA Journal, 68*(11), 15-16.

Nisar, T. (2004). E-learning in public organizations. *Public Personnel Management, 33*(1), 79-88.

Parks, E. R. (2004). *Calculating the total cost of e-learning.* Retrieved September 6, 2005, from http://www1.astd.org/TK04/pdf/TU405.pdf

Paulsen, M. F. (2003). Experiences with learning management systems in 113 European institutions. *Educational Technology & Society, 6*(4), 134-148.

Schaaf, D. (1997). A pipeline full of promises: Distance training is ready to delivery. *Training, 34*(10), A3-A22.

Schaaf, D. (1999, September). Bandwidth basics. *Training, 36*(9), OL23-OL37.

Schneider, M. (, 2001, April). GM gives log-on learning a boost. *Businessweek*, 2. Retrieved March 7, 2003, from http://www.businessweek.com

Schoenfeld, J., & Berge, Z. (2005). Emerging ISD models for distance education. *Journal ofEducational Technology Systems, 33*(1), 29-37.

Siemens saves $2,000 per employee per week. (2000). Lotus Development Corporation. Retrieved June 21, 2000, from http://www.lotus/com/home.nsf/welcom/learningspace

Sloan C-View. (2003). *Business issues in online education.* Retrieved September 5, 2005, from http://www.sloan-c.org/publications/view/v2n8/editorletterv2n8.htm

Sloan C-View. (2004). *Perspectives in quality online education.* Retrieved August 27, 2005, from http://www.sloan-c.org/publications/view/v2n4/coverv2n4.htm

Sloman, M. (2002, October). Breaking through the e-barriers. *Training & Development*, *10*, 36-41.

Strandberg, J. E. (1999). Instant answers.com. *Training, 36*(5), 40-44.

Strother, J. (2003). *International review of research in open and distance learning*. Retrieved June 3, 2005, from http://www.irrodl.org/content/v3.1/strother.html

Swanson, S., (2000, November 20). *Companies emerge as online teacher.* Retrieved March 7, 2003, from http://www.informationweek.com/bizint/biz813/teaching.htm

Tomlinson, M. B. (2005). *Instructional design considerations for Web-based instruction*. Unpublished manuscript, Pennsylvania State University, State College, PA.

Trombley, B. K., & Lee, D. (2002). Web-based learning in corporations: Who is using it and why, who is not and why not? *Journal of Educational Media, 27*(3), 137-146.

Voci, E., & Young, K. (2001). Blended learning working in a leadership development program. *Industrial and Commercial Training, 33*(4/5), 157-161.

Weinberger, D. (n.d.) *What is a podcast?* Retrieved September 5, 2005, from http://www.epnweb.org/index.php?view_mode=what

Wentling, T. L., Waight, C., Strazzo, D., File, J., La Fleur, J. A., & Kanfer, A. (2000). *The future of e-learning: A corporate and an academic perspective.* Retrieved June 10, 2005, from http://learning.ncsa.uiuc.edu/papers/elearnful.pdf

Wiley, D., South, J., Bassett, J., Nelson, L., Seawright, L., Peterson, T., et al. (1999). *Three common properties of efficient online instructional support systems.* Retrieved April 16, 2000, from http://www.aln.org/alnWeb/magazine/Vol3_issue2/wiley.htm

Williams, R. (1998). *Challenges to the optimal delivery of a training program via the World Wide Web.* Retrieved September 23, 1999, from http://www.trainingplace.com/source/wbtlimit.html

Young, A. C., & Young, J. D. (2002). A new look at the old ISD process. *Performance Improvement, 41*(5), 35-44.

Zenger, J., & Uehlein, C. (2001, August). Why blended learning? *Training and Development, 55*(8), 56-60.

Section III

Coordination, Collaboration, and Communication Technologies for CSL

Chapter XI

Awareness Design in Online Collaborative Learning: A Pedagogical Perspective

Curtis J. Bonk, Indiana University, USA

Seung-hee Lee, Indiana University, USA

Xiaojing Liu, Indiana University, USA

Bude Su, Indiana University, USA

Abstract

Collaboration in online learning environments is intended to foster harmonious interactions and mutual engagement among group members. To make group performance effective, it is essential to understand the dynamic mechanisms of online groupwork and the role of awareness supporting dynamic online collaboration. This chapter reviews the nature of online collaboration from the standpoint of task, social, and technological dimensions and reconceptualizes the importance of awareness support into these three dimensions of online collaboration. Further, this chapter suggests key knowledge elements in each type of awareness. Detailed pedagogical examples and technological features for awareness support for online collaboration are proposed.

Introduction

In the midst of the emergence of advanced Web technologies, groupwork has arisen as one of the most promising and innovative practices in online as well as face-to-face teaching and learning. For decades, educators have been arguing that a technologically sophisticated learning environment can provide support for online inquiry and knowledge-building in a learning community. However, decisions about which technologies to use and the ways they that are used for collaboration greatly impact the quality and depth of computer-supported learning. Effective communication and productive groupwork across time zones and geographic distances are highly dependent on whether the technological tools are used in conjunction with appropriate pedagogical guidelines and technological support.

Groupwork in real world situations often relates to working together for a key part of a project. In educational settings, groupwork often entails learners building collective knowledge via dialogues while working together. The process of groupwork produces unexpected synergistic ideas between group members, the intense discussion or debate of ideas, and creative final products that extend far beyond the talents of any one individual.

Many groupware tools and course management systems offer a variety of advanced features, but most of these serve the function of delivering communication rather than supporting group activities (Kirschner & Van Bruggen, 2004). Given that deep understanding of peer interactions within a shared workplace impacts the success of group performance (Gutwin & Greenburg, 1999), problems within current groupwork environments often lie in their lack of support of intricate group tasks and dynamic group processes.

In order to make group performance successful, different types of awareness support as well as instructional design focused on groupwork are critical for online interactions (Dias & Borges, 1999; Kirsch-Pinheiro, Lima, & Borgers, 2003). Given that awareness is defined as "an understanding of the activities of others, which provide a context for your own activity" (Dourish & Bellotti, 1992, p. 1), any contextual information provided by instructional design and systems supports helps coordinate the collaborative work process. In other words, awareness can assist in building harmonious interactions by allowing learners to be aware of basic information such as what is going on, what the assigned task or learning goal is, and what and how they can work together in online environments. Importantly, a sense of awareness of others, of the assigned tasks or activities, and of the multiple communication modes available plays a crucial role in ordinary work processes. Given that the success of online collaboration is contingent on group member interactions in the learning process with support of awareness information, awareness should be a major concern when designing groupware tools and systems.

Up to now, system development approaches for supporting awareness in online learning environments have not addressed all of the dimensions of online collaboration. A key reason for these limitations is that most studies in this area have been approached from system development or technological perspectives, rather than from pedagogical ones. As a result, such studies have failed to explore the dynamic mechanisms involved in the online collaborative process.

In response, in this chapter, we discuss the importance of awareness as a way of supporting the process of online collaborative learning, and introduce some related previous studies. Second, we present a framework of awareness support for online collaboration. In detail, the framework describes how we can design awareness, both pedagogically and technologically, for online collaboration. At the same time, the conceptual framework illustrates how different technological applications can support pedagogical strategies that facilitate collaborative teaching and learning. From the standpoint of human factors research, this chapter suggests a set of focal points wherein pedagogical and technological supports may foster awareness within online collaboration.

Literature Review

Dimensions of Online Collaboration

Learning is truly a social endeavor. Learning typically takes place when students work in a group, though the size and duration of such a group drastically varies. Given that meaningful group learning experiences typically do not occur naturally, many researchers and scholars have suggested more intense investigations of issues related to creating meaningful group learning environments.

Broadly defined, group learning is an activity in which two or more people learn or attempt to learn something together (Dillenbourg, 1999). In a work setting, groupwork can be defined as an activity wherein learners pursue possible solutions related to a mutual problem (Roschelle & Teasley, 1995). Meanwhile, in an online environment, a "group" refers to "people with complementary competencies executing simultaneous, collaborative work processes through electronic media without regard to geographic location" (Chinowsky & Rojas, 2003, p. 98). In effect, the online group can be dispersed anywhere and can contact each other regardless of time and place.

In particular, in online learning environments, the value of groupwork lies as much in the process of learning as it does in the ultimate product(s). Accordingly, groupwork is a dynamic and complex force that generates outputs and products that are difficult for learners and instructors to predict. A variety of input variables in groupwork (e.g., expectations, experiences, cultural backgrounds, assigned tasks, etc.) influence one another and produce different learning results or outcomes. This dynamic learning process within a group becomes a part of the learning experience. Thus, it is important that instructional designers and practitioners consider how to design learning environments in ways that support groupwork both pedagogically and technologically.

On the other hand, the features of online collaboration can be well described using the framework of online collaborative learning, which is comprised of three dimensions: (1) task, (2) social, and (3) technological dimensions (Carabajal, LaPointe, & Gunawardena, 2003). In face-to-face collaboration, much attention is made within the task dimension regarding integrating good strategies for effective task performance. Instructors and practitioners generally do not need to consider social and technological dimensions because simultaneous contact in the same space creates social climates naturally. Moreover, technological tools are minimally used, or at most, are supplemental devices in the support of collaborative work. However, due to geographic and time-related distances, online collaboration brings new situations and contexts to both instructors and learners. Thus, instructors need to recognize the multiple dimensions of online collaboration as well as the various roles needed to create successful online collaboration. Key aspects of the task, social, and technological dimensions in online collaboration (Lee, Bonk, Magjuka, Su, & Liu, in press) are summarized next.

- **Task dimension:** Group members accomplish group tasks through mutual engagement, idea negotiation, and the clarification of the key group goals or tasks. In the collaborative learning process, group members benefit from the group process through giving and receiving feedback and other assistance, exchanging information and resources, and challenging each other's thinking and reasoning patterns (Johnson & Johnson, 1996). This collaboration process fosters cognitive dissonance and conflict among group members, and, thus, encourages new knowledge construction. Due to the loss of explicit contextual cues in online environments, online collaborative groups may have more difficulty in reaching consensus than traditional residential groups. In this case, developing a shared mental model is important for motivating students to pursue high task performance. Setting mutual goals, achieving consensus, and providing groupwork guidelines are critical steps to assist students in effective group processes of completing a common task (Carabajal et al., 2003).

- **Social dimension:** The social dimension of online collaboration concerns the socio-emotional needs of group members and interpersonal relationships between group members. The richness of in-person communication comes from cues such as facial expression, eye contact, body gestures, and feelings of closeness. These types of cues often get lost or substantially reduced in online environments. Given the limited social cues, it is vital to explore various techniques to enhance the social dimension of groupwork in online environments. In addition, a rich social atmosphere helps minimize feelings of isolation in an online learning context, and cultivates a sense of community. Wegerif (1998), for instance, points out that group members are prone to be defensive, nervous, and reluctant to collaborate unless a sense of community is present. Social communications also promote mutual understandings and help build group norms. Such group norms often lead to group discipline which is especially important in online collaboration for enhancing group effectiveness and efficiency. More importantly, social engagement helps build trust among group members, which is essential for providing a social context that is conducive to virtual group collaboration.
- **Technological dimension:** The technological dimension is another distinct feature of online collaborative groups. Collaborative technologies often require the modification and transformation of traditional pedagogical approaches by both online instructors and students to new patterns of communication and learning. The appropriate choices of technologies as well as effective uses of them have important consequences for the quality and depth of online collaborative group processing and task performances (Carabajal et al., 2003; Duarte & Snyder, 1999). With a plethora of technologies currently available for online collaborative group members, the importance of identifying technologies that optimize the performance of online groups cannot be overstated (Durate & Snyder, 1999). One critical factor to consider in terms of the effective use of technologies is its potential to facilitate a shared dialogue and information exchange among group members (Carabajal et al., 2003). Technologies, when used appropriately, can also facilitate socio-emotional well-being of the group entity as a whole as well as increase the social awareness among group members or participants that enhances the effectiveness of collaboration and coordination among instructors and students (Durate & Snyder, 1999).

Awareness in Online Collaboration

While awareness is a widely-known concept in the fields of computer science and human computer interactions, many researchers have pointed out that there is no overall comprehensive depiction of awareness in the prevailing research literature (Gutwin, 1997). Schmidt (2002) claims that awareness is perhaps not really a distinct concept due to its diverse and sometimes even contradictory definitions and usage.

Awareness can be defined in several ways, but, as noted earlier, awareness is generally considered as an understanding of the activities of others and their learning context (Dourish & Bellotti, 1992). This definition underscores that individual contributions are important to the group activity as a whole, and to assessing individual actions with regard to group performance.

The concept of awareness has recently gained increasing attention among researchers in the study of computer-supported environments, a field that considers awareness crucial for creating effective online collaboration. In a shared face-to-face workspace, effective groups naturally develop a shared knowledge and practice through group members continuously checking on the actions of other people as well as the evolution of group products. Such a shared mental model of a group requires minimal conscious effort (Gutwin & Greenberg, 1999). However, in online environments, knowledge of others is not available unless the system makes it explicit. Knowledge sharing is the key to group interaction. Lack of this awareness when collaborating online (e.g., awareness of group members and their associated skills, collaboration tasks and goals, role within the group, group progress, resources available, and knowledge gaps) creates continuous breakdowns in the flow of knowledge, and it has a negative impact on learning (Prasolova-Førland & Divitini, 2002).

Several researchers, in fact, have identified awareness support as a factor in effective group performance (Kirsch-Pinheiro et al., 2003). They argue that awareness can be a key mediator for effective group communication and coordination. Awareness can assist in simplifying the need for verbal communication, in assisting with coordination, in providing a context for assistance and anticipation, and generally in helping people recognize opportunities for getting closer as a team or workgroup (Gutwin, 1997).

Although the concept of awareness has been widely used in designing groupware and information systems, the use of such design concepts is rare in existing educational collaborative tools and systems. It is not an exaggeration to say that currently popular course management systems do not adequately maintain awareness to support group process and performance. In response, in this chapter, we extend the concept of awareness in the context of online collaborative learning environments, and, thus, propose a framework of awareness design to support online collaboration.

How to Enhance Awareness in Online Collaboration

In the above sections, we have pointed out that in online collaborative environments, learners should recognize what is happening and know how to act and respond appropriately. In this section, we propose a framework of awareness design in online collaborative learning environments from the perspective of task, social, and technological dimensions of collaboration. First, we present how previous studies address awareness design from these three dimensions of online collaboration. Second, we address key elements of knowledge that constitute awareness, which support three different dimensions of online collaboration. The key elements of knowledge will be addressed with four "w" words and one "h" word: who, what, where, when, and how. Finally, based on the implications of previous studies and key knowledge elements of awareness design, we propose a substantial number of pedagogical examples and technological features for enriched awareness support.

Awareness Design for Task Dimension of Online Collaboration

Implications from Literature Review

A learning task is designed to achieve specific learning goals. A successful collaborative learning process involves setting task goals, coordinating efforts, and evaluating the progress of collaboration (Carroll, Neale, Isenhour, Rosson, & McCrickard, 2003). The task dimension of online collaboration requires learners to be aware of task goals and structure as well as other people's activities in relation to progress toward task goals. Such understanding is essential for group members to maintain the awareness of overall situations to accomplish common collaboration goals.

The literature has identified several characteristics of awareness including four categories of task awareness. First, task-oriented collaborations operate on shared goals and plans. Well conceptualized goals stimulate effective strategies, timelines, and collective activities for effective group performance (Marks, Mathieu, & Zaccaro, 2001). In online environments, it is critical that all members of a group have a sense of goal awareness, which, according to Endsley (1995), is a shared understanding of the goal and plans.

Second, a complex project involves a variety of activities taking place in different time periods. According to research on activity awareness, knowledge about the task related activities of other group members (Jang, Steinfield, & Pfaff, 2002) falls under the rubric of task awareness. To coordinate with other members of the group in a learning task, it is important to be aware of other people's situations. Different types of collaboration tasks require task-specific awareness. In real time collaboration situations, when several learners operate simultaneously on a learning task, they need detailed information about their group members' activities. In a long-term task, when group members' actions are interdependent, they usually need to be aware of the progress, completions, and actions of others (Gutwin, 1997).

Third, to simply learn the status of others' activities may not be enough for effective coordination. In addition to knowing about group member activities, one must be aware of how others in the group perceive the general situation (Endsley, 1995) and interpret particular situations and activities. To enhance such awareness, a group needs regular communicative actions to support perspective awareness.

Fourth, another aspect of task awareness is to understand the resources that are available or potentially available for online collaboration (Espinosa, Cadiz, Rico-Gutierrez, Kraut, Scherlis, & Lautenbacher, 2000). Whether in its initial planning stage or group progress stage, the process of monitoring available resources critical to the tasks, along with effective communication of this information, leads to situational awareness (Marks et al., 2001).

Key Knowledge Elements for Task Dimension

Based on the awareness literature, we propose that task awareness for online collaboration should reflect the nature of the group task, awareness of group progress, awareness of group perceptions, and awareness of resources. Awareness within the task dimension can revolve around the four "w" and one "h" words: who, what, where, when, and how.

Awareness of the nature of group tasks. Group members need to build a shared mental model of the task goals and structure:

- What is the goal of the task?
- What is the structure of the task?
- What steps must we take to complete the task?

Awareness of group progress. Group members need to know the activity status of others and the overall situations of tasks in relation to the common goal:

- When do we have to finish the sub-goals and final goals of the task?
- How much have we done as a group?
- What more do we have to do?
- Who is doing what?

Awareness of group perceptions. Group members need to be aware of others' perceptions of group activities and group process:

- What are they thinking?
- Why do they think this way?

Awareness of resources. Group members need to have knowledge of available resources to complete their own tasks and assist in other members' tasks:

- What resources (tools/materials/skills/expertise) are needed to complete the task?
- What resources are available for the task?

Pedagogical Examples for Task Dimension

Listed next are a few pedagogical examples and possible groupware system features that support task awareness in online collaboration.

Setting mutual goals and expectations. Besides being encouraged to do initial goal-setting, online groups also need to have a codified document related to their overall goal statement and task structure. For example, in a groupware space, a graphical view of a project timelines that includes group deadlines for goal or sub-goal accomplishment can serve as a situational status reminder (Carroll et al., 2003).

- **Encouraging role assignment and task responsibilities.** In a collaborative learning task, the assigning of explicit roles to learners is an effective way of making learners aware of their task roles in the group. Groupware can use icons or avatars to indicate explicit roles that learners have been assigned (Gutwin, 1997).
- **Encouraging group discourse.** A group needs regular communicative actions to support perspective awareness. Regularly scheduled online conversations or explicit comments regarding tasks or artifacts provide awareness of other group members' understandings and will contribute to a shared understanding of the group's purpose.
- **Providing work flow guidelines where a procedural map of task and sub-tasks is presented**. Monitoring groupwork flow is important to make effective collaboration. A workflow system that can present the tasks as a sequence of actions following a defined order is one example of a practice that keeps the group focused on task goal.
- **Reflecting group progress periodically.** Besides setting up regular meetings to update group progress and coordinate actions, many system features in groupware assist in awareness of group progress. To improve activity awareness, a system log of all tasks or activities is helpful for group members to understand what has happened (Jang et al., 2002). In addition, an activity notification system can send e-mail notices to the group to keep group activities up-to-date (Jang et al., 2002). A chronological visualization of project artifact histories and evolution is helpful to catch group members up with group progress on different fronts (Carroll et al., 2003). A simple calendar in a groupware system that displays the critical dates and provides detailed descriptions of the events might also serve the purpose of process awareness and assist in task progress (Jang et al., 2002).
- **Getting and sharing available resources.** A resource analysis should be conducted at the initial stage of groupwork. Group members are encouraged to share their expertise and personal resources that contribute to the group goals. Groups need to keep up-to-date on the availability of new information resources as well as emerging themes or patterns within those resources. A designated group folder or private groupwork space in groupware facilitates the sharing of resources within the group.

A summary of awareness design for the task dimension in online collaboration is shown in Table 1.

Table 1. Awareness design for task dimension of online collaboration

Key Elements	Pedagogical Examples	Technological Features
Awareness of the nature of group tasks • What is the goal of the task? • What is the structure of the task? • What steps must we take to complete the task? *Awareness of group progress* • When do we have to finish the sub-goals and final goals of the task? • How much have we done as a group? • What more do we have to do? • Who is doing what? *Awareness of group perceptions* • What are they thinking? • Why do they think this way? *Awareness of resources* • What resources (tools/materials/skills/expertise) are needed to complete the task? • What resources are available for the task?	• Setting mutual goals and expectations • Encouraging role assignment and division of responsibilities • Encouraging cognitive discourse • Providing work flow guidelines where a procedural map of task and sub-tasks is presented • Reflecting on group progress periodically • Getting and sharing available resources	• Calendar • Graphical view of project timelines • Avatars or icons for role structure • Reflection note for group progress • Activity notification • Activity log • Electronic workflow guidelines • Group note pad • Private groupwork space or folders

Awareness Design for Social Dimension of Online Collaboration

Implications from Literature Review

In the context of collaborative learning, awareness support for the social dimension is defined as "the awareness that students have about the social connections within the group" (Gutwin, Stark, & Greenberg, 1995, p. 2). Several types of awareness that have been identified in the literature can be categorized under the larger umbrella of social awareness support. For example, informal awareness, which is concerned with who is around and whether they are available, is a part of social awareness (Gutwin, 1997). On the other hand, some scholars (Caselles, François, Metcalf, Ossimitz, & Stallinger, 2000) point out that social awareness should not merely be concerned with superficial awareness such as the existence of another entity. Non-superficial awareness that involves understanding and trust should also be a concern. Non-superficial social awareness is crucial to nurturing a context that is conducive to collaboration for group members where differences and conflicts can be resolved through mutual understanding and trust. This point can be further supported by social-cultural theory that highlights the importance of member relationship mutuality and the significance of interaction in collaborative learning (Sfard, 1998). To provide a comprehensive picture of social awareness, we can discuss it in relation to the emergence of online communities, group norms, and member trust.

Key Knowledge Elements for Social Dimension

Awareness support for the social dimension reflects the knowledge about a sense of learning community, group norms, and member trust. Similar to other kinds of awareness, social awareness also can revolve around the four "w" and one "h" word(s) mentioned earlier.

Awareness of a sense of community. To minimize feelings of isolation, members need to sense the existence of other members and need a sense of belonging to their group.

- Who is around?
- Who are they?
- How much do I know them?
- How much do they know me?
- How can I get in touch with them?
- When are they available?

Awareness about group norms. To be efficient, group members need to follow the explicit and implicit rules that have evolved over the period of collaboration.

- What are the appropriate ways to approach the group?
- What role should I take in this group?
- What roles will other members of the group assume?
- When/where is the appropriate time/location to work with them?
- How should I interact with other group members?

Awareness about member trust. To be effective, groups should demonstrate high levels of trust among members to decrease possible misunderstandings and unnecessary conflicts.

- What do I expect from my group members?
- What do they expect from me?
- How comfortable do I feel when I communicate with others?
- How comfortable do they feel when they communicate with me?
- How much do my group members trust me?

Pedagogical Examples for Social Dimension

Enhancing social awareness in the context of online collaborative learning can be approached from both technological and pedagogical aspects. Some pedagogical examples to support social awareness in online collaborations are listed below.

- **Encouraging discourse among group members:** A number of tactics can encourage discourse in virtual collaboration. For instance, instructors can read online discussions once in a while to provide feedback or even grade the quality and quantity of the discussions. In-depth and frequent communications among members definitely contribute to their mutual understanding.
- **Setting up regular communication patterns:** One approach to online collaborative learning is that group members attempt to minimize the time that they spend on communication since most of them have full-time jobs or other responsibilities. Asking group members to establish a regular communication pattern from the beginning can help establish a routine that will facilitate effective and perhaps seamless group communication.
- **Establishing and clarifying group norms:** Making the group rules clear—especially clarifying the implicit ones—can help members predict others' actions, and, thus, help support awareness.
- **Encouraging role negotiations:** Asking group members to assign roles during collaboration can help clarify who is supposed to do what.
- **Arranging peer teaching and peer evaluations:** Asking group members to provide feedback and generally assist each other will create communication opportunities through which members can deepen their mutual understanding.

Table 2. Awareness design for the social dimension of online collaboration

Key Elements	Pedagogical Examples	Technological Features
Awareness of a sense of community • Who is around? • Who are they? • How much do we know each other? • Whether and when are they available? *Awareness about group norms* • What are the appropriate ways to approach the group? • What roles should I and others play? • When/where is the appropriate time/location to work with other group members? • How should I interact with them? *Awareness about member trust* • What do group members expect from each other? • How comfortable are we to communicate with each other? • How much do my group members trust me?	• Encouraging social discourse among group members • Setting up regular communication patterns • Establishing and clarifying group norms • Encouraging role negotiations • Arranging peer teaching and peer evaluations • Arranging group reflection opportunities	• Threaded discussion spaces • Weekly logbook • Displaying multiple screens during synchronous collaboration • Virtual meeting place such as a "coffee house" where learners can bump into each other like in real life situations • Build-in artifacts that reflect member identity and activities that help trace collaboration patterns • Annotation and brainstorming tools, desktop videoconferencing, electronic whiteboards, knowledge management portals and tools, mentoring exchange systems, translation tools, virtual classrooms or online presentation tools (Bonk, Wisher, & Nigrelli, 2004)

- **Arranging group reflection opportunities:** To enhance social cohesion and member trust, instructors may provide group reflection activities so that misunderstandings and conflicts can be discussed and solved among group members.

A summary of awareness design for the social dimension in online collaboration is shown in Table 2.

Awareness Design for Technological Dimension

Implications from Literature Review

Awareness support for the technological dimension of online collaboration links the task and social dimensions of online collaboration. Technological awareness allows effective collaboration. Minimal research has considered awareness support from the technological dimension, when compared to the attention paid to supporting awareness from both the task and social dimension standpoints.

In the context of collaborative learning, we define technological awareness through two aspects. Not surprisingly, the first part is the general knowledge of technology tools used in groupwork. The other key part is workspace awareness, defined as up-to-date knowledge about other learners' interactions with the shared technological workspace, including past, current, and future traces of activity in the groupware (Gutwin, 1997). While knowledge of online pedagogy is vital, the effectiveness of online collaborative environments greatly depends on how technological tools are applied for learning and how learners use them to make their groupwork meaningful. The general knowledge of technological tools is a critical aspect for group effectiveness but is often neglected in practice. For example, group members may have failed to take advantage of the potential interactive tools in a groupware system due to insufficient orientation sessions related to those tools. Technological tools should function as cognitive tools (Gao, Baylor, & Shen, 2005; Jonassen & Carr, 2000; Teasley & Roschelle, 1993), rather than as just communication or message delivery tools. This cognitive tool focus implies that the technological dimension needs to help expand learners' capacity to create, filter, share, and represent collective knowledge.

In addition, in online learning environments, a group workspace is sometimes the only central space that links different task activities of group members. The artifacts in a group space represent the shared repertoire of the community. Group members leave traces of their actions on the artifacts, reflecting various activities and resource ownerships (Prasolva-Førland & Divitini, 2002). The awareness of others' interactions within a group space not only facilitates effective coordination in the space but also facilitates task and social awareness for collective goals.

Key Knowledge Elements for Technological Dimension

Key knowledge of technological awareness covers awareness of general technology tool use and awareness of the groupwork space. Similar to other types of awareness, technological awareness cues can revolve around the key "w" and "h" words noted earlier.

Awareness of general technological tool uses. Group members need to have a good understanding of different tools for group communications.

- What technologies are available for the group?
- How do they function?
- How much time and energy do they require to learn and to use?

- How compatible are the available technologies that I have access to with the technologies of others in my group?

Awareness of groupwork space. To foster effective use of tools for collaboration, group members need to be aware of the status of others' interactions with the technological space.

- Where have they been in the workspace?
- What have they already done in the workspace?
- Where are they now?
- What are they doing in the workspace?
- Are they online or off-line at this moment?

Pedagogical Examples for Technological Dimension

Some pedagogical examples to support technological awareness in online collaborations are listed next.

- **Understanding what tools are available:** Learners need to be aware of the facility or system that they have for online groupwork. In effect, they should be aware of what technological tools and features are available for groupwork, including hardware and software. For instance, is there a group workspace or a place to post shared documents? Are there threaded discussions or synchronous chat tools?
- **Orientating features/functions of tools and how to get support for their use:** One concern raised by online educators is that many learners do not know about the current technological tools that are embedded in course management systems or groupware systems, their pedagogical purpose or potential, how much time and energy they require to learn and to use, and whether different technologies are compatible with others. This lack of technology knowledge blocks learners' effective use of online collaborative environments. As a result, many learners need to acquire this knowledge while collaborating online. Instructor orienting tasks and activities as well as available system supports are highly valuable in fostering this knowledge and awareness as well as general system use.
- **Understanding the usefulness of tools for certain groupwork:** Setting expectations for technology requirements up front can help learners to have an idea of how to use given technological tools for their groupwork. One

suggestion is to list relevant technologies with their pros and cons to help learners understand the usefulness of tools.

- **Matching appropriate tools with groupwork:** Knowledge of how to use technological tools, when to use them, and for what purposes they should be used, will help determine the effectiveness of online collaboration.
- **Making a joint decision on types of tools used for group communication:** Group members need to discuss and reach a consensus on the types of tools used in the group and be consistent in their use.
- **Keeping group members aware of actions in groupwork space:** Group members should make it explicit when their actions in the groupwork space could impact others' activities. Some groupware features help support this awareness. Activity notifications and logs in a groupware system or courseware usually track the changes within the artifacts and provide a history of actions in the groupware space. Data mining tools can help visualize such activity patterns and usage statistics, thereby providing more insights on group member participation and functioning.

A summary of awareness design for the technological dimension in online collaboration is shown in Table 3.

Table 3. Awareness design for the technological dimension of online collaboration

Key Elements	Pedagogical Examples	Technological Features
Awareness of general technological tool uses • What technologies are available for the group? • How do they function? • How much time and energy do they require to learn and to use? • How much are my technologies compatible with others? *Awareness of group workspace* • Where have they been? • What have they already done in the workspace? • Where are they? • What are they doing in the workspace? • Are they online or offline at this moment?	• Understanding what tools are available • Orienting to features and functions of tools and how to get support to use them • Understanding the usefulness of tools for certain groupwork • Matching appropriate tools with groupwork • Making a joint decision on types of tools used for group communication • Keeping group members aware of actions in groupwork space	• Tutorials • Tool use guidelines • Activity notification • Activity log • Annotations • Private groupwork space/folders

Summary

Collaboration is not simply a collection of individual work. Optimal collaboration pursues mutual engagement for problem solving, rather than just communication transmissions or simple message delivery. Collaboration in online learning environments requires that learners have an appropriate sense of understanding of themselves, their peers, the required activities, and other important situational context information.

This chapter revisits the concepts of "awareness," which has been studied among computer science and is now being introduced into various educational fields. In this chapter, we have examined the importance of awareness in online collaboration and presented an awareness framework from a pedagogical perspective, rather than a groupware development perspective. In particular, we addressed how to support awareness from the standpoint of the task, social, and technological dimensions of collaboration.

Yet, there are several concerns to be considered. First, though task awareness has been proposed as one important principle for designing effective groupware systems to support collaboration and coordination, several issues also have been raised regarding embedding features to support task awareness. For example, information overload is a well-known phenomenon resulting from over-designed task awareness tools and features (Kirsch-Pinheiro et al., 2003). When task awareness is not designed to accommodate individual needs, awareness information can also be extremely distracting and harmful to individual activities. On the other hand, the design of awareness tools should be complementary to other communication and coordination tools preferred by collaborators. Without such considerations, awareness tools may be redundant and need extra effort from collaborators in using awareness supports (Jang et al., 2002).

Second, individuals working in a group inevitably use other members' visible or predictable actions to pace and plan their own actions (Ackerman & Starr, 1995). Therefore, supporting social awareness can help group members to understand their overall situations better and make more suitable decisions about their own actions. However, the support of social awareness itself does not guarantee positive effects in group collaboration. Building social awareness definitely is a precondition for creating cohesive relationships among students. At the same time, providing social awareness activities or tasks with learners during online groupwork can be another burden for learners to address or take care of in addition to conducting task assignments. Careful determination of what social awareness information to provide and appropriately timing its delivery during virtual teaming or different stages of group collaboration would significantly impact task performance.

Figure 1. Relationship of three dimensions for awareness support in online collaboration

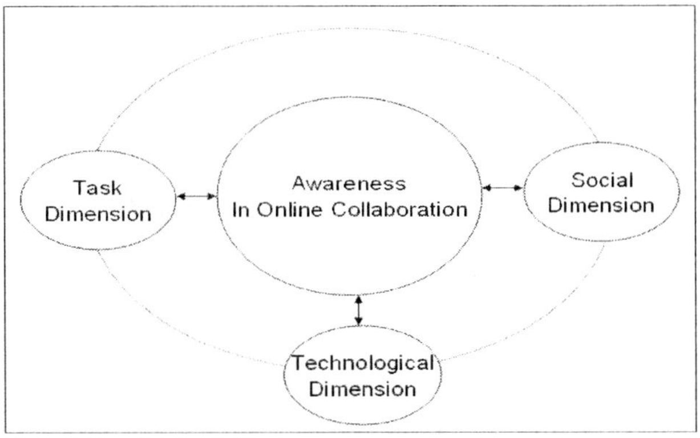

Third, technological awareness is definitely the most salient and probably the most significant portion of awareness in online collaboration. Still, support for technological awareness has received scant attention compared with other aspects of awareness.

As shown in Figure 1, awareness support from task, social, and technological dimensions positively connects to the effectiveness of online collaboration. Considering three dimensions are closely interrelated with one another, online educational practitioners, instructional designers, and instructors should consider balancing support and embedded cues when designing awareness in online learning environments.

In conclusion, the current groupware tools and course management systems provide some pedagogical examples and technological features for awareness support. The pedagogical examples and technological features discussed in this chapter contribute to online learning environments functioning not just as virtual spaces but also as cognitive tools. As online groupware and Web collaboration continue to emerge and educational theory and use related to such tools simultaneously evolves, there will be a plethora of interesting research and development avenues to enhance online collaborative group functioning and success. In addition, there will be interesting windows on previously hidden or unknown aspects to human learning and social interactions as well as countless opportunities for research that explores these innovative forms of group functioning and human learning and performance. These are exciting times for becoming aware of how online collaborative groups function, negotiate roles, foster new insights, and ultimately succeed or fail. It is definitely time for those in education to become more aware of online collaboration awareness.

Acknowledgment

This work was supported by Korea Research Foundation Grant (KRF-2003-037-B00071).

References

Ackerman, M., & Starr, B. (1995). Social activity indicators: Interface components for CSCW systems. In *Proceedings of the 8th ACM Symposium on User Interface Software and Technology (UIST'95)* (pp. 159-168). Retrieved April 16, 2006, from http://portal.acm.org/citation.cfm?id=215969&col=GUIDE&dl=ACM&CFID=69623356&CFTOKEN=139753&ret=1#Fulltext

Bonk, C. J., Wisher, R. A., & Nigrelli, M. L. (2004). Learning communities, communities of practice: Principles, technologies, and examples. In K. Littleton, D. Miell, & D. Faulkner (Eds.), *Learning to collaborate, collaborating to learn* (pp. 199-219). Hauppauge, NY: Nova Science Publishers.

Carabajal, K., LaPointe, D., & Gunawardena, C. N. (2003). Group development in online learning communities. In M. G. Moore, & W. G. Anderson (Eds.), *Handbook of distance education* (pp. 217-234). Mahwah, NJ: Lawrence Erlbaum Associates.

Carroll, J. M., Neale, D. C., Isenhour, P. L., Rosson, M. B., & McCrickard, D. S. (2003). Notification and awareness: Synchronizing task-oriented collaborative activity. *International Journal of Human-Computer Studies, 58*(5), 605-632.

Caselles, A., François, C., Metcalf, G., Ossimitz, G., & Stallinger, F. (2000). Awareness and social systems. In G. Chroust & C. Hofer (Eds.), *Social systems and the future* (pp. 31-42). Österreichische Studiengesellschaft für Kybernetik, Reports of the Austrian Society for Cybernetic Studies, Vienna, Australia.

Chinowsky, P., & Rojas, E. (2003). Virtual teams: Guide to successful implementation. *Journal of Management in Engineering, 19*(3), 98-106.

Dias, M. S., & Borges, M. R. S. (1999). Development of groupware systems with the COPSE infrastructure. In *Proceedings of String Processing and Information Retrieval Symposium & International Workshop on Groupware* (pp. 278-285). Retrieved April 6, 2006, from http://csdl.computer.org/dl/proceedings/spire/1999/0268/00/02680278.pdf

Dillenbourg, P. (1999). What do you mean by collaborative learning? In P. Dillenbourg (Ed.), *Collaborative-learning: Cognitive and computational approaches* (pp. 1-19). Oxford: Elsevier.

Dourish, P., & Bellotti, V. (1992). Awareness and coordination in shared workspaces. In *Proceedings of the ACM Conference on Computer-Supported Cooperative Work (CSCW'92),* Toronto, Ontario (pp. 107-114). New York: ACM Press. Retrieved April 16, 2006, from http://portal.acm.org/citation.cfm?id=143468&coll=GUIDE&dl=GUIDE&CFID=73906796&CFTOKEN=24042431&ret=1#Fulltext

Duarte, D., & Snyder, N. (1999). *Mastering online collaborative groups: Strategies, tools and techniques that succeed.* San Francisco: Jossey-Bass.

Endsley, M. R. (1995). Toward a theory of situation awareness in dynamic systems. *Human Factors, 37*(1), 32-64.

Espinosa, A., Cadiz, J., Rico-Gutierrez, L., Kraut, R., Scherlis W., & Lautenbacher, G. (2000). Coming to the wrong decision quickly: Why awareness tools must be matched with appropriate tasks. In *Proceedings of the SIGCHI Conference on Human Factors in Computing Systems CHI 2000, 2(1)* (pp. 392-399). New York: ACM Press.

Gao, H., Baylor, A. L., & Shen, E. (2005). Designer support for online collaboration and knowledge construction. *Educational Technology & Society, 8*(1), 69-79.

Gutwin, C. (1997). *Workspace awareness in real-time distributed groupware.* Unpublished dissertation transcripts. University of Calgary, Alberta, Canada.

Gutwin, C., & Greenberg, S. (1999). *A framework of awareness for small group in shared-workspace groupware* (Tech. Rep. No. 99-1). Saskatoon, Canada: University of Saskatchewan, Department of computer science.

Gutwin, C., Stark, G., & Greenberg, S. (1995). Support for workspace awareness in educational groupware. In J. L. Schnase & E. L. Cunnius (Eds.), *Proceedings of Computer Supported Collaborative Learning (CSCL'95)* (pp. 147-156). Mahwah, NJ: Lawrence Erlbaum Associates.

Jang, C., Steinfield, C., & Pfaff, B. (2002). Virtual group awareness and groupware support: An evaluation of the GroupSCOPE system. *International Journal of Human-Computer Studies, 56*(1), 109-126.

Johnson, D. W., & Johnson, R. T. (1996). Cooperation and the use of technology. In D. H. Jonassen (Ed.), *Handbook of research for education communications and technology* (pp. 1017-1044). New York: Simon and Schuster Macmillan.

Jonassen, D. H., & Carr, C. S. (2000). Mindtools: Affording multiple knowledge representations for learning. In S. P. Lajoie (Ed.), *Computers as cognitive tools, volume II: No more walls: Theory change, paradigm shifts, and their influence on the use of computers for instructional purposes* (pp. 165-196). Mahwah, NJ: Lawrence Erlbaum Associates.

Kirsch-Pinheiro, M., Lima, J. V., & Borges, M. R. S. (2003). A framework for awareness support in groupware systems. *Computer in Industry, 52*(1), 47-57.

Kirschner, P., & Van Bruggen, J. (2004). Learning and understanding in virtual teams. *Cyberpsychology & Behavior, 7*(2), 135-139.

Lee, S., Bonk, C. J., Magjuka, R. J., Su, B., & Liu, X. (in press). Understanding the dimensions of virtual teams. *International Journal on E-learning.*

Marks, M. A., Mathieu, J. E., & Zaccaro, S. J. (2001). A temporally based framework and taxonomy of group processes. *Academy of Management Review, 26*(3), 356-376.

Prasolova-Førland, E. (2002). Supporting awareness in education: Overview and mechanisms. In *Proceedings of the International Conference on Engineering Education (ICEE 2002)* (Manchester, UK). MUIST. Retrieved April 16, 2006, from http://www.idi.ntnu.no/grupper/su/publ/ekaterina/ICEE2002.pdf

Prasolova-Førland, E., & Divitini, M. (2002). Supporting learning communities with collaborative virtual environments: Different spatial metaphors. In *Proceedings of the IEEE International Conference on Advanced Learning Technologies (ICALT 2002)* (Kazan, Russia). IEEE Press. Retrieved April 16, 2006, from http://lttf.ieee.org/icalt2002/proceedings/t605_Icalt114_End.pdf

Roschelle, J., & Teasley, S. (1995). The construction of shared knowledge in collaborative problem solving. In C. E. O'Malley (Ed.), *Computer supported collaborative learning* (pp. 69-97). Berlin: Springer-Verlag.

Schmidt, K. (2002). The problem with 'awareness': Introductory remarks on 'awareness in CSCW'. *Computer Supported Cooperative Work, 11*(3-4), 285-298.

Sfard, A. (1998). On two metaphors for learning and the dangers of choosing just one. *Educational Researcher, 27*(2), 4-13.

Teasley, S. D., & Roschelle, J. (1993). Construction a joint problem space: The computer as a tool for sharing knowledge. In S. P. Lajoie, & S. J. Derry (Eds.), *Computers as cognitive tools* (pp. 229-258). Hillsdale, NJ: Lawrence Erlbaum Associates.

Wegerif, R. (1998). The social dimension of asynchronous learning networks. *Journal of Asynchronous Learning Networks, 2*(1), 34-49. Retrieved September 4, 2005, from http://www.sloan-c.org/publications/jaln/v2n1/pdf/v2n1_wegerif.pdf

Chapter XII

Communication, Coordination, and Cooperation in Computer-Supported Learning: The AulaNet Experience

Carlos J. P. Lucena, Catholic University of Rio de Janeiro, Brazil

Hugo Fuks, Catholic University of Rio de Janeiro, Brazil

Alberto Raposo, Catholic University of Rio de Janeiro, Brazil

Marco A. Gerosa, Catholic University of Rio de Janeiro, Brazil

Mariano Pimentel, Catholic University of Rio de Janeiro, Brazil

Abstract

This chapter introduces an approach based on the 3C (communication, coordination, and cooperation) collaboration model to the development and analysis of collaborative systems, by means of a case study of a learningware (AulaNet) and the methodology of a Web-based course, both designed based on the model. The 3C model is presented through the analysis of each of its three elements, followed by the case study of its application in the AulaNet environment and in the ITAE (Information Technology Applied to Education) course, an entirely online course that has been taught since 1998.

Introduction

Collaboration may be seen as the combination of communication, coordination, and cooperation. The 3C model was originally proposed by Ellis, Gibbs, and Rein (1991), with some terminology differences. It appears frequently in the literature as a means to classify collaborative systems or as a basis for groupware development methodologies (Borghoff & Schlichter, 2000; Laurillau & Nigay, 2002). In this chapter, we explore the 3C model as a means to represent a learningware application domain and also as a basis for a system development.

The relationship among the 3Cs of the model facilitates the understanding of a groupware application domain. In this chapter, we are focused on the group work domain, which is represented in Figure 1. According to this instantiation of the 3C model, communicating people negotiate and make decisions. The commitments generated during communication are organized into tasks managed by coordination. While coordinating themselves, people deal with conflicts in such a way as to avoid the loss of communication and cooperation efforts. Cooperation is the joint operation of members of the group in a shared space to complete tasks and generate and manipulate cooperation objects. The needs of renegotiation and making decisions about unexpected situations that appear during

Figure 1. 3C collaboration model instantiated for group work

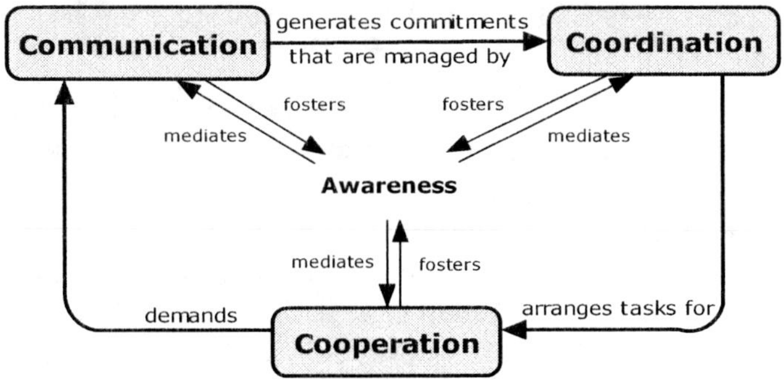

cooperation may demand a new round of communication, which will require coordination to reorganize the tasks to be executed during cooperation.

In this chapter, we show how the 3C model has been applied to the development of the AulaNet environment and to the dynamics of a course titled Information Technology Applied to Education (ITAE), currently in its 14th edition. In the next section, AulaNet and the ITAE course are introduced. The following sections detail each aspect of the 3C collaboration model, namely communication, coordination, and cooperation, using AulaNet and the ITAE course as a case study.

The AulaNet Learning Environment

The manner in which people work has changed with the advent of the connected society. Accustomed to the paradigm of command and control that is taught in the classroom and widely disseminated on the factory floor or, rather, conditioned by it, workers are not up to the new demands of the connected society. They are taught to react to clear orders, well-defined procedures, and specific activities. Their understanding of communication is vertical—memorandums come down from above, and reports are sent up the line. Thus, like in the classroom, horizontal communication—communication with a shift colleague—besides being hardly well thought of is also given no technological support. Knowledge workers, on the other hand, constantly interact with their work colleagues in order to carry out their tasks. The organization that was imposed top-down in the command and control paradigm loses effectiveness and is replaced by one that is peer-to-peer, where communication, coordination, and cooperation predominate.

AulaNet is a freeware Web-based environment for teaching and learning. It has been under development since June 1997 by the Software Engineering Laboratory of the Catholic University of Rio de Janeiro (PUC-Rio). Besides Portuguese, AulaNet is also available for download (http://www.eduweb.com.br) in English and Spanish versions. A comparison with other environments can be found at Zaina (2001).

In its first versions, AulaNet resources were subdivided into administrative, assessment, and didactic services, a common approach in educational tools (Edutools, 2004). Unfortunately, this approach led teachers to use the environment to teach in the traditional vertical way: broadcasting information with a low degree of learner-teacher interaction and no interaction among learners at all. Collaborative learners are expected to have a high degree of interaction among themselves and with their teachers, who are now supposed to act as coordinators

Figure 2. Classification of AulaNet services based on the 3C Model. The 3C triangle appears in Borghoff and Schlichter (2000).

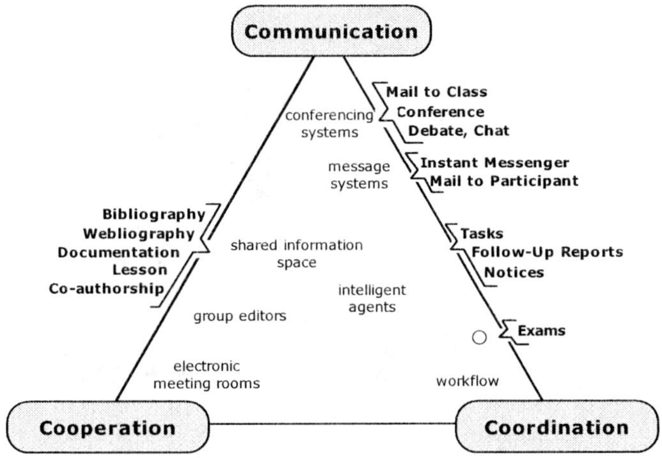

or mediators rather than as information deliverers. Hence, the services were reorganized based on the 3C collaboration model, which is suitable for a collaborative learning approach (Fuks, 2000).

The AulaNet environment's services are currently subdivided into communication, coordination, and cooperation services, as can be seen in Figure 2. The communication services provide tools for forum-style asynchronous text discussion (*Conferences*), chat-style synchronous text discussion (*Chat* and *Debate*), instant message exchange between simultaneously connected learners (*Instant Messenger*), and individual electronic mail with the mediators (*Mail to Participant*) and with the whole class, in a list-server style (*Mail to Class*). Coordination services support the management and the enforcement of group activities. In AulaNet, coordination services include tools for notification (*Notices*), evaluation (*Tasks* and *Exams*), as well as a tool that allows monitoring group participation (*Follow-Up Reports*). Cooperation services in AulaNet include *Lessons* and *Documentation*, a list of course references (*Bibliography* and *Webliography*), and course co-authoring support, both for teachers (*Teacher Co-Authoring*) and for learners (*Learner Co-Authoring*).

In AulaNet courses, teachers can have three different roles, which may or may not be assumed by the same person. The coordinator's role is to design the course, defining and configuring the services that are made available to learners.

Figure 3. The AulaNet interface

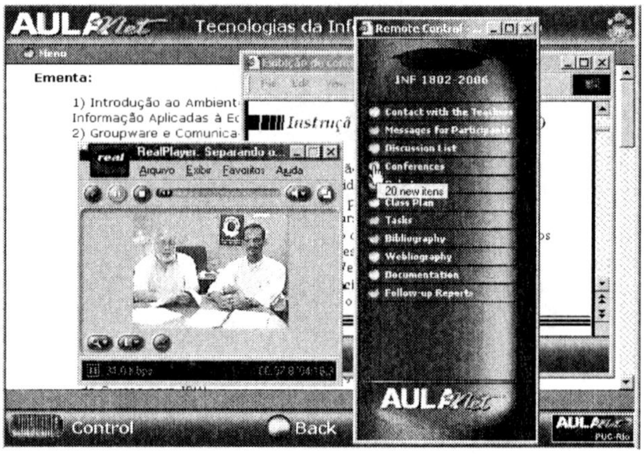

The author's role is to produce and insert content. The mediator's role is to animate the group, maintaining order, motivating and evaluating learner participation. In the ITAE course (introduced in the following section) there are two coordinators who also assume the author's role, and there are mediators, who vary from one semester to the next.

The AulaNet services are placed at the disposal of coordinators during the creation and maintenance of a course, enabling them to select those they wish to make available to learners in the menu represented as a remote control unit (Figure 3). During the ITAE course, the teacher gradually makes more AulaNet services available to help the learners understand the environment in which they are studying.

Although Internet offers advantages and facilities for teaching/learning, there are also many difficulties associated with its use. To produce interactive Web-based content, for instance, if an institution does not provide support for it, teachers must comprehend technologies that sometimes are not part of their expertise. To reduce these difficulties they can use environments, like AulaNet, that separate content from navigation. This lets them concentrate on the production of content, using habitual tools such as word processing programs, while leaving the management of learner navigation to the environment. Additionally, integrated communication, coordination, and cooperation services can be added to courses, and some environments supply reports so that teachers can follow up learner participation.

It was with this scenario in mind that the Information Technologies Applied to Education (ITAE) course was designed. The aim of the course is to get students to learn to work in groups with information technology, turning them into Web-based educators.

The ITAE Course

The ITAE course has been taught since 1998 as one of the courses of the Computer Science Department at PUC-Rio entirely online, using the AulaNet environment. The course methodology was envisaged to change the behavior of students used to be passive receivers into learners who actively generate knowledge. This process encourages learners to look for their own sources of information, to deal with information overload and to turn information into knowledge collaboratively. Learners are graded for their contributions that add value to the group and not for their individual activities (Fuks, Gerosa, & Lucena, 2002).

In the first part of the course, learners study the contents according to the weekly topic, reading contents in the *Lesson* service, and discussing the topic asynchronously in the *Conference* service and synchronously in the *Debate* service (Figure 4). In the ITAE course, learners conduct the discussions and take turns playing the Conference Leader and Debate Moderator roles throughout the course. All learners are expected to contribute discussing with their colleagues, developing and refining concepts, and having their work observed, commented upon, and evaluated by their peers (Benbunan-Fich & Hiltz, 1999).

In the second part of the course, learners develop an educational multimedia interactive content, working in small groups of two or three, which are formed

Figure 4. Portion of dialogue from the Conference *(left) and* Debate *(right) services*

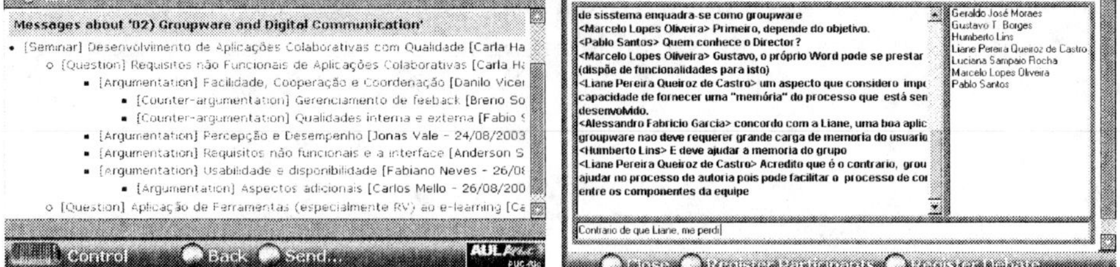

according to previously submitted profiles plus their performance in the course's learning activities. Based on this information, AulaNet suggests group formations that best satisfy the criteria defined by mediators (degree of skill, interest, and competence) (Cunha, Fuks, & Lucena, 2003). After the initial submission, a period of collaborative peer reviews begins. Members of at least three other groups evaluate each group's content. This evaluation takes place asynchronously in *Conferences* created specifically for this purpose, where learners discuss problems they found in the prototypes. Once this period is over, groups are given a new deadline to present a revised version that incorporates the contributions of their colleagues.

More detail about the course and the AulaNet environment is given in the following sections.

Communication

In the command and control paradigm, communication is considered successful when the sender is informed that the receiver has received the message. On the other hand, the success of communication in the collaboration paradigm entails the understanding of the message by the receiver. The only way of obtaining indications about the receiver's understanding is by observing his/her actions and reactions, since they are guided by commitments assumed during communication. The receiver reads the message and interprets it, changing his/her commitments and knowledge in a certain way. That will prompt him/her to reason about the newly acquired knowledge and react. Thus, sender and receiver move into a discussion where they reason about their actions.

The designer of a communication tool defines the communication elements that will define the communication channel between the interlocutors, taking into consideration the specific usage that it is being planned for the tool (time, space, objective, dynamics, and type of participants) and other factors such as privacy, development and execution restrictions, information overload, and so forth. Then, these elements are mapped onto software components that give support to the specific needs.

Communication elements related to the message characteristics are particularly important in the computer supported learning area. Data and examples collected from several editions of the ITAE course enable us to present an analysis of crucial message characteristics.

Figure 5. Examples of discussion structure

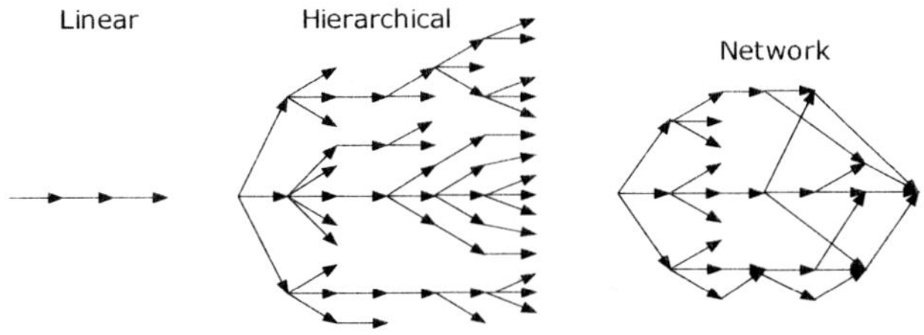

Message Chaining

Communication tools have different ways of structuring messages: linear (list), hierarchical (tree), or network (graph), as can be seen in Figure 5. Despite the fact that a list is a specific case of a tree, and this is a particular type of graph, no one structure is better than another is. Linear structuring is appropriate for communication in which the chronological order of the messages, such as the sending of notices, reports, and news, is important. Hierarchical structuring on a forum, on the other hand, is appropriate when the relationships between messages, such as questions and answers, need to be quickly identified. However, it is relevant to point out that, since there is no way to link messages from two different branches, the tree can only grow wide and, thus, the discussion takes place in diverging lines (Stahl, 2001). Network structuring can be used to seek convergence of the discussion.

In the ITAE course, the forum, based on the AulaNet Conferences service, is used for the in-depth discussion of the course's subject matter. The format of the resulting tree indicates the depth of the discussion and the level of interaction (Gerosa, Pimentel, Fuks, & Lucena, 2005).

The hierarchical structure is also useful to provide indications about the evolution of the class and to identify discussions that moved out from the expected pattern. For example, in the resulting trees presented in Figure 6, it is possible to observe the declining interaction in the 2002.1 edition of the ITAE course. In the first four conferences of this edition, the average level of the tree was 3.0, and the percentage of unanswered messages (leaves) was 51%; in the last four conferences, the average tree level was 2.8, and the number of leaves was 61%. This illustrates that the conversation structure is useful to detect undesired characteristics, such as the low level of the trees and high number of leaves, which, in this case, indicate a low level of interaction among learners.

Figure 6. Conversation structure of some ITAE conferences

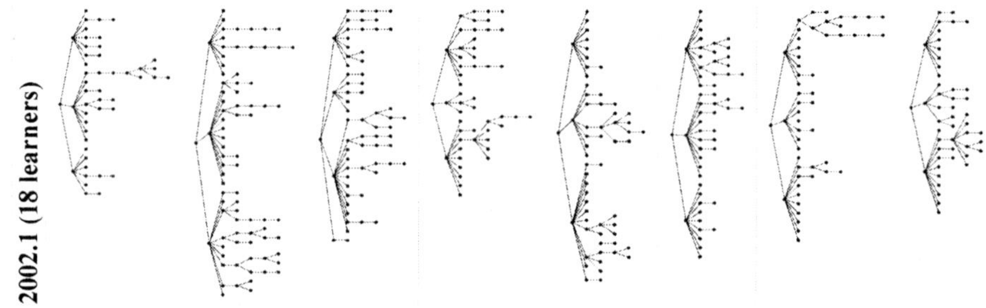

Figure 7. Tree derived from a conference with the message categories.

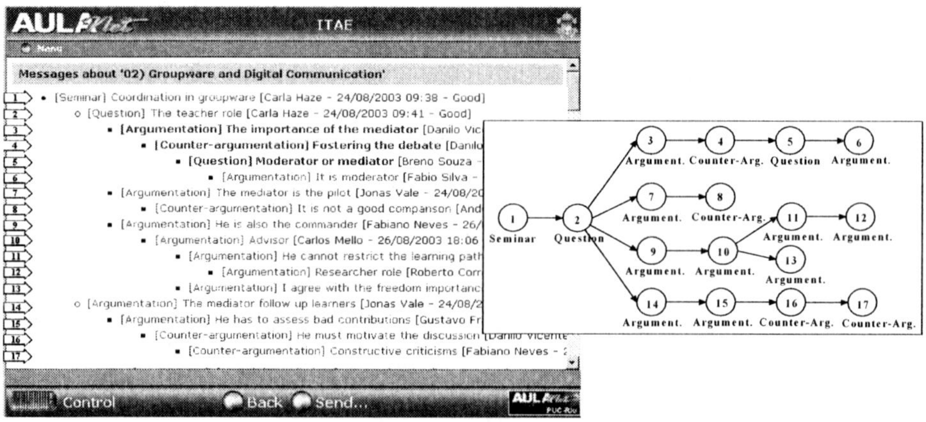

Message Categorization

Upon preparing a message, the author chooses the category that is most appropriate to the content being developed, providing a semantic aspect to the relationship between messages. Looking at the categories, learners and mediators estimate how the discussion is progressing and the probable content of the messages. AulaNet does not force the adoption of a fixed set of categories. The teacher who plans the course can change the category set to the objectives and characteristics of the group and their tasks.

The categories adopted in the ITAE conferences were originally based on the IBIS' node types (Conklin, 1988). Currently, the categories being used are: Seminar, for the root message of the discussion; Question, Argumentation, Counter-Argumentation, and Clarification. Figure 7 presents a portion of a dialogue from a conference showing numbered messages mapped to a tree.

Categories clearly help to understand the relation between messages without having to inspect their content, thus complementing the information provided by the message structure and helping to identify the direction that the discussion is taking. For example, in a tree or a branch that only contains argumentation messages, there is no confrontation of ideas taking place, while an excessive number of counter-argumentations may indicate that the group has gotten into a deadlock or there may be interpersonal conflicts taking place (Gerosa, Pimentel, Fuks, & Lucena, 2004).

In order to provide proper support for communication, the designer should also take into account coordination and cooperation elements. Coordination elements deal with access policies to the communication channel, while cooperation elements deal with information rendering and registration. These elements are discussed in the following sections.

Coordination

Coordination organizes the group in a way that avoids the loss of communication and cooperation efforts and ensures that the resulting tasks are carried out in the correct order, at the right time, and in compliance with the restrictions and objectives, enforcing the fulfillment of the commitments assumed during communication (Raposo, Magalhães, Ricarte, & Fuks, 2001).

Coordination involves the pre-articulation of the tasks, their management, and post-articulation. Pre-articulation involves actions that are necessary to prepare coordination, usually concluded before cooperation begins, such as the identification of goals, the mapping of these goals into tasks, the selection of participants, and the distribution of tasks among them. The post-articulation stage occurs after the end of the tasks and involves the evaluation and analysis of tasks and the documentation of the collaborative process. The management of the tasks being carried out is the act of managing interdependencies between tasks that are carried out to achieve a goal (Malone & Crowston, 1990).

The great challenge in designing coordination mechanisms in groupware is to achieve flexibility without loosing the regulation, which is necessary in some situations where the social protocol is not enough. Collaborative systems should not be designed based on the assumption that the systems will automate all the articulation work. The system should not impose rigid work or communication patterns, but rather offer the user the possibility to use, alter, or simply ignore them. This way, coordination flexibility and accessibility should be pursued by learningware designers.

Activities' Flow

ITAE's learning activities exemplify a typical situation that requires pre- and post-articulation to define and refine the coordination itself. ITAE has been continuously evolving based on the feedback provided in previous editions. Learning activities that had been planned in advance for an edition were analyzed and afterward reformulated in the light of the results obtained in that edition.

Figure 8 shows the sequence of tasks planned for the ITAE course. After the initial introductions, there are eight topics for content studies, each of them comprising content reading, asynchronous conference, and synchronous debate. Finally, there is the content-generation activity, which is also subdivided into three sub-tasks, and the course finalization, when the final grade is announced.

The overall view of the course workflow indicates that it is necessary to have a hierarchical representation of activities. In Figure 8, for example, the composed activities represented inside the boxes are internally subdivided into more

Figure 8. ITAE flow of activities

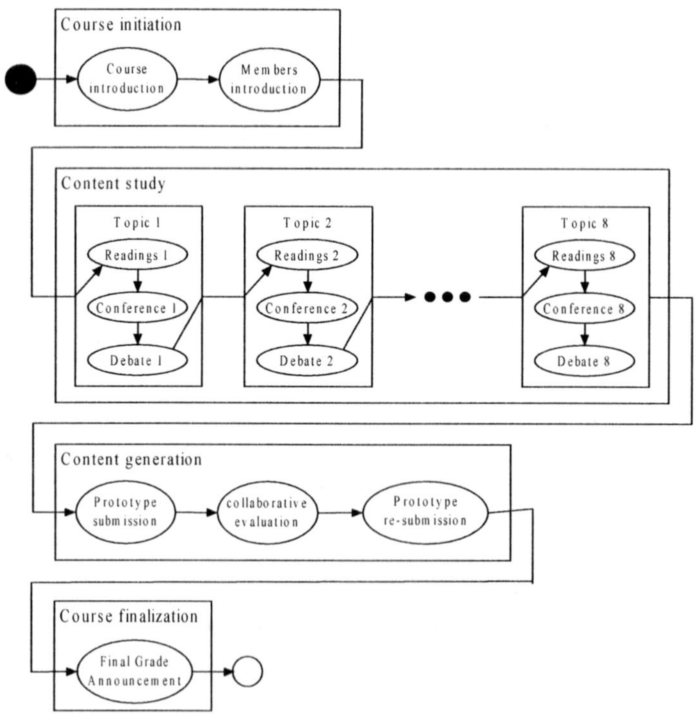

Figure 9. Expanded workflow of a conference

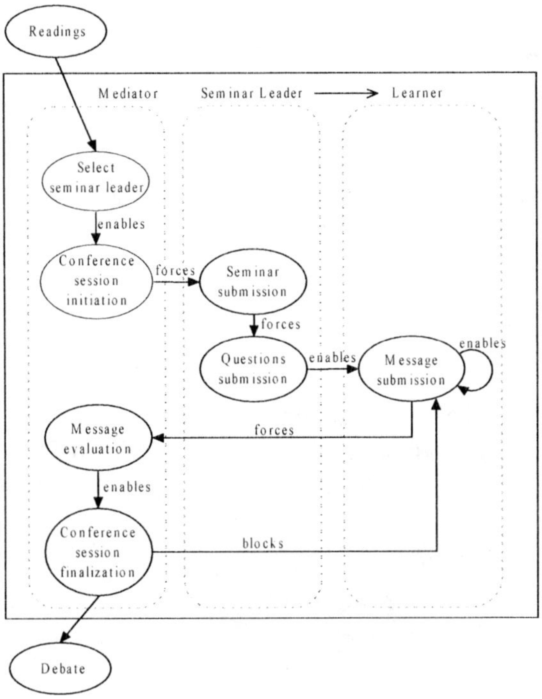

detailed sub-activities. For example, the content generation by the learners has three sub-activities, namely, prototype submission, its evaluation by other groups of learners, and prototype re-submission. Getting into an even lower abstraction level, it is necessary to decompose some activities until atomic ones and detail the kinds of interdependency that exist among these activities. Figure 9 presents the expanded workflow for the weekly conference activity. This activity involves three roles. The mediator (teacher) selects the learner that will play the seminar leader in that week and initializes the seminar session. The leader must then submit the seminar message to the conference and propose a number of questions to be discussed. The discussion takes place by means of message submissions by the learners to the conference. Each of these messages is evaluated by the mediator, who may also finalize the session.

In Figure 9 there are also indications of the kind of interdependency among activities, expressed by *enables*, *forces*, and *blocks* operators (Raposo et al., 2001). An example of *enables* relation takes place between the leader's question submission and the learners' message submission. Learners are not able to submit messages before the leader's questions, but these questions do not oblige each learner to submit messages. Actually, the non-participation of a learner may have a negative impact on his/her degree, but this does not harm the procedural flow of the seminar. Other activities are connected with a stronger relation. For example, the session initialization by the mediator *forces* the leader to submit his/her seminar, followed by the questions; otherwise the seminar would fail. The *blocks* operator is also used, indicating that learners cannot submit messages after the mediator finalizes the seminar session. This does not imply that the mediator will not be able to continue evaluating the remaining questions. The mediator must evaluate all questions; some of them may be evaluated after the seminar finalization.

The examples of Figures 8 and 9 show that the teacher should model the course activities, specifying the services, learners, and sub-activities involved. An activity may comprise several sub-activities, different participant roles, and also different services. This is not an easy task, but it is important not only to enable the course coordination, but also to offer a pictorial view of the course dynamics, facilitating its re-design. Once the course is modeled, it will be straightforward to modify its dynamics.

Another important feature that will be obtained with the use of a workflow-based coordination approach within AulaNet is the possibility to create different workflow paths for different learners or groups over a single course. For example, a more advanced class may skip introductory contents, while novices should study them.

Assessment Rules

The ITAE weekly conference is an interesting example showing how coordination can be used to enhance communication. Previous editions of the ITAE course have taught us that most of the content should be self-studied and that most of the discussion should be conducted asynchronously in order to enhance reflection. However, by reducing the time pressure to respond, it is easier for a learner to drop out of the group (Graham, Scarborough, & Goodwin, 1999). Each conference session lasts 50 hours: from 12 noon Monday to 2 pm Wednesday. Until the 2003.2 edition, there was a burst during the last five hours of the conference. In some cases, more than 50% of the messages were sent during this period. This phenomenon of students waiting until the last possible moment to carry out their tasks is well known and has been dubbed "Student Syndrome" (Goldratt, 1997). The act of sending contributions near the deadline disturbs in-depth discussions, for those last-minute messages will neither be graded nor be answered during the discussion.

Figure 10. Average hourly rate of messages in conferences

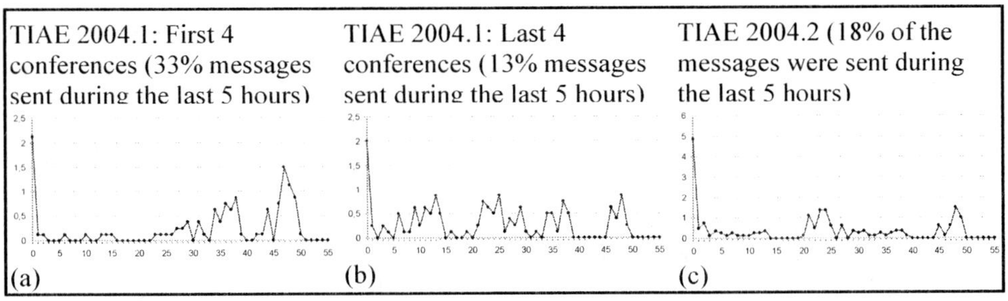

In order to avoid this unwelcome behavior mediators have to encourage the earlier sending in of contributions. Unfortunately, our experience with this course has shown that this encouragement does not work. In the 2004.1 edition, the following experiment was conducted. The last four conferences had a different assessment rule than the first four conferences, this different assessment being that if until the 25th hour the learners had not sent half of the expected amount of messages, the grade of all the messages sent during the following 25 hours would be divided by two.

Figure 10a shows the 50th hour message bursts, that happened for the four first conferences of 2004.1 ITAE edition. In Figure 10b, representing the last four conferences, the chart does not show the 50th hour message bursts, which indicates that the assessment rule has worked. The percentage of messages sent during the last five hours of conference fell from 33% in the first half of the course to 13% in the second half. Nevertheless, there are lower 25th and 50th hour peaks. However, now mediators and learners have room to access and answer the first batch of messages. The same can be seen in Figure 10c, where all eight conferences of the 2004.2 edition were assessed based on the aforementioned rule. In this edition, an average of 18% of the messages was sent during the last five hours.

Communication and coordination, although crucial, are not enough: "it takes shared space to create shared understandings" (Schrage, 1995). Given that coordination is required to manage the tasks, according to the 3C model it is also necessary to provide a shared workspace where cooperation will take place. In the specific case of ITAE, where knowledge production is the main goal, the example for shared space is the *Conference* service; another choice would be the *Debate* service.

Cooperation

Group members cooperate by producing, manipulating, and organizing information, and building and refining cooperation objects, such as documents, spreadsheets, artwork, and so forth.

In a face-to-face situation, a large part of how we maintain a sense of who is around and what is going on is by being able to see and hear events or actions such as people arriving or leaving, phones ringing, conversations, interjections, and so forth. "These are all things we can potentially use to coordinate our work and play together and we often do so with little conscious effort" (Fitzpatrick, Kaplan, Mansfield, Arnold, & Segall, 2002). On the other hand, in a digital environment, awareness support is less effective since the means for making information available to sensory organs are limited; however, irrelevant information can be filtered in a way that reduces distractions that usually affect face-to-face collaboration.

The designer of a digital environment must identify what awareness information is relevant, how it will be obtained, where awareness elements are needed, and how to display and give individuals control over them. Excessive information can cause overload and disrupt the collaboration flow. To avoid disruption, it is necessary to balance the need to supply information with the care to avoid distracting the attention required to work. The supply of information in an asynchronous, structured, filtered, and summarized form can accomplish this balance (Kraut & Attewell, 1997). The big picture should be supplied, and individuals may select which parts of the information they want to work with, leaving further details to be obtained when required. There must also be some form of privacy protection. The shared space must be conceived in a way that group members could seamlessly move from awareness to work.

Awareness Elements in the AulaNet

Awareness elements are the interface elements through which information designed to provide awareness is made available. These elements should be taken into account when designing groupware. Which awareness elements will be needed, how they should be generated, how to join them up, and how to distribute them must be foreseen. In this section, we will discuss some of these aspects with regard to the AulaNet environment.

The awareness information must provide individuals with a vision of what they will find in each one of the services, to enable them to decide which one to use and to have a notion about the total volume of work that is pending. This information must be summarized in a manner that the participants may quickly obtain a notion about the quantity and the characteristics of the work to do, avoiding information overload.

In AulaNet, whenever a list of topics is presented, as is the case of the class topics in the *Lessons* and the *Conferences*, the quantity of unread items and the total of items of that topic are shown. Other awareness elements include the name and a description of the topic, previously supplied by the teacher, and the name of the content provider who created it. At the end of the list, totals of the quantity of topics, of the items and of the unread or unsolved items are provided.

In order to navigate around the course, participants use a menu of services graphically represented by a remote control unit (Figure 3) that supplies navigational facilities built upon previous selections by the course coordinator. Awareness information can be observed on the remote control unit. In the upper part is the course code, offering an individual awareness element for localization and context. The remote control items make the participant aware of the services available at a given moment. Next to each menu item there is a circular button. This button changes color in order to provide information about the services. A blue button indicates the service that the participant has selected, showing his/her location. A light orange button indicates that possible actions need to be taken. Upon moving the mouse over the button, one sees the number of items upon which some action should be taken (items not read or not solved). A dark orange button indicates a service where no changes have taken place since the last access. This awareness information is designed for individuals and helps them coordinate themselves.

Upon listing the messages of the environment's asynchronous communication services, awareness information is offered in order to help participants contextualize the message, to decide if it is the proper moment to access it or to locate something that is being sought. The category, the subject, the author, the date, and the assessment of each message are shown. Besides this information, the messages that still have not been read are in bold face, indicating that action needs to be taken. In the specific case of *Conference* and *Mail to Class*, where it is possible to explicitly answer the messages, another piece of awareness information that is presented is the nesting of the messages. Through nesting it is possible to identify the connections between the messages, facilitating the understanding of the context. These awareness elements mix individual awareness (things related to the individual work, like the indication of unread messages) with group awareness. The group awareness is related to the cooperation objects, which in this case are the messages exchanged and the discussion threads.

The AulaNet also offers a service called *Follow-Up Reports* (Figure 11) that seeks to enhance the group awareness about its members' activities, providing

Figure 11. Follow-Up Report *interface*

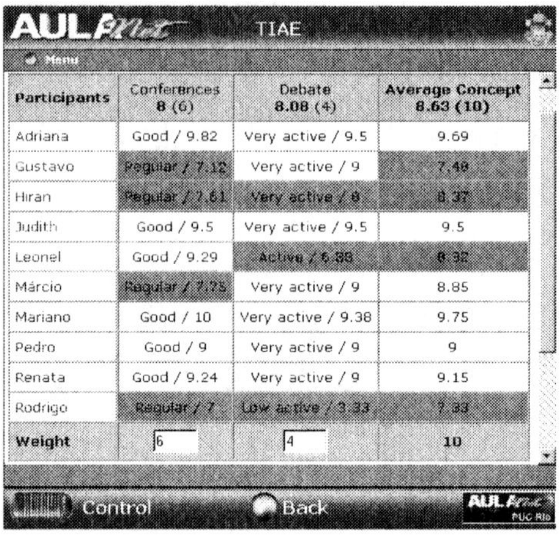

subsidies for coordination. The reports summarize the quantity, extracted automatically by the environment, and the quality of contributions, supplied by the course mediator. Each contribution—messages, participation in debates, submission of content, and resolution of tasks—are marked and, in the majority, commented upon by the teacher.

The reports give an average rating of each participant per service, an average percentage for effective contributions, frequency of participation in the debates, the number of contributions per service, and detailed reports for each service of the course. These reports make it possible for learners to check their performance and compare them with that of colleagues through information that is continuously updated. Furthermore, it helps the participants get to know each other better, to have a notion of how the course is going, of their roles within it, and to choose other colleagues to form work groups. It also lets the mediator organize, motivate, and evaluate the learners and check up on pending tasks.

Shared Workspace and Shared Objects

Knowledge and multimedia content are the ultimate production of the ITAE course. Given that the latter is created off-line and outside AulaNet, we are focusing on the former, which takes place in the *Conference* service. It is worth pointing out that AulaNet does not contemplate content authoring. Learners develop educational content using their habitual tools, and the environment supports navigation around the course's shared space.

The *Conference* service provides a shared workspace where learners cooperate by producing and refining knowledge by means of an argumentation process. In ITAE the conference session lasts 50 hours. Learners generate new cooperation objects, in this case conference messages. Learners also construct and handle conference messages (the cooperation objects) and receive feedback from their actions and feedthrough for their colleagues' actions by means of awareness information. In the conference shared space, awareness information about the cooperation objects is displayed, including their authorship, date, category, subject, and the assessment made by course mediators. The 3Cs for the conferences are shown in Figure 12.

The register of group interactions is filed, catalogued, categorized, and structured within cooperation objects. This is how group memory is saved in AulaNet. Ideas, facts, questions, points of view, conversations, discussions, decisions, and so forth are retrievable, providing a history of the collaboration and the context in which learning took place (Kanselaar, Erkens, Andriessen, Prangsma, Veerman, & Jaspers, 2003).

Figure 12. Production in the Conference *shared workspace*

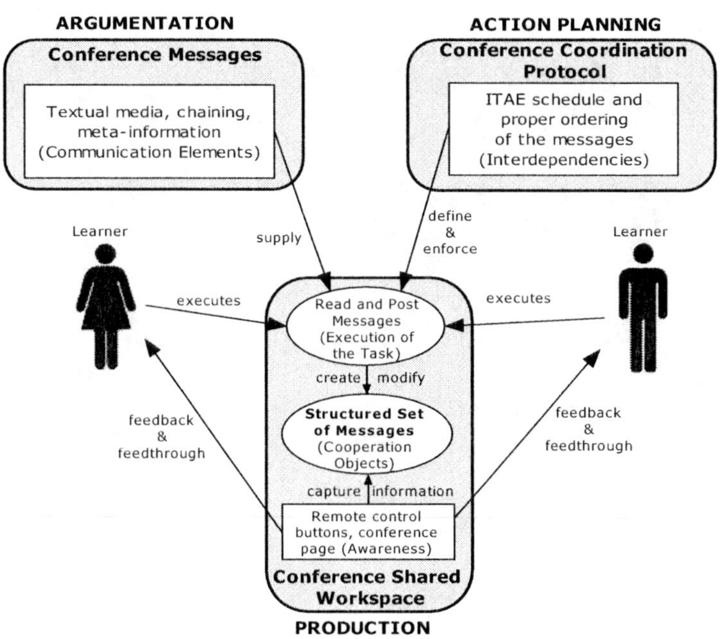

Integrating the 3Cs: The Debate Service Case Study

In the initial versions of AulaNet, the *Debate* service was a plain chat tool, holding an expression element, where learners could type their messages, and awareness elements, where learners participating at the chat session were presented (Figure 4). This version of the Debate was implemented using a communication component, which implements synchronous communication protocols, and a cooperation component, which implements the shared space. This version gives no computer support to coordination, leaving it to the standing social protocol. However, this is not always the case, because some courses use a well-defined procedure to the debate activity, like the one shown in Figure 13, which represents the procedure adopted in a course.

In this procedure, for each debate, the course mediator selects a learner to be the session moderator. It is also up to the mediator to declare the session initiated and finalized and to evaluate learners' participation. The debate moderator posts a summary of the discussion that took place during the week's conference and then poses three questions. For each question, each learner posts a comment, and

Figure 13. Flow of activities in a debate

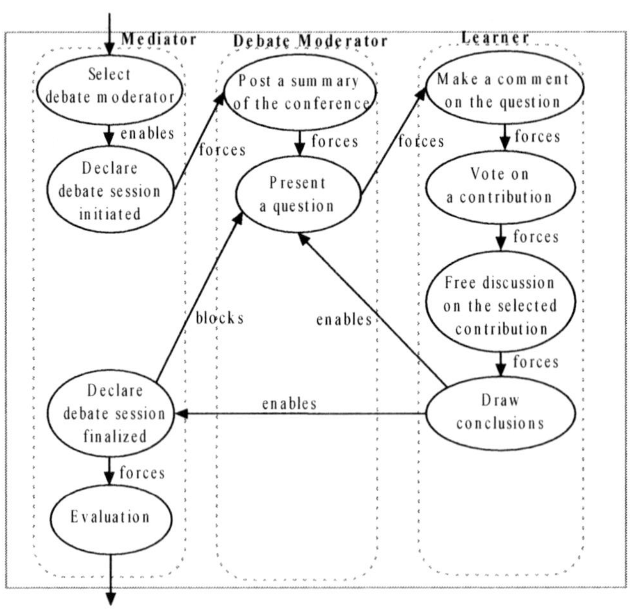

after every learner has posted its comment, they vote and decide which one will be discussed. Then, a free discussion takes place. Before the moderator poses a new question, learners have to draw their conclusions.

In order to better support tightly integrated activities, like the one exemplified above, in the following version of the *Debate* service (presented in Figure 14), coordination mechanisms were implemented. Floor control, participation order, and shared space blocking ability were added to the service. The shared space was also enhanced by new awareness elements, like session title, message timestamp, and the identification of mediators.

In this new *Debate* version, the same communication component was used, as the synchronous communication protocols and the characteristics of the messages did not change. The cooperation component, which implements the shared space, however, was enhanced by the new awareness elements mentioned above. The main difference, however, is the insertion of a coordination component, which implements the floor control coordination mechanisms.

This example illustrates the benefits of having an architecture that deals with the three Cs of the collaboration model, namely, communication, coordination, and cooperation.

Conclusion

The 3C collaboration model defines three types of services that a learningware may support. The concepts and representation models described in this chapter can be used to guide the functional specification and to provide a common language for representing and describing the collaboration aspects of a workgroup. The application of the 3C model was illustrated throughout this chapter using the AulaNet learning environment and the ITAE course.

The groupware component-system architecture used in the AulaNet environment mirrors the 3C model. Communication, coordination, and cooperation functionalities were directly mapped into the implementation of AulaNet's collaboration services. AulaNet services are being developed using a component-framework-based architecture, as can be seen in Figure 15. There is a common structure implemented by the collaboration framework, which defines the skeleton of the services, and plugged to this framework there are the communication, the coordination, and the cooperation component frameworks, which support each C of the model. Class frameworks are used to implement components, which are plugged to the corresponding C-framework and implement the specific functionalities of the service (Fuks, Raposo, Gerosa, & Lucena, 2005).

Figure 14. Debate service mediator interface

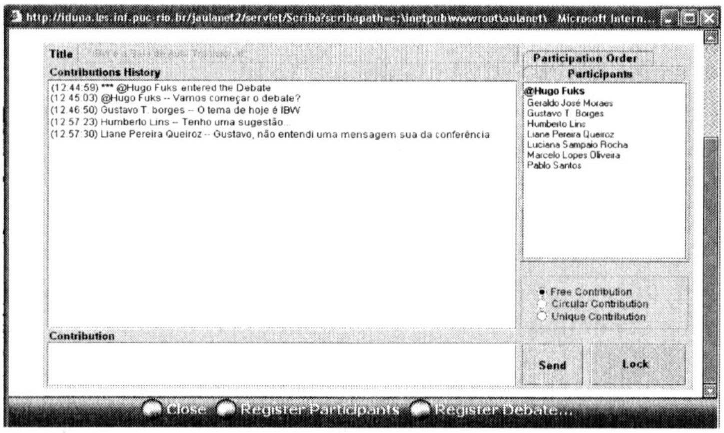

Figure 15. Architecture of a collaboration service in AulaNet

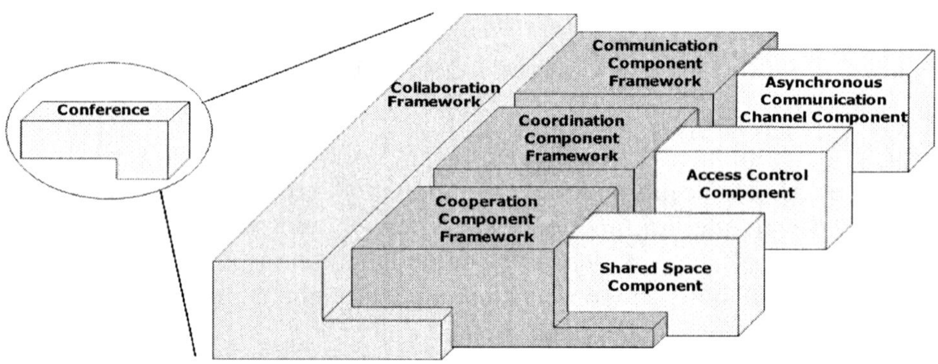

The application of the 3C model was also illustrated through the ITAE course, whose objective is to train learners to become workers capable of operating in a knowledge society. In the ITAE, the learners are encouraged to work in groups, to seek updated information, to argue, to take on and accomplish commitments—at the end of the day, to communicate, coordinate, and cooperate.

Acknowledgments

The AulaNet project is financed by the Ministry of Science and Technology through its Program Multi-Agent Systems for Software Engineering Project (ESSMA) grant n° 552068/2002-0. It is also financed by individual grants awarded by the National Research Council to: Carlos José Pereira de Lucena n° 300031/92-0, Hugo Fuks n° 303055/02-2, and Marco Aurélio Gerosa n° 140103/02-3. Mariano Pimentel received an individual grant from the Council for the Improvement of Higher Teaching of the Ministry of Education. Thanks to Professor Marcelo Gattass, Head of Tecgraf/PUC-Rio, a group mainly funded by Petrobras, Brazilian Oil & Gas Company.

References

Benbunan-Fich, R. & Hiltz, S. R. (1999). Impacts of asynchronous learning networks on individual and group problem solving: A field experiment. *Group Decision and Negotiation*, *8*(5), 409-426.

Borghoff, U. M., & Schlichter, J. H. (2000). *Computer-supported cooperative work: Introduction to distributed applications.* Heidelberg, Germany: Springer-Verlag Berlin.

Conklin, J., & Begeman, M. (1988). gIBIS: A hypertext tool for exploratory policy discussion. In I. Greif (Ed.), *Conference on computer-supported cooperative work (CSCW)* (pp. 140-152). New York: ACM Press.

Cunha, L. M., Fuks, H., & Lucena, C. J. P. (2003). Setting groups of learners using matchmaking agents. In V. Uskov (Ed.), *IASTED International Conference on Computers and Advanced Technology in Education (CATE 2003)* (pp. 321-326). Alberta, Canada: Acta Press Calgary.

Edutools. (2004). Retrieved July 27, 2004, from http://www.edutools.info

Ellis, C. A., Gibbs, S. J., & Rein, G. L. (1991). Groupware—Some issues and experiences. *Communications of the ACM, 34*(1), 38-58.

Fitzpatrick, G., Kaplan, S., Mansfield, T., Arnold, D., & Segall, B. (2002). Supporting public and accessibility with Elvin: Experiences and reflections. *Computer Supported Cooperative Work, 11*(3-4), 447-474.

Fuks, H. (2000). Groupware technologies for education in AulaNet. *Computer Applications in Engineering Education, 8*(3-4), 170-177.

Fuks, H., Gerosa, M. A., & Lucena, C. J. P. (2002). The development and application of distance learning on the Internet. *Open Learning Journal, 17*(1), 23-38.

Fuks, H., Raposo, A. B., Gerosa, M. A., & Lucena, C. J. P. (2005). Applying the 3C model to groupware development. *International Journal of Cooperative Information Systems (IJCIS), 14*(2-3), 299-328.

Gerosa, M. A., Pimentel, M., Fuks, H., & Lucena, C. J. P. (2004). Analyzing discourse structure to coordinate educational forums. In J. C. Lester, R. M. Vicari, & F. Paraguaçu (Ed.), *The 7th International Conference on Intelligent Tutoring Systems (ITS-2004)* (LNCS 3220, pp. 262-272). Heidelberg, Germany: Springer-Verlag Berlin.

Gerosa, M. A., Pimentel, M., Fuks, H., & Lucena, C. J. P. (2005). No need to read messages right now: Helping mediators to steer educational forums using statistical and visual information. In T. Koschmann, T.-W. Cha, & D. D. Suthers (Eds.), *Computer supported collaborative learning (CSCL 2005)* (pp. 494-498). Mahwah, NJ: Lawerence Erlbaum Associates.

Goldratt, E. M. (1997). *Critical chain*. Great Barrington, MA: The North River Press Publishing.

Graham, M., Scarborough, H., & Goodwin, C. (1999). Implementing computer mediated communication in an undergraduate course—A practical experience. *Journal of Asynchronous Learning Networks, 3*(1), 32-45.

Kanselaar, G., Erkens, G., Andriessen, J., Prangsma, M., Veerman, A., & Jaspers, J. (2003). Designing argumentation tools for collaborative learning. In P. Kirschner, S. Shum, & C. Carr (Eds.), *Visualizing argumentation: Software tools for collaborative and educational sense-making* (pp. 51-73). London: Springer-Verlag.

Kraut, R. E., & Attewell, P. (1997). *Media use in global corporation: Electronic mail and organisational knowledge. Research milestone on the information highway*. Mahwah, NJ: Erlbaum.

Laurillau, Y., & Nigay, L. (2002). Clover architecture for groupware. In E. F. Churchill, J. McCarthy, C. Neuwirth, & T. Rodden (Eds.), *Conference on Computer-Supported Cooperative Work (CSCW)* (pp. 236-245). New York: ACM Press.

Malone, T. W., & Crowston, K. (1990). What is coordination theory and how can it help design cooperative work systems? In F. Halasz (Ed.), *Conference on Computer-Supported Cooperative Work (CSCW)* (pp. 357-370). New York: ACM Press.

Raposo, A. B., Magalhães, L. P., Ricarte, I. L. M., & Fuks, H. (2001). Coordination of collaborative activities: A framework for the definition of tasks interdependencies. In M. R. S. Borges, J. M. Haake, & H. U. Hoppe (Eds.), *7th International Workshop on Groupware* (CRIWG) (pp. 170-179). Los Alamitos, CA: IEEE Computer Society Press.

Schrage, M. (1995). *No more teams! Mastering the dynamics of creative collaboration.* New York: Currency Doubleday.

Stahl, G. (2001, July 6). WebGuide: Guiding collaborative learning on the Web with perspectives. *Journal of Interactive Media in Education,* 1. Retrieved April 10, 2006, from http://www-jime.open.ac.uk/

Zaina, L. A. M., Bressan, G., Silveira, R. M., Stiubiener, I., & Ruggiero, W. V. (2001). Analysis and comparison of distance education environments. In T. Clausen, D. Budney, T. Larkin-Hein, R. J. Herrick, & L. Richards (Eds.), *Proceedings of the International Conference on Engineering Education (ICEE)* (pp. 7E8-19-7E8-24). Arlington, VA: International Network for Engineering Education and Research. Retrieved April 10, 2006, from http://www.ineer.org/Events/ICEE2001/Proceedings/papers/335.pdf

Chapter XIII

Video Annotation in Online Collaborative Discussion: A Constructivist Tool for Computer-Supported Learning

Myint Swe Khine, Nanyang Technologicial University, Singapore

Abstract

Computer-supported collaborative learning has become one of the important areas in the education and training field, and online discussion is the predominant mode in the meaning-making process. While many of the software available in online discussion are text-based, recent development in such tools includes the capability of viewing video. This chapter introduces the use of software that allows users to engage in collaborative discussion by attaching notes to video footage. This type of software is relatively new in education applications. This chapter also reports findings from the study and suggests how such tool can be applied to improve the interaction among learners in other training situations in computer-supported learning environments.

Introduction

Many of us will agree that we have entered an information age where we will treat knowledge as power. Accessing information and networking among people with the use of computers and communication technologies are becoming important. Under the influence of information and communication technologies there is also an increased tendency toward collaborative learning among students and with their teachers. Many educational institutions embark on projects that involve information-sharing activities among students and teachers regardless of time and location differences. There are evidences that computer-supported collaborative learning processes help students to achieve deeper levels of knowledge generation through the creation of shared goals, shared exploration, and a shared process of meaning making. The common features of collaborative learning are reflection on the learning process and dialogic inquiry. The dialogue carries a flow of meaning, and discussion involves exchanging of views between participants. In collaborative discussions each participant advocates and defends a point of view based on his or her own observations, interpretation, and generalization.

One of the major shifts in education under the influence of information and communication technologies is an increased tendency toward collaborative learning among students and with their teachers. The notion of collaboration also stems from the fact that people are social creatures who like to talk with each other about topics of common interest. Computer-supported learning allows flexibility in the acquisition and transformation of knowledge among the community of learners and practitioners. The number of active and interactive discourse communities has expanded in recent years due to the easy access to the computers and telecommunication services. Lewin's prediction of the dealing with human beings not as isolated individuals, but in the social setting of groups is becoming a reality in technological society.

There are evidences that computer-supported collaborative learning processes help students to achieve deeper levels of knowledge generation through the creation of shared goals, shared exploration, and a shared process of meaning making (Lipponen, Hakkarainen, & Paavola, 2004). The common features of collaborative learning are a reflection on the learning process and dialogic inquiry. The dialogue carries a flow of meaning, and discussion involves exchanging of views between participants. In collaborative discussions each participant advocates and defends a point of view based on his or her own observations, interpretation, and generalization.

Vygotsky's sociocultural theory of learning emphasizes that human intelligence originates in our society or culture, and individual cognitive gain occurs first through interpersonal (interaction with social environment) than intrapersonal (internalization). The major theme of Vygotsky's theoretical framework is that social interaction plays a fundamental role in the development of cognition (Wink & Putney, 2002). This indicates that learning is more than the accumulation of facts, and it includes a process of enculturation through social interaction and discourse.

At the time of writing this chapter, most software available for online discussion are text-based. Such software allows users to interact with each other by reading one another's text messages. These threaded discussions can occur in either a synchronous mode, chat, or asynchronous mode, list servers. Using this type of online, text-based discussion, viewers would have to watch the video footage separately before entering the online discussion. Without the facility to attach a comment to a specific location on the video, each discussant has the additional burden of referring back to the actions that occurred at the remembered location of an event on the video.

In this chapter, the author describes existing learning management systems that allow text-based collaborative discussions and reviewed existing video annotation systems that allow the users to view the particular video frame and make annotation of the content. The main mission of this chapter is to introduce the use of software that allows users to engage in collaborative discussion by attaching notes to video footage. This type of software is relatively new in education applications.

Computer-Supported Collaborative Learning

In recent years computers and communication technologies have evolved to support collaborative activities through different forms of networks such as Internet and World Wide Web. These computer-supported learning communities may use e-mail, chat, newsgroup, conferencing, forums, and bulletin boards to discuss wide ranging topics. These technologies support networked learning communities consisting of students and teachers that may enhance teaching or learning.

There is no doubt that both computer accessibility and connectivity in schools and community have been greatly enhanced in the recent years. As a result of the marriage between education and Internet, the way we teach and learn in formal and informal settings is permanently altered. A lot of enthusiasm for online learning has emerged, and there is no shortage of courses available on the World Wide Web. With the use of Web-based instruction, learners can involve in active participation beyond time and space boundaries to continue their learning. In this information age, lifelong learning and collaboration are essential aspects of most innovative work (Stahl, 2000). It is imperative that educators need to nurture our next generation learners in the habit of community participation and collaboration. Computer supported collaborative learning (CSCL) systems are the tools designed to support the building of shared knowledge and knowledge negotiation (Stahl, 2004).

Video Annotation and Discussion Systems

At the time of writing this chapter, most software available for online discussion are text-based. Such software allows users to interact with each other by reading one another's text messages. These threaded discussions can occur in either a synchronous mode, chat, or asynchronous mode, list servers. Using this type of online, text-based discussion, viewers would have to watch the video footage separately before entering the online discussion. Without the facility to attach a comment to a specific location on the video, each discussant has the additional burden of referring back to the actions that occurred at the remembered location of an event on the video.

Schroeter, Hunter, and Kosovic (2003) described that indexing and annotation systems for digital video files have been developed only to use within stand-alone environments in which the annotations can be saved and shared asynchronously. They have surveyed the existing video annotation systems and noted the features of each system. According to them, IBM's MPEG-7 Annotation tool provides support for both MPEG-1 and MPEG-2 files, and the interface is easy to use. They concluded, however, that user interface is restricted to a preset video size and aspect ration.

They also described two other Web-based video annotation systems. Those are continuous media (CM) Web browser by CSIRO and Microsoft's research annotation system (MRAS). These are Web-based applications designed to enable students to asynchronously annotate Web-based lectures videos and to share their annotations. The systems described above are not designed to be used within a collaborative videoconferencing environment. They have noted that the ability to engage in real-time video-based discussion collaboratively is of the great interest to the education, medical, scientific, cultural, defense, and media communities.

They have attempted to develop a unique prototype application that combines videoconferencing over access grid nodes with collaborative, real-time sharing of an application that enables the indexing, browsing, annotation, and discussion of video content between multiple groups at remote location.

Kipp (2001) developed a video annotation tool, Anvil (Annotation of Video and Language), which offers frame accurate, hierarchical multilayered annotation driven by a user-friendly annotation scheme. According to Chong and Soskul (2003) one form of adding interactivity to online learning is video annotation, which is an active field of research in content-based video retrieval and summarization. They have presented a framework for video-centered discussions on the Web and developed a system that allows users to attach notes to video segments and share their notes with other users asynchronously.

For some collaborative activities, discourse and simultaneous viewing of video clips are necessary to ensure that the discussants keep in view the video content. Here, the details of specific action in the video are important to the content of the discussion. The recent development of a mediated learning tool extends learning communities into cyberspace by integrating video viewing and online discussion at the same time. It allows for threaded asynchronous discussion in computer-supported learning environment.

Functions of Conversant Media

The mediated learning tool, which will be explained in this chapter, consists of a media player and some administrative functions. On selecting a movie, the screen consists of a media player on the left-hand side of the screen and a commentary frame on the right-hand side of the screen. Each line in the commentary frame represents the title of a comment, which can be clicked open and viewed in the bottom, card display frame. Each video frame has a unique time-coded, which is inherited by the attached comment. Clicking on a comments title automatically displays the card and brings the video to the attached frame.

While viewing a particular segment of a video, if the user is ready to post a comment, the video can be stopped. By using the "Comment" button, a commentary can be created in a dialog box and submitted to the system. The commentary is recorded, and the author (commentator's name) is displayed along side the title of the commentary. In this manner other users are able to add their own comments or react and reply to other users' comments.

As each annotation is added, a mark is drawn at the corresponding time code position on the timeline for playing the video. Over time, it becomes possible to locate "hot spots" on the video where higher densities of comments are located. The combination of the spatial display of comments attachment locations and the results of peer ratings of the comment allows discussants to keep track of the online discussion. Such an annotation track also allows users to retrieve the records of the commentaries from the database easily. The user can open up to 10 annotation cards that are arranged in cascades in the card display area.

Because the system is designed to encourage thoughtful comments, there is an option for drafting comments before submitting them to the public forum. Here the user creates his or her comment in a "private space," which cannot be viewed by other members of the group. When the user is ready to share his or her views, he or she can then make his or her comments public by publishing them from the private to the public space.

Another feature that attempts to encourage better commentaries is a peer rating system. Every card that is opened by a discussant has to be rated before the user is allowed to proceed. Rating is done on a 1 to 5 scale of overall value and informativeness of the comment. Once the user rates the commentary, he or she can close the window to proceed to the other tasks.

In order to encourage users to find their own commentary voices, there is a feature that constrains discussants to make their initial comments without access to the public debate. The user must add a set number of comments before he or she can read other's comments. Once the user has submitted the required number of comments, he or she can log off, and upon logging back in, view his or her own and all the other comments in the public space.

The other concern of this chapter is to report the findings from the use of such mediated learning tool in teacher training. The investigation was conducted in the teacher-training institute in Singapore to find out how this tool helps to engage students in reflective analysis of authentic classroom teaching episodes so that they will have a deeper understanding of how the theories are translated to actual practice in classroom situations. This new approach for teaching and learning online was considered appropriate to augment the face-to-face situation. This electronic discussion provides an opportunity for the students to work in private and post their commentary for others to review and comment. This chapter reports findings from the study and suggests how such tool can be applied to improve the interaction among learners in other training situations in computer-supported learning environments.

Advancement in the field of information and communication technologies has brought about new opportunities to develop software for delivering instruction in innovative ways in many educational settings and training situations. *Conversant Media* is server-based application software developed by Laboratories of Information Technology, Singapore that allows users to engage in collaborative discussion based on video footages. Although there is a possibility that the user

Figure 1. Online discussion with video viewing

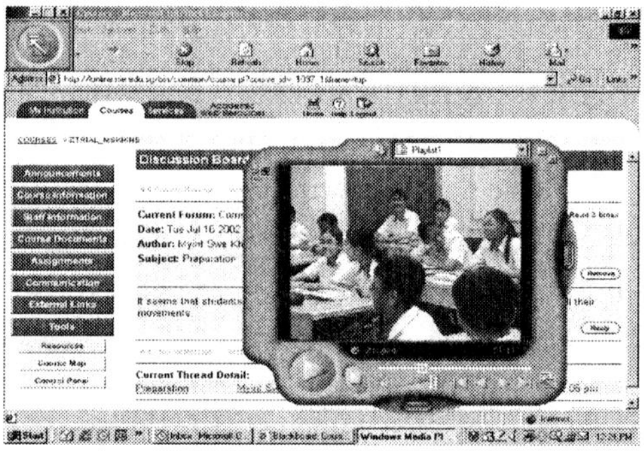

Figure 2. Conversant Media screen

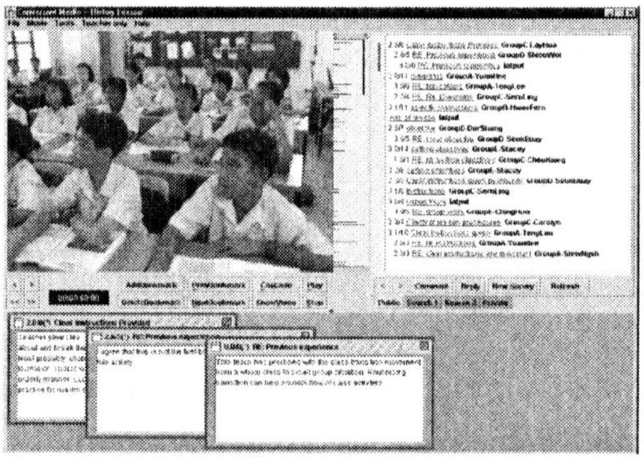

can watch a video footage before and during the online discussion (see Figure 1), integration of video viewing and interaction at the same time was not possible in the past. For some collaborative activities, discourse and simultaneous viewing of video clips are necessary to ensure that the discussants keep in view the video content. The recent development of *Conversant Media* builds learning communities in the cyberspace by integrating video viewing and online discussions. The online discussion can be done both synchronously and asynchronously. The prototype version of the software has client-server architecture, and a Web-based version will be developed in the future.

The *Conversant Media* system consists of a Media Player and some administrative tools. Once the user launches the software, a default screen pops up. As shown in Figure 2, the screen consists of a media player on the left-hand side of the screen and a commentary box on the right-hand side of the screen. Video footages are time-coded, and each commentary is synchronized with the timeline (see Figure 2).

After viewing a particular segment of a video, if the user is ready to post a commentary, the video can be stopped. By using the "Comment" button, a commentary can be added to the system. The commentary is recorded, and the author (commentator's name) is displayed along side the title of the commentary. In this manner other users are able to add their own comments or react and reply to other users' comments. All the commentaries are annotated in the left-hand side of the screen.

This process of annotation (recording comments, time, and author) allows keeping track of the online discussion. Such an annotation track also allows users to retrieve the records of the commentaries from the database easily. The user can open up to 10 annotation cards that are arranged in cascades.

Another feature of the Conversant Media is the use of "public space" and "private space." After the user has seen a particular segment of the video, he or she can add a comment in "Private Space," not allowing it to be viewed by other members of the group. When the user is ready to share his or her views, he or she can then make his or her comment public.

Conditions can be set such that the user must first add a comment before he or she can read other's comments. By looking at the annotation track, the user can choose any one of the commentaries and open an annotation card posted by other discussant. To ensure that the user read the content, the system will prompt the user to rate the comment. The rating can range from "high" to "low" depending upon how the survey question has been designed. Once the user rates the commentary, he or she can close the window to proceed to the other activities.

The *Conversant Media* software was used in the delivery of the Module, *Instructional Strategies and Effective Learning*, as one of the means to engage students in reflective analysis of authentic classroom teaching episodes so that they will have a deeper understanding of how the theories are translated to actual practice in classroom situations. This video-based media tool was considered appropriate because students in Singapore do not normally express their views freely and openly. This tool provides an opportunity for the students to work in private and post their commentary for others to review and comment.

Study on the Impact of Conversant Media

An experiment was conducted to find out the impact of *Conversant Media* on collaborative learning and on the development of commentary skills of trainee teachers to analyze classroom episodes. The overall objective of this experiment was to find out the advantages of the software and how it works in a collaborative learning environment. Another aspect of this study is to explore the benefits of the Conversant Media in teacher education.

Experimental Process and Method

Twenty-five pre-service trainee teachers who were involved in this study were introduced to the features of the *Conversant Media* software, and they were given opportunity to practice in the use of the different features. The practice consisted of two one-hour sessions. Then they were engaged in three different activities over a period of three weeks. For the activities the students were divided into five groups consisting of five students in each group. To facilitate these activities the computer laboratory was reserved for the use of the students one hour a week. Students also had access to the lab when not in use by other users.

For example, the video episode used in activity #1 shows a teacher using the class project approach to engage the students in the learning process. The length of the video footage is three minutes and 12 seconds. The trainee teachers were asked to view the video and comments on various aspects of teaching and classroom management such as preparation, clarity of instruction, student accountability, and other related aspects.

In activity #2, trainee teachers were asked to view the video episode that showed a teacher teaching the concept of number sequences using a real life experience. The video lasted for five minutes and 25 seconds. For this episode trainee teachers were asked to comment on how the teacher in the video organized pupils to learn, what kind of instructional strategies he used, and how the lesson was delivered. The trainee teachers were also asked how the teacher established rapport with his students.

The third video episode contained a scene with a teacher teaching a pre-lab science lesson. The video shows the teaching explaining and demonstrating the technique of reading the volume of a liquid in a measuring cylinder. The trainee teachers were asked to comments the aspects of planning and preparation of the lesson, selection of instructional strategy, and lesson delivery. They were also

Table 1. Descriptions of video episodes and learning activities engaged by the students

Video episode	Description	Activity
1	The video episode used in this activity shows a teacher using the class project approach to engage the students in the learning process. The class was divided into three groups, the scientists' group, the reporters' group and the counselors' group. The video clip showed the session where the teachers set the task to the groups and the section where she received the report from the different groups. (length of video footage: 3mins 12 secs.)	Trainee teachers were asked to view the video clip and comments on the following aspects of teaching and classroom management: ▪ Preparation ▪ Clarity of instruction ▪ Student accountability ▪ Appraisal of student efforts ▪ Any other aspects
2	The video episode used in this activity showed a teacher teaching the concept of number sequence using a real life experience – breeding of rabbits. The teacher used presentation approach in the lesson to introduce the topic with the help of a transparency. (length of video footage: 5 mins. 25 secs.)	Trainee teachers were asked to view the video clip and comments on the following aspects of teaching and classroom management: ▪ Getting pupils ready to learn ▪ Selection of instructional strategy ▪ Lesson delivery ▪ Teacher-pupil interpersonal relationship
3	The video clip shows a teacher teaching a pre-lab science lesson. The teacher explains and demonstrates the technique of reading the volume of a liquid in a measuring cylinder (5 min. 0sec). The pre-lab lesson is in preparation for a laboratory activity to determine the volume of irregular objects. (length of video footage: 5 mins. 0 secs.)	Trainee teachers were asked to view the video clip and comments on the following aspects of teaching and classroom management: ▪ Planning and preparation ▪ Selection of instructional strategy ▪ Lesson delivery and use of body language ▪ Engaging pupils in lesson ▪ Any other aspect

asked to comment on how the teacher engaged pupils in learning. Details of the descriptions of the video episodes and learning activities engaged by the students during the experiment are shown in Table 1.

The level of participation was assessed by counting and recording the number of comments made by each participant. The quality of the comments was judged by the rating given to each of the comments made by group members. An average rating of 3.2 on the 5-point scale was considered a good commentary as it corresponds to a B grade in the university assessment system. The instructor also graded the final exercise to assure quality control. The views of the participants on the use of Conversant Media were obtained through a survey questionnaire.

Descriptive statistics are used to describe the usage, quality of the comments, and the views of the trainee teacher related to the different aspect of Conversant Media use.

Findings and Discussion

Degree of Participation and Quality of Comments

Activity 1

The students were required to make at least two comments. The 25 students in all made 82 comments and responded to the comments of their group members 69 times. The mean peer rating on the comments and responses on the 5-point scale are 2.93 (SD = .37) and 2.88 (SD = .38) respectively. Of the 67 comments and 53 responses that were rated by the participants, 12 and 10 attempts received a 3.2 and above mean rating respectively (Table 2).

Activity 2

The students were required to make four comments and respond to the comments of their group members. All the students submitted four comments each. The mean peer rating on the comments and responses are 3.17 (SD = .353) and 3.11 (SD = .34) respectively. Fifty-four of the 100 comments received 3.2 and above mean ratings. They also responded 180 times to the comments of their

Table 2. Activity 1: Participation and quality of comments and responses

Type	Total	Rated	≥3.2 (%)	Mean rating (SD)
Comment	82	67	12 (17.9)	2.93 (.37)
Response	69	53	10 (18.9)	2.88 (.38)

Table 3. Activity 2: Participation and quality of comments and responses

Type	Total	Rated	≥3.2 (%)	Mean rating (SD)
Comment	100	100	54 (54.0)	3.17(.35)
Response	180	113	34 (30.1)	3.11 (.34)

Table 4. Activity 3: Participation and quality of comments and responses

Type	Total	Mean rating		≥3.2	
		Peer	Instructor	Peer	Instructor
Commentary	25	3.26 (.60)	3.22 (.37)	15	15

group members. One or more peers rated 113 of these comments. Thirty-four of these response comments received a 3.2 and above mean rating (Table 3).

Activity 3

For this activity the students were required to view the whole video clip, five minutes in length, and write a commentary on the teaching scenario presented. All the students submitted the commentary. Each of this commentary was read and rated by the four other members in the group. The mean peer rating of the commentaries on the 5-point scale is 3.26 (SD = .597). Fifteen (60.0%) of the commentaries were given a rating of 3.2 and above. The instructor also assessed the commentaries. The mean rating given by the instructor was 3.22 (SD = .372), and also 15 of the commentaries received a 3.2 and above rating (Table 4).

From the results discussed above it is clear that the trainee teachers have participated enthusiastically in this exercise. They have engaged themselves in the interactive collaborative learning processes more than the minimum requirement set for them. Trainee teachers' views of writing comments and reading the peers' comment are discussed below. The ratings indicate that the commentary skills of the trainee teachers have improved progressively as they participated in the activities. The mean rating for comments in Activity #1 was 2.93, and it increased to 3.17 and 3.26 for Activity #2 and #3 respectively. Also, the percentage of good commentary has improved over the activities. This seems to suggest that *Conversant Media* can be a useful tool to help trainee teachers develop commentary-writing skills, which can come in handy in their self-assessment effort of their teaching.

Participants' Views on Writing and Reading Comments

Table 5 shows the response to the four items related to writing comments. All the responses indicate that they have a favorable attitude to the activity of writing comments with "writing comments force me to think through what I believed about good teaching" receiving the highest mean rating. From this it can be

Table 5. Views related to writing comments

No.	Writing comments	Frequency (%)					Mean/ SD
		Strongly Disagree	Disagree	Not Sure	Agree	Disagree	
1	Writing comments helped me apply pedagogical theories into actual classroom events.	1 4.3%	1 4.3%	10 43.5%	11 47.8%		3.35 0.78
2	*Conversant Media* helped me to think critically and write about my own ideas concerning teaching and management.			10 43.5%	11 47.5%	2 8.7%	3.65 0.65
3	Writing comments force me to think through what I believed about good teaching.			5 21.7%	15 65.2%	3 13.0	3.91 .60
4	*Conversant Media* helped me to apply pedagogical theories into actual classroom events.	1 4.3%		14 60.9%	8 34.8%		3.26 0.69

concluded that this writing comments exercise makes the students think critically about teaching. They also seem to view writing comments as a meaningful and useful exercise. Close to 50% of the students responded that Conversant Media helped them to think critically and write about their own ideas concerning teaching and management of the classroom. Similarly, a high majority of the students felt that software helped them to apply pedagogical theories into actual classroom settings.

Table 6 shows the responses to the nine items related to reading peer comments. Here again we see positive views expressed about reading the comments of the peers. The opportunity to compare views (#7) and see alternative points of view (#4) is highly valued. A general comment offered by one of the participant summarizes the value of sharing views: "*Conversant Media provides the trainee teachers with a medium to converse and criticise each other's comments*." The views expressed by the trainee teachers are in line with what the literature has said about the benefits of collaborative learning (Palloff & Pratt, 2001).

The trainee teachers felt that their peer's comments and opinions expressed in the notes broadened their perspective of teaching and classroom management and also help them with how to interpret classroom events. They further expressed that reading their peers' comments about the classroom events helped

Table 6. Reading comments

No.	Reading comments	Frequency (%) Strongly Disagree	Disagree	Not Sure	Agree	Strongly Agree	Mean/ SD
1	My peer's opinion broadened my perspective of teaching and class management.		1 4.3%	6 26.1%	15 65.2%	1 4.3%	3.70 0.63
2	Reading my classmates' comments helped me how to interpret classroom events.		1 4.3%	5 21.7%	17 73.9%		3.70 0.56
3	Reading my peers' comments about the classroom events helped me understand better the theories discussed in class.	1 4.3%	1 4.3%	8 34.8%	11 47.8%	2 8.7%	3.52 0.90
4	Responses from my peers on my comments helped me see the alternative point of view.			5 21.7%	13 56.5%	5 21.7%	4.00 0.67
5	Reading my peers' comments made me write better comments.		4 17.4%	10 43.5%	7 30.4%	2 8.7%	3.30 0.88
6	I came to know my classmates' opinions on classroom teaching much better with *Conversant Media* than in a normal class situation.		3 13.0%	7 30.4%	11 47.8%	2 8.7%	3.52 0.85
7	Reading comments helped me to compare my classmates' way of viewing the events to my own.			5 21.7%	10 43.5%	8 34.8%	4.13 0.71
8	My peers' view provoked critical self-reflection on my view.			13 56.5%	9 39.1%	1 4.3%	3.48 0.59

them to understand better about the theories discussed in the class. However, the majority of them were not sure about whether the views of the peers provoked critical self-reflection on their own view.

Qualitative Data

The face-to-face interviews with training teachers revealed that they are satisfied with the use of software. Many indicated that there was an obvious advantage in collaborative learning. The following are some of their comments:

I found that the Conversant Media *is interactive and fun, interesting, and enjoyable to use in certain tasks.*

The software allows me to add greatly to my understanding and enjoyment of learning this task.

I really enjoyed participating in this discussion. I found it easier to relate to the reading when seeing the video. I strongly suggest using this for future classes.

The Conversant Media *is the perfect tool as an addition to class discussion. I know that I would not have paid more attention if we were to discuss the same topic in the class.*

I enjoyed the use of Conversant Media. *It helps me to understand the topic a great deal.*

Future Trends

The objective of this chapter is to review the existing video annotation systems that allow the users to view the particular video frame and make annotation of the content and share with the other users. The chapter also explores the benefit of using the *Conversant Media* in teacher education and to obtain the views of the participants on writing and reading comments on authentic classroom episodes. The results of the experiment indicate that the students have benefited from the use of the software in the delivery of this elective course. The commentary writing skills have improved over the three activities in which they were engaged. The quality and quantity of good comments increased over the three activities. The instructor's rating of the comments indicates that the trainee teachers have developed the ability to analyze teaching episodes and make quality comments. This suggests that *Conversant Media* could be used not only to engage trainee teachers in collaborative learning about instructional and management strategies but also to help students develop their commentary-writing skills.

Writing comments on authentic cases has forced them to think and see the relationship between theory and practice. Reading the feedback comments of peers was also highly valued by the students. They feel that it provides them the opportunity to compare views and see alternative points of view. They also feel that *Conversant Media* can provide a means to create a community of learners who can benefit from each other by sharing their views on topics of common interest. The most appreciated aspect of *Conversant Media* is the opportunity it provides for those who are shy to express their views directly to do so through this electronic medium.

The *Conversant Media* provides many opportunities for trainee teachers to participate in collaborative online discussion, which is not possible with other existing software. The software has a potential of being used in any teaching and training situation where video can be used to visualize the scenario. The software provides a rich leaning environment where a community of learners can take advantage of its features.

Conclusion

Judging from the enthusiastic participation of the trainee teachers in this preliminary investigation, the potential use of *Conversant Media* in creating a collaborative learning environment is noteworthy. On the whole it can be said that *Conversant Media* is versatile software to help students participate actively in the learning process. This tool can be specifically useful in teacher education as it provides an alternative to school visits to see the action in the classroom and hold discussion. Through this software it is possible to bring the classroom to the computer laboratory of the teacher education institutions and engage trainee teachers in powerful learning activities. Most trainee teachers often complain that the teacher education programs are too theoretical and seldom see the authentic case studies during the training period. *Conversant Media* can provide the means to help them see theory in action in the classroom even before they set foot in school to teach.

There is a relentless advancement of educational technology as a means of delivering and enhancing, and it is becoming an integral part of the teaching and learning process (DeBard & Guidera, 2000). These technologies are at the disposal of the teachers and trainers to use for effective teaching and training in their own context.

References

Chong, N., & Sosakul, T. (2003, June). *A framework for video-centered discussions on the Web*. Paper presented at ED-MEDIA 2003 World Conference on Educational Multimedia, Hypermedia and Telecommunications, Hawaii, USA.

DeBard, R., & Guidera, S. (2000). Adapting asynchronous communication to meet the seven principles of effective teaching. *Journal of Educational Technology Systems, 28*(3), 219-230.

Hough, B., Smithey, M., & Evertson, C. (2004). Using computer-mediated communication to create virtual communities of practice for intern teachers. *Journal of Technology and Teacher Education, 12*(3), 361-386.

Kipp, M. (2001). Anvil: A generic annotation tool for multimodal dialogue. In *Proceedings of the 7th European Conference on Speech Communication and Technology* (pp. 1367-1370). Aalborg, Denmark.

Lipponen, L., Hakkarainen, K., & Paavola, S. (2004). Practices and orientations of CSCL. In J. Strijbos, P. Kirschner, & R. Martens (Eds.), *What we know about CSCL and implementing it in higher education* (pp. 31-50). Dordrecht: Kluwer Academic Publishers.

Palloff, R. M., & Pratt, K. (2001). *Lessons from the cyberspace classroom: The realities of online teaching.* San Francisco: Jossey-Bass.

Schroeter, R., Hunter, J., & Kosovic, D. (2003, October). *Vannotea—A collaborative video indexing, annotation and discussion system for broadband network.* Paper presented at K-CAP 2003 Workshop on knowledge markup and semantic annotation. Florida, USA.

Stahl, G. (2000). Collaborative information environments to support knowledge construction by comments. *AI and Society, 14,* 1-27.

Stahl, G. (2004). Building collaborative knowing. In J. Strijbos, P. Kirschner, & R. Martens (Eds.), *What we know about CSCL and implementing it in higher education* (pp. 53-86). Dordrecht: Kluwer Academic Publishers.

Wink, J., & Putney, L. (2002). *A vision of Vygotsky.* Boston: Allyn and Bacon.

Chapter XIV

Educational Geosimulation

Vasco Furtado, University of Fortaleza, Brazil

Eurico Vasconcelos, Integrated Colleges of Ceará (FIC), Brazil

Abstract

In this work we will describe EGA (educational geosimulation architecture), an architecture for the development of pedagogical tools for training in urban activities based on MABS (multi-agent based simulation), GIS (geographic information systems), and ITS (intelligent tutoring systems). EGA came as a proposal for the lack of appropriate tools for the training of urban activities with high risk and/or high cost. As a case study, EGA was used for the development of a training tool for the area of public safety, the ExpertCop system. ExpertCop is a geosimulator of criminal dynamics in urban environments that aims to train police officers in the activity of preventive policing allocation. ExpertCop intends to induce students to reflect about their actions regarding resources allocation and to understand the relationship between preventive policing and crime.

Introduction

Simulation aims to represent one phenomenon via another. It is useful to measure, demonstrate, test, evaluate, foresee, and decrease risks and costs. Computational simulation can be considered as experimentation based on a computer model that provides a safe experimental environment for the inquiry of system properties. In educational terms, simulation is important because it allows learning through the possibility of doing (Piaget, 1976). Simulation has proven to be a good teaching tool, especially for complex situations, with high cost and risk. Practical application can be seen in various areas, such as in the aeronautical industry, nuclear industry, space exploration, petrochemical industry, and military research (Roger, 1994).

Multi-Agent paradigm has been widely adopted in the development of complex systems. In particular, if there are heterogeneous entities or organizations with different (possibly conflicting) goals and proprietary information, then a multi-agent system (MAS) is useful to handle their interactions. A MAS is also appropriate whenever there is a need to represent each entity of the modeled domain individually or if these entities have an intelligent behavior to be modeled.

Social or urban environments are dynamic, non linear, and made of a great number of interacting entities, characterizing a complex system. The use of MAS to simulate social environments has become broadly used (Billari & Prskawetz, 2003; Gilbert & Conte, 1995; Khuwaja, Desmarais, & Cheng, 1996). Aggregating a GIS (geographical information system) to an MAS in the simulation of social or urban environments characterizes geosimulation (Benenson & Torrens, 2004). With the computational development of GIS, bringing precision and realism to simulation (Wu, 2002), multi-agent based simulations (MABS) benefited from them in terms of geographical representation of the areas to be simulated.

Analyzing the existing proposals and tools, and in accordance with Gibbons (Gibbons, Lawless, Anderson, & Duffin, 2001), there are few or even no adequate tools for developing educational computer systems where intelligent agents support the interaction between the simulation model and the user. Despite recent proposals on new models and implementations of instructional layers in simulators (Gibbons et al., 2001; Mann & Batten, 2002), few tools have been created specifically for urban activities, none of them with adequate support to the education process.

This chapter describes the educational geosimulation architecture (EGA), an architecture for training in urban activities based in the synergy among MABS, GIS, and ITS (intelligent tutoring systems) that we consider an optimal and complementary set of technologies for building educational geosimulation. We also describe the ExpertCop system, a training tool developed for the area of public safety based on EGA. ExpertCop is a geosimulator of criminal dynamics in urban environments, which aims to train police officers in the activity of preventive policing allocation. ExpertCop intends to induce students to reflect about their actions regarding resources allocation. Assisting the user, the pedagogical agent aims to define interaction strategies between the student and the geosimulator in order to make simulated phenomena better understood.

This software, based on a police resource allocation plan made by the user, produces simulations of how crime behaves in a certain period of time based on the defined allocation. The goal is to allow a critical analysis by students (police officers) who use the system, allowing them to understand the cause-and-effect relation of their decisions.

With the aim of helping the user to understand the causes and effects of his/her process of allocation, ExpertCop uses an intelligent tutorial agent provided by the architecture endowed with strategies and pedagogical tools that seek to aid the user in understanding the results obtained in the simulation. The agent offers the student a chronological, spatial, and statistical analysis of the results obtained in the simulation. Using a machine learning concept formation algorithm, the agent tries to identify patterns on simulation data, to create concepts representing these patterns, and to elaborate hints to the student about the learned concepts. Moreover, it explores the reasoning process of the domain agents by providing explanations, which help the student to understand simulation events.

ExpertCop was applied in a set of training classes, making it possible to analyze its effectiveness quantitatively as an educational tool.

Background Knowledge

Geosimulation and Intelligent Tutoring Systems

The MABS is a live simulation that differs from other types of computational simulations because simulated entities are individually modeled with the use of agents. There is a consensus about the adoption of multi-agent approach (bottom-up) to the study of social and urban systems (Benenson & Torrens, 2004; Billari & Prskawetz, 2003; Gilbert & Conte, 1995; Gimblett, 2002). Social or urban environments are dynamic, nonlinear, and made up of a great number of variables. MAS are also appropriate when the environments are composed of a great amount of entities whose individual behaviors are relevant in the general context of the simulation.

Figure 1. Components of an ITS architecture.

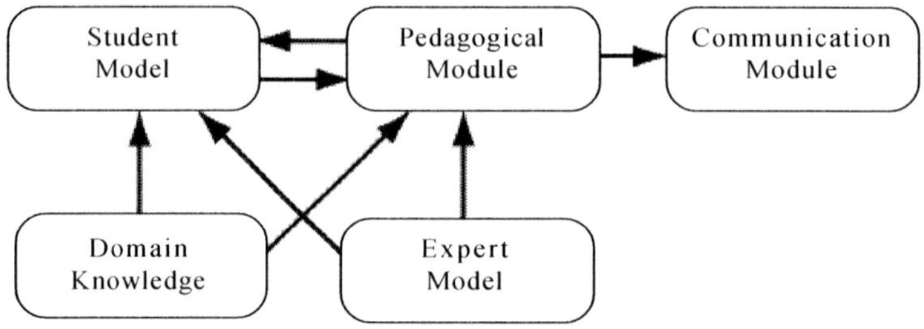

A particular kind of simulation, called geosimulation, treats an urban phenomena simulation model with a multi-agent approach to simulate discrete, dynamic, and event-oriented systems (Benenson & Torrens, 2004). In geosimulated models, simulated urban phenomena are considered a result of the collective dynamic interaction among animate and inanimate entities that compose the environment. Geosimulation has been applied in the study of a variety of urban phenomena (Torrens, 2002). The GIS is responsible to provide the "data ware" in geosimulations.

Simulation is widely used as an educational tool because computerized simulation of the studied activity allows the user to learn by doing (Piaget, 1976) and to understand the cause-and-effect relationship of his/her actions.

The simulation *per se* is not a sufficient tool for education. It lacks the conceptual ability of the student to understand the simulation model. Therefore, some works (Siemer, 1995; Taylor & Siemer, 1996) have tried to integrate the notions of intelligent tutoring system (ITS) and simulation in order to better guide learning and to improve understanding of the simulation process. The idea of an ITS is the integration of artificial intelligence in computer learning systems. It aims at emulating the work of a human teacher that has knowledge of the content to be taught, and how and to whom it should be taught. To achieve this, we need to represent I) the domain of study, II) the pedagogical strategies, and III) the student to whom the teaching is provided. A fourth component may also be considered (Kaplan & Rock, 1995; Woolf & Hall, 1995) the interface with the user. Figure 1 shows the most common architecture for an ITS.

The user interface determines how the interaction with the system will be. Through the interaction of these components, the ITS adapts pedagogic strategies on a domain at the level of the student for his/her individual needs.

Educational Geosimulation Architecture

Motivation and Proposal

A major part of the world's population today lives in large urban centers, dynamic environments composed of an infinity of heterogeneous entities that are interrelated in a series of activities.

Good management of these urban centers depends on an understanding of the dynamics of the urban social relationships and activities occurring among the entities that make up these environments as well as of the environment itself.

Public safety, urban traffic control, migration control, population growth, and urbanization are a few of the complex examples of urban activities or processes that are part of urban relationships. The management of such activities demands an understanding of the factors, entities, and processes involved directly or indirectly in these activities. In addition to the various factors involved and the natural complexity of the relationships between these factors, such activities involve, for the most part, very high risks and costs since they deal with values of public domain and mainly because they involve human lives. This complexity inherent to urban activities makes it difficult, if not impossible, to study and manage such activities.

One can observe a lack of support to the study of these areas, means, or tools that allow a broader base for actions undertaken in such areas.

It is fitting in this context to construct computational tools that make it possible to represent the complexity of the entities and relationships involved in urban activities, in a way as to provide subsidy to studies, training, and management by those persons responsible directly or indirectly for the administration or enforcement of such activities.

Focusing on the complexity of studying urban social activities and the lack of tools to support the study of such activities, a bibliographical search was performed in the area of the educational computational tools, seeking proposals, architectures, or even tools that could aid in the understanding and training of urban activities.

By means of this research, it was possible to verify there are no specific pedagogical tools, nor even approaches, geared toward the presented problematic. We thus confirmed Gibbons' affirmation that there are no, or very few, educative tools that give adequate support to the interaction between the student and studied environment (Gibbons et al., 2001).

However, it was possible to identify approaches geared toward parts of our problem. We observed, for example, that when the object of study is dynamic and the practical study of which is impracticable by involving high risks and costs, the computational simulation of this object proves to be a good strategy. Simulating allows for the representation of the dynamics of the studied object and prevents or minimizes the risks and costs of onsite study, and according to Piaget, simulating offers the pedagogical advantage of "learning by doing." The urban activities we propose to study are made up of a great number of different interrelating entities. In order to simulate the activity of these entities, it is necessary to represent them appropriately. Various authors (Gilbert & Conte, 1995; Khuwaja et al., 1996) describe the approach of multi-agent systems as appropriate for the computational representation of independent entities that interrelate within the same environment. In this way, the multi-agent based simulation seems to encompass two interesting characteristics for our study—process and entities. A third important characteristic in the process of study of urban activities is the representation of the environment. For such, the geographic information systems allow for the appropriate representation and study of geographic environments. The aggregation of the MABS with the GIS in representing the urban environment was named geosimulation by Benenson and Torrens (2004). Finally, another practice noted in the research is the adoption of Intelligent Tutorial Systems as support to computerized learning.

Based on the observations made in our research, we elaborated an architecture that brings together what we consider ideal for the development of urban activities training systems—the architecture for educational geosimulation.

The Architecture

Educational geosimulation architecture is composed of four main components: a user interface, an MAS, a GIS, and a database as is shown in Figure 2. Each part of EGA architecture will be discussed in detail in the following items.

Figure 2. Educational geosimulation architecture

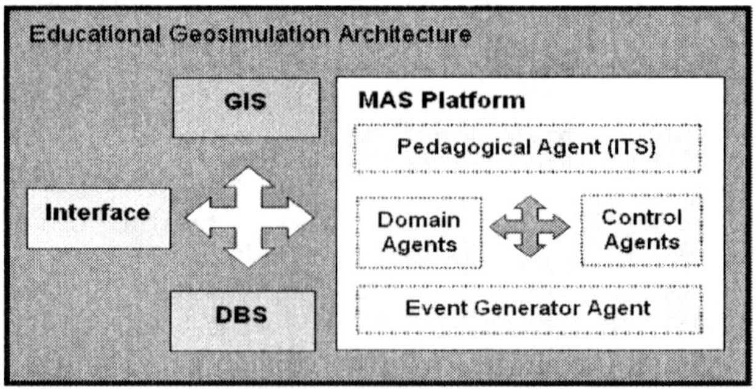

User Interface

The interface is the means of interaction between the user and the rest of the system. It contains the map of the region to be studied, generated by the GIS, whereby the user will interact with the agents of the system in the simulation process. It is also the means by which the pedagogical agent will apply its pedagogical techniques, aimed at assisting the user. The interface is constructed in a logical and organized way and in accordance with ergonomic standards.

Geographical Information System

The GIS is responsible for generating, manipulating, and updating a map on a small scale of the studied region. The map contains a set of layers, representing the geographic, social, and urban characteristics of the area as quadrants, streets, avenues, buildings, parks, slums, and so forth. The GIS offers a set of controls that allows the user and the other parts of architecture to manipulate the map, by amplifying, minimizing, or demarcating areas or by creating, manipulating, or moving objects on the map, among other functions.

System Database

The system database contains (a) information about each user and about his/her simulations, (b) configuration data, (c) statistical data about the studied domain, (d) the domain ontology. Such an ontology is a definition of basic concepts used in the domain and was produced by an expert of the domain.

MABS Platform

The structure, communication, administration, and distribution of the agents, the simulation process, and flux are provided by the MABS platform. The multi-Aagent based simulation platform is made up of four groups of agents: control agents, domain agents, the event generator agent, and the pedagogic agent.

Control Agents

The control agents are responsible for the control, communication, and flow in the system. The control agents are:

- **GIS agent,** which is responsible for answering requests from the graphical interface, domains, and control agents. It is responsible for updating the map with the generated simulation data. The GIS agent represents the environment.
- **Manager agents,** which manage the types of agents of the studied domain. They are responsible for the coordination and interaction with agents of their type or class. This agent is a middleware among agents of its own group and the rest of the system. They control pre-programmed activities of their agents as activation and deactivation and controlled events.
- **Log agent,** which is responsible for recording all interactions among system agents in order to contain all data about the simulation and the configuration.
- **Graphical agent,** which compiles pertinent data to the domain, exchanging information with the log agent, and dynamically generating statistical graphics to the graphical interface.

Domain Agent

Domain agents are the actors of the domain, acting actively in the simulation process. The number, kind, behavior, and relations of these agents depend on the studied problem. The idea is that these agents are modeled with the most representative characteristics and actions of the behavior of the entities being proposed for representation.

Event Generator Agent

The event generator agent is responsible for generating the events that will motivate the simulation process. If the studied domain were that of traffic of urban vehicles, it would generate, for example, events such as traffic accidents. If the domain were that of the dynamics of the fire department, it would generate fires or other occurrences to be responded to. If the domain were that of natural disaster control, the generator could be responsible for generating floods, landslides, or earthquakes. The type of event generated by the agent depends on the domain to be studied, being up to the developer to define what he/she wishes to be generated by the agent. This definition is provided by filling in statistical tables in which the agent bases itself on data about the events in question. These tables associate the type of event with its geographical or temporal pattern of occurrence. Each type of event is characterized by sets of geographic and temporal factors, each factor with a set of possible values and each value with weights that define its probability in relation to the event.

The parameters assessed by the agent for the process of events generation are: the period to be simulated, the area selected, and the student's level of experience. The agent simulates the occurrence of events for the entire period to be simulated, making the geographic and temporal distribution of the events according to statistical data from the system database. This process occurs within of a set of successive steps:

1. **Input of parameters:** Initially the agent receives, as input parameters, the period, the area, and the user of the simulation.
2. **Total events calculation:** Based on the parameters received, the agent searches through specific tables of the database, statistical information referring to the occurrences of the events.

   Data of the occurrence of events in similar and previous periods are joined with those that the user desires to simulate, taking into account the seasonableness of the occurrence of such events.

   Based on these statistical data, the agent makes a projection (prediction) of the tendency of the total number of events per type for the selected period. For such, we used one of the analysis methods of time series represented by formula Y = TCSI, where "Y" represents the value of time series to be estimated, "T" represents the trend, "C" represents the cyclical movements, "S" represents the seasonal movements, and "I" represents the irregular movements. The method in question is the method of moving averages that allows us to ignore the cyclical, seasonal, and irregular variations, analyzing only the tendency. To analyze the tendency, the agent will consider the tendency of the last periods and the tendency of periods similar to the desired one as in Figure 3.

Figure 3. Selection of data for calculation of the totals of an event for any given period

Seasonableness is observed by the fact that only periods similar to the one selected were studied (month of January).

PERIODS	Events
January 1998	20
January 1999	21
January 2000	24
January 2001	24
January 2002	26
January 2003	27
January 2004	30
January 2005	?

The projection of **tendency** (temporal series) observes the behavior of the values in a temporal way; in this case in particular there is a tendency of growth over the years, especially for the months of January.

3. **Temporal and geographical distribution of events:** Once the numbers of events per type are obtained for the period, the second step is to distribute them geographically and temporally within the area to be simulated. For temporal distribution, the generator verifies the statistical data of the selected area in relation to the number of events of each type per day of the week and per shift. These statistics allow the agent to make the distribution of the total of events per type (calculated in the first step), on each day to be simulated.

   For the geographical distribution (latitude and longitude) of the events, the simulator uses the map's geographical and social information seeking to associate the type of event to its geographic pattern of occurrence. A geoprocessed map is composed of various layers of information and characteristics. For this reason it is possible to subdivide the map by sets of characteristics. These characteristics are mapped in a table (by the developer) with the association among areas with specific characteristics and types of events. In Figure 4 we can see four layers of a map (A, B, C, D), each layer showing areas demarcated by a specific type of characteristic. In this way we can create a table relating, on a percentile basis, the types of events to the characteristics of the environment in which they occur.

4. **Adequacy to the student's level:** The final step is to consider the student's level of experience. The system can characterize the student as beginner, intermediary, and experienced. Each level functions as a type of filter for steps 2 and 3 described. For example, at the inexperienced level, the simulator—after calculating the total number of events per type—applies a percentile reduction to the total, and when geographically distributing this total of crimes on the map for the given period, the simulator will

Figure 4. Association between area characteristics and event types

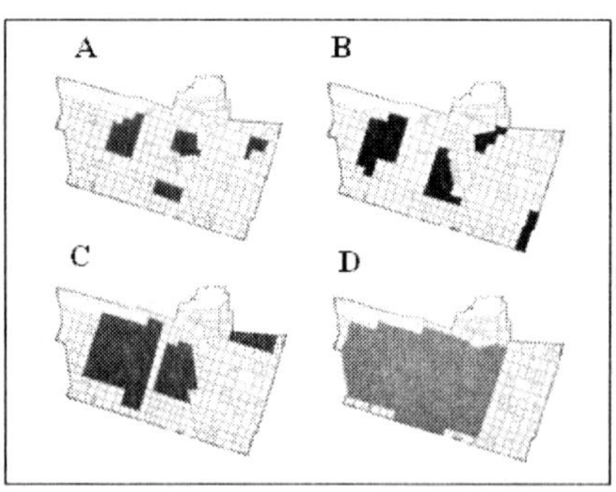

Characteristics / Events	Event X	Event Y	Event Z
Characteristic A	10 %	20%	30%
Characteristic B	20 %	5%	10%
Characteristic C	0%	25%	25%
Characteristic D	70%	50%	35%

seek to encase the event into a smaller and more accurate number of geographic, social, and temporal characteristics, so as to facilitate the student's analysis and identification of patterns. These characteristics are defined previously in a table for each level of student. At the professional level, instead of having a percentage of reduction, there is a percentage of increase. When registering with the system, the student is automatically placed at the beginner level. This presumption will be validated and readjusted according to the results obtained by the student during his or her simulation. Since the results of the simulations are kept individually per student in the system's database, the student's growth in using the system can be accompanied and adapted according to the student's performance. The system does not delimit the number of simulation that one user can perform nor the area and period that the student wishes to simulate; the accompaniment is done according to the results.

The agent also permits the simulation to be focused on a specific type of event, for example, if the student/user is showing results of a certain type of event with discrepancies in relation to the others, the simulator increases the percentage of events of the type with which the user has the most difficulty, reducing the percentage of the type that the user shows better performance.

The level of difficulty rises with the increase of factors that characterize each type of event and with each increase in the total number of events.

Pedagogical Agent

The pedagogical agent will be discussed in detail in the pedagogical proposal of the EGA section.

Pedagogical Proposal of EGA

The pedagogical model of EGA is based on the concept of intelligent tutoring simulation system where in addition to the simulation itself, an agent provides adaptive explanations to the student at different levels.

The Simulation as a Pedagogical Tool

In EGA we consider simulation as one part of a pedagogical tool. The student can learn by doing. He/she initially interacts with the system by allocating the police.

It is a moment to expose his/her beliefs on the allocation of the resources. A simulation of the interaction of the agents is then done, and the students' beliefs can be validated by means of a phase of result analysis. This cycle can be repeated as many times as the student finds necessary.

The Learning Process

According to Kolb (1984), learning is favored when the learning process occurs within successive steps as shown in Figure 5. These steps are:

- **Concrete experience:** Obtained through the activity itself or its simulation in a virtual environment.
- **Reflexive observation:** The experience is followed by the reflection phase. It is recreated internally in the user's mind under different perspectives.
- **Abstract conceptualization:** In this stage, the experience is compared, and its patterns, processes, and meanings are analyzed. In this context, abstract concepts and new knowledge are created. The knowledge is generated in two moments of the cycle, in this step and in that of solid experience. The knowledge generated in the solid experience phase comes only from the simple observation of the external event, while the knowledge generated in the abstract conceptualization phase emerges as a consequence of an internal cognitive process of the student.

The Pedagogical Agent as a User Support

The pedagogical agent gives support to the user during the reflexive observation and abstract conceptualization steps of the simulation process. It uses two

Figure 5. Steps that enhance learning

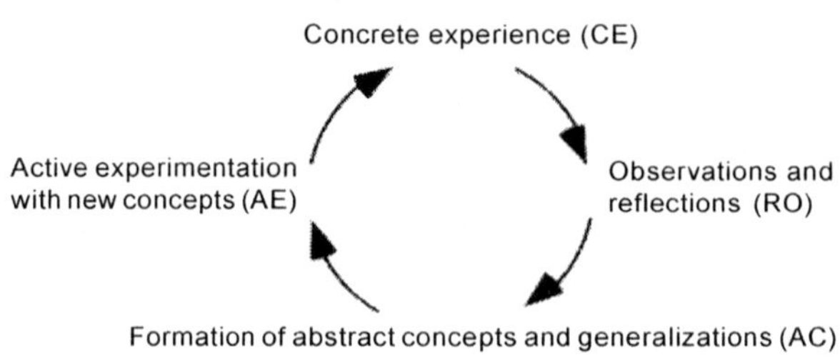

distinct strategies to help the user in the comprehension of the simulation results. The explanation is provided at a micro level and at a macro level.

The ExpertCop System

Motivation

Police resource allocation in urban areas in order to perform preventive policing is one of the most important tactical management activities and is usually decentralized by sub sectors in police departments of the area. What it is intended by those tactical managers is that they analyze the disposition of crime in their region and that they perform the allocation of the police force based on this analysis. We agree with the principle that by knowing where the crime is happening and the reasons associated with this crime, it is possible to make an optimized allocation of resources and consequently, to decrease the crime rate.

The volume of information that police departments have to analyze is one of the main factors to provide society with efficient answers. Tactical managers who perform police allocations, for instance, have a lack of ability related to information analysis and decision-making based on this analysis. In reality, understanding criminal mapping activities, even using GIS, is a nontrivial task. In addition to that, experiments in this domain cannot be performed without high risks because they result in loss of human lives. In this context, simulation systems for teaching and decision support are a fundamental tool.

Objectives

The ExpertCop system aims to support education through the induction of reflection on simulated phenomena of crime rates in an urban area. The system receives as input a police resource allocation plan, and it makes simulations of how the crime rate would behave in a certain period of time. The goal is to lead the student to understand the consequences of his/her allocation as well as understanding the cause-and-effect relations.

In the ExpertCop system, the simulations occur in a learning environment and along with graphical visualizations that help the student's learning. The system allows the student to manipulate parameters dynamically and analyze the results.

ExpertCop Architecture

ExpertCop Architecture is based totally on EGA. As the generic parts of the architecture were previously described, we will deal only with the specification of the domain agents and how the pedagogical agent implemented the pedagogical strategies.

MABS Platform in ExpertCop

There is a great diversity of existing frameworks for the development and maintenance of an MABS platform. We adopted the JADE (Java Agent Develop Framework) (TILab, 2003) due to the fact that it is based on FIPA specifications, to offer tools for creation, maintenance, and control of the agents in addition to being open source, freeware, offering a good documentation, and being based on a robust freeware and simple programming language, JAVA.

ExpertCop Domain Agents

Domain agents are the actors of the domain, performing actively in the simulation process:

- **Police teams:** The mission of the police teams is to patrol the areas selected by the user during the work period and work shifts scheduled for the team. An agent represents each team and has a group of characteristics defined by the user, such as means of locomotion, type of service, and work shift that will influence his patrol. The team works based on its work period and work shift. The work period determines the beginning and end of work, and the work shift determines the work and rest periods. The patrol areas are composed of one or more connected points. The patrol areas are given to the police team as a mission. These areas are associated with intervals of time so as to fill out the work period of the team.
- **Criminals:** The criminal manager creates each criminal agent in the simulation, with the mission of committing a specific crime. After the selection of the area and simulation period by the user, the criminal manager loads, from the system database, all the crimes pertaining to the area and selected period and places the crimes in chronological order. When beginning the simulation, observing the chronological order of the events, it creates a criminal agent for each crime. The criminal's task is to evaluate the viability of committing the crime. The evaluation is based on risk,

benefit, and personality factors, defined on the basis of a set of interviews with specialists in crime of the public safety secretariat and on research in the area of criminal psychology.

The values of the variables regarding crime (type of crime, type of victim, geographical location of crime, date, and time) are sent to the criminal by the criminal manager. But to obtain the data on the environment (geographical factors), the criminal exchanges messages with the GIS agent who furnishes the geographical location, date, and time of the crime.

Having collected all the necessary information for the decision support process of the crime to be executed, the agent uses a PSM of evaluation (abstract and match) (Pinheiro & Furtado, 2004) that will evaluate the viability of committing the crime. The PSM is made up by sets of inference rules containing the structure of the decision support process and an inference machine, in our case JEOPS (Figueira & Ramalho, 2000), that sweeps these rules associating them with the data collected on the crime. This process results in the decision of committing the crime or not. In the sequence below, we demonstrate an example of rules contained in the PSM:

IF **distance_police** = *close* AND **type_crime** = *robbery* AND **type_victim** = *bank* THEN **risk** = *high*

IF **type_victim** = *bank* THEN **benefit** = *high*

IF **benefit** = *high* AND **risk** = *high* AND **personality** = *bold* THEN **decision** = *commit_crime*

We observed the logical structure of the rule with capital letters, the variables that make up the agent's internal state in boldface type, and the values of the variables coming from the data of the crime and the exchange of messages with the GIS Agent in italic type.

After deciding, the criminal sends a message to the GIS Agent informing his decision so that the GIS Agent may mark on the map exhibited by the user, the decision made—in red if the crime is committed and in green if it is not.

- **Notable points:** Notable points are buildings of a region relevant to the objective of our simulation, such as shopping centers, banks, parks, and drugstores. They are located on the simulation map having the same characteristics of the buildings they represent.
- **Pedagogical agent (PA):** PA represents the tutorial module of an ITS proposal. Endowed with pedagogical strategies, this agent aims to help the user in the understanding of the simulation process and results. PA will be discussed in detail in the pedagogical proposal section of this work.

ExpertCop Pedagogical Proposal: Adaptive Explanations

The pedagogic agent uses two distinct forms to explain the events of the system, the explanation at a micro level and at a macro level.

Individual Explanation of the Events of the System (Micro-Level)

To explain the simulation events (crimes), the system uses a tree of proofs describing the steps of reasoning of the criminal agent responsible for the event. This tree is generated from the process of the agent's decision making. The agent's evaluation of a crime is represented by a set of production rules explored by an inference engine called JEOPS (Figueira & Ramalho, 2000). The student can obtain the information on the crime and the process that led the agent to commit it or not, by just clicking with the mouse on the point that represents the crime on the map. Each crime represented by mean of a point at the screen is associated with a proof tree. An example of this can be viewed in Figure 6.

Figure 6. Individual events explanation

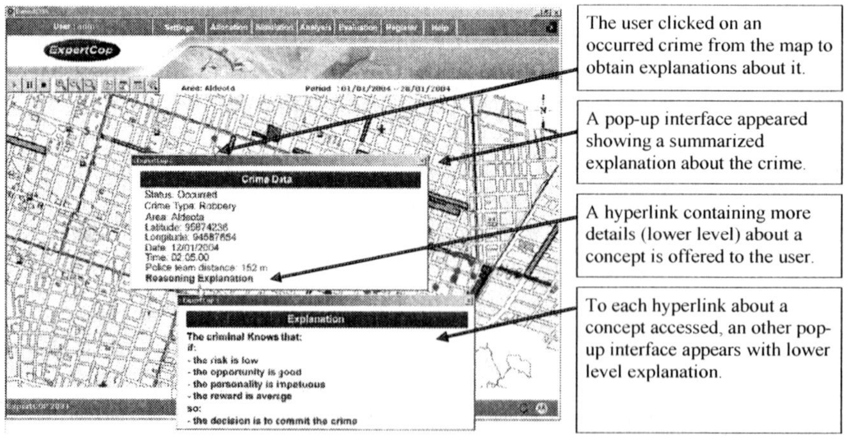

Figure 7. Macro-level explanation process

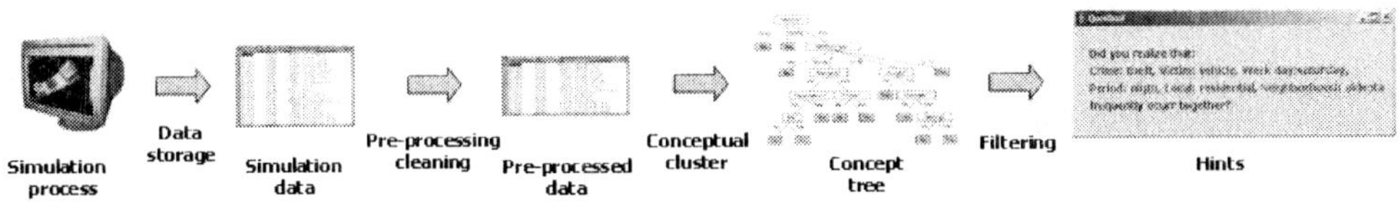

Explanation of the Emerging Behavior or Starting at the Agents' Interactions (Macro-Level)

In ExpertCop, we understand as emerging behavior, the effects of individual events in crime, its increase or reduction, criminal tendencies, and seasonableness. For the explanation of the emerging behavior of the system, the pedagogical agent tries to identify patterns of behavior from the database generated in the simulation. The pedagogical agent (PA) does the KDD process automatically, illustrated in Figure 7.

First, the agent takes (requesting the LOG agent) the simulation data (events generated for the interaction of the agents as crimes (date, hour, motive, type) and patrols (start time, final time, stretch), and preprocesses it, adding geographic information such as escape routes, notable place coordinates, distance between events, agents and notable places, and social and economical data associated with geographic areas. After preprocessing, in the mining phase, PA identifies patterns by means of a probabilistic concept formation algorithm. This algorithm generates a hierarchy of probabilistic concepts. The generated concepts are characterized according to their attribute/value conditional probabilities. That is to say, a conceptual description is made of attribute/values with high probability. Having the probabilistic concept formation hierarchy constructed, the agent identifies and filters the adequate concepts for being transformed in questions to the student. The heuristics used to filter which concepts will generate questions to the student and which features will compose these questions follow the next steps:

- The root of the hierarchy is ignored (not appraised), because it aggregates all the concepts being too generic.
- The hierarchy is read in a bottom-up fashion from the most specific to the most generic concepts.

- The criteria used in the analysis of the concepts for selection are:
  - A concept must cover at least 10% of the total of examples. We believe that less than 10% of the examples would make the concept little representative.
  - An attribute value is only exhibited in the question when it is present in at least 70% of the total of the observations covered by an example.
  - A question must contain at least three attributes.
- When going through a branch of the tree considering the previous items, in case a concept is evaluated and selected, the nodes superior to this concept (parent, grandparent...) will no longer be appraised in order to avoid redundant information. This does not exclude the nodes in the same level of the hierarchy of this node that may be appraised in the future.

An example of COBWEB result displayed to the user in a simulation process is the following hint: "Did you realize that: *crime*: theft, *victim*: vehicle, *weekday*: Saturday, *period*: night, *local*: residential street, *neighborhood*: Aldeota frequently occur together?" Having this kind of information, the user/student can reflect on changes in the allocation, aiming to avoid this situation.

System Functioning

Initially, the student must register with the system and configure the simulation parameters using a specific interface. After that he/she determines the number of police teams to be allocated and the characteristics of these teams. Based on the geographical and statistical data available on the map about the area and his/her knowledge about police patrol, the student determines the areas to be patrolled and allocates the police teams available on the geoprocessed map. To perform the allocation process, the student selects the patrol areas on the map for each team. After that he/she defines the period of time that the police team will be in each patrol area. The sum of each period of time must be equal to the team's workload.

Agents representing the police teams monitor the patrol areas defined by the user following the programmed schedule. The patrol function is to inhibit possible crimes that could happen in the neighborhood. We presume that the police presence is able to inhibit crimes in a certain area scope. The goal of the student is to provide a good allocation, which prevents to the greatest extent the occurrence of crimes.

After the configuration and allocation process, the user can follow the simulation process in the simulation interface. At the end of the simulation process, the user accesses the pedagogical tools of the system.

In addition to the visualization functionalities, the student can access the explanation capabilities. A micro-level explanation can be obtained from the click of the mouse on any red or green point on the screen that indicates crimes that have occurred or have been avoided, respectively. Figure 6 is a screen-shot of the screen at the moment of a micro-level explanation. The student can request a macro-level explanation pushing the hint button represented on the screen. Figure 7 also shows how the concepts discovered by the probabilistic concept formation algorithm are presented on the screen. A set of questions is shown to the student in order to make him/her reflect about possible patterns of crimes.

Upon each new performed allocation, the system will comparatively evaluate the simulated moments, showing the student whether the modification brought a better effect to the crime rate or not. PA also makes comparisons among results obtained in each simulation tour for evaluating learning improvements done by the student. The student can also evaluate the results among a series of simulation at the evaluation screen. On this screen, the results of all simulations made by the student are shown in a bar graphic.

EGA and ExpertCop Evaluation

ExpertCop was used to support a course at the Ministry of Justice and the National Secretariat of Public Safety—SENASP. The course had the objective of emphasizing the importance of information technologies in public safety. ExpertCop was intended to help police officers reflect on the forms of treatment and analysis of information and how these influence the understanding of crime. The audience was made up of three groups of 30 professionals in the area of public safety: civil police officers, chiefs of police, and military police (which are the majority). This use of the system allows us to validate the tool itself and the proposed architecture.

The use of the system was introduced in a training context, which allows us not only to teach the students how to evaluate the tool regarding its usability and effectiveness for the learning proposals. Regarding the architecture, the tool was completely implemented according to the proposal, showing itself to be appropriate for representing and simulating the studied domain. According to the analysis of the obtained results, we observed a significant statistical growth (test T-Test mean-pair with 1% of error) in students' performance, which we consider as learning. We used a dispersion graph to evaluate the relation between the results obtained and the use of the system's support tools. According to the graph, a positive linear relation indicates that the use of the pedagogical tools made it possible for the students to gain from their performance. We also observed that the tool showed itself to be ergonomic regarding its usability and aroused interest in the students, who showed themselves to be motivated to use it even after the course was over. More specific data on the methodology of application for the course and the methods of attainment and analysis of the results can be obtained in Furtado and Vasconcelos (2005).

Related Work

MAS simulation in education (Gibbons, Fairweather, & Anderson, 1997; Khuwaja et al., 1996; Querrec et al., 2003), ITS (Johnson, Rickel, & Lester, 2000; Ryder, Scolaro, & Stokes, 2001), social simulation to support decision-making, and GIS works (Gimblett, 2002) strongly influenced this research work. These propose an intersection among these areas. There are a great number of works that describe solutions with parts of our proposal:

- Virtual environments for training as SECUREVI proposed by Querrec (Querrec et al., 2003). The system is based on MASCARET model that uses multi-agents systems to simulate realistic, collaborative, and adaptive environments for training simulation.
- Intelligent GIS as the proposed system by Djordjevic (Djordjevic-Kajan, Mitrovic, Mitrovic, Stoimenov, & Stanic, 1995) that intends to provide computer support in fire rescue. The system has a "Fire Trainer," an intelligent agent that covers the activities connected to education.
- Multi-agents with GIS in urban simulation (geosimulation) as a computer model in the approach of Wu (2002) and Benenson (2004).
- Intelligent tutoring systems as those proposed by Wisher (Wisher, MacPherson, Abramson, Thorndon, & Dees, 2001) that describe an intelligent tutoring for field artillery training or Sherlock system by Lesgold (Lesgold, Lajoie, Bunzo, & Eggan, 1992), which provides advice when impasses appear while using a simulated system.
- Phoenix system (Cohen, Michael, David, & Adele, 1989), a discrete event simulator based on an agent architecture. The system is a real-time, adaptive planner that simulates the problem of forest fires.
- The architecture proposed by Atolagbe (Atolagbe & Hlupic, 1996) and Draman (1991) for educational simulation also has similar points with this

work although they do not emphasize the power of simulation in GIS with the use of KDD to improve student learning.

- Pedagogical agents in virtual environments as proposed by Jondahl and Morch (Jondahl & Morch, 2002).
- Several works in games and entertainment (Galvão, Martins, & Gomes, 2000; Leemkuil, Jong, Hoog, & Christoph, 2003) use simulation with an educational propose. Even though they present some similarities with our approach, game simulators have a different pedagogical strategy. They focus on the results of the simulation while we believe that most important is the process itself. Another differential is that few games are adapted to the student level. In order to diminish this, some have proposed to insert ITS features in games (Angelides & Siemer, 1995).

Conclusion and Future Work

This work described the educational geosimulation architecture, an architecture for the development of tools for training in urban activities based on the interaction among MABS, GIS, and ITS. As a case study, we develop a system based on EGA for the area of public safety, the ExpertCop system. ExpertCop is a pedagogical geosimulator of crime in urban areas. The ExpertCop architecture is based on the existence of MAS with a GIS to perform geosimulations and of a pedagogical agent that follows the simulation process and can define learning strategies as well as use a conceptual clustering algorithm to search relations in the facts generated in the simulation. ExpertCop is focused on education for police officers, in relation to resources allocation.

Initial training courses with police officers interacting with the system were performed aiming to evaluate learning by using this tool. As a complement to the use of the system, a course was made where ExpertCop was used as a tool for analysis and reflection of practical situations. The methodology adopted to analyze the learning of students in ExpertCop has shown a significant improvement in the students' data analysis abilities, in the process of resource allocation with ExpertCop, and in the identification of factors that influence crime.

We intend to continue this research on the ExpertCop system, enhancing its functionalities, and increasing the training support, aiming to make it not only an educational tool but a decision-making support tool as well. The next steps are to implement systems based on EGA in other domains of urban activities.

References

Angelides, M. C., & Siemer, J. (1995). Evaluating intelligent tutoring with gaming-simulations. In C. Alexopoulos & K. Kang (Eds.), *Proceedings of 1995 Winter Simulation Conference* (pp. 1376-1383). Arlington, VA: ACM.

Atolagbe, T., & Hlupic, V. (1996). A generic architecture for intelligent instruction for simulation modelling. In J. M. Charnes, D. J. Morrice, & D. T. Brunner (Eds.), *Proceedings of the 1996 Winter Simulation Conference* (pp. 856-863). San Diego, CA.

Benenson, I., & Torrens, P. M. (2004). Geosimulation: Object-based modeling of urban phenomena. *Computers, Environment and Urban Systems, 28*(1-2), 1-8.

Billari, C. F., & Prskawetz, A. (2003). *Agent-based computational demography: Using simulation to improve our understanding of demographic behaviour.* Germany: Phisica-Verlag.

Cohen, P. R., Michael, L. G., David, M. H., & Adele, E. H. (1989). Trial by fire: Understanding the design requirements for agents in complex environments. *AI Magazine, 10*(3), 32-48.

Djordjevic-Kajan, S., Mitrovic, D., Mitrovic, A., Stoimenov, L., & Stanic, Z. (1995). Intelligent GIS for fire department services. In S. Folving, A. Burrill, & J. Meyer-Roux (Eds.), *Proceedings of Eurocarto XIII* (pp. 185-196). Ispra, Italy: Joint Research Centre, European Commission.

Draman, M. (1991). A generic architecture for intelligent simulation training systems. In *Proceedings of the 24th Annual Symposium on Simulation*, (pp. 30-38). New Orleans, LA: IEEE Computer Society.

Fayyad, U. M., Piatetsky, G., Smyth, P., & Uthurusamy, R. (1996). From data mining to knowledge discovery: An overview. In U. Fayyad, G. Piatesky-Shapior, P. Smith, & R. Uthurusamy (Eds.), *Advances in knowledge discovery and data mining* (pp. 1-34). Menlo Park, CA: AAAI Press.

Fensel, D., Motta, E., Benjamins, V. R., Decker, S., Gaspari, M., Groenboom, et al. (2003). The unified problem-solving method development language UPML. *Knowledge and Information Systems, An International Journal, 5*(1), 83-127.

Figueira, F. C., & Ramalho, G. (2000). JEOPS—The Java Embedded Object Production System. In M. Monard & J. Sichman (Eds.), *Advances in artificial intelligence* (pp. 52-61). London: Springer-Verlag.

Fisher, D. (1987). Knowledge acquisition via incremental conceptual clustering. *Machine Learning, 2*(2), 139-172.

Furtado, V., & Vasconcelos, E. (2005). A pedagogical agent on mining, adaptation and explanation of geosimulated data. In M. M. Veloso & S. Kambhampati (Eds.), *Proceedings of the 18th International IAAI* (pp. 1521-1528). Pittsburgh, PA: AAAI Press.

Galvão, J. R., Martins, P. G., & Gomes, M. R. (2000). Modeling reality with simulation games for a cooperative learning. In P. A. Fishwick (Ed.). *Proceedings of the 2000 Winter Simulation Conference* (pp. 1692-1698). Orlando, FL: Society for Computer Simulation International.

Gibbons, A. S., Fairweather, P. G., & Anderson, T. A. (1997). Simulation and computer-based instruction: A future view. In C. R. Dills & A. J. Romizowski (Eds.), *Instructional development: State of the art* (pp. 772-783). Englewood Cliffs, NJ: Educational Technology Publications.

Gibbons, A. S., Lawless, K. A., Anderson, T. A., & Duffin, J. (2001). The Web and model-centered instruction. In B. H. Khan (Ed.), *Web-based training* (pp. 137-146). Englewood Cliffs, NJ: Educational Technology Publications.

Gilbert, N., & Conte, R. (Eds.). (1995). *Artificial societies: The computer simulation of social life*. London: UCL Press.

Gimblett, H. R. (Ed.). (2002). *Integrating geographic information systems and agent-based modeling techniques for simulating social and ecological processes*. University of Arizona & Santa Fe Institute: Oxford University Press.

Johnson, W. L., Rickel, J. W., & Lester, J. C. (2000). Animated pedagogical agents: Face-to-face interaction in interactive learning environments. *International Journal of AI in Education, 11*(1), 47-78.

Jondahl, S., & Morch, A. (2002). Simulating pedagogical agents in a virtual learning environment. In G. Stahl (Ed.), *Proceedings of Computer Support for Collaborative Learning* (pp. 531-532). Boulder, CO: Lawrence Erlbaum.

Kaplan, R., & Rock, D. (1995). New directions for intelligent tutoring systems. *AI Expert, 10*(1), 30-40.

Khuwaja, R., Desmarais, M., & Cheng, R. (1996). Intelligent guide: Combining user knowledge assessment with pedagogical guidance. In C. Frasson, G. Gauthier, & A. Lesgold (Eds.). *Proceedings of International Conference on Intelligent Tutoring Systems* (pp. 225-233). Berlin: Springer Verlag.

Kolb, D. A. (1984). *Experiential learning: Experience as the source of learning and development*. Englewood Cliffs, NJ: Prentice Hall.

Leemkuil, H. H., Jong, T. de, Hoog, R. de, & Christoph, N. (2003). KM quest: A collaborative internet-based simulation game. *Simulation & Gaming, 34*(1), 89-111.

Lesgold, S., Lajoie, M., Bunzo, G., Eggan. (1992). SHERLOCK: A coached practice environment for an electronics troubleshooting job. In J. Larkin & R. Chabay (Eds.), *Computer assisted instruction and intelligent tutoring systems* (pp. 201-238). Hillsdale, NJ: Lawrence Erlbaum Associates.

Piaget, J. (1976). *Le comportement, moteur de l'évolution*. Paris: Ed. Gallimard.

Pinheiro, V., & Furtado, V. (2004). Developing interaction capabilities in knowledge-based systems via design patterns. In A. Bazzan & S. Labidi (Eds.), *Proceedings of Brazilian Symposium of Artificial Intelligence-* (pp. 174-183). São Luis, Brazil: ACM.

Querrec, R., Buche, C., Maffre, E., & Chevaillier, P. (2003). SecuReVi: Virtual environments for fire fighting training. In S. Richir & B. Taravel (Eds.), *Proceedings of Conférence Internationale sur la Réalité Virtuelle* (pp. 169-175). Laval, France.

Roger, B. (1994). *The swarm multi-agent simulation system* (Tech. Rep.). In Object-Oriented Programming Systems, Languages, and Applications (OOPSLA) Workshop on "The Object Engine." (Request report number and publisher/publication location)

Ryder, J. M., Scolaro, J. A., & Stokes, J. M. (2001). An instructional agent for UAV controller training. In *Proceedings of UAVs—16th International Conference* (pp. 3.1-3.11). Bristol, UK: University of Bristol.

TILab S.p.A. Java Agent Development Framework—JADE. (2003). Retrieved January 20, 2005, from ttp://sharon.cselt.it/projects/jade

Torrens, P. M. (2002). Cellular automata and multi-agent systems as planning support tools. In S. Geertman & J. Stillwell (Eds.), *Planning support systems in practice* (pp. 205-222). London: Springer-Verlag.

Wisher, R. A., MacPherson, D. H., Abramson, L. J., Thorndon, D. M., & Dees, J. J. (2001). *The virtual sand table: Intelligent tutoring for field artillery training* (ARI Research Report 1768). Alexandria, VA: U.S. Army Research Institute for the Behavioral and Social Sciences.

Woolf, B., & Hall, W. (1995). Multimedia pedagogues—Interactive systems for teaching and learning. *IEEE Computer, 28*(5), 74-80.

Wu, F. (2002). Complexity and urban simulation: Towards a computational laboratory. *Geography Research Forum, 22*(1), 22-40.

Chapter XV

Balancing Tradeoffs in Designing, Deploying, and Authoring Interactive Web-Based Learn-By-Doing Environments

Lin Qiu, State University of New York at Oswego, USA

Abstract

Computer-based learn-by-doing environments have been used to provide students supportive and authentic settings for challenge-based learning. This chapter describes the design tradeoffs involved in interactive learning environment design, deployment, and authoring. It presents a combination of design choices in INDIE, a software tool for authoring and delivering learn-by-doing environments. INDIE's design balances the tradeoffs and leverages Web technologies to improve the accessibility and deployability of learning environments as well as feedback generation and authorability. It explores a vision of learning environments that are more accessible and usable to students, more supportive and customizable to instructors, and more authorable to software developers.

Introduction

The constructivist theory of learning has shown that learning is a process where the learner actively constructs understanding rather than passively receiving knowledge (Bransford, Brown, & Cocking, 1999; Bransford, Goldman, & Vye, 1991; Brown, 1988; Chi, Leeuw, Chiu, & LaVancher, 1994). This learning theory has become one of the dominant theories in education. It provides us a strong theoretical base about the nature of learning and calls for changes to the traditional didactic-based methodology of instruction. Meanwhile, greater demands are being placed on education systems at all levels to teach students the ability to apply knowledge and skills learned in classrooms to solve real-world problems. In response to these emerging needs, challenge-based learning has become a popular new paradigm of teaching. It centers learning on investigation and development of solutions to complex and ill-structured authentic problems (e.g., Boud, 1985; Bridges, 1992). Students acquire content knowledge and problem-solving skills through self-directed learning. Instructors work as facilitators providing resources and coaching to students. While challenge-based learning offers an effective approach to improve teaching and learning, a number of difficulties occur in implementing it in schools (Hoffman & Ritchie, 1997). For example, activities in solving realistic problems can be expensive, time-consuming, and even dangerous. Students need extra support to have successful learning experiences in complex real-life contexts.

Scenario-based learn-by-doing environments have been built to support challenge-based learning. They put students in fictional scenarios and provide tools such as simulations and data portfolios for solving challenges embedded in the scenarios. For example, Alien Rescue (Liu, Williams, & Pedersen, 2002) is a learning environment where students need to find a new home in the solar system for aliens to survive. BioWorld (Lajoie, Lavigne, Guerrera, & Munsie, 2001) is a learning environment where students need to diagnose patients in a simulated hospital setting. The goal-based scenario (GBS) (Schank & Neaman, 2001; Schank, Fano, Bell, & Jona, 1993) is a framework for scenario-based learn-by-doing environments. It engages students in a real-life role to solve some realistic problem in a simulated world. Students can carry out activities that are not feasible in classrooms and receive just-in-time individualized feedback. For example, Sickle Cell Counselor (Bell, Bareiss, & Beckwith, 1994) is a GBS where students work as reproductive counselors advising couples on the level of risk their children would have for sickle cell disease.

Recent advances in technology such as the Web and inexpensive and powerful computers have been particularly promising in making computer-based learning environments more accessible and deployable. This chapter describes INDIE, a software tool for authoring and delivering learn-by-doing environments. While

INDIE is based on the GBS framework, it leverages the Web technology to improve its deployability, authorability, and usability. We begin with an overview of INDIE and description of Corrosion Investigator, a learning environment delivered by INDIE. We then focus on the design choices in INDIE to illustrate how to balance the design tradeoffs in deployment, authoring, and learning support.

INDIE

INDIE is a software tool for authoring and delivering Web-based learning environments where students can run simulated experiments, collect data, generate hypotheses, and construct arguments. INDIE includes an authoring tool and a content-independent runtime engine. The authoring tool provides a form-based Web interface (Figure 1) for constructing the content in an INDIE learning environment. The runtime engine reads in the content and delivers a Web-based learning environment.

Learning environments delivered by INDIE consist of a common set of Web interfaces: a *challenge* screen showing a statement describing the challenge scenario, a *reference* screen where students can browse materials describing the scenario and domain content, an *experiment* screen where students can order tests and collect results, a *feedback* screen where students can read and respond to comments from the instructor on their work, and a *report* screen

Figure 1. The INDIE authoring tool interface

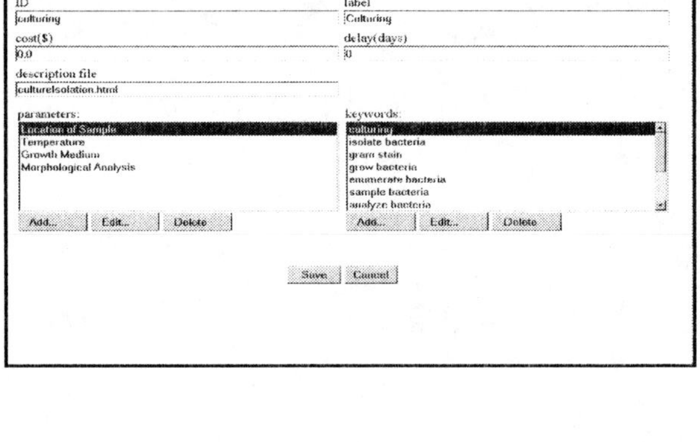

where students can construct arguments for or against possible hypotheses. INDIE learning environments automatically generate lab test results based on requests from students and provide support for students to construct arguments.

An Example: Corrosion Investigator

INDIE has been used to deliver Corrosion Investigator, a learning environment on biofilms in which environmental engineering students take the role of consultants helping a paper processing company find the cause for recurring pipe corrosion. In the following, we use Corrosion Investigator as an example to describe the INDIE learning environment.

When students first enter Corrosion Investigator, a *challenge* screen (Figure 2) explains the problem context to the students. After reading the challenge, students can then go to the *reference* screen (Figure 3) to read background materials. Students can send e-mails to characters in the scenario for additional information. There are four people in the scenario: the plant foreman, the plant manager, the scientific consultant, and the supervisor. E-mails sent to these characters are forwarded to the instructor. The instructor plays the role of these characters and provides responses to students. Students need to direct different questions to different persons according to their specialty. Communicating with these characters allows students to involve in social interactions commonly seen in real workplaces.

Figure 2. The challenge *screen in Corrosion Investigator*

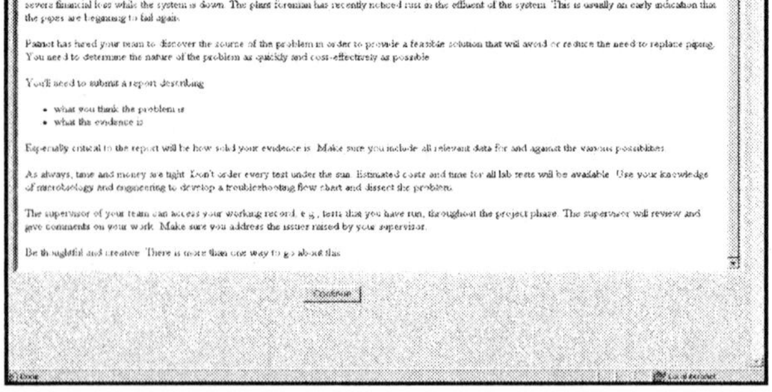

Figure 3. The reference *screen in Corrosion Investigator*

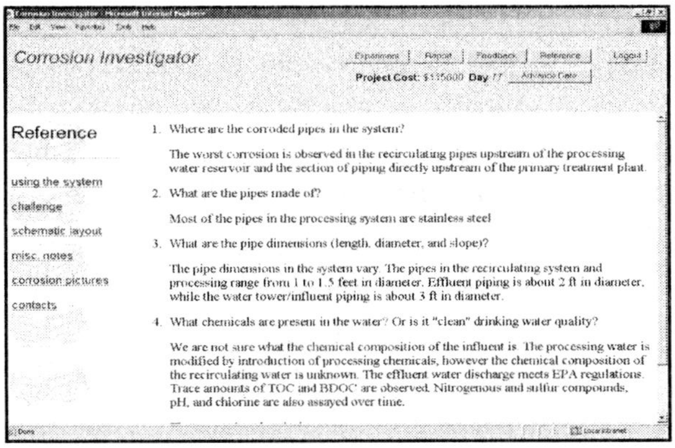

Figure 4. The experiment *screen in Corrosion Investigator*

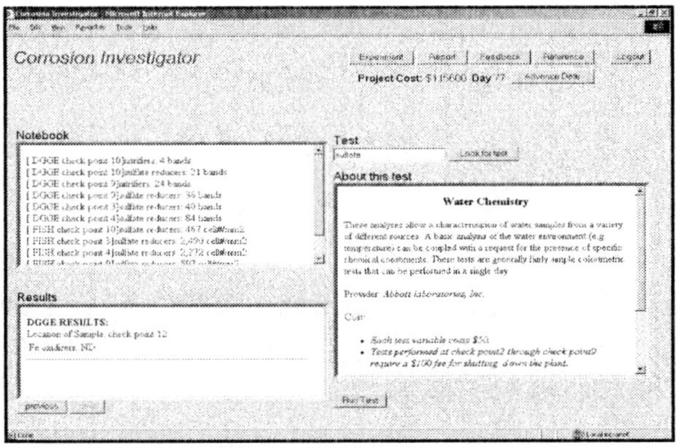

To run tests, students go to the *experiment* screen (Figure 4). The left side of the screen has the *notebook* and *result* area. The *notebook* automatically collects all the test results that students have received from the system and splits them into single items with labels indicating their test names and conditions. This helps students keep track of all the test results received from the system. Test results in the notebook are clickable items. Students can easily identify and select them to use as evidence in their reports. The *result* area displays test results in a readable form, typically a table with labeled columns and rows.

The right side of the *experiment* screen allows students to look for tests by entering test names into a textbox. Tests matching the name will be shown. Students can view the description of the tests and possible variable values for the tests. If no test matches the name that a student enters, the student will be asked to try another name, or e-mail the scientific consultant character for help.

When students decide to run a test, they can specify the parameters for the test on a separate screen (Figure 5). For example, there are two parameters for the water chemistry test, Location of Sample and Test Variable. Students can

Figure 5. The parameter value selection screen in Corrosion Investigator

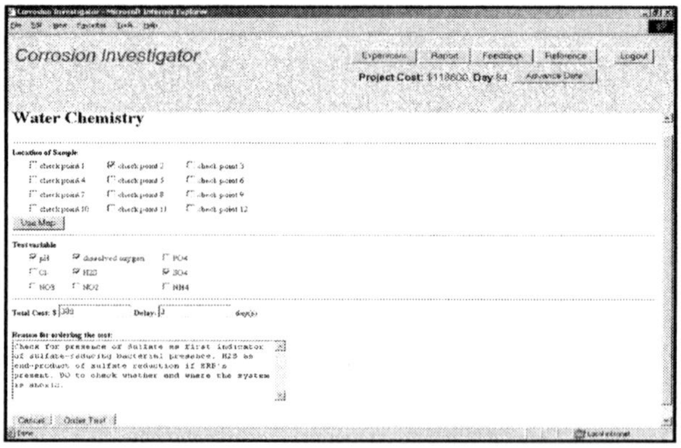

Figure 6. The interactive map in Corrosion Investigator

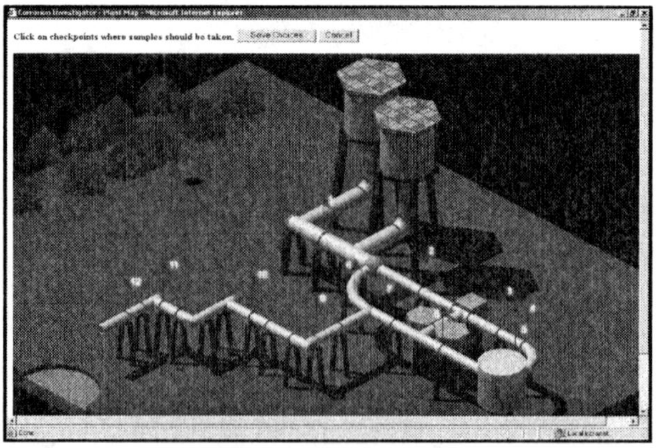

specify where to take water samples by clicking on appropriate checkboxes in the "Location of Sample" section or clicking the Use Map button to use an interactive map (Figure 6). The map allows students to pick checkpoints for taking water samples on a schematic layout of the pipeline. The *cost* and *delay* field on the parameter selection screen displays the simulated amount of money and the days the test will take. These values are dynamically calculated and displayed based on the parameter selection. They will be added to the value of the *project cost* and *day* field at the top of the screen respectively. In addition to selecting values for each test parameter, students also need to enter reasons for ordering the test.

To receive test results, students need to press the *advance date* button at the top of the screen to advance the simulated project date to the time when the most recent test results are available. Newly available test results will appear in both the *notebook* and *result* area on the Experiment screen.

When students feel they have gathered enough information, they can go to the *report* screen (Figure 7) to make claims and use test results in the *notebook* as evidence to support their claims. Students can pick a corrosion location and enter their diagnosis. When they select a result in the *notebook*, a window will pop up allowing them to enter the reason for using the test result as evidence. Newly added evidence will appear in the report on the right side of the screen. When students finish constructing the report, they e-mail their report to their client in the scenario. The report will be evaluated by the instructor in terms of the correctness of their diagnoses and the relevance of the evidence to the diagnoses.

Figure 7. The report *screen in Corrosion Investigator*

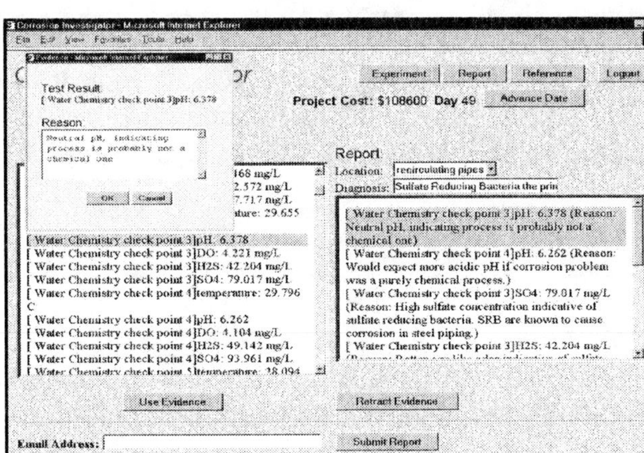

Figure 8. The feedback *screen in Corrosion Investigator*

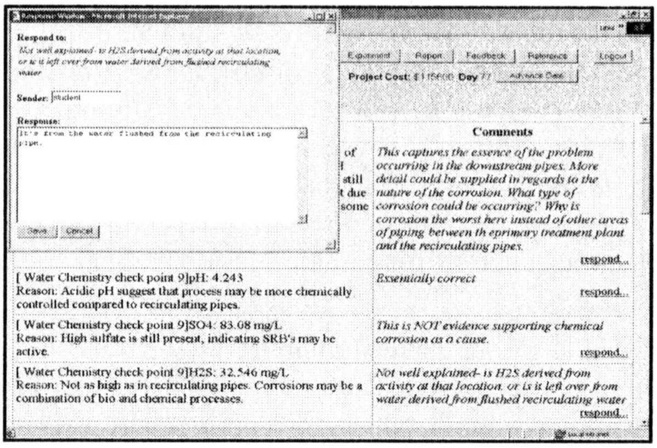

While students are working in the system, their work is under review by their supervisor (role-played by the instructor). The supervisor can add comments to the student's work such as the tests students have run and reasons for running the tests. These comments will appear on the *feedback* screen (Figure 8). Students can respond to these comments by clicking the *respond* link and enter their responses in a pop-up window.

Design Choices

INDIE presents a combination of design choices that balance deployability and interactivity, generality and usability, authenticity and simulation, openendedness, and feedback generation. The following describes each design choice.

Web-Based Client-Server Architecture

Up until the mid-90s, most educational software systems were monolithic systems. They could have rich multimedia interfaces and fast response time, but they needed to be installed on individual machines. For example, previous GBSs such as *Return of the Wolf* (Schank & Neaman, 2001) and *Volcano Investiga-*

Figure 9. The client-server architecture of INDIE

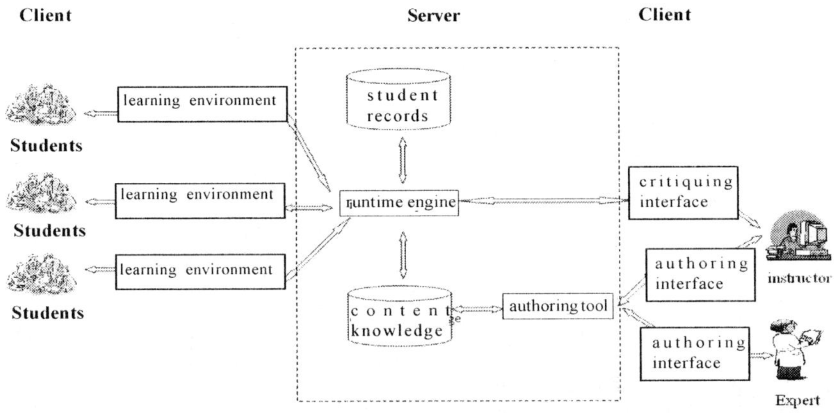

tor (Dobson, 1998) used extensive videos to create engaging problem contexts. They were deployed using CDs. This could create installation problems when conflicts occurred between the system and other software on the machine. Furthermore, when updates needed to be installed, each copy of the system needed to be updated. This required additional effort in all the places where the system was used.

To avoid the above installation and update problem, a Web-based client-sever architecture in INDIE was used (see Figure 9). The architecture stores the code and content of the learning environment on the server so that there is no need to install any program on the student's machine. The architecture provides a Web interface for students to access the learning environment through their Web browsers. Student interactions with the learning environment are recorded on the server.

Saving learning content on the server allows students to have access to it anytime, anywhere through the Web. It also prevents students from having access to key information that they need to explore by themselves. For example, students would not be able to look at the code and find out all the tests in the learning environment without doing the research by themselves. Nor would they be able to find out the results for each test without running the tests.

Figure 10. A pop-up window for adding comments to student records

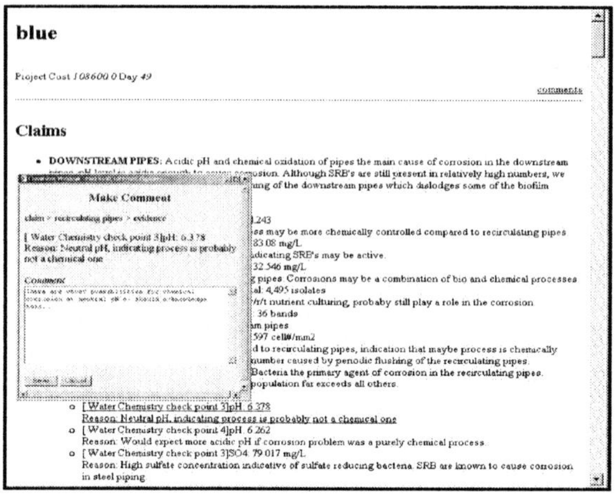

The storage of learning content on the server also facilitates authoring. With a Web-based authoring tool, authors can modify the learning content anytime, anywhere through Web browsers. When the learning content is modified, there is no need to update each copy on the students' machines. Learning environments in student Web browsers are automatically updated because they are always constructed from the current content on the server.

Student records saved on the server allow instructors to have easy access to them in a centralized location. Instructors do not need to collect student records from individual machines. INDIE further displays student records with a Web interface so that instructors can review and critique them from Web browsers. The record includes the time and money that students have spent, tests that students have scheduled and run, and diagnoses and supporting evidence that students have created (see Figure 10). Items in the record are clickable links. Instructors can click on any of them and a pop-up window will allow the instructor to enter critiques. These critiques will appear in the feedback screen in the learning environment. The student record is updated every time the student makes a move in the learning environment so that the instructor sees the most recent student activity.

Standards-Based Platform-Independent Implementation

There is a range of options to implement Web-based learning environments. Standard HTML pages are easily accessible from Web browsers on any platform. They are, however, typically not very interactive. JavaScript Web pages introduce more interactions, but they can only provide limited options such as textboxes and drop-down menus. Plug-in based tools such as Flash and Authorware Web Player support integration of video, text, audio, and graphics for richer interfaces and greater interactivity. They are, however, not fully supported on all platforms. They typically run on Windows, sometimes on Mac OS, and less often on other platforms such as Linux.

To provide wider deployability with the least commitment to third-party vendor support, a platform-independent implementation was used in INDIE.

In INDIE learning environments, student activities do not require complex interactions such as drawing pictures. Therefore, standard JavaScript is used for the user interface. This implementation allows the interface to be accessible from modern Web browsers such as Internet Explorer 6 and Netscape 7 without special software plug-ins. It provides quick response to user interactions because the JavaScript is downloaded into client Web browsers and executed on the local machine. For example, JavaScript is used to display the cost and delay of a test requested by students. Students can see the cost and delay change immediately when they pick different test parameter values. Handling such interactions on the client machine reduces the need to send information to the server for processing. It gives students fast interactivity even when connection bandwidth is low.

Interactions that require intensive computation but do not need instant feedback are sent to the server for processing. For example, student test requests are sent to the server because generating results for these requests requires complex algorithms to produce random numbers under multiparameter constraints. Processing complex interactions on the server reduces the workload on the client and leverages the computing power on the server.

Besides the learning environment, INDIE provides a Web-based authoring tool. User interactions in the authoring tool are different from the user interactions in the learning environment. In the authoring tool, users constantly modify the data on the server. This requires the interface to be kept consistent with the data on the server. We used JavaServer Pages (JSP) to implement the authoring interface. These JSP pages are reconstructed from the data on the server every time the user performs an authoring operation. The latest changes of the data on the server are reflected immediately on the authoring interface, which keeps the interface up-to-date.

We used Java and extensible markup language (XML) to implement the code on the server. The Java code runs as a servlet to accept and process requests from the learning environment and authoring tool. The XML code records the scenario information such as test descriptions and result generation methods, as well as student work in the learning environment. The Java and XML implementation along with the standard Web interface provides INDIE cross-platform deployability with minimum requirements on both the client and server side. See Qiu, Riesbeck, and Parsek (2003) for further information on system architecture and implementation.

Predefined Interface Framework with Data-Oriented Authoring Approach

In authoring tool design, there is a tradeoff between usability and generality. Usability means how easy it is for an author to use the tool to build a specific application. Generality refers to the number of different applications that can be created using the same authoring tool. During the design phase usability and generality are usually in tension. In order to make the authoring tool easy for creating a specific type of application, the tool usually needs to provide application-specific support, that is, a tool for constructing certain types of interface or processing certain types of data. This support, however, inevitably limits the variety of the applications that the authoring tool can create. For example, generic authoring tools such as Authorware or Flash allow authors to build any kind of interface, but they lack the support for building a specific type of application because they require authors to know how to design a good user interface and write code to handle user interactions and data processing. In contrast, authoring tools designed for specific kinds of problems, for example, balancing chemical equations, allow authors to define new problems with a relatively small amount of information and effort, but they can only create applications in specific domains with a fairly fixed interface.

INDIE is designed to situate between application-specific authoring tools and generic authoring tools. It provides authors with a general but standard interface framework. This framework includes an interface for specifying test parameters, a persistent structured collection of received test results, an argument construction tool, and an interface for reviewing and responding to critiques. The framework includes the underlying code to handle user interactions with the above components. It allows authors to specify virtually all contents using static data. This includes the names of tests (e.g., "measure temperature"), the possible options for each test (e.g., "at checkpoint 1"), the costs of tests (e.g., "$1,000"), the durations of tests (e.g., "15 days"), and the generation of test results (e.g., "102 degrees, plus or minus 0.5"). Authors do not need to write rules or scripts. They only need to specify the scenario content.

In addition to providing code for handling user interactions, the INDIE framework structures the authoring process to help authors develop a learning-by-doing environment based on sound educational principles. The framework requires the author to show a challenge statement upfront to motivate students. Authors also need to provide tests and results that students need to use in solving the challenge. The framework makes sure that the student's learning activity is investigative problem solving rather than reading essays and answering multiple choice questions.

INDIE's framework provides a relatively fixed learning environment interface with predefined components and layout. The framework, however, is not application-specific because it can be used for scenarios in different domains. For example, a previous version of INDIE (Dobson, 1998) produced learning environments for students to diagnose a patient or investigate the likelihood of the eruption of a volcano. Even though the main activity in the framework is always running tests and constructing arguments, various tests can be designed, and results can have different formats. This makes INDIE capable of creating different learning environments for diagnostic reasoning. In addition, because INDIE learning environments use Web-based interface, authors can use off-the-shelf graphical Web page editors to customize the appearance of the interface. Web-based materials such as graphics, audios, or videos can be easily incorporated into the learning environment as content. This avoids the need to have a specialized graphical authoring tool for constructing multimedia learning materials.

Rich Problem-Solving Options with Authentic Constraints and Feedback

In learning environment design, there is a tradeoff between providing accurate computer-based feedback and supporting authentic and open-ended problem solving. This is because natural language understanding by computers is still an unsolved problem. Texts freely entered by students cannot be understood by the system. In order to provide accurate feedback, all the actions that students can perform and their corresponding feedback in the system have to be specified in advance. Open-ended interface elements such as text boxes are usually avoided to limit student inputs to information that the system can understand. Once deployed, students are only allowed to do what the system is prepared to support. Most interactions with the system become choosing existing options or paths in the system. Students will not be able to explore options beyond the ones supported in the system. Their problem-solving activity is restricted and becomes less authentic. For example, systems such as Wayang Outpost (Arroyo, Walles, Beal, & Woolf, 2003) can provide accurate feedback, but only allow students to enter numbers or "true" or "false" selections. Other systems allow for less fixed inputs, but they require significant domain knowledge to analyze and understand student inputs. For example, the LISP Tutor (Anderson, Conrad, & Corbett, 1989) allows students to write LISP code in the learning environment. It uses more than 300 production rules to detect misconceptions in the user's code and provide feedback. AutoTutor (Graesser, Wiemer-Hastings, Wiemer-Hastings, Harter, Person, & the TRG, 2000) allows students to enter texts in natural language. It evaluates student inputs by using Latent Semantic Analysis (LSA) (Foltz, 1996; Landauer & Dumais, 1997; Landauer, Foltz, & Laham, 1998) to compare student inputs against examples of good and bad answers stored in the system. Systems such as WorldWatcher (Brown & Edelson, 1998) allow students to freely write texts and draw pictures, but they cannot provide any feedback.

INDIE uses two approaches to address the above problem. The first approach is to make core choices that students have to make in the learning environment rich enough so that the problem solving process is as complex as in the real world. These choices are provided with authentic constraints and feedback. This approach keeps student inputs easy to understand by the system while making the scenario authentic and challenging. For example, the most complex test in Corrosion Investigator has four parameters, with three to 12 possible values for each parameter. Students have a total of over 500 different test options from which to choose. Such complexity of test options requires students to fully understand each test and make conscious decisions about which tests to run. One important feature of real-life tests is that tests take time and cost money. To simulate this feature, INDIE was designed to allow its tests to have simulated, differing time and money values depending on the student's choice of parameter values. For example, the time and cost of the culturing test in Corrosion Investigator varies from seven to 14 days and $1,000 to $10,000 respectively based on its parameter values. If students order the test, they need to spend a certain amount of money (in simulated cost) and wait a certain amount of days (in simulated time) for the results to be available. The system keeps track of the total time and money that students have spent in solving the challenge. The instructor can use the time and cost to compare and evaluate student performance. Therefore, students have to think hard about what tests to run and when tests should be run in order to solve the challenge in a time- and cost-effective manner. Another feature of real-life tests is that test results rarely remain exactly the same when the same test is conducted again. To simulate this effect, INDIE allows its test results to be generated randomly based on the constraints set during scenario authoring. This gives students different results every time they run a test. INDIE further allows authors to use HTML templates to display test results in authentic formats. Students can receive test results as they would receive them in the real world.

Hybrid Feedback Generation for Open-Ended Inputs and Incremental Authoring

The second approach that we used in INDIE to balance the tradeoff between feedback generation and open-ended inputs is to use different feedback generation mechanisms for different types of inputs. We used the system to generate feedback to inputs that require immediate response or computational-intensive process, and let the instructor generate feedback to inputs that are open-ended.

In INDIE, the system generates the cost and delay of a test. This is because these values needed to be generated immediately so that students know them before they make decisions on whether to run the test. The system also handles test result generation because it is fairly complex. The instructor is introduced into the feedback loop to provide feedback to open-ended inputs such as e-mails sent to characters in the scenario and reasons for requesting a test. INIDE provides a Web interface for instructors to add comments to the student's work.

To fully support challenge-based learning, it is important to allow students to explore options not available in the learning environment. Having instructors in the feedback loop lets students obtain additional information and coaching. Being a part of the feedback loop allows instructors to have access to the student's work in the learning environment. Instructors are facilitated in becoming a "guide on the side" rather than a "sage on the stage." Assessment becomes an iterative process where students make progress, the instructor provides feedback, the students utilize the feedback and make improvement, and the instructor reviews the progress and provides more feedback. This process continues until the students correct all the mistakes and reach expected learning goals. Our experience indicates that instructors want to be in the feedback loop. For example, the designer and instructor of the Corrosion Investigator scenario requested to have students enter reasons for their test requests in the system so that he could review these reasons.

Furthermore, having instructors in the feedback loop allows instructors to incrementally author the learning content as part of responding to requests from students. The design choices made in INDIE, especially the Web-based client-server architecture and the instructor in the loop, naturally supported runtime adaptation and extension of scenario content. Instructors can use the authoring tool to add new materials such as tests, test results, or background information, into the system after deployment. This in turn leads to a possible alternative model to scenario development—incremental authoring—that makes runtime extension the prime mode of authoring, rather than the exception. In this model, a learning environment is initially built with a challenge statement, relevant background information, the obvious actions that students will take, and feedback for those actions. It does not need to have all the possible resources and feedback, but should be complete enough so that students can start working within the learning environment. When the learning environment is put into use, it is the agent that students primarily interact with. When student inputs can be handled by the system, the system provides automatic feedback to these inputs. The instructor is in the feedback loop and can opt to verify and improve the feedback before it is given to students. When student inputs cannot be handled by the system, they are sent to the instructor. The instructor provides feedback to these inputs, and the feedback is automatically incorporated into the system. During the process of providing feedback, the instructor gradually incorporates new materials into the system to improve its performance.

The incremental authoring model amortizes the significant upfront development effort that many learning environments have into "use time." Authoring is done in the context of using the system to deliver a scenario. There is no need to anticipate and implement all possible situations upfront. Authoring is driven by real needs from students. Issues not anticipated during system design can be explored and incorporated into the system after deployment. The system is kept from totally depending on pre-programmed content. In addition, by having an instructor in the feedback loop, the system can be put into use during early development stages where automatic feedback generation is not yet mature and reliable.

Classroom Implementation

Corrosion Investigator was used in a class by six first-year environmental engineering graduate students. The students formed into two groups of three. The pipe corrosion challenge was first introduced in class by the instructor. After a week, each group gave a presentation on their thoughts about what might be the cause of the corrosion problem. Then, the software was introduced to the students. The students were given three weeks to finish the project by themselves. They mainly interacted with the learning environment, but also had the option of contacting characters in the scenario role-played by the instructor. All communications were via e-mail except the in-class midterm and final presentations where student reported their progress and received feedback from the instructor. All software interactions were recorded, and after the project the students completed a survey regarding their experiences.

Students reported that they spent an average of 10 to 15 hours on the project, including interacting with the system, doing background research, participating in group discussion, and so forth. Overall the system was satisfying for doing the project. Students largely benefited from immediate feedback generated from the system. Timesaving from test simulations reduced the project time from eight weeks (the time it took when all the test results were generated manually by the instructor) to three weeks.

To test the effect of the time and cost mechanism, students were asked, "How much does the time and cost feature in the system force you to think hard on what tests to run and when to run them?" Students gave an average rating of 2 on a scale from 1 to 5, with 1 being "always" and 5 being "never." This suggests that the time and cost mechanism caused the desired impact as intended.

During the project, e-mails between the instructor and the students were much fewer (14 e-mails) compared to the situation where the scenario was delivered without the software (71 e-mails). This significantly reduced the instructor's effort in generating responses to students. It, however, does not mean that interactions between students and instructor were discouraged. When responding to the statement, "I had sufficient communication with the characters (plant foreman, plant manager, and scientific consultant) in the system," students rated an average of 2 on a scale of 1 to 5, with 1 being "strongly agree" and 5 being "strongly disagree." This suggests that students were satisfied with the level of communication with the instructor.

A survey was filled out by the instructor comparing his experience in using the Corrosion Investigator software with his experience in delivering the same challenge without the software. The instructor reported that the effort in delivering the scenario and the time students needed to complete the scenario were considered much less when using the software. The instructor's workload was reduced from 24 total person-hours to four. It was most evident in reducing the work in generating test results. The quality of the data generated by the system was considered slightly better. The quality of the students' final reports and their learning of the target skills were considered identical to the ones when the scenario was delivered without the software.

When Corrosion Investigator was first created, there were 39 keywords to match student test inquiries. During the project, 34 new keywords were discovered in student inputs and added to the system. The addition resulted in a total of 87% increase of keywords in the system. The system's coverage of student test inquiries was significantly improved. Furthermore, one student's input pointed out that the parameter value Fe was missing from the water chemistry test. The parameter value and its corresponding test results were then added using the authoring tool without interrupting the on-going project.

Related Work

INDIE learning environments are based on a framework where students are engaged in a fictional scenario, working with a simulation, constructing arguments using data from the simulation, and receiving feedback. Other scenario-based learning environments have been built to engage students in such learn-by-doing activities. For example, Alien Rescue (Liu et al., 2002) is a learning environment teaching astronomy and space travel. It engages 6th graders in a scenario where they need to find a home in the solar system for a group of aliens arrived in Earth orbit. BioWorld (Lajoie, 1998) is another scenario-based learning environment. It teaches biological terminology by engaging students in a simulated hospital setting where they need to diagnose patients.

Alien Rescue and BioWorld use multimedia such as videos and graphics to create a motivating setting. The current INDIE does not have special support for multimedia materials such as videos and graphics. However, because INDIE uses a Web-based interface, such materials could be incorporated using standard Web page mechanisms for multimedia objects.

The focus of Alien Rescue and BioWorld is to provide cognitive tools (Lajoie, 1993) such as information libraries and graphics tools to reduce the cognitive load involved in problem solving. INDIE provides a notebook to help students collect and organize data, and a report construction interface for students to use the data to generate arguments. However, the focus of INDIE is not to provide cognitive tools but to support the delivery of a challenge by providing just-in-time feedback and a simulated environment.

Like Alien Rescue and BioWorld, most scenario-based learning environments are closed systems. They do not support instructors participating in the feedback loop to respond to student requests and provide feedback. INDIE learning environments, however, allow instructors to receive e-mail requests from students and critique student work.

A number of simulation-based learning environments (Van Joolingen & de Jong, 1991) have been built to support learners performing tasks with simulations. For example, SHERLOCK (Lesgold, Lajoie, Bunzo, & Eggan, 1993) is a system where avionic technicians practice electronics troubleshooting in a simulated work environment. STEAMER (Hollan, Hutchins, & Weitzman, 1984) is an environment where students explore and manipulate a simulated steam propulsion plant. Using complex domain models, these systems provide students simulated results of their actions, explanations of mistakes, and intelligent coaching during the learning process.

Different kinds of simulations have been used in learning environments. Van Joolingen and de Jong (1991) categorized them into two types: operational model-based simulations and conceptual model-based simulations. Operational models use sequences of cognitive and non-cognitive operations or procedures to represent the simulation. One example of an operational model can be found in a radar control simulation (Munro, Fehling, and Towne, 1985). Conceptual models use principles, concepts, and facts to represent the simulation. Mendelian genetics (Brant, Hooper, & Sugrue, 1991) and HUMAN (Coleman & Randall, 1986) are two example systems that use conceptual models in their simulations.

Articulate software is a particular type of educational software that supports students building or interacting with a simulation, as well as receiving conceptual explanations of simulation outputs (Forbus, 2001). For example, CyclePad (Forbus & Whalley, 1994; Forbus, Whalley, Everett, Ureel, Brokowski, Baher, & Kuehne, 1999) is an articulate virtual lab where students design thermodynamic cycles and receive simulated results of their design, explanations of values or procedures involved in the simulation, and suggestions for improvement. Evaporation Laboratory is an example of articulate software called active illustration (Forbus, 2001). It provides a simulated environment where students can set up experiments to observe simulated water evaporation in cups made of different materials in different environments. Students can receive data recorded during the simulated process as well as explanations of casual qualitative relationships between the factors involved in the process. Explanations generated in articulate software are not specifically entered by authors, but are produced by the simulation based on qualitative physics. This saves authors from specifying every example-specific explanation, and makes sure that the explanations are consistent with the simulation.

Systems with extensive domain knowledge can automatically handle different problems and construct responses to student inputs. They, however, require significant development effort. The focus of INDIE is not on the simulation but on the challenge and task. Simulations in INDIE are the minimum necessary to support the challenge. This is to minimize upfront development cost and allow authors to quickly construct a scenario without building a model first.

A major learning activity in INDIE is to collect test results and use them to construct arguments. A number of systems have also been built to support students collaboratively constructing arguments. CoVIS (Edelson, Pea, & Gomez, 1995) and CSILE (Scardamalia & Bereiter, 1991) are two representative systems. They allow students to post data such as images and documents in a common electronic workspace to refute or support different claims. The purpose of these systems is to facilitate students sharing information and ideas so that they can collaborate on a problem. It encourages students to bring information from various sources to generate different perspectives. Instructors can review student work in the workspace and provide commentary.

INDIE differs from the above collaborative argument construction systems from two aspects. First, in INDIE, the data that students collect are primarily for use in report construction, not for collaborative problem solving. INDIE provides an interface that supports students selecting test results, attaching explanations, and inserting them into a report. It, however, does not provide facilities for sharing such information among students. Second, most of the data that students collect are generated internally by INDIE. This makes it possible for the computer to recognize them in the report and perform automatic critiquing.

Conclusion

The goal of this chapter was to describe the design tradeoffs in designing, deploying, and authoring interactive learning environments, and illustrate an example of balancing these tradeoffs. We described INDIE, a software tool for authoring and delivering learn-by-doing environments. INDIE presents a particular combination of design choices that leverages Web technologies to improve the accessibility and deployability of learning environments as well as feedback generation and authorability. It explores a vision of learning environments that are more accessible and usable to students, more supportive and customizable to instructors, and more authorable to software developers.

INDIE includes an authoring tool and a content-independent software engine. INDIE has been used to deliver Corrosion Investigator, a learning environment where students take the role of consultants helping a paper processing company determine the cause of recurring pipe corrosion. Classroom use of Corrosion Investigator suggested that the software successfully facilitated the delivery of the challenge.

To make INDIE easily deployable and accessible, a Web-based client-server architecture and platform-independent implementation was used. To simplify and structure authoring, a predefined interface framework with a data-oriented approach was used for authoring the learning environment. To enable authors to create more authentic and challenging learning environments, INDIE was designed to support fairly complex test options with time and cost constraints and authentic test result generation. To provide feedback to open-ended inputs, instructors were introduced into the feedback loop complementing automatic feedback generation. Having instructors in the feedback further supports an incremental authoring model where the instructor improves the learning environment based on demands from actual students during usage. The synergy of the above design choices makes INDIE a highly deployable and accessible tool for authoring and delivering learn-by-doing environments.

Acknowledgments

This work was supported primarily by the Engineering Research Centers Program of the National Science Foundation under Award Number EEC-9876363.

References

Arroyo, I., Walles, R., Beal, C. R., & Woolf, B. P. (2003). Tutoring for SAT-Math with Wayang Outpost. In *Demo paper AIED.*

Anderson, J. R., Conrad, F. G., & Corbett, A. T. (1989). Skill acquisition and the LISP Tutor. *Cognitive Science, 13*, 467-505.

Bell, B. L., Bareiss, R., & Beckwith, R. (1994). Sickle cell counselor: A prototype goal-based scenario for instruction in a museum environment. *Journal of the Learning Sciences, 3*, 347-386.

Boud, D. (1985). Problem-based learning in perspective. In D. Boud (Ed.), *Problem-based learning in education for the professions* (pp. 13-18). Higher Education Research Society of Australia.

Bransford, J. D., Brown, A. L., & Cocking, R. R. (Eds.). (1999). *How people learn: Brain, mind, experience, and school.* Washington, DC: National Academy Press.

Bransford, J. D., Goldman, S. R., & Vye, N. J. (1991). Making a difference in people's ability to think: Reflections on a decade of work and some hopes for the future. In R. J. Sternberg & L. Okagaki (Eds.), *Influences on Children* (pp. 147-180). Hillsdale, NJ: Erlbaum.

Brant, Hooper, G. E., & Sugrue, B. (1991). Which comes first the simulation or the lecture? *Journal of Educational Computing Research*, 7, 469-481.

Bridges, E. M. (1992). *Problem-based learning for administrators* (ERIC Document Reproduction Service No. EA 023 722).

Brown, A. L. (1988). Motivation to learn and understand: On taking charge of one's own learning. *Cognition and Instruction, 5*, 311-321.

Brown, M., & Edelson, D. C. (1998). Software in context: Designing for students, teachers, and classroom enactment. In A. S. Bruckman, M. Guzdial, J. L. Kolodner, & A. Ram (Eds.), *Proceedings of the International Conference of the Learning Sciences* (pp. 63-69). Charlottesville, VA: AACE.

Chi, M. T. H., de Leeuw, N., Chiu, M., & LaVancher., C. (1994). Eliciting self-explanations improves understanding. *Cognitive Science*, 18, 439-477.

Coleman, T. G., & Randall, J. E. (1986). *HUMAN-PC: A comprehensive physiological model* [Computer software]. Jackson: University of Mississippi Medical Center.

Dobson, W. D. (1998). *Authoring tools for investigate and decide learning environments.* Unpublished doctoral theses, Northwestern University.

Edelson, D. C., Pea, R. D., & Gomez, L. (1995). Constructivism in the collaboratory. In *Constructivist learning environments: Case studies in instructional design*. Englewood Cliffs, NJ: Educational Technology Publications.

Foltz, P. W. (1996). Latent semantic analysis for text-based research. *Behavior Research Methods, Instruments, and Computers, 28, 197-202.*

Forbus, K. (2001). Articulate software for science and engineering education. In K. Forbus, P. Feltovich, & A. Canas (Eds.), *Smart machines in education: The coming revolution in educational technology.* AAAI Press.

Forbus, K., & Whalley, P. B. (1994). Using qualitative physics to build articulate software for thermodynamics education. In *Proceedings of the 12th National Conference on Artificial Intelligence* (pp. 1175-1182). Menlo Park: American Association for Artificial Intelligence.

Forbus, K. D., Whalley, P., Everett, J., Ureel, L., Brokowski, M., Baher, J., et al. (1999).CYCLEPAD: An articulate virtual laboratory for engineering thermodynamics. *Artificial Intelligence, 114*(1-2), 297-347.

Graesser, A. C., Wiemer-Hastings, P., Wiemer-Hastings, K., Harter, D., Person, N., & the TRG. (2000). Using latent semantic analysis to evaluate the contributions of students in AutoTutor. *Interactive Learning Environments*, *8*, 128-148.

Hoffman, B., & Ritchie, D. (1997). Using multimedia to overcome the problems with problem based learning. *Instructional Science, 25*(2), 97-115.

Hollan, J., Hutchins, E., & Weitzman, L. (1984). STEAMER: An interactive inspectable simulation-based training system. *AI Magazine*, *5*(2), 15-27.

Landauer, T. K., & Dumais, S. T. (1997). A solution to Plato's problem: The latent semantic analysis theory of acquisition, induction, and representation of knowledge. *Psychological Review, 104*(2), 211-240.

Landauer, T. K., Foltz, P. W., & Laham., D. (1998). An introduction to latent semantic analysis. *Discourse Processes*, *25*, 259-284.

Lajoie, S. P. (1993). Computer environments as cognitive tools for enhancing learning. In S. P. Lajoie & S. J. Derry (Eds.), *Computers as cognitive tools* (pp. 261-288). Hillsdale, NJ: Lawrence Erlbaum Associates, Inc.

Lajoie, S. P. (1998). Promoting argumentation in face to face and in distributed computer-based learning situations: Constructing knowledge in the context of BioWorld. In M. A. Gernsbacher & S. J. Derry (Eds.), *Proceedings of the 20th Annual Conference of the Cognitive Science Society* (p. 5). Mahwah, NJ: Lawrence Erlbaum Associates.

Lajoie, S. P., Lavigne, N. C., Guerrera, C., & Munsie., S. (2001). Constructing knowledge in the context of BioWorld. *Instructional Science, 29*(2), 155-186.

Lesgold, A., Lajoie, S. M., Bunzo, M., & Eggan., G. (1993). SHERLOCK: A coached practice environment for an electronics troubleshooting job. In *Computer assisted instruction and intelligent tutoring systems: Establishing communication and collaboration* (pp. 201-238). Hillsdale, NJ: Lawrence Erlbaum Associates.

Liu, M., Williams, D., & Pedersen, S. (2002). Alien Rescue: A problem-based hypermedia learning environment for middle school science. *Journal of Educational Technology Systems, 30*(3).

Munro, A., Fehling, M. R., & Towne, D. M. (1985). Instruction intrusiveness in dynamic simulation training. *Journal of Computer-Based Instruction, 2*, 50-53.

Qiu, L., Riesbeck, C. K., & Parsek, M. R. (2003). The design and implementation of an engine and authoring tool for Web-based learn-by-doing environments. In *Proceedings of World Conference on Educational Multimedia, Hypermedia & Telecommunications* (ED-MEDIA), Hawaii.

Scardamalia, M., & Bereiter, C. (1991). Higher levels of agency for children in knowledge building: A challenge for the design of new knowledge media. *Journal of the Learning Sciences, 1*(1), 37-68.

Schank, R., Fano, A., Bell, B., & Jona, M. (1993). The design of goal-based scenarios. *Journal of the Learning Sciences, 3*(4), 305-345.

Schank, R., & Neaman, A. (2001). Motivation and failure in educational simulation design. In K. D. Forbus & P. J. Feltovich (Eds.), *Smart machines in education* (pp. 99-144). Menlo Park, CA: AAAI Press/MIT Press.

van Joolingen, W. R., & de Jong., T. (1991). Characteristics of simulations for instructional settings. *Education & Computing, 6*, 241-262.

About the Authors

Francisco Milton Mendes Neto received a bachelor's degree in computing science from the State University of Ceará, Brazil, in 1997. He received an MSc degree in informatics in 2000 from the Federal University of Paraíba, Brazil, for his work on environments to support Web-based collaborative learning. Dr. Mendes Neto received a PhD degree in electrical engineering from the Federal University of Campina Grande, Brazil, in 2005 for his work on knowledge management and computer-supported learning. In 1998, he joined the Superintendence of Corporate Systems of the Federal Service of Data Processing, where he is currently the manager of projects of computer-supported learning and of learning communities of the Brazilian Federal Government. Dr. Mendes Neto is a member of the Brazilian Computing Society and the Brazilian Knowledge Management Society.

Francisco Vilar Brasileiro received a bachelor's degree in computing science and an MSc degree in informatics from the Federal University of Paraíba, Brazil, in 1988 and 1989, respectively. He received a PhD in computing science in 1995 from the University of Newcastle upon Tyne, England, for his work on fail-controlled nodes and agreement protocols. In 1989, after a brief incursion in industry, he joined the Department of Systems and Computing of the Federal University of Paraíba, where he is currently a senior lecturer. His main research areas are in fault tolerance and distributed systems and protocols. Dr. Brasileiro is a member of the Brazilian Computing Society, the ACM, and the IEEE Computer Society.

* * * *

Cengiz Hakan Aydin, PhD, is an assistant professor at the School of Communication Sciences of Anadolu University, Turkey. Dr. Aydin holds an ME degree from Arizona State University's educational media and computers program and a PhD from Anadolu University's communication sciences program. His research interest mainly focus on different aspects of computer mediated communications, online learning and teaching, readiness for online learning, roles and competencies for online teaching, communities of practice, building online learning communities, sense of presence, and community in online environments.

Curtis J. Bonk is a professor of instructional systems technology at Indiana University (USA). Dr. Bonk is also a senior research fellow with the DOD's Advanced Distributed Learning Lab. He has received the CyberStar Award from the Indiana Information Technology Association, Most Outstanding Achievement Award from the U.S. Distance Learning Association, and Most Innovative Teaching in a distance education program from the State of Indiana. Dr. Bonk is in high demand as a conference keynote speaker and workshop presenter. He is president of CourseShare and SurveyShare. More information about Dr. Bonk is available at http://mypage.iu.edu/~cjbonk/.

Steve Borland, MEd, received his master's degree from the instructional systems program at Pennsylvania State University, USA, and is a project coordinator of information systems at Temple University Health Systems, PA (USA).

Juan Manuel Adán-Coello received a BSc degree in computer science in 1980, an MSc degree in electrical engineering in 1986, and a PhD in electrical engineering in 1993, all from the State University of Campinas (Unicamp), Brazil. He is currently a professor in the school of computer engineering at Pontifical Catholic University of Campinas (PUC-Campinas). His current research interests are focused on the application of intelligent systems for education.

John W. Coffey holds a BS degree in psychology from the College of William and Mary in 1971, and a BS in systems science in 1989, an MS in computer science in 1992, and an EdD in instructional technology in 2000 from The University of West Florida (USA). He received a software patent in 1996. Since 1992 John has divided his time between the computer science department at UWF, where he is an associate professor, and the Florida Institute for Human and Machine Cognition, where he is a research scientist. In his work for the FIHMC, John served as the principle software developer on the NUCES Project and developed the software for the VNet portion of the Quorum project. He has also served as a knowledge engineer on projects with NASA Glenn Research Center, the Electrical Power Research Institute, the Chief of Naval Education and Training, several of the nations Intelligence Agencies, and others.

Ricardo Luís de Freitas received BSc and MSc degrees in computer science from, respectively, the Federal University of São Carlos in 1988, and University of São Paulo in 1991, and a PhD in electrical engineering from the University of São Paulo in 1996. He is currently a professor at the school of computer engineering at the Pontifical Catholic University of Campinas (PUC-Campinas), Brazil. His research interests are focused in intelligent systems for education.

Carlos J. P. Lucena is the software engineering professor in the Department of Informatics at the Catholic University of Rio de Janeiro, Brazil, where he coordinates the software engineering laboratory, and adjunct professor of computer science and senior research associate, computer systems group, University of Waterloo, Canada. His research interests include formal methods for software engineering, multi-agent systems, reuse, ontologies, frameworks, aspect oriented programming, object oriented programming, Web engineering, and Web-based instruction. Lucena received a PhD in computer science from the University of California in Los Angeles. He is a member of the Brazilian Computer Society.

Rogério Patrício Chagas do Nascimento received his undergraduate degree at Universidade Federal de Sergipe, Brazil, his MSc in computer science at Universidade Federal de Pernambuco, Brazil, and his PhD in informatics engineering at Universidade de Aveiro, Portugal. He was lecturer in the CEFET-SE and coordinator of the Industrial Informatics Department at UNED Lagarto. Since July of 2005, he has been an invited auxiliary professor at Universidade do Algarve, Portugal. At the present, he collaborated with 39 coauthors, wrote 41 papers, created 17 processes or products, and received five awards or prizes.

Bernhard Ertl earned his diploma in computer science from the Ludwig Maximilian University Munich in 1998 and his PhD in education in 2003. Currently, he is a research assistant at the Institute of Educational Psychology, Ludwig Maximilian University of Munich. Since 1999 he has been working with Professor Heinz Mandl in DFG-funded research projects focusing on collaborative learning, namely "collaborative learning in graphics-enhanced tele-learning environments" and "collaborative knowledge construction in desktop videoconferencing." His current research interests lie in the research on video-mediated learning, Internet collaboration, and online-courses with a particular focus on the support of collaborative knowledge construction by structured communication interfaces.

Eurico Vasconcelos obtained a bachelor's and master's degree, both in computer science, at the University of Fortaleza. Since his graduation, he has worked with academic research making scientific initiation works in the field of multi-agents and social security. In parallel, he worked at software houses and consulting companies as a system analyst. In 2002 he earned a national scholarship from the Brazilian National Center of Research—CNPQ to work in the ExpertCOP project, researching in the field of multi-agents simulation in education. He teaches intelligent systems and multi-agent systems at Integrated Colleges of Ceara—FIC.

Hugo Fuks is an associate professor in the Department of Informatics at the Catholic University of Rio de Janeiro, Brazil, and a researcher of the software engineering laboratory. His research interests include computational support for collaboration and interaction, groupware, computer supported collaborative learning, and information systems. Fuks received a PhD in computing from Imperial College, London University. He is a member of the Brazilian Computer Society.

Vasco Furtado graduated from Federal University of Ceara as data processing technical in 1986. He was a specialist in computer science at UFC in 1988. He finished his master's degree at Federal University of Paraíba in 1993, with the thesis "A4 Um Ambiente de Apoio a Aquisição Automática de Conhecimento." His PhD thesis was "Formation de Concepts Dans Le Contexte Des Langages de Schemas" at Universite d'aix—Marseille III—France in 1997. He works at Social Security Public Department as director of technology and teaches at the University of Fortaleza. For more information, visit his homepage at http://www.seguranca.ce.gov.br/vasco.

Marco A. Gerosa is a researcher of the Software Engineering Laboratory of the Department of Informatics at the Catholic University of Rio de Janeiro, Brazil. His research interests include component-based groupware development, computer supported collaborative learning, and information systems. Gerosa received a DSc in computer science from Catholic University of Rio de Janeiro, Brazil. He is a member of the Brazilian Computer Society.

Fethi Ahmet Inan is in the instructional design and technology program at The University of Memphis (USA). He received his MS, BS, and teaching degree in computer education and instructional technology from Middle East Technical University, Turkey. Fethi worked for Appalachian Technology in Education Consortium as a research associate. Currently, he is responsible for the research design and data analysis of various projects for the Center for Research in Educational Policy. Fethi also teaches technology integration courses in the University of Memphis. His recent research interests are design, development and implementation of online learning environments, individual differences, adaptive hypermedia, and integration of technology into various learning environments.

Vinícius Medina Kern has applied and researched peer review in graduate and undergraduate education since 1997, in Brazil. He holds a PhD in production engineering from UFSC in 1997, with research stages at Virginia Tech and NIST, USA. He is currently on the board of directors of Instituto Stela. He is a professor of computing science at Univali and researcher of the graduate program in knowledge engineering and management. His main research, development, and teaching areas of interest are databases, knowledge engineering, and peer review in education.

Myint Swe Khine is an associate professor and coordinator of the master's degree program in learning sciences and technologies at the National Institute of Education, Nanyang Technological University, Singapore. He received his master's degrees from the University of Southern California, USA, and University of Surrey, UK, and a PhD in education from Curtin University of Technology, Australia. He has co-authored and published books including *Studies in educational learning environments: An international perspective* (World Scientific), *Engaged learning with emerging technologies* (Springer), and *Technology-rich learning environments: A future perspective* (World Scientific). He is also an editorial board member of *Educational Media International*.

Doris Lee, PhD, is an associate professor and coordinator of the instructional systems program at Pennsylvania State University, Great Valley School of Graduate Professional Studies, Malvern, USA. Dr. Lee received both her MA and PhD degrees from the University of Texas at Austin, USA, and her areas of expertise include: systematic instructional and training programs design, computer-based instruction, Web-based instruction, e-learning, and adult learning.

Seung-hee Lee is a research fellow at Kelley Direct Online Program within Kelley School of Business at Indiana University (USA). Dr. Lee earned her PhD from Hanyang University, Korea, in 2003. Previously, she had worked in the Center of Learning and Teaching of the Korean National Open University in Seoul, where she consulted promoted faculty development, and instructional design and development for e-learning. She had conducted several postdoctoral research projects at Indiana University for a couple of years. Major research interests of Dr. Lee are online collaboration, reflective technologies, e-learning in higher education, and online moderating/mentoring.

Sunnie Lee has a bachelor's degree in educational technology from Ewha Womans University and a master's degree in instructional systems technology from Indiana University (USA). She is currently studying in the department as a doctoral student pursuing research in systemic change in education and instructional design. She has done instructional design for such companies as McDonalds, Walgreens, and Accenture as a contractor with WisdomTools, Inc. Prior to coming to Indiana University, she was an instructional designer for Solvit Media, Inc. and a high school teacher of English in Seoul, South Korea.

Xiaojing Liu is a PhD candidate in instructional systems technology and a research fellow at Kelley Direct Online Program at Indiana University, Bloomington (USA). Previously she was an assistant professor at the Institute of Higher Education in Beijing University of Aeronautics and Astronautics in China. She worked on various research projects sponsored by World Bank on educational investment in China. Her research interests focus on online learning, information systems, communities of practices, and knowledge management.

Deborah L. Lowther is currently an associate professor of instructional design and technology at The University of Memphis (USA). She received her PhD in educational technology from Arizona State University in 1994. She has co-authored *Integrating Computer Technology into the Classroom* (3rd ed.), several book chapters, refereed journal articles, and is a current consulting editor for the *Educational Technology Research* and *Development Journal*. Her scholarly activities also include numerous presentations at national and international educational conventions, co-guest editing a special edition of a national journal, working with multiple grants focused toward technology integration, and providing professional development to educational institutions across the country.

Heinz Mandl is a professor of education and educational psychology at Ludwig Maximilian University of Munich, Germany. He was president of the European

Association for Research on Learning and Instruction (EARLI; 1989-1991). He got the Oeuvre Award for outstanding contributions to the Science of Learning & Instruction of the European Association for Research on Learning and Instruction. Main research areas are knowledge management, acquisition and use of knowledge, netbased knowledge communication, and design of virtual learning environments. In research and development projects he cooperates with companies and organizations like Siemens, BMW, Telekom, ALTANA, VW, and Bundesrechnungshof.

Marina S. McIsaac earned her PhD in educational technology from the University of Wisconsin, Madison, USA. She is currently professor emerita of Arizona State University. She is president of ICEM, the International Council for Educational Media, a UNESCO affiliated nongovernmental organization. Dr. McIsaac is also director of international relations for CARDET, the Center for the Advancement of Research and Development in Educational Technology, based in Singapore and Cyprus. She has published more than 100 articles, book chapters, and reports on distance education, teacher training, and Internet-based course development. Her work focuses on intercultural issues as they relate to Web-based teaching and learning in developed and developing countries. McIsaac has received three Fulbright Scholar Awards; two Fulbright Senior Scholar/Researcher Awards; and a Fulbright Alumni Initiatives Award to Anadolu University in Eskisehir, Turkey.

Mehmet Emin Mutlu, PhD, is an assistant professor at the Open Education Faculty of Anadolu University where he also serves as one of the vice-deans. In addition, Dr. Mutlu is the director of the Computer-Based Learning Centre of the university. After receiving his master's degree in the industrial rngineering program of the Anadolu University, he has completed his PhD degree in Osmangazi University's Operations Research Program. Since Dr. Mutlu has been focusing more on development, his research interest is in general related to design and development processes of computerized instruction and online learning.

Wilson Castello Branco Neto is a professor of information systems at the University of Planalto Catarinense, Brazil. His current research interests lie in the areas of Semantic Web, Web-based education, and adaptive educational systems. He received his master's degree from the Federal University of Santa Catarina, where he is finishing his PhD in computer science.

Roberto Carlos dos Santos Pacheco is principal researcher at Instituto Stela, professor of information systems at INE/UFSC, and professor of the graduate program in knowledge engineering and management, UFSC, Brazil. He holds a DrEng in production engineering from UFSC in 1996 with research stage at USF-Tampa, USA. He led the conception, development, and deployment of Plataforma Lattes in 1999 and Portal Inovação in 2005, both world premiere projects. Plataforma Lattes grew the Brazilian curriculum database from 35,000 to 500,000 in 4.5 years. Portal Inovação uses information from Plataforma Lattes and other sources to promote university-industry interaction.

Joyce Munarski Pernigotti holds a PhD in psychology from PUCRS. She worked for 23 years as a teacher, counselor, and member of the directing council of Colégio de Aplicação, UFRGS, Brazil. She coordinated several distance learning courses at PUCRS, from 2000 to 2004, at the graduate and undergraduate levels. Her main research area is educational psychology with emphasis on curricular restructuring. Dr. Pernigotti is currently the lieutenant municipal secretary of education at Porto Alegre—a system of 92 schools, 133 child care units, and about 3,900 teachers and 60,000 students from kindergarten to high school plus lifelong learning.

Mariano Pimentel is a PostDoc student in the department of informatics at the Catholic University of Rio de Janeiro, Brazil, and researcher of the Software Engineering Laboratory. His research interests include computational support for collaboration and interaction, computer supported collaborative learning, and information systems. Pimentel received a DSc in computer science from Catholic University of Rio de Janeiro, Brazil. He is a member of the Brazilian Computer Society.

Lin Qiu is an assistant professor in the Department of Computer Science at State University of New York at Oswego. He received his PhD in computer science with a graduate specialization in cognitive science from Northwestern University in 2005. His dissertation was on computer-based interactive learning environments. His research interests lie in the area of human-computer interaction and artificial intelligence, with a focus on the design and authoring of educational software. He has broad interests in learning technologies, cognitive science, and education.

Alberto Raposo is a senior researcher and area coordinator at the Computer Graphics Technology Group (Tecgraf) and part-time professor in the Department of Informatics at the Catholic University of Rio de Janeiro, Brazil. His research interests include groupware, virtual reality, and collaborative virtual environments. Raposo received a DSc in computing from Electrical and Computer Engineering School, University of Campinas, Brazil. He is a member of the Brazilian Computer Society.

Charles M. Reigeluth has a BA in economics from Harvard University and a PhD in instructional psychology from Brigham Young University. He taught high school science for three years. He has been a professor in the Instructional Systems Technology Department at Indiana University since 1988, and was chairman of the department for three years. He cofounded the Council for Systemic Change in AECT and founded the Restructuring Support Service at Indiana University. He has worked with several school districts to facilitate their change efforts. He served on the Indiana Department of Education Restructuring Task Force and made a significant input to the recommendations that resulted in the appropriation and subsequent RFP; he served on the proposal review team; and he advised several of the six pilot schools on how to conduct systemic change. He has been facilitating a systemic change effort in a small school district in Indianapolis since January 2001, and is using that as an opportunity to develop more knowledge about a guidance system for transforming public education.

João Luís Garcia Rosa graduated in electrical engineering in 1983, got an MSc degree in computer and electrical engineering in 1993, and PhD in computational linguistics in 1999, all of them at State University of Campinas, Brazil. He teaches formal languages and automata and artificial intelligence disciplines (artificial neural networks, natural language processing), advises graduate students, and does research at Pontifical Catholic University of Campinas (PUC-Campinas), State of São Paulo, Brazil. His main research interests are on natural language processing applications and biologically plausible connectionist models.

Luciana Martins Saraiva has a BSc in psychology, Unisinos. Her doctoral thesis in production engineering, UFSC, investigated the effectiveness of peer review as pedagogical approach. She is presently conducting research on distance education at Instituto Vias and teaching for psychology at Univali, Brazil. She leads projects in the areas of psychology of health, organizational psychology, and educational psychology. She led the creation, as coordinator, of the course of psychology at Univali, Biguaçu-SC, as well as the psychological services at Regional Hospital of São José-SC.

Bude Su is a PhD candidate in instructional systems technology and works as the assistant Web director of School of Education in Indiana University

Bloomington (USA). She is also a research fellow at Kelley Direct Online MBA program at Indiana University. Previously she was the national director of international education and resource network in China (http://www.iearn.org). Her major research interests include online teaching and learning, technology integration in education, organizational behavior, and knowledge management.

Carlos Miguel Tobar received BE and MS degrees in computer science from, respectively, the State University of São Paulo, Brazil, in 1978, and State University of Campinas, in 1989, and a PhD degree in computer and electrical engineering from the University of Campinas (Unicamp), in 1998. He is currently a professor at the School of Computer Engineering, Pontifical Catholic University of Campinas (PUC-Campinas). His research interests are focused in intelligent systems for education.

William R. Watson is a lecturer of computer and information technology in the school of engineering and technology at Indiana University - Purdue University Indianapolis (USA). He has a BA in English and a master's degree in information science from Indiana University and is currently pursuing a PhD in instructional systems technology at Indiana University. His research interests include systemic change in education and the incorporation of video and computer games for instruction.

Katrin Winkler earned her Master in Education from the Ludwig Maximilian University Munich (Germany) in 2000 and her doctorate in education in 2004. Currently, she is a research assistant at the Institute of Educational Psychology, Ludwig Maximilian University of Munich. Since 2000, she has been working with Professor Heinz Mandl in research projects focusing on knowledge management, community building in virtual and face-to-face environments, and e-learning and blended learning environments.

Index

D

E

F